D1496079

Lavish Self-Divisions

Lavish Self-Divisions

The Novels of Joyce Carol Oates

BRENDA DALY

University Press of Mississippi
Jackson

Manufactured in the United States of America
99 98 97 96   4 3 2 1
The paper in this book meets the guidelines for permanence and durability of the
Committee on Production Guidelines for Book Longevity of the Council on Library
Resources.

Library of Congress Cataloging-in-Publication Data

Daly, Brenda O., 1955–
      Lavish self-divisions : the novels of Joyce Carol Oates / Brenda Daly.
         p.   cm.
      Includes bibliographical references and index.
      ISBN 0-87805-885-0 (cloth : alk. paper)
      1. Oates, Joyce Carol, 1938–   —Criticism and interpretation.   2. Women
and literature—United States—History—20th century.   3. Self in literature.
4. Authorship.   I. Title.
      PS3565.A8Z635   1996
      813'.53—dc20   96-11684
                                                                                          CIP

British Library Cataloging-in-Publication data available

Contents

Acknowledgments

My friends and colleagues—Maureen Reddy at Rhode Island College, Marie Lathers and Marty Graham at Iowa State University, and Laurin Porter at the University of Texas at Arlington—have supported my work on Oates for many years, sometimes reading drafts of chapters, sometimes inviting me to present at conferences. I am grateful for their love and support. In addition, I am thankful to the following editors who, by publishing my work on Oates, sustained my dream of completing this book: Elaine Showalter, Barbara Lounsberry, Michael J. O'Shea, Dale Bauer and Susan Jaret McKinstry, S. E. Sweeney and Carol J. Singley, Olivia Frey and Diane Freedman, Katherine Ackley, Ray Browne, and Nancy Kobrin. My thanks also to the many conference chairs who have invited me to present on Oates. This book bears traces of all these collaborations.

Because I began reading the fiction of Joyce Carol Oates more than twenty years ago, I sometimes think of myself as a fiction—an "I"—created by JCO. Had I not yearned to write about Oates's fiction, I might not have applied for doctoral studies at the University of Minnesota. I completed my studies with the help of Chester Anderson who, as my dissertation director, provided valuable criticism and support. Thanks to feminists at the University of Minnesota—Madelon Sprengnether, Shirley Nelson Garner, and Toni McNaron—I became a much stronger reader, a feminist reader. I also thank the Center for Advanced Feminist Studies at the University of Minnesota which appointed me a Fellow in 1993, providing me with library privileges while I was on leave and working on this book.

The leave itself was provided by Iowa State University, which has also supported my work on this project with a faculty grant from the College of Liberal Arts and a number of research releases from the English department. I thank my colleagues at Iowa State University, many of whom have encouraged and supported my work on Oates. I am grateful to Billie

Green, who typed portions of the manuscript, and to Don Payne and David Russell, who taught me to use the computer.

Finally, I thank my son Stephan for his love and understanding. But most of all, I thank John for believing in me and in this book.

Introduction

Lavish Self-Divisions: The Novels of Joyce Carol Oates

The "Joyce Carol Oates" in *Lavish Self-Divisions* refers, not to an absent author, but to the many selves, the contending voices and texts graphically represented in her novels. As Oates herself has pointed out, "Most writers divide themselves up lavishly in their novels" (*New Heaven, New Earth* 278n.4). It follows, once the writer is perceived as plural—as divided into all the characters in her novels, past and present—that the "Joyce Carol Oates" of the 1960s is not the same as the "Joyce Carol Oates" of the 1980s. Oates explains her creation of "alternative" selves, over time, in these words: "Each angle of vision, each voice, yields (by way of that process of fictional abiogenesis all story tellers know) a separate writer-self, an alternative Joyce Carol Oates" ("Stories That Define Me" 1). Yet how is it possible to understand such an intersubjective and historical conception of authorship? In my view, Mikhail Bakhtin provides such a concept of authorship when he describes the author as "orchestrating" the social heteroglossia of her era; in other words, authorial consciousness mediates among the voices—the embodied points of view—struggling for social control in a particular time and place. Because Bakhtin's theory of language is grounded "in the social struggle over meaning" (Ebert 887),[1] his concept of multivocal authorship can provide a useful framework for analyzing Oates's answers, as a novelist, to the social struggles that have taken place in the United States over the past three decades.

The body of Oates's work certainly provides evidence that she has, as critics have noted, many voices or styles. Lorna Sage remarks that "few contemporary writers have inhabited more styles than Joyce Carol Oates. She is the author as picaresque character, the travelling writer equally at home with Gothic, realism, romance and detection" (186). Or, as Henry Louis Gates comments, "She picks up and discards generic forms at will . . . . She refuses to restrict herself to one subject, to one stratum of society, one personality type. Indeed her very productivity stands as a reproach" (29). Fortunately, despite criticism of her productivity,[2] Oates has continued her ambitious project: an examination of American society, past and present, especially in terms of the distribution of power among institutions, such as medicine, law, politics, psychiatry, religion, education, business, the military-industrial complex, and the family—especially the family. Since all of these discourses, along with a wide range of generic forms, can be found in Oates's novels, Bakhtin's argument—that a novelist's style cannot be identified with a single genre—is useful in an analysis of Oates's relationship to discourses. It is the very nature of the novel, according to Bakhtin, to absorb other genres, both literary and extraliterary. In addition, as this study will demonstrate, Oates's relationship to genres is complex. Often, for example, she deliberately transgresses generic conventions in order to challenge implicit hierarchies of gender, race, and class. Such resistance illustrates how, though one may be born a daughter (as every woman invariably is), it is possible to resist the constraints of sociolinguistic codes. Certainly it has been possible for Oates—a woman born into a white, working-class family—to create a wide range of alternative selves of different times and places, as well as different races, genders, and classes.

At the same time, Oates's novels yield graphic traces of a struggle to free her imagination from linguistically imposed constraints of gender. As Oates has acknowledged, as a child reader she chose to identify with the male author of "Alice in Wonderland" rather than with his female character, Alice. "Though a child like me," she says of Alice, "she wasn't telling her own story: That godly privilege resided with someone named, in gilt letters on the book's spine, 'Lewis Carroll.'" She explains that "being Lewis Carroll was infinitely more exciting than being Alice, so I became Lewis Carroll" ("Stories That Define Me" 2). For the youthful Joyce Carol Oates, then, authorship was a masculine role, "a godly privilege" denied to female characters. Oates's struggle to free her imagination from such gendered literary conventions is particularly evident in her efforts to redefine her authorial relationship to female characters. As I shall illustrate, over the past three decades she has redefined the act of authorship itself while at the same time opening up new possibilities for the young women in her novels. The Alices in Oates's novels do not remain characters in plots designed by that male impersonator, author Joyce "Carroll" Oates; instead, with increasing frequency, they become authors of their own lives. She may have begun writing as a male impersonator—as Joyce "Carroll" Oates— but she has actively revised novelistic conventions in order to emancipate her characters and her authorial self.

In *Lavish Self-Divisions*, I demonstrate that between 1964 and 1994 Oates has created a number of different author-selves,[4] each of whom functions as a means of resistance to novelistic conventions, as well as a response to social struggles taking place in the United States. For example, during the 1960s, the period of Oates's "anxious authorship," she had to resolve the dilemma of the (woman) writer's relationship to a literary tradition defined, according to Sandra Gilbert and Susan Gubar, as a struggle between fathers and sons. "Where," they ask, "does such an implicitly or explicitly patriarchal theory of literature leave literary women?" (7). During the 1970s, a period of "dialogic" authorship, as defined by Bakhtin, Oates began to resist the Law of the Father, the law of one (Bakhtin's monologic), not only by "writing beyond the ending" of the romance plot, as Rachel Blau Du Plessis would phrase it, but with a series of metaphorical "marriages" and "infidelities" to the Father-Author. During the 1980s, which I define in Susan Lanser's terms as a period of "communal" authorship, Oates began to address complex issues of gender and authorial voice.[5] Employing communal narrators— women who speak not as "I" but as "we"—Oates began to redefine narrative voice as multivocal rather than individual, and as mothered as well as fathered. In short, Oates challenges novelistic conventions that perpetuate a "masculine," individualistic concept of authorship.

As Oates points out, "While there are 'women writers' there are not, and have never been, 'men writers.' This is an empty category, a class without specimens; for the noun 'writer'—the very verb 'writing'—always implies masculinity" ([*Woman*] *Writer* 27). This linguistic practice makes it more difficult for a woman to imagine herself an author, whether in social or linguistic terms; indeed, both linguistically and socially, a woman seems fated to become a character in some (male) author's plot. What, then, is the ontological status of a writer *who is also a woman?* Oates raises this question not only in critical essays but in many novels, short stories, and plays. For example, in "The Girl," a short story first published in 1966, a nameless young woman becomes an actor in a (male) author's movie.[6] Again, in *Ontological Proof of My Existence*, a play first staged in 1970, a young woman named Shelley struggles to become the author of her own life, first by resisting her dominating father and then her lover, both of whom insist on making her a character in their plots. As Oates says in the play's 1986 preface, "Shelley of *Ontological Proof of My Existence* begins her play strongly and even defiantly; but she loses it, as she loses the audience, to the superior imagination—the strength and bravado—of her entertaining lover, Peter V" (*Three Plays* viii). How, then, is a woman to become the author of her own text, her own life?

Oates has been attentive to this ontological puzzle—which is also the puzzle of socially constructed gender identities—from the outset of her career. Beginning in 1964 with the publication of her first novel, *With Shuddering Fall*, through the publication of *Foxfire, Confessions of a Girl Gang* in 1993, where this study ends, Oates has attempted again and again to transform the daughter's part. In fact, each of Oates's female protagonists might be described as yet another attempt to re-vision the daughter's part. As Gilbert points out, the daughter continues to be defined in terms of a kinship system that leaves the daughter "no choice but to be *for* the father— to be his treasure, his land, his voice" ("Life's Empty Pack" 265). For this reason, I use the term "daughter"[7] to foreground the woman's place in an ancient kinship system that, though it may be defunct, is perpetuated by linguistic practice. According to Nelly Furman, a daughter is born into a society and a language in which "she is at once an object of desire and an object of exchange, valued on the one hand as a person in her own right, and on the other considered simply as a relational sign between men" (61). Since the daughter's identity is situated "at the intersection of two incompatible systems," according to Furman, she is both person and sign, both individual and object, "an impossible duality" (61).

How this impossible duality, which Oates envisioned as tragic in her early novels, later became the occasion for the brilliant emancipatory strategies of her subversively comic novels is my topic in *Lavish Self-Divisions*. The sociolinguistic fact that every woman is born a daughter, that she has no choice about this relationship, creates her dilemma. My thesis is that the daughter's dilemma prompted Oates, herself a daughter, to experiment with a wide range of literary conventions, including plot, closure, narrative voice, imagery, and genre, in order to expand the range of sociolinguistic options available to her, as an author, and to her female characters. Such sociopolitical concerns inspire many of Oates's literary experiments, as well as her frequent allusions to other literary works. "Experimentation for its own sake doesn't interest me" (*Conversations* 71–72), Oates told Robert Phillips. As Eileen Teper Bender has demonstrated, Oates's allusions to other writers are frequently parodic, a strategy for resisting the Law of the Father, including the laws governing genres. Oates's desire to transform the daughter's part is one reason why, as Gates says, she "picks up and discards generic forms at will." Although Oates's relationship to genres may confuse critics—especially those who want to categorize her as a realist, a naturalist, or a gothic novelist—her parody of genres is one means by which she articulates a feminist vision. At other times, Oates's feminist voice can be heard in relationship to the authorial voice(s) in her novels. In the 1980s, for example, Oates transforms many of her daughter-characters into narrators whose authority comes from the feminist communities in which they participate.

The mother-daughter tradition from which these narrators derive their authority subverts the traditional notion of authorship in which authority passes from father to son. It is no accident, for example, that Michel Foucault uses the male pronoun when he suggests that "it would be worth examining how the author became individualized in a culture like ours, what status he has been given . . . at what point we began to recount the lives of authors rather than of heroes, and how this fundamental category of 'the-man-and-his work criticism' began" (720). Yet if Foucault's "author function" is conceived, in Bakhtinian terms, as a site for "the dynamic interplay between the male and female" (Finke 99), it has considerable value for the feminist critic. On the other hand, if we are to understand authorship in terms of power relations, it makes a difference who is speaking, who is authoring. As feminist critics have pointed out, the linguistic position of the (woman) writer, like the social position of her fictional daughters, differs from that of her male counterparts. Until recently, for example, a (woman) writer could not look to literary foremothers because they had been "lost." It is likely that Oates, who began publishing in the late 1950s, had studied such a traditional father-son canon. Hence, I agree with Cheryl Wall that, given the exclusion of women from the traditional canon, "to erase a woman poet as the author of her poems in favor of an abstract indeterminacy is an act of oppression" (571).

Nevertheless, when Oates asks, "What is the ontological status of a writer *who is also a woman?*" she answers: "In the practice of her craft, she may well become bodiless and invisible, defined to herself fundamentally as what she thinks, dreams, plots, constructs" ([*Woman*] *Writer* 22–23). In Oates's view, then, writing may be understood as an act of imagination by which a woman becomes "invisible,"[8] free of those categories, including gender stereotypes, imposed on her by others. Where, then, are we to find that invisible woman, author "Joyce Carol Oates"? The answer, as Oates herself suggests, is that she can be found "in what she thinks, dreams, plots, constructs." Hence, the emphasis in *Lavish Self-Divisions* is on Oates's imaginative experiences, on what she "thinks, dreams, plots, constructs," rather than on her actual lived experiences. Following Domna Stanton's example in *The Female Autograph*, I excise the *bio* from auto*bio*graphy in order to "bracket the traditional emphasis on the narration of 'a life,' and that notion's facile presumption of referentiality" (vii). Oates herself places emphasis on the graphic when she says, in a comment on her plays, that "no form of art is perhaps so graphically autobiographical in essence—in emotional essence—as the drama; yet no form of art can appear so distant" (*Three Plays* ix). As stated above, in *Lavish Self-Divisions* "Joyce Carol Oates" refers to the many selves, the contending voices and texts, graphically represented in her novels. As Oates explains, " 'JCO' is not a person, nor even a personality, but a process that has resulted in a sequence of texts" (" 'JCO' and I" n.p.).

Lavish Self-Divisions is, in addition, a feminist analysis of the intriguing sociolinguistic parallels between author Oates and her daughter-characters. I argue that Oates's linguistic dilemmas—in particular her struggles with the Law of the Father—mirror the social dilemmas that her fictional daughters must struggle to resolve in order to become authors of their lives. These struggles differ, both for Oates and her female characters, reflecting changes in the women's movement in the United States during the past three decades. It is important to note, however, that in contrast to a biographical analysis, an auto-graphic analysis of a (woman) writer's oeuvre does not require that the author live through all that her characters experience. Quite the contrary: by writing about an experience, it is sometimes possible to avoid enacting it. As Oates once explained to interviewer Sally Quinn, by writing "The Dead" she had avoided the fate of her female protagonist, Ilena. Furthermore, although the inarticulate characters in her fiction often " 'do not understand . . . that they have been destroyed' " (72), Oates herself wanted, as she explained in a 1972 interview with Walter Clemons, "to move toward a more articulate moral position, not just dramatizing nightmarish problems but trying to show possible ways of transcending them" ("Joyce Carol Oates" 77). Clearly, because of her ability to portray a wide range of human beings, Oates differs from her inarticulate characters. However, even when, as in novels such as *Unholy Loves* or *Marya, a Life*, she depicts women who are, like Oates herself, teachers and writers, her novels are not necessarily auto*bio*graphical—that is, the experiences of even her most articulate women are not necessarily the same as hers.

In my view, critics can do great damage to the reputation of a (woman) writer by using an autobiographical approach. Some, for example, have diminished Oates's creative accomplishment by equating her with her female characters—mistakenly assuming that the author suffers from the same problems as her characters. Such critical misconceptions date from the early 1970s, but since they continue to exert a negative effect on the reception of her novels, it is important to address them here.

For example, in a 1971 review of *them*, Benjamin DeMott charged that Oates failed to distance herself from the values and attitudes of her lower-class characters, a charge that critics repeated for another decade. According to DeMott, Oates's failure to distance herself from her characters indicated a lack of reflective intelligence; therefore, he concluded, she did not deserve the literary prizes—in this instance, the National Book Award for *them*—she had been awarded. Even though Oates's "Author's Note" to *them* had described the brutal experiences of the Wendalls as "remote" ("Because their world was so remote from me," she wrote, "it entered me with tremendous power" [n.p.]) DeMott insisted upon interpreting the novel as autobiographical. Oates, he said, "repeatedly stresses that, in substance as in detail, *them* is no imaginary voyage. The basis of the whole was solid fact" (*Critical Essays* 20). In short, DeMott diminished Oates's accomplishments by claiming that she did not *imagine* her novel *them*, but only *experienced* it. According to DeMott, Oates is a writer who, like her working-class characters, lacks "reflective intelligence," and therefore, "registers no distinctions among qualities of experience," a writer "whose characters' responses never are set in any perspective broader or subtler than their own" (21).

Other critics mistakenly assume that, in order to write about violence, Oates must have personally experienced it. So frequently has Oates been asked, "Why Is Your Writing So Violent?" that in a 1981 essay that uses this question as its title she responded that this is an "insulting," an "ignorant," a "sexist" question ("Why Is Your Writing So Violent?" 35). As Oates says, "War, rape, murder and the more colorful minor crimes evidently fall within the exclusive province of the male writer, just as, generally, they fall within the exclusive province of male action" ("Why" 35). It must be, she says, that "there is a violation of some unspoken rule in the very fact that a woman writes—that is, thinks" ("Why" 15). Despite evidence of violence everywhere on the globe, her questioners—whether "in Oslo, in Helsinki, in Brussels, in Budapest and in that dramatically 'Western' city in Eastern Europe known for its encircling wall" (15)—assumed that she writes about violence because she has personally experienced it. "Why," she was asked by Europeans, "was my writing so violent? Might it be that my 'personal experience,' 'perhaps my childhood' and, in any case, my 'unique temperament' had so 'distorted my vision of mankind and of history'?" ("Why" 15). One questioner in West Berlin, apparently unaware of his own city's history of violence, actually suggested that her writing might be violent because she had lived in that "violent" city, Detroit, Michigan, the setting of *them.* In short, although Oates sympathetically imagined the characters in *them,* readers continue to assume that, because she is a woman, her novels are autobiographical.

Unfortunately, feminist critics have sometimes subjected Oates to the same kind of criticism. For example, beginning in the early 1970s, feminists began to echo DeMott's attack, creating a negative climate for Oates's fiction for at least a decade. Feminist hostility toward Oates began, as Jane Gallop notes, with the publication in 1972 of Susan Koppelman's *Images of Women in Fiction.* Since Gallop expected the first collection of feminist criticism to "trash" male writers, she was surprised, she says, to find in Koppelman's "unusually vehement" essay, an especially harsh attack on *them* (*Around 1981* 82). According to Koppelman, " '[A]t no time does Miss Oates separate herself from her characters and say, 'This sexism, like their racism, their ignorance . . . their poverty, is part of their victimization' " (qtd. in Gallop, *Around 1981* 94). Echoing DeMott, Koppelman charges that Oates lacks sufficient critical and moral distance from her poor, bigoted characters. Subsequent critics have repeated this charge, though usually in milder tones. Gary Waller says, for example, that "with Oates, we are never provided with a firm moral perspective; instead we are taken into the maelstrom of feelings" (118), while Linda Wagner asks, "What kind of moral judgment underlies her fiction?" (xix).

This chapter in the history of feminist criticism may explain, in part, why many feminist critics remain hostile to Oates's fiction. Another possibility

is that some critics, confusing the author with the victimized female characters in her early fiction, mistakenly conclude that Oates lacks a feminist
consciousness. As Marilyn Wesley points out, such confusion is often most
evident when "critics address the implications of Oates' largely ignored
incest motif" ("Father-Daughter Incest" 252). The most blatant example
of such confusion, Wesley argues, is Anne Z. Mickelson's argument that
Oates is " 'working out her own fears and obsessions through the medium
of fiction' " (qtd. in "Father-Daughter Incest" 252). On the topic of father-
daughter incest, which, as I shall demonstrate, is pervasive in Oates's oeuvre,[9] it is critical to differentiate between the author and her characters.
Nevertheless, Oates's linguistic struggles with the Law of the Father often
mirror the struggles her female characters enact with their seductive or
sexually violent fathers or father surrogates. Yet, in the mid-1970s, Oates
began to shift her narrative focus from father-daughter to mother-daughter
stories. As this shift took place, Oates's vision began to change from tragic
to comic.

   To state the matter too simply, Oates's vision is tragic when the daughter
submits to a father's incestuous desires, but her vision is comic, in a subversively feminist sense, when the daughter has a strong bond with a mother
who encourages her daughter's quest for self-definition. Tragic action is
averted when the patriarch, acknowledging love for his aging wife, along
with his fear of death, lets go of his daughter, despite his incestuous desires.
Denying such incestuous desires is not effective, for, if the patriarch re-
presses these powerful emotions, they will be projected in paranoid fashion
onto the outside world. Hence, as Oates points out, Lear is terrified of the
truths Cordelia utters: "Very exciting it is, extremely convincing—Lear's
dread of the daughter who will speak her mind, the chaos of nature that will
not be governed, the female impulses that leap, uncontrolled, to the most
forbidden of all objects, the illegitimate son" (*Contraries* 76). Shakespeare
may have sacrificed Cordelia, Oates suggests, not because the logic of the
plot demanded it, but because the playwright himself had mistaken Cordelia
for the "enemy." Why would a father, whether Lear or Shakespeare, mistake
his youngest daughter for the enemy?

   Again and again, Oates dramatizes this problem in short stories and
novels, demonstrating that the departure of the youngest daughter signals,
for the father, his impending death. Like Lear, many of the fathers in
Oates's fiction mistake the departure of a last and youngest daughter with
the threat of death; hence, the father demands that the daughter love him

"all," just as she is about to leave him behind. Psychologically, the patriarch's fear is understandable; however, as Oates argues in "Is This the Promised End?" the patriarch's paranoia blinds him, causing him to conflate the "feminine" with "evil," and imagine as enemies those who "love him best" (*Contraries* 78). From the sixties through the early nineties, many fathers in Oates's fiction display such paranoia: like Lear before them, Herz in *With Shuddering Fall* (1964), Jessie Vogel in *Wonderland* (1971), Ian McCullough in *American Appetites* (1989), and Jerome Corcoran in *What I Lived For* (1994) confuse their youngest daughters' departure with betrayal, chaos, death. Nevertheless, following Oates's re-vision of the tragic ending of *Wonderland* in 1973, she began to shatter the looking glass, re-visioning the daughter's role in an increasing number of subversively feminist comic novels. In *Childwold* (1976), for example, Oates employs a plot that will become, in the 1980s, the pervasive pattern in most of her novels: the daughter's return to her culturally devalued mother. Furthermore, as these changes take place in Oates's daughter-characters—as they acquire the ability to author themselves—they mirror changes in Oates's conception of authorship from anxious to dialogic and, in the 1980s, to a feminist-communal authorship.

As I demonstrate in Part One, during Oates's period of anxious author-ship, her imagination remained circumscribed by the Law of the Father. She was able to move beyond this period of authorship only when she began to transgress the convention of aesthetic unity, especially as it governs tragic closure. Oates employs tragic closure in *With Shuddering Fall* (1964) and in two novels of her early trilogy, *A Garden of Earthly Delights* (1966) and *Expensive People* (1968). With the publication of *them* (1969), this pattern began to change, but Oates used tragic closure in her next novel, *Wonderland* (1971), although she revised the ending before allowing the novel to be reissued in 1973. Oates's struggle with closure was, in part, a response to the violence taking place in the United States, as some groups—white women and blacks, especially—struggled for social change. The novel, unlike tragedy, was shaped by such decentralizing, centrifugal forces, ac-cording to Bakhtin.[10] During the period of the novel's development, Paula Cohen argues, it was the daughter's role, through an incestuous alliance, psychological or actual, with the father, not only to save the family, but "to save a theory of representation that corresponds to it" (181). The ideology of "the closed family is reflected," Cohen states, "in the nineteenth century aesthetic practice of tying up loose ends to achieve a unified close," which was, at the same time, "an effort to retain a belief in empirical reality, in the unitary nature of truth" (181).[11]

This very problem—the desire to achieve the aesthetic perfection of a unified close, a desire that required the sacrifice of a daughter-character to an incestuous father—brought Oates to "the edge of impossibility." As she wrote in a 1975 journal entry, following the publication of *Wonderland*: "In 'Wonderland' I was dictated to by an organizational clarity that forbade expansion, wanting the work to be 'perfect' in its form. Its curve is tragic. It was a deliberate tragedy, worked out in detail, structurally meticulous"("Delirium and Detachment" 134). She adds, "I must have been listening to or reading old-fashioned critics, though it might have been simply that I saw, in the mid- and late sixties, that certain American pathways were tragic and those who took them lived out a tragic curve, a tragic destiny" ("Delirium and Detachment" 136). Almost twenty years later, in an "Afterword" to the 1992 edition of *Wonderland*, Oates offered this analysis of her fictional daughter: "My graphic vision of Shelley, wasted and ungendered and sickly-yellow with jaundice at *Wonderland*'s end, is an exaggerated self-portrait, meant perhaps to exert authorial control over the torrential experience of novel-writing—which is the formal, daylight discipline of which novel-imagining is the passion" (508). Here is an example, then, of how author Oates experiences, on a linguistic or "graphic" register, what her fictional daughter, Shelley, enacts.

In an effort to emancipate her daughters from victimization, Oates began to transgress and transform generic conventions beginning in the early 1970s, the decade that I define as the period of "dialogic" authorship. By this time Oates had recognized, as did the emerging feminist movement, that daughters need stories of their own. Oates says, for example, "In retrospect, it seems that Shelley Vogel was crying out for a novel of her own, a story that was not a mere appendage of her father's, but this was a novel I could not, or would not write. The material was simply too devastating" (1992 "Afterword" 511). In her next novel, *Do with Me What You Will* (1973), Oates began to transform her daughters into more autonomous and assertive human beings; at the same time, she was struggling to affirm the dialogic or I/thou nature of identity (the law of two), rather than the isolated, competitive "I." Oates has consistently resisted the myth of the isolated author-self, the "I" in competition with all others, to affirm what Patricia Waugh calls the "positional 'I,'" the dialogic author-self defined only through relationships.[12] On a linguistic plane, this meant that Oates would define her own artistic vision, or voice, through her relationship to other voices and texts absorbed into her novels. As I demonstrate in Part Two, Oates committed "infidelities" to patriarchal linguistic codes in a series of "marriages" to literary fathers such as Joyce and James, as well as to extraliterary fathers, who embodied the voices (and discourses) of lawyers, politicians, and businessmen.

Where, then, are we to find author Oates during this "dialogic" decade? My answer is that she can be found in the dialogic tensions between the languages or discourses she absorbs into her novels. In "Discourse in the Novel," Bakhtin explains, "Dialogic tension between two languages and two belief systems permits authorial intentions to be realized in such a way that we can acutely sense their presence at every point" (*Dialogic Imagination* 314). Many examples of such tensions are evident in Oates's satires of literary, legal, political, religious, and business discourses. One such tension (of great significance in Oates's oeuvre, as I have suggested above) is her marriage/infidelity to tragic closure. As Oates began to transform the father-daughter romance plot into the mother-daughter romance, a parallel shift took place in her vision: the tragic vision of the sixties became the comic vision of the 1970s. A parallel change is evident in Oates's criticism. In the 1972 Preface to *The Edge of Impossibility: Tragic Forms in Literature*, she wrote, "Art is built around violence, around death; at its base is fear. The absolute dream, if dreamed, must deal with death, and the only way toward death we understand is the way of violence" (7), but by 1976 she apparently had changed her mind. As Oates began to transform the daughter's part, she began to parody the conventions of tragedy.

As I argue in Part Two, the scene of dismemberment in *The Assassins* (1975) should be read as a parody of the tragic vision—and also as a metaphor of the (woman) writer's lavish self-division into all her characters. As evident in Oates's critical essays written during the early 1970s, she was becoming increasingly critical of what she describes as "the pretensions of tragedy." For example, in 1972, while revisiting the question of tragedy in an essay on D. H. Lawrence, she found in him "a curious and probably unique equation between the exalted pretensions of tragedy and the rationalizing, desacralizing process [that] he sensed in operation everywhere around him" (*New Heaven, New Earth* 58). The Joyce Carol Oates who wrote *The Assassins* seems to agree with Lawrence, for this novel implies that the tragic vision is "representative of a distorted claim to prominence in the universe, a usurpation of the sacredness of the Other, the Infinite" (*New Heaven, New*

Earth 58). This change in Oates's view of the tragic vision explains why, in *The Assassins*, she satirizes a father-identified female protagonist who writes as a "male impersonator," while, for the first time, she portrays in *Childwold* a daughter's return to her working-class mother. What Mary Kathryn Grant describes as "the tragic vision of Joyce Carol Oates" is transformed, with the publication of *Childwold*, into a feminist comic vision. In 1976, the same year Oates published *Childwold*, she declared in an essay on Joyce: "The impulse of comedy is gregarious; it is really comedy, rather than tragedy, that 'breaks down the dykes' between people (to use Yeats's expression) and unlooses a communal music" (*Contraries* 186). In Oates's novels, this communal voice can be identified as a society's yearning to acknowledge the repressed, the (m)other in us.

Although the mother-daughter story has been at the margins of cultural consciousness for centuries, as Adrienne Rich reminds us in *Of Woman Born*, it has rarely been told. How, then, do (women) novelists—in what voices and in what manner—tell mother-daughter stories when, historically, as Du Plessis and others have pointed out, this relationship has been marginalized by the heterosexual romance plot? As Susan Lanser explains in *Fictions of Authority*, if a (woman) writer is to overcome the authority of this heterosexual plot, she must "construct narrative voices that seek to write themselves into Literature without leaving Literature the same" (8). Such narrators may be "skeptical of the authoritative aura of the male pen and often critical of male dominance in general," as Lanser says, but they are constrained "by social and textual convention to reproduce the very structures they would reformulate" (8). As a result, somewhat contradictorily, "as they strive to create fictions of authority, these narrators expose fictions of authority as the Western novel has constructed it" (Lanser 8). These fictions of authority include both heterosexual conventions of plot, as well as individualistic, "masculine" conventions of narration. In other words, if women are to say "we"—as mothers and daughters, as sisters, as communities of women—they must overcome conventions of plot and narration which separate them.

As I demonstrate in Part Three of *Lavish Self-Divisions*, Oates often creates communal narrators of a feminist kind in order to solve these problems in her female-centered novels of the 1980s. Many of these novels illustrate Marianne Hirsch's argument in *The Mother/Daughter Plot:* that the mother-daughter story can be found in "postmodern plots" in contemporary novels by women that are "structured around the motif of return" to the mother

(139). Oates employs this plot in almost every novel of this decade, not only in her postmodern novels, set in the nineteenth century—*Bellefleur, A Bloodsmoor Romance,* and *Mysteries of Winterthurn*—but also in her so-called realistic novels, set in the twentieth century, *Angel of Light, You Must Remember This, American Appetites,* and *Marya, a Life.* Oates also examines eroticism and power struggles in female relationships in *Solstice* (1985) and *Foxfire, Confessions of a Girl Gang* (1993). Even in Oates's realistic novels, as Sally Robinson has noted, she "raises questions about the politics of representations. Such questioning can produce a sharp critique of our assumptions about social positions" ("Heat and Cold" 401). In order to produce such a critique, Oates, along with other contemporary feminist novelists, has repeatedly challenged established conventions of the novel.

In my view, the novel is amenable to such feminist re-visionings of its conventions; it is not a genre whose very structure, as Myra Jehlen speculates, requires "an impotent feminine sensibility" ("Archimedes" 214). The novel is far more plastic, as Bakhtin emphasizes, than has sometimes been recognized, and, as feminist critics revise the history of the novel, they are discovering the genre's hidden potential. For example, although it is true, as Cohen says, that male modernists placed more emphasis on fathers and sons than on mothers and daughters, in a revised feminist canon the mother-daughter story becomes central. Through a study of this feminist canon, as Marianne Hirsch argues in *The Mother/Daughter Plot,* it is possible to identify historical changes in the daughter's part. Hirsch found that daughters often refuse to identify with their mothers and sisters in nineteenth-century novels by women, but in the modernist novel—as, for example, in Virginia Woolf's *To the Lighthouse*—this pattern begins to change as more emphasis is placed upon the daughter's artistic ambitions. Nevertheless, as Hirsch points out, daughters rarely show a mature desire for affiliation with other women, including mothers and sisters, until the present era. Even in contemporary novels, such a desire for female affiliation does not always occur since daughters may continue to privilege their alliances with the fathers.

Yet the fiction of Joyce Carol Oates suggests at least one powerful mode of resistance to the incestuous father: a daughter's strong bond with a healthy, self-assertive and self-defining mother. As illustrated in Oates's novels of the 1980s, and as Jessica Benjamin argues in *The Bonds of Love,* a mother's right to establish boundaries is rarely put forward as a model of her children's mental health, let alone of her own. Society's expectation of mothers—

that they sacrifice themselves to others—remains much the same even after three decades of struggle by the second wave of the women's movement. In fact, feminist criticism, as well as feminist fiction, suffers from a tendency toward "daughter-centricity,"[13] a privileging of the daughter's perspective that results in the silencing and marginalizing of the mother. This problem occurs not only because of the constraints of traditional Oedipal narrative—narrative based upon father-son relationships—but also because many daughters suffer from what Elizabeth Spelman calls "somatophobia," a fear and hatred of the maternal body. As Adrienne Rich reminds us, we are all "of woman born," and to deny this fact is to deny our kinship with our mothers.

In an "adolescent" society, with its romantic denial of aging, daughters find it difficult to resist the temptation to ally themselves with seductive father figures, both socially and linguistically. In the 1980s, Oates's daughter-heroes frequently overidealize their fathers, but a significant change can be discerned: in varying degrees, daughters begin to value their maternal inheritance, and as the mother-daughter romance becomes central in their life-narratives, they begin to resist incestuous alliances, psychological or actual, with their fathers. In contrast to novels of the 1960s, in which mothers are generally victimized, in these later novels mothers are human beings with voices and aspirations of their own. In *American Appetites,* for example, Glynnis McCullough is both a traditional homemaker and a writer of cookbooks; in *Marya, a Life,* Marya's mother, who is "found" in the last chapter of the novel, has a face much like her daughter's and a name, "Vera"; and in *You Must Remember This,* Enid's mother Hannah starts a sewing business, claiming the value of her own artistry, a value her daughter Enid belatedly discovers, and one that nurtures her own desire to become a pianist. A similar pattern can be discerned in the postmodern novels in which daughter-narrators—Germaine, Deirdre, and Perdita—draw upon their mothers' stories in order to become authors of their own lives and texts. Indeed, the daughter's "empty pack" is finally being filled, for she now carries with her the mother's story.

Thus, the question—What happens when women write?—is complex. Yet Joyce Carol Oates has been equal to the sociolinguistic challenge: her novels critique, transgress, and transform literary genres or conventions that perpetuate unjust social hierarchies. To illustrate this feminist critique, I analyze the sociolinguistic parallels between the (woman) writer and her daughter-characters in novels published over the past three decades. In

Part 1 I argue that during the 1960s and early 1970s, the period of "anxious authorship," Oates was struggling to leave the linguistic Law of the Father, while on the social plane her female characters tried repeatedly, usually without success, to leave the houses of seductive or incestuous fathers. In Part 2 I illustrate how, in the mid-1970s through the early 1980s, the period of "dialogic authorship," Oates made a series of "marriages" to literary and extraliterary fathers in order to commit "infidelities" to their rule; during this same decade, her increasingly transgressive daughters began, however tentatively, to author their own lives. Finally, I demonstrate that during the 1980s and early 1990s, the period of Oates's "communal authorship," she began to acknowledge her literary foremothers and create feminist communal narrators, while her literary daughters, many of whom were also artists, began seeking alliances with their devalued mothers and sisters.

Lavish Self-Divisions

PART I

Anxious Authorship in the 1960s: Daughters Leaving Home

In a story called "Images," published in her first collection *By the North Gate* (1963), Joyce Carol Oates depicts a young woman haunted by memories. As she turns to her lover, having just left the bedside of her dying father, she "sees a little girl, a pale, thin-faced little girl with astonished, ashamed eyes; she sees her mother, her grandfather, her father—all staring in amazement at her, trying to call her back, claim her, transform her back to herself. This is not you, they cry, this is not you! You are someone else!" (119). Out of the desire to keep their daughter, the family wants to fix its image upon her in defiance of the passage of time emphasized in the story's temporal divisions: "Thirteen Years Ago," "Eleven Years Ago," "Eight Years Ago," "Five Years Ago," "One Year Ago." But, like Oates herself, the girl has found a way to leave her family—the way of the imagination—long before she actually leaves home. The desire to leave, whether literal or figurative, is a strong characteristic of women's fiction of the early 1960s, according to Gayle Greene. Yet, as Greene says, "Leaving home is not enough. Change requires more than moving out, resolution or will: it requires a process of re-envisioning which allows an evolution and alteration of desire and consciousness" (*Changing the Story* 14).[1]

"Images" does not achieve such a re-envisioning, but it does indicate a desire for change, and it identifies the daughter's imagination as the proper site for such a transformation. By simply standing at the screen door and looking into the darkness, the daughter had "slipped out of herself and, if surprised by her mother, she would stare at the woman in horror: horror at herself, at her shame in appearing naked face set to face, mask askew. She would grope about her in the dark of the kitchen for her other face, her role. Blind, she would grasp anything—an outgrown face, a ten-year-old face" (113). Moreover, by locating consciousness on the threshold—at a gate, a doorway, a wall—this early story carnivalizes the notion of a stable self, suggesting the imagination's fluidity, its ability to transform social roles such as daughter, wife, or mother. We can leave home anytime, through our "images," this story suggests, as long as we are also willing to risk leaving behind the self by which we are known to others. This equally powerful desire to stay, to remain where we are known—however oppressive home may be—often conflicts with a daughter's desire to leave. As a result, at least in the early fiction, Oates's characters are frequently defeated in their efforts to leave, just as they are defeated in their attempts to author themselves. As Robert Fossum says, in Oates's fiction " 'all human beings are artists, whether consciously or unconsciously,' " but they are "notably unsuccessful artists" (285).

In certain respects this pattern of failure for Oates's daughters is symptomatic of her own "failures" as an author during this decade. For even though, as Oates says, "Most novelists divide themselves up lavishly in their novels" (*New Heaven, New Earth* 278n), during the 1960s she most often projected her power of self-authoring onto her male characters, while projecting a willingness to be authored or defined onto her female characters. The early fiction reveals a pattern of authorial self-division that conforms to gender conventions: her male characters, such as Richard Everett in *Expensive People* and Jules Wendall in *them*, assume the right to define themselves, whereas her female characters, such as Nada Everett in *Expensive People* or Maureen Wendall and Nadine Greene in *them*, act as characters in some (male) author's fiction. Indeed, in the final pages of *them* lower-class Maureen asserts herself more effectively than does her counterpart from the upper-middle-class suburb of Grosse Point, a passive princess whose problems are also explored in "How I Contemplated the World," first published in 1969.[2] Like Nadine Green in *them*, the unnamed narrator of "How I Contemplated the World" refers to herself only in the third person, as "the girl," whereas Richard Everett, as narrator of *Expensive People*, begins his memoirs with the bold statement, "I was a child murderer."

Although both are economically and educationally privileged children, only Richard readily assumes an authorial persona, speaking from the place of a violently preestablished, coherent authorial "I." By contrast, the girl, who has no preestablished I, illustrates Judith Kegan Gardiner's point that female identity is a process that does not conform to the Oedipal myth of a unique, whole, and coherent self (179). Moreover, though Gardiner suggests that women often define themselves through the act of writing, the girl in "How I Contemplated the World" does not. Both of these adolescents have been educated in elite private schools, but only Richard writes well, and only he has the audacity to criticize America. The girl has no awareness of the irony involved in her use of an outline, a form most readers will recognize as quite unsuited to the girl's disorganized statement of identity. By contrast, Richard's memoirs savagely satirize the values of a consumer society. His confession that he has killed his mother, not his father, is even more sophisticated satire—an inversion of the Oedipal plot. This inversion functions as a critique of the Freudian concept of identity, the very concept of identity used by the Freudian psychiatrists who, of course, fail in their attempts to cure him.

The socially determined personae adopted by both of these adolescents—the male "author" and the female "character"—are ultimately self-destructive. For example, it is apparent from the girl's essay, a disorganized outline of her experience of running away from home, that she is a character still in search of a (male) author, a lover to replace her father; whereas Richard, the girl's mirror image, is already an accomplished author, but one whose authority has been established by violence, by matricide. His satire reeks of aggression, not only against his parents but against most adults, including his anticipated readers. Helplessly acting out the script of the passive female character and the aggressive male author, these adolescents clearly acquiesce to traditional gender roles. In this way, they are like other adolescents in Oates's early fiction whom Fossum describes as feeling as if they are "actors in a script written and directed by someone else" (286). Both illustrate Fossum's point that "repeatedly, Oates's people crave an order associated with 'home' and the loving protection of the father. Repeatedly, this conflicts with the yearning for the 'road' and freedom from the father" (286).

Of course, "lighting out for the territory" is hardly a new metaphor for the struggle for self-definition in American fiction. Huck Finn and Holden Caulfield are well-known examples of adolescents who not only leave home but who narrate their stories of flight with considerable insight. This male tradition may have led Fossum to argue that the yearnings of Oates's adolescents, whether for home or for the road, are "expressions of a struggle to control their own lives against the forces of 'accident,' circumstances, [and] other people" (286). Although Fossum's statement is accurate, it tends to minimize the desire for relationship suggested in the metaphor of "home." Perhaps because Fossum's model of identity formation is based upon male experience, it places more emphasis on control and autonomy than upon connectedness. Yet whether we are at home or in flight, we define ourselves only in relationship to others; even our declarations of independence must be acknowledged by someone, as Jessica Benjamin points out in *The Bonds of Love*. In both her criticism and fiction Oates emphasizes, as Benjamin does, that the self is socially embedded, or "interconnected," and that this relational self is constructed by language. Once we accept the notion that identity is formed through language, it follows that, as Bakhtin asserts, "we must all, perforce, become authors" (quoted in Holquist 314). For if we do not make a conscious effort to resist the gender scripts encoded in language, they author us.

Thus, the problem of self-definition is complex, but especially for daughters. While a son expects to inherit cultural—and authorial—power, a daughter does not. As Lynda Boose and Betty Flowers point out in *Daughters and Fathers*, a daughter's inheritance from her mother is not parallel to a son's inheritance from a father. Daughters are therefore more anxious about assuming authorship over their lives. As a result, the problem of how to "leave home" developed into a gender riddle for Oates, for the problem of leaving home differs for sons and daughters. In fact, Oates commented in 1973 that the theme of her story "How I Contemplated the World" had "so obsessed" her that she had "treated it half a dozen times, perhaps more" ("Appendix" 542). That theme, she says, is "why we leave home or make vain attempts to leave home, or failing that, yearn to leave home. There are many ways of leaving" (542). As she intimates, one way of leaving home is literal; another way is imaginative; the problem is that "while you're away, trying to map out another life, new parents or stray adults or simply anyone with an I. Q. one point above yours conquers you. They just walk up to you and take hold. That's that" (542). Whether you're trying to "map out another life" on the street or in a work of fiction, the problem is greater for young women. "The puzzle is," Oates says, with an emphasis on gender, "how do we become these people who victimize us? They are so charming, so much in control of their bitten-off part of the world; they are so very masculine" (542).

The problem of how to free young people from debilitating notions of selfhood continued to puzzle Oates throughout the 1960s, and she worried aloud about the possible "moral failure" of her writing in an interview with Walter Clemons in 1972, because she had depicted problems, but no solutions, in her early fiction. Yet in "How I Contemplated the World," it is possible to see, however faintly, a notion of selfhood that is suggestive of a different conception of the female as well as the authorial self. Although the female adolescent writer's effort to define an "I" does not succeed, her "Notes for an English class" illustrate Judith Kegan Gardiner's point that, while the myth of male identity posits a "unique, whole, and coherent" self defined after a single crisis, female identity is not achieved by way of such a catharsis. Since the right to an "Oedipal" identity is denied to daughters, women must establish identity, Gardiner says, "in defiance of conventional generic boundaries and of conventional characterization" (179). As reformulated by Gardiner, and as suggested in this early Oates story, female identity may be imagined as a "process," just as writing is a process (178).

Oates recognized that in order to challenge socially constructed identities, she had to do something more than simply reverse male and female gender roles. Transforming her female adolescents into questors—into heroes who would "kill" the father in order to claim his cultural authority—would merely perpetuate myths of violent self-definition. Gardiner suggests a partial answer to this riddle when she proposes a maternal metaphor of authorship, "the hero is her author's daughter." This transforms the old heroic authorial "I" into "a maternal metaphor of female authorship [that] clarifies the (woman) writer's distinctive engagement with her characters" (179). Gardiner's metaphor of authorship does seem appropriate for defining Oates's nurturant relationship to her characters, both male or female, but it does not completely solve the riddle of gender, a problem that puzzled her in the late 1960s. During this decade, Oates continued to divide herself into violently articulate sons who, in order to become authors, dominate passively inarticulate daughters, whom they claim as characters in their own fictions. Such authorial self-division is characteristic of women writers, past and present, as Charlotte Goodman points out, partly because of the conventions of the traditional bildungsroman. In other words, even as Oates attempted to transform the daughters in her short stories and novels, literary conventions worked against her efforts.

As previously stated, Oates herself says of *Ontological Proof of My Existence* that her female character, Shelley, "begins her play strongly and even defiantly; but she loses it, as she loses her audience, to the superior imagination—the strength and bravado—of her enterprising lover Peter V" (*Three Plays* viii). Peter V, an aggressive male character, simply takes over as Shelley's director. A similar fate befell most of the daughters in Oates's novels and short stories: they would try to leave home, only to be conquered by more powerful males, many of whom acted as their author-fathers. These problems of plot and characterization are probably the reason that in a 1980 preface to *Ontological Proof of My Existence*, written almost ten years after the play's performance, Oates defines it as "graphically autobiographical." In this retrospective description of the play, Oates acknowledges that the riddle of identity is, more specifically, a riddle of gendered identity. Her female protagonist is a graphic trace of Oates's own authorial dilemma. For example, in "Stories That Define Me" (1982), she acknowledges that Alice "wasn't telling her own story; That godly privilege resided with someone named, in gilt letters on the book's spine, 'Lewis Carroll' " (15). As I demonstrate in the next three chapters, Oates's desire for an alternative model of authorship becomes increasingly evident in her depictions of male-female relationships in the novels of the 1960s.[3]

I

Not Strictly Parallel: The Sacrificial Plots of Daughters and Sons *in* With Shuddering Fall

Joyce Carol Oates published her first novel in 1964, a few years prior to the emergence of the second wave of the women's movement; nevertheless, her recognition of the destructive effects of narrowly defined gender roles is critical to an understanding of plot and character in *With Shuddering Fall.* In fact, although Oates docs not succeed in "writing beyond the ending" (Du Plessis) of the romance plot in this early novel, she does begin to explore conventions of plot and narrative authority. If the novel is read not as a romance but as a contemporary variation upon ancient stories of sacrifice, it can also be understood as a probing analysis of the destructive effects of patriarchal plots—religious, socioeconomic, political, and literary—upon the lives of the young, both male and female. The novel announces its focus upon patriarchal plots through an early and explicit reference to the biblical story of Abraham's near-sacrifice of Isaac. Its portrayals of three contemporary Old Testament fathers are all variations on the Abraham-Isaac plot: the story of Old Rule, a poor hermit who is dying and whose son arrives just as the novel opens; the story of Mr. Herz, an aging but wealthy farmer who fears the loss of his daughter; and also the plot of Max, a wealthy businessman who "owns" his race car driver, Shar Rule, and who wants to possess Karen Herz. When Shar Rule comes home to bury his father, he is attracted to Karen, the seventeen-year-old daughter of Herz. Oates may have seen both Shar and Karen as Isaac-figures sacrificed to the father, but daughters and sons are not, she would discover, structural equivalents.

Nevertheless, the novel develops both plots—the plot of the obedient daughter and the disobedient son—in order to dramatize the quote from Nietzsche that prefaces the novel: "What is done out of love always takes place beyond good and evil" (6). As Oates explained in a 1969 interview, *With Shuddering Fall* was meant to be a "religious" novel in which "the father was the father of the Old Testament who gives a command as God gave a command to Abraham, and everything was parallel, very strictly parallel," and she added, "how we obey it or not obey it, and if we do obey it we're not going to be rewarded anyway" (Kuehl 309). In fact, the novel does make the point that neither the patriarch's "good" nor his "evil" is rewarded, for Karen's passive obedience leads to Shar's death, while Shar's aggressive disobedience leads to the death of their unborn child. In this way the novel illustrates Nietzsche's view that mature love takes place beyond "good" or "evil," beyond the binary logic and morality of childhood. Indeed, the novel's point is that human beings become loving adults only by transcending this paternal logos. The novel does not, however, make the point that these plots—the disobedient son and the obedient daughter— are "strictly parallel." A lack of symmetry is already obvious when, at the outset, Karen functions as the object of the struggle between Shar and Herz. Furthermore, although Karen appears to be active in the quest for Shar, she is actually an "innocent" instrument of her father's will as long as she remains sexually frigid in obedience to her father's command to "kill" her lover. It is a psychological game that confuses Shar, who finally kills himself on the race track.

Unlike the son, the daughter is the "exchangeable" figure who marks the boundary between inside and outside the family, threatening the father's rule. As Lynda Boose says, "To an institution that fears loss, the daughter's presence by definition constitutes a threat to its maintenance of closed boundaries. In multiple ways, she signifies all that the father desires and simultaneously cannot have" (31). Ordinarily the marriage ceremony, with its gift-giving rhetoric, disguises this loss, giving the appearance that the father controls the exchange when, in fact, the daughter's maturation makes the loss inevitable. "The bestowal design places the daughter's departure from the father's house and her sexual union with another male into a text defined by obedience to her father—not preference for an outside male," (32), according to Boose. *With Shuddering Fall* lays bare the paternal plot, a plot in which the father's possessiveness, or latent incest, may be seen as a form of resistance to the natural and inevitable process of aging. Since no marriage takes place, there is no disguise for Herz's desire to keep his daughter for himself. Just at the moment the daughter is to leave her father's house[1]—the moment Herz sees Karen with Shar—he becomes violent. In retaliation, Shar almost kills Herz, but the aging father, relying upon his daughter's loyalty, commands her to "Get him. Kill him" (50).

Hence, the novel is an analysis of the psychological effects of this paternal command upon the daughter, as well as an analysis of the effects of paternal hostility toward the son. The asymmetry between daughters and sons becomes most obvious at the end of *With Shuddering Fall* when Karen Herz, who has returned to her father's home, receives Communion in a Catholic church. Shar has become a sacrifice, while Karen is perceived as fallen. Having moved beyond this notion of good and evil, Karen thinks, " 'I can accept them but they will never accept me' " (223). She understands that Shar has been crucified and that the spectators, the community, are as guilty of causing his death as she is. Therefore, although the community regards Karen as "guilty," as having played her part in a narrative of "sin and penance and expiation" (221), she sees the community as sharing in her guilt by perpetuating such dramas of crucifixion out of their own need for scapegoats, the desire for someone else to bear their guilt, so that they may preserve the illusion of innocence. They see themselves as "good," but Karen sees that "they have initiated me into the communion of killers, murderers" (221). Unfortunately, the disparity between Karen's sudden insight and her previous actions is too great to be credible. Yet this disparity points to a surplus of authorial consciousness, not fully developed in the novel, that has attached itself to the daughter's part.

For example, it is Karen who acts the part of a submissive daughter, returning home and attending Mass with her father—"Karen, you are my girl, my good girl!" says Herz, and Karen whispers, "I love you too, Father" (224)—but it is more believable that author Oates herself is thinking, " 'They know that something is wrong with me, that my mind is wrong, put together wrong. Am I to blame for that? Can I help my mind? It is insane to look for meaning in life, and it is insane not to; what am I to do?' " (223). Karen's question comes as a surprise since, throughout most of the novel, she has acted the part of the daughter without analyzing her role. This statement is certainly credible as that of her author, the young and brilliant Joyce Carol Oates, for even if we accept Karen's recognition of her complicity in Shar's death this awareness would not necessarily lead her to conclude that the search for meaning is "insane." Yet Karen herself has shown little interest in intellectual growth prior to the novel's conclusion; in fact, during her pursuit of Shar, she doesn't read even a newspaper. Thus, when her intellectual hunger surfaces at the end of the novel, it is too sketchy and belated to be persuasive. Whereas it might be credible that Karen actually cures herself by acknowledging her share of guilt in causing Shar's death, it does not follow that by reading many books in a few months—mysteries, medical books, as well as psychology and philology texts—she suddenly possesses the insights of her author.

This weakness in characterization is intriguing, for if the now eighteen-year-old Karen Herz cannot plausibly think that "something is wrong with me, that my mind is wrong, put together wrong," then it must be her author—whose anxieties cannot be fully contained in her female character—who concludes that it is "insane to look for meaning and insane not to," and who cries, "What am I to do?" What, indeed, is a brilliant (woman) writer to do? In this novel, for example, Oates seems torn between the necessity of acknowledging that tragedy is communal—that Shar's death is the result of a sacrificial plot, or myth, in which we all play a part—and also acknowledging that the gendered parts we play in mythical plots often severely limit our potential as human beings. In other words, the conflict between a desire for knowledge and a desire for communion—the conflict dramatized in the daughter's part in *With Shuddering Fall*—is auto-graphical.[2] I am not suggesting that Oates lived through the same events as Karen Herz, but rather that she experienced, imaginatively, linguistically, the conflicts Karen enacted. Oates dedicated *With Shuddering Fall* to Donald Dike, one of her creative writing professors at Syracuse, who described Oates as "the most brilliant student we've ever had here," adding "she had some conscience problems about her writing in those days; she was afraid it was 'not nice' and might offend her parents, and I tried to reassure her" (Clemons, "Joyce Carol Oates" 73).

Oates's problem of conscience was not idiosyncratic. Although writers of both genders may experience authorial anxiety, this particular kind of authorial anxiety, the belief that the act of writing is "not nice," is more typically a female ailment, as Sandra Gilbert and Susan Gubar have pointed out. According to Harold Bloom, males experience writing anxiety because they have a long tradition of father-writers to overcome, but women writers experience "anxiety of authorship," according to Gilbert and Gubar, because they lack a tradition of mother-writers. As a consequence, for women the act of writing is experienced as disobedient, as "not nice." As Gilbert and Gubar argue, the act of writing "caused enormous anxiety in generations of the women who were 'presumptuous' enough to dare such an attempt [at the pen]" (7). But can this diagnosis of anxious authorship in nineteenth-century women writers also be applied to twentieth-century women? For those women writing prior to the women's movement, the answer must certainly be yes, for they would have studied male writers almost exclusively. As a consequence, American women writers would suffer from "anxious authorship" as a result of not knowing of the existence of literary foremothers. Such a literary education is clearly reflected in Oates's first collection of critical essays, *The Edge of Impossibility: Tragic Forms in Literature*, which includes essays on Shakespeare, Melville, Chekhov, Yeats, Mann, and Ionesco, but not a single essay on a (woman) writer. During the 1960s Oates published only one essay on a woman writer, and it is significant that in this essay, called "The Art of Relationships: Henry James and Virginia Woolf," she considers the woman writer only in relationship to a male writer, although Woolf had already been accepted into the canon.

My point is that, despite the differences in education, Joyce Carol Oates and her female protagonist do share at least one problem: both are daughters who, in the eyes of the community, are not equal to sons. As a daughter, Oates's writing is not viewed as equal to that of a son's, just as Karen's sacrifice is viewed as not equal to Shar's. The novel makes this point when, during the Mass that Karen attends after returning home, she imagines her father exclaiming, "Here is a real sacrifice," as he gestures to the sacrifice of God's only begotten Son. He reminds Karen that a daughter's sacrifice pales in comparison: "You think you have given yourself, you think you have been fed upon—and so in a way you have—but still you are alive, you have your health and youth and beauty" (222). While it is true that Karen survived, it is also true that the sacrifice of Shar and her unborn child are as real to Karen as the sacrifice of Jesus. Thus, though Karen has tried to be a "good" daughter who obeys her father, her sacrifice—the loss of her lover and her unborn child—is not seen as heroic. In fact, Karen now sees her father's idea of "goodness" as a form of willed innocence. Understandably, then, Herz's morality is no longer compelling to his daughter. The tragedy is that Karen understands—too late—that her love for Shar might have allowed her to move beyond the good and evil of her father's monologic (binary) morality. Karen finally recognizes that Herz's hunger to preserve his power, and the community's desire to preserve the unjust status quo, actually require such sacrifices: the sacrifice of the young to the fathers or (to state the matter in the graphic imagery of the novel) the feeding of the young to old men who hunger for godlike immortality.

However, when the novel opens, Karen certainly does not view her father as implicated in the community's sacrificial morality. She simply enjoys being her father's favorite, and so she becomes Herz's accomplice in seeking to outmaneuver Shar, using the psychological power of icy passivity to defeat her lover's passion for her. Only when Karen meets Shar's boss, Max, does she begin to resist the competitive game, a plot manipulated if not entirely controlled by powerful patriarchs. Significantly, Karen's change from a passive into a resisting daughter is portrayed in scenes of reading: the first scene portrays Karen as listening to her father read the Old Testament story of Abraham's sacrifice of Isaac; the second portrays Karen, who is by this time pregnant, as listening to and resisting Max's interpretation of *Paradise Lost*. Since Karen is portrayed only as a listener, not as a reader (at least until her hospitalization late in the novel) these moments encode the author, rather than her character, as a resisting reader of patriarchal plots. In fact, *With Shuddering Fall* illustrates Sandra Gilbert's thesis in "Life's Empty Pack" that "since the daughter has inherited an empty pack and cannot be a father, she has no choice but to be for the father—to be his treasure, his land, his voice" (265).

Oates projects her rebellion into the son and her submissiveness into the daughter, but neither role satisfies her. Yet Oates's desire to rewrite the old father-son stories from the daughter's point of view can be inferred from the change in Karen: a change from Herz's submissive virgin daughter into a mother-to-be who resists Max's incestuous hunger. By the end of the novel, in fact, Karen is actually voicing Oates's own cry, "What am I to do?" As Oates develops the presumably parallel plots of a son and daughter, of Karen and Shar, her resistance to mythically defined gender roles also becomes apparent in the novel's doubles—a prostitute identified as Karen's shadow self, and a man named Ponzi who functions as Shar's double—who dramatize the destructiveness of the narrowly defined gender roles. The nameless prostitute who looks so eerily like Karen, and who is paid to attend Shar's needs after Karen's departure, performs without disguise the daughter's function as an object of exchange in the homosocial order.[3] And Ponzi (who, unlike Shar, has strong feelings of sympathy that he is capable of expressing) functions as the repressed "feminine" of the presumably emotionless, nerves-of-steel race car driver.

These inhibiting gender roles seem mandated by the ancient biblical plots that are foregrounded early in the novel. For example, as Karen listened to her father read the Old Testament story of Abraham's near-sacrifice of Isaac, she had thought, "What strange dignity to fulfill one's destiny in that way—forever bound by the inhuman plot of a story, manipulated by God Himself!" (34). In her next sentence, author Oates adds this disclaimer: "It was a queer thought and Karen did not really understand it" (35). Listening obediently, Karen readily accepts the power of the father by imagining herself as the obedient son Isaac. Yet the brilliant insight, that we are "bound by the inhuman plot of a story," is more credible as Oates's. At the time that she wrote the novel, Oates herself may not have fully understood the full import of Karen's "queer thought" for, as already stated, she viewed the part of the disobedient son and the obedient daughter as "parallel, very strictly parallel" (Kuehl 309). Perhaps Oates assumed that Karen's middle-class social standing made her equal to lower-class Shar, despite his gender advantage. Nevertheless, in the process of projecting her more submissive self into daughter Karen and her more rebellious self into Shar, the author of *With Shuddering Fall* could not discover a way beyond an ancient tragic plot. Yet the author's analysis of gender is apparent in the novel's contrasting images: ice signifies Karen's mute passivity, her lack of physical response to Shar's passion, whereas fire signifies Shar's angry rebellion, his burning down of his own father's shack to prevent Herz from burying his father's body in the Herz family plot. Both seem trapped in a violent game.

Although Karen and Shar are the players, the game itself—the couple's unvoiced power struggle—is controlled by the competitive fathers; mothers are conspicuously absent. Rule's wife has left him, and Herz has buried four wives. Oates calls attention to this maternal absence when, early in the novel, Karen walks at her father's side, in the place a wife would ordinarily walk, to carry food to Shar's father, the Herzes' ailing neighbor. Karen's older sister had "gotten out of it somehow, and her father would not go alone carrying food; that was woman's work" (7). Immediately following this passage, a superfluous detail surfaces: "The girl, hugging a paper bag, walked clumsily—she wore old shoes of her father's, great cracked shoes hardened with mud but suited well for this trip; she did not want to ruin her shoes" (7). Thus, though Karen may occupy only a woman's place, she nevertheless wears her father's shoes, shoes better suited for a son than a daughter. This telling detail hints at the fact that a son can inherit the role of the father, with all that role's attendant cultural authority, whereas a daughter cannot. As Lynda Boose explains in her introduction to *Daughters and Fathers*, the son's role is to displace the father, whereas the daughter, the father's property, is "the exchangeable figure."

In this instance, daughter Karen, the property of Herz, functions as the exchangeable figure whom Shar Rule, Herz's young rival, attempts to claim as his. In this action the novel dramatizes what Boose defines in "The Father's House and the Daughter in It" as the central presumption of myths, Christian, Hebrew, and Greek: that fathers and sons are "homologous," whereas daughters are "subsumed as mothers and their independent contributions are obscured by their loss of name" (21–22). Indeed, as Karen moves from Herz to Rule, from being the property of her father to becoming the property of her lover, according to the legal and religious conventions of marriage, she would lose the name of her father and acquire the name of her lover. She has no right to claim (or name) herself; Karen enters culture only through her capacity as a vessel, a "receptacle," as Boose puts it, in the "male-chain" linkage of succession. Since no ceremony disguises the violence of male succession in *With Shuddering Fall*, Karen's "fall" may be redefined, not as a fall from "innocent" virginity but as a fall into male violence, violence precipitated by the male struggle to possess her.

This fall "herz" Karen (*hurts*, though *herz* also means "heart" in German), a point made with these almost too-obvious paternal names. The "Old Rule" hurts Karen, who loses her lover and their unborn child through passive obedience to her father's command, but the old rule also hurts the (woman) writer. For just as Karen tries to leave her father's house—a departure marked by violence when Shar nearly kills Mr. Herz—author Oates is also trying to leave behind this "inhuman [sacrificial] plot." Ironically, it is through Karen's obedience to her father's command that Karen "'Get him,'" and "'Kill him,'" (50) that the violent plot is fulfilled. In other words, however passive the daughter's part as an object of exchange, she participates in violence by accepting this gendered role. Oates imagines this ancient plot as a psychological drama: Karen kills her lover by way of her sexual frigidity; that is, by remaining psychologically a virgin, the prisoner of her father's locked-in ego.[4] Yet Oates's own disobedience, as a daughter who claims the cultural authority of the son—the authority to walk in the father's boots, the authority to write—does not enable her to transform the inhuman plot. In her first three novels, sons sacrifice themselves to the father by committing suicide: first Shar Rule in *With Shuddering Fall*, then Swan Revere in *A Garden of Earthly Delights*, and next Richard Everett in *Expensive People*. Only gradually, with her fourth novel, *them*, does Oates resist the sacrifice of her male protagonist.

Like author Oates, Karen Herz moves gradually from obedience to resistance. Initially, as the "good" Karen listens passively as Herz reads the story of Abraham and Isaac, she thinks, "What strange dignity to fulfill one's destiny in that way—forever bound by the inhuman plot of a story, manipulated by God Himself!" (34), but at the time she has had little experience with violence. Only later, after observing the violence of the race track—violence fueled by Max's money—does Karen begin to resist the father's will. Significantly, Karen is pregnant when her resistance to the wealthy patriarch finally emerges. At one point Max tries to buy sexual favors from Karen, while reminding her that "we are all kin," that each soul is "defined only in terms of what it had surrendered: to claims of blood and duty, to love, to religious ecstasy" (111). Although Karen knows that Max is right, knows that she "had no existence without the greater presence of someone to acknowledge her (her father: God)," this thought does not comfort her. For Karen also knows that kinship imprisons us, a point the omniscient narrator makes in her next sentence: "If some men supposed themselves free it was only because they did not understand that they were imprisoned—bars could be made of any shadowy substance, any dreamy loss of light" (111–12).

Bound as we are by cultural stories, by myths that create our sense of community, we also become prisoners of their shadowy bars, their "inhuman plots." These patriarchal myths consume the lives of daughters as well as sons, as illustrated in the scene in which Max interprets *Paradise Lost* to the now-pregnant Karen. As the obese Max eats "a plate of soft eggs, mixed with colorless strips of bacon and little sturdy-looking globules of fat" (127), Karen understands, intuitively, that he wants to consume her— and the egg/fetus growing in her womb—just as he consumes Milton's poem.[5] Of *Paradise Lost*, Max says, " 'Men make the error that things will turn out for the good—we religious people make that error, though our experiences contradict us. In literature, now, things are different; this long poem I've been rereading . . . temptation, sin, fall, and expiation, all around in a circle, into the garden and out of it, many angels, great blazes of rhetoric and light—an immense scheme of tautological relationships you need never believe in!" (127). Yet Karen's contradictory desires—which she acts out by leaving her father's house while, at the same time, remaining psychologically a "Daddy's girl"—precipitate the tragedy, for it is her rejection of Shar's love that leads to his death. In an act of self-sacrifice that sets off a race riot, Shar commits suicide on the race track, the novel's "giant circle." Violence is never gratuitous in Oates's fiction even though critics often make this charge; it is always, as in *With Shuddering Fall*, a result of the myths that we live by, however shadowy the bars of these myths.

"As if it mattered that there was ever a paradise, or in what way it was lost to us," (127) Max says, arguing that literature is unrelated to life. Oates's repudiation of this formalistic premise is apparent in her portrayal of contemporary adolescents as enacting rituals (or plots) of sacrifice to the Father. Karen understands, for example, that "even the child growing within her—a speck of life, a ghostly image, a mockery of life—would not escape his wrath; but she did not care" (97). Just as Shar is sacrificed to the wrath of the father on the race track, a circle of death, their child is sacrificed to the circular plot. Max controls the game, a game that destroys (Max/mocks) love. Yet he describes racing, just as he describes literature, as if it were only a philosophical problem: " 'What keeps them on it?' " Max wonders aloud. " 'By common sense you would expect them all to fly off like that—drawn off—so!' " Then he answers, " 'It's the law of the circle, the one pressure on the outside and the other on the inside, they push together—the little car, it is caught in the middle' " (96). But Karen, seeing Shar compete with another driver whose car is forced out of the circle, declares him a "killer," and Max a killer too. " 'It's a theory to you, it's nothing to you—Shar kills a man and it's nothing to you!' " Karen screams (97). Likewise, the circular narrative—in which the father resists passing on his power to the son—is filled with death. Karen voices her author's resistance to this master plot, but she does not escape it. Nor does Oates find a way to revise this script in the fiction of the 1960s.

In *With Shuddering Fall*, Karen sends her lover to his death when she tells him, "You make me sick" (181). As Karen understands, they have been playing a competitive game, "an elaborate dance" in which they compete by "luring and entrapping each other," a game that Shar comes to see as a "mockery of love." Karen continues the game even after Shar has given it up, revealing his feelings for her and telling her, following her miscarriage, " 'If you want a baby, you can have a baby.' " But Karen has learned to be a competitor, to defend herself from feeling vulnerable; for this reason, when her "heart went out to him, she felt shame in her emotion. I can't help it if I have fallen in love, she thought defensively" (178). Karen understands that her choice to send her lover off to die will affect the entire community, and again she serves as the thinly disguised authorial voice: "But if he dies, she thought, then I will die too. If he dies, everyone will die. No one will survive" (181). Here, again, Karen articulates her author's vision of the tragic, establishing a causal relationship between her "private" failed union with Shar to the "public" violence following his death, the "mock communion" of the race track. Unlike earlier races, during which Shar had felt hostile toward spectators, in this final race, "Shar felt none of his usual antagonism for the crowd, but felt instead a peculiar tenderness toward them" (183). He finally recognizes—as a tragic figure usually does—that the community wants to share in his heroic deed, "in the skill and triumph . . . of such speed and courage" (183); most of all, Shar understands that the spectators want to share in his confrontation with death.

The crowd, we are told, "thirsted for death, they were fascinated by it, and envious of it; they gave up their identities to risk violence, but were always cheated because the violence, when it came, could not touch them" (183); it could touch only the drivers, the heroes. The "mock communion" of the race track in *With Shuddering Fall* illustrates a view of tragedy also stated in *The Edge of Impossibility:* "Art is built around violence, around death; at its base is fear. The absolute dream, if dreamed, must deal with death, and the only way toward death we understand is the way of violence" (7). Nevertheless, even as she was writing the fiction of the 1960s, Oates sought alternatives to the way of violence. One possible alternative was the daughter's refusal to play her part in the ritual, a refusal requiring her to act upon her own desires, her own authority. However implausibly, Karen Herz finally acknowledges both her power and her responsibility, and this knowledge "cures" her. It is a view of psychological healing that departs radically from that of Karen's psychiatrist, a man who sees his patient as an innocent victim, as a woman mentally disoriented by violence, by, as he says, "the man killed, the miscarriage because of the shock, the involvement in that riot" (207). The psychiatrist is unaware of Karen's responsibility for any of the events surrounding her "shuddering fall" into madness. In fact, as we know, Karen's miscarriage occurs before Shar's death, not after; furthermore, we know that Karen has willfully refused to tell Shar of her pregnancy and that, after Shar's violent lovemaking causes the miscarriage, she sends him to his death. Shar's death, in turn, triggers the riot that takes other lives.

But just how much responsibility does Karen bear for the tragedy? Initially, Karen appears willing, as Shar was, to act the part of the community's scapegoat. That is why, during the riot, she leaves the safety of her room, exposing herself to the violence of the crowd, sobbing, "My God, forgive me . . . forgive me. Forgive me for what I did" (201). Deliberately, she endures being brutally kicked and nearly raped, apparently inviting such punishment out of a sense of guilt. Yet Karen's initial willingness to bear complete responsibility for Shar's death drives her into madness, a madness cured only when she assumes an existentialist, rather than a Christian, view of responsibility.[6] Oates explains the difference, as she sees it, in an essay on *The Brothers Karamazov:* "The existentialist accepts all responsibility for his actions and does not beg forgiveness, but he accepts absolutely no responsibility for actions that are not his own" (*Edge of Impossibility* 107). During her stay in the hospital Karen cures herself by becoming an existentialist, an attitude that requires a repudiation of the Christian notion of responsibility which, as Oates sees it, would cast her in the role of a "creature."

Oates explains that "the essentialist (in this context, the ideal Christian) accepts all guilt for all his actions, is morally ubiquitous, has no singular identity, and can be forgiven any sin, no matter how terrible, because ultimately he has no freedom and no responsibility, not simply for his own sins, but for the sins of mankind; he is a "creature" (107). Following her cure, Karen voices Oates's view of the Christian sense of moral responsibility. After returning to her father's house, she is attending church with him when she comes to understand that, despite her existential view of events, the congregation sees her as one "who had suffered to prove to them the justice of the universe"—a universe they perceive in terms of good or evil. Lacking awareness of their own complicity in rituals of sacrifice, they remain "innocent" Christians, "creatures" incapable of acknowledging that they too are "killers." An existentialist, Karen is alienated from members of the community, whom she now sees as "killers," including her own father, "whose command she had so well fulfilled" (213). In obeying the paternal command to "get" Shar, to "kill" him, Karen understands that she has helped to fulfill the community's need for a scapegoat, thereby participating in the ritual of violence: the sacrifice of the son, the Christ, to the father.

Prefacing her first novel with Nietzsche's aphorism, "What is done out of love takes place beyond good and evil," Oates affirms Karen's existential morality, the ethic that she voices at the novel's conclusion. Tragedy occurs, then, not because of Karen's "fall" from innocence, but rather because Karen has resisted the so-called "fall" from innocence, preferring the "virginity" of childhood obedience to her father. As Karen recognizes, too late, she has been schooled for such icy virginity by her father's beliefs, beliefs shared by the entire community. Yet there is a lack of symmetry, a lack of parallelism, in Oates's portrayal of a tragic death for the son, while she rejects such a death for her daughter-hero. An asymmetry occurs when Karen refuses the role of scapegoat, whereas Shar, who accepts the role, becomes a tragic sacrifice. Oates's resistance to Christianity is evident in Karen's rejection of self-sacrifice; nevertheless, Oates's plot follows a tragic curve in this first novel. Karen Herz is the first of many fictional daughters who choose survival rather than death, but no other female protagonist in novels of 1960s achieves her measure of insight. As I demonstrate in the next chapter, neither Clara Walpole in *A Garden of Earthly Delights* nor Maureen Wendall in *them* achieves much insight into her struggles; however, like Karen, they do manage to survive.

Yeats's Daughter: Images of "Leda and the Swan" in the Trilogy of the 1960s

We are all "interconnected," all part of the same family, Joyce Carol Oates believes, yet we live in a society "in which the concept of 'divinity' was snatched up by a political/economic order, and the democratic essence of divinity denied" (*Where are you going* 8). A desire to reclaim this lost dream, a dream in which all of "us" recognize our kinship to "them," shapes Oates's tragic vision in the trilogy of the 1960s—*A Garden of Earthly Delights* (1966), *Expensive People* (1968), and *them* (1969). Even though the trilogy does not transform gender roles, these novels portray human suffering with a keen eye for the connections between individuals and society, past and present, personal and political acts. Oates is also aware in this early trilogy that the conventions of discourses, literary and extraliterary, may perpetuate social injustices. *Expensive People* is, for example, a satire not only of the rich but of the discourses of literary criticism and psychoanalysis, while *them* criticizes the conventions of naturalism as well as the romance plot. In all three novels Oates's vision is tragic, as suggested in her allusions to Yeats and, with the exception of *them*, the curve of her plots is tragic. Invariably, allusions to Yeats's "Leda and the Swan" surface just at those moments when Oates's desire to transform our unjust society is most intense. Oates's language in *A Garden of Earthly Delights* is, according to Eileen Teper Bender, a Yeatsian rhetoric of "feathered visions, clamorous wings, diving predators, and unwitting prey, 'hawks of the mind'" (*Joyce

Carol Oates 26), a rhetoric I find throughout the entire trilogy. But is the tragic vision capable of affirming a democratic kinship, despite the genre's encoding of hierarchies of gender, race, and class? Oates seems uncertain how to answer this question.

Her ambivalence is illustrated in an essay on Yeats that first appeared in the *Bucknell Review*, Winter 1969–70, just at the time she completed the trilogy. She begins this essay, which later appeared in *The Edge of Impossibility* (1972), by quoting Yeats's view that "tragedy seems to break down the "dykes that separate man from man [sic]," but she adds—contradictorily— that "the experience is aesthetic rather than humanistic. It is the strange 'emptiness' of tragedy that appeals to us, not its communal nature" (*Edge of Impossibility* 156). A few pages later, however, she reasserts the argument that tragedy has a communal nature: "The only fruition honored is that of death, which produces an ecstasy that comes from a sudden enlargement of vision—the breaking-down of the dykes that separate man from man— so that personality is finally lost" (158–59). Oates asks: is the flowing forth of passion in this genre only an aesthetic experience, leaving behind emptiness, or does tragedy create a sense of community that overcomes nihilism? Oates's view that Yeats's heroes are tragic by virtue of "their ritualistic enactment of the common human dilemma" (167) implies that, regardless of class or consciousness, human beings participate in tragic action. In the introduction to *The Edge of Impossibility*, again echoing Yeats, she suggests that tragedy is communal: "In the various works examined in this collection of essays . . . nihilism is overcome by the breaking-down of the dikes between human beings, the flowing forth of passion" (7). Because Oates believes that tragedy is communal (or should be) she challenges the notion that tragedy is for the upper classes, while naturalism is for the poor—a critique particularly evident in *them*.

Yet Oates's early critics often failed to recognize her critique of genres as related to her critique of the evils of injustice. It is understandable, for example, given the generational cycles of violence in the U.S.—cycles portrayed as ritualistic sacrifices of the young to hungry patriarchs—why the young in these novels are preoccupied with acquiring control over their own lives. Surprisingly, however, when critics comment upon this desire for control,[1] they rarely mention that some characters have too much control, whereas others have too little, nor do they notice that the rich are swollen with political-economic power, whereas the poor have only a thin chance of achieving even material security, however intelligent and determined they may be. Oates also recognizes, as some of her critics apparently do not, that generic conventions can perpetuate such evil. For example, Frank Cunningham claims that Oates's characters lack the divinity of tragic figures; thus her vision is not tragic, but naturalistic. "Sanctity cannot be possible," Cunningham argues, "without awareness and self-realization" ("Enclosure" 23–24). But if sanctity is possible only for those who have "awareness and self-realization," then only well educated human beings— those who can afford an excellent education—are fit subjects for tragedy. Apparently unaware of the class implications of his argument, Cunningham asserts that Oates's "fascination with the inevitably circumscribed situation, the inevitably determined character" leads mainly to "monochromatic case studies in Naturalism rather than multi-faceted representations of the complex human condition" (24). In other words, tragedy is for the upper class, naturalism for the lower.

Benjamin DeMott echoes Cunningham's sentiments in his review of *them*. Mistakenly assuming that the novel is autobiographical, he charges Oates with failing to establish aesthetic distance. "Not once," he says, "not even in the tone-shattering, clumsy moment midway in the book when Miss Oates enters in her own person . . . does she enable her reader to believe that a mind subtler than that of the characters has been silently viewing the action with an appropriately compassionate and critical decency" (21). Yet Oates created the character "Miss Oates" to parody the naturalistic convention of a distanced, ironic author. According to naturalistic convention, the author—whose masculine intelligence is capable of the godlike objectivity of a scientist—is situated above the social reality he records, at too great a distance to feel sympathy toward his characters. According to DeMott, Oates betrays her own working-class origins through a lack of refinement: in "clumsy" words that reveal a mind lacking in "appropriately compassionate and critical decency." Having defined Oates as lacking the capacity for "aesthetic distance" as a result of both her gender and class, DeMott charges that her attempts at ironic distance in other novels, such as the obvious satire in *Expensive People*, also lack "wit and grace" (22). Only those authors of a certain gender and class, he implies, understand how to establish the "appropriate" critical distance from their inferior characters.

In fact, Oates uses the "Author's Note" in *them* to emphasize her sympathy with the poor, with "them," despite their social differences, as, for example, between her student, Maureen Wendall, and herself, a professor of English. At the same time, she emphasizes certain similarities between herself and

Maureen, such as the fact that they were both born into working-class families, and that both love to read. She says of Maureen, "I became aware of her life story, her life as the possibility for a story, perhaps drawn to her by certain similarities between her and me" (n.p.). Sadly, primarily as a result of the differences between author and character (Maureen's step-father was sexually violent toward her, crippling her ability to think and learn, while Oates's father nurtured her creativity)[2] their stories end differently: "Maureen is now a housewife in Dearborn, Michigan; I am teaching in another university" (n.p.). Nevertheless, in *Images of Women in Fiction,* the earliest collection of feminist essays, Susan Koppelman Cornillon criticized *them* because of the author's supposed failure to differentiate her moral vision from the sexist or racist views of her characters (120). Following this attack, Gary Waller says that "with Oates, we are never provided with a firm moral perspective" (118), and Linda Wagner comments that Oates's "readers have sometimes expressed dismay that such unpleasant things happen to characters, while Oates as author appears to have little opinion about these reprehensible situations—little opinion, little sympathy, little outrage. What kind of moral judgment underlies her fiction?" (xix).

Yet Oates herself has stated repeatedly that she is concerned with only one thing, "the moral and social conditions" of her time, a comment reiterated in her epigraphs to *Upon the Sweeping Flood, With Shuddering Fall,* and *them.* My view is that Oates's moral vision is complex, challenging both traditional moral categories, such as "good or evil," "moral or immoral," as well as the hierarchies implicit in the conventions of traditional genres. As Oates says in her 1974 Preface to *Where are you going, Where have you been?* "A new morality is emerging in America, in fact on the North American continent generally, which may appear to be opposed to the old but which is in fact a higher form of the old—the democratization of the spirit, the experiencing of life as meaningful in itself, without divisions into 'good' or 'bad,' 'beautiful' or 'ugly,' 'moral' or 'immoral'" (9). To transform such binary thought (and binary morality) Oates employs myths for the purpose of challenging and re-visioning them. Though critics do not always recognize Oates's re-visionary strategies, they can be identified even in her first novel, which invokes *Paradise Lost* in order to parody it. As Teper Bender argues, "An artist's dream of 'final form,' the grand design, is simultaneously evoked and parodied in the Miltonic structure of *With Shuddering Fall.* In Oates's second novel *A Garden of Earthly Delights,* she is once again revising a myth—the myth of the godlike author—

by dramatizing "the failure of 'various claims of the artist, the supposed controller of will' " (Teper Bender, *Joyce Carol Oates* 27).

I agree with Mary Kathryn Grant that Oates's novels are "efforts to raise the consciousness of ordinary people . . . to encourage us to continue the struggle to put some meaning into human life" (3). In contrast, Cunningham states that in most of Oates's writings "the crucially significant function of human struggle is absent" ("Enclosure" 24). Despite Cunningham's claim, Oates frequently portrays young people, including the poor, as struggling to achieve full humanity in a society that, while claiming to be democratic, perpetuates social injustices. According to Grant, in the early novels Oates's vision of a society powerless to change the waste of war, assassinations, and riot is tragic. Because of Oates's sympathy with victims—with women, as with minorities and the poor of any gender—she is also critical of the Renaissance ideal of the self, the imperial "I." This concept of the self—a "masculine" concept—may have been healthy at one time, Oates argues, but in the present era it has become "pathological." She explains this view, placing particular emphasis on the gender implications of the Renaissance ideal, in an essay on Sylvia Plath, "The Death Throes of Romanticism," first published in 1973: "Where at one point in civilization this very masculine, combative ideal of an 'I' set against all other 'I's'—and against nature as well—was necessary in order to wrench man from a hermetic contemplation of a God-centered universe and get him into action, it is no longer necessary, its health has become a pathology, and whoever clings to its outmoded concepts will die" (*New Heaven, New Earth* 115). These outmoded concepts, she believes, killed Plath. In other words, a woman who accepts her culture's belief in "this very masculine, combative ideal of an 'I' set against all other 'I's,' " will die, as Plath did.

The trilogy alerts readers to the pathology, the inherent violence and immorality of the masculine, combative Renaissance ideal. David Bakan defines this pathology as the disease of "unmitigated agency," and it is especially apparent in the wealthy patriarchs whom Oates depicts in Yeatsian rhetoric, as the Zeus (or swan) figures: Herz and Max in *With Shuddering Fall*, Revere in *A Garden of Earthly Delights*, Mr. Everett in *Expensive People*, and the absent father of Nadine Greene in *them*. The wealthy fathers in her novels view all others, including their own children, as competitors. As they age and as their fear of death intensifies, these men try to swallow up all they see—the land, the crops, finally even "the garden of earthly delights" itself. This boundless greed, unmitigated by a vision of the self as part of a community, is the pathology that, according to Oates, our society has inherited from the Renaissance.[3] Bakan makes a similar argument when he says that "our so-called affluent society is evidence of the success of the agentic strategy. But at this historical moment we are in danger of becoming like Don Quixote, equipped to cope with life problems in one way while the nature of the world has been so changed that this approach is becoming archaic" (14). Thus, Bakan argues that "the moral imperative is to mitigate agency with communion" (14). This moral imperative has informed Oates's fiction from the outset of her writing career.

Historicizing old myths, Oates weds them to specific historical periods in order to critique them. Her early novels usually begin with the Great Depression and end with the violence of the 1960s, violence portrayed as the tragic consummation of three generations of socioeconomic injustice. Patriarchs such as Mr. Herz and Max in *With Shuddering Fall* are the agents of socioeconomic injustice, aging men who use their greater economic and psychological power to devour the young. In *With Shuddering Fall*, as I illustrated in chapter 1, Karen Herz recognizes that Max wants to possess even her unborn child; Shar's suicide and the riot that follows are the violent consequences of Max's (and Herz's) unmitigated agency. The violence in *A Garden of Earthly Delights*, which ends in fratricide and suicide, is the tragic consequence of Revere's devouring ego; the violence in *Expensive People*, which ends in matricide and the promise of suicide, is the consequence of the Everett's egocentricity and materialism; and the violence in *them*, which concludes with a riot in a Detroit ghetto, is the tragic consummation of three generations of socioeconomic injustice in the United States. Oates portrays these acts of violence not as isolated and meaningless but as the consequence of a collective failure of imagination, a failure to see "them" as "us." All of us were meant to partake in our democratic society's garden of delights, but this dream has been denied in the United States. Violence often follows moments when the imagination fails, moments of passion when the self—the ego—might have been lost through the love of an other.

Allusions to "Leda and the Swan" surface at just such moments in Oates's trilogy. Yet, as Helen Sword points out, a (woman) writer's use of Yeats's well-known image raises the problem of point of view, a problem with both moral and aesthetic implications. Sword reminds us, "For women, of course, rape is not merely an abstract concept, for even if no woman actually fears being violated by a swan (or, one would hope, by Zeus in any form), tales like the Leda myth, in which human contact with the divine is couched in the vocabulary of sexual conquest, can serve as telling metaphors both for female poets' real-life experiences of male domination and for their anxieties of male literary influence" (306). Oates always identifies with the victim (as is characteristic of women writers, according to Sword), yet she varies the gender of the rape victim in the trilogy. How, then, are we to interpret the gender and class implications of this image, as least for Oates? As a scholarship student at Syracuse University in the 1950s, the first in her working-class family to attend college, Oates would have been keenly aware of her supposed inferiority, both as a woman and as a member of the working class. Thus, while it is evident that Yeats exerted a powerful influence on her imagination, it is likely that the imagery of a male god raping a female and carrying her away in his "indifferent beak" was also deeply disturbing to her. As Sword says, "Women writers confronting the Leda myth . . . might reasonably be expected to identify, at least in imagination, with Leda and her plight; that is, one can hardly conceive of a woman writing about the myth solely from Zeus's point of view, except perhaps with heavy irony" (306).

In fact, in *A Garden of Earthly Delights*, Oates does "identify, at least in imagination, with Leda and her plight," for Leda/Clara is both female and poor. Indeed, when Leda/Clara gives birth to a son, she names him Swan because she wants her son to claim the kind of "indifferent" power her husband, Revere, a wealthy landowner, possesses. Implicitly, then, Oates acknowledges that Leda cannot, at least not directly, claim Zeus-like power for herself: Leda/Clara cannot "put on his knowledge with his power." Even though Swan achieves Zeus-like power, enacting a role for which his mother and father have scripted him, the story ends tragically, as Swan kills first his father and then himself. Thus, the tragic plot of *A Garden of Earthly Delights* bears out Sword's argument that a woman would write from Zeus's point of view only with "heavy irony." In *A Garden of Earthly Delights*, as in the entire trilogy, Oates employs such irony in order to critique the Renaissance ego, particularly those who perpetuate Zeus-like visions of authority—regardless of their gender. For example, the parents of Richard Everett in *Expensive People* are implicated in social violence, for, by transforming their Leda-like son into a swan, they create a killer. A similar transformation occurs in *them* when Nadine Greene—daughter of a Zeus-like father in an expensive suburb—rejects Jules, her Leda-like lover from a Detroit ghetto. The questions remains, Is Oates concerned, in these novels written just as the women's movement began, with the gender implications of Yeats's poem? I argue that Oates began to address the issue of gender more directly, more sharply, in *them* when, for the first time, the Leda figures are portrayed not in generational sequence, as a mother and son, but as brother and sister. In this reconfiguration of Yeatsian imagery, Oates highlights gender differences. By twinning the Leda figures, Maureen and Jules, a brother and sister from a working-class family, she dramatizes differences in the lives of brother and sister, male and female.

However, in these early novels daughters do not find ways to resolve the dilemma of gender: those who do not claim male-defined agency remain powerless, relegated to the silence of the maternal realm, whereas those who do claim male-defined agency, or authority, privileging the "I" over family and community, become agents of death, not nurturers of life. In terms of Yeats's imagery in "Leda and the Swan," whether a woman does or does not struggle to "put on his knowledge with his power," she is doomed to failure, for according to a Yeatsian vision of sociohistorical struggle, women are fated for victimization. Four years after publishing *them*, Oates announced her rejection of such a vision in "The Death Throes of Romanticism," the same essay in which she says that women writers who are "male in their aggression and their cynical employment of rhetoric" (*New Heaven, New Earth* 113) perpetuate their own victimization. Even in the trilogy, however, Oates is critical of women who, in imitation of men, strive to become Zeus-like, as if, through identifying with male power, they can escape the fate of Leda. For example, in *A Garden of Earthly Delights*, Clara struggles to obtain Zeus-like power while recognizing that she can gain access to it only indirectly, through marriage to a man of high social standing and through her son, who can directly claim his father's economic power. Again, in *Expensive People*, Nada strives for Zeus-like power, but indirectly, through a husband and son. In *them*, only Jules dares imagine himself in Zeus-like terms, while his sister—like Clara and Nada before her—seek economic security through marriage.

For example, in *A Garden of Earthly Delights*, Clara Walpole determines to marry a wealthy farmer named Revere after being abandoned while pregnant with another man's child. Clara consciously chooses this means of survival, using her beauty to gain economic security for herself and her unborn child. Within the constraints of historical and economic realities, Clara does plot her life: "The day Clara took her life into control was an ordinary day" (189), we are told, though she thinks, while in Revere's arms, that "the son she had, hers and Lowry's, was delivered over to Revere forever" (214). As if to underscore the conscious nature of her decision—

and her eligibility as a tragic figure—Oates gives Clara an opportunity to change her mind, to leave Revere and go with her lover. Tragically, Clara chooses not to go with the father of her child. "There was only this child between herself and Lowry: without him she would throw some things together and the two of them would run out to his car and drive off, and that would be that" (246). But because she wants her child to inherit material wealth, to have what she did not have, she refuses. Looking at Swan, the son he does not know is his, Clara's working-class lover, Lowry, makes a prediction: "You're going to kill lots of things," he says; "I can see it right there—all the things you're going to kill and step on and walk over" (247). This prediction turns out to be correct, not because Lowry is clairvoyant, but because he understands the system of values that lies behind Clara's rejection of him. Clara chooses the rich older man.

After becoming part of the Revere family, Swan, a sensitive, listening child, tries to understand the power, or lack of power, of those around him. "As Revere talked," for example, "Swan saw behind this tall dark-haired man another man, vague and remote but somehow more vivid than Revere, whose presence seemed to be descending over this house like a bird circling slowly to earth, its wings outstretched in a lazy threat" (261). Lowry's power over his mother was much greater than Revere's, Swan recalls, but finally he loses the memory of this more expansive consciousness. Clara's passion for the child's biological father—passion that is her only experience of divinity—becomes instead a passion for political-economic power, a choice that, though Clara does not understand it, spiritually diminishes both her son and herself. Even though Clara is not aware, as Oates is, that she is enacting a sacred drama, she is not completely devoid of awareness. For example, because Clara understands that "the son she had, hers and Lowry's, was delivered over to Revere forever" (124), she tries to preserve some sense of personal agency by naming the child in honor of her own secret dream. Revere prefers the name "Steven," but Clara's "own name for him was 'Swan' [and] she liked to whisper 'Swan, Swan' to him," though she refuses to tell Revere why. Of course the almost illiterate Clara, reader of comic books and women's magazines, would not recognize the name "Swan" as an allusion to Greek myth; nevertheless, she has the intelligence to understand that since she cannot inherit directly from Revere, she must prepare her son for this Zeus-like role.

To engineer her plot, Clara first waits patiently for Revere's wife to die; then she waits patiently for her son to grow old enough to defeat his stepbrothers and take over his father's farms. Clara, we are told, "could outwait anyone, outlast anyone" (215). In the meantime, Clara is determined that her son shall learn how to become a god-like patriarch: "My little Swan will grow up like his father and be big and strong and rich" (259). The idea for her son's name comes, not from reading Yeats, but from a movie magazine. Yet a Yeatsian image of power is implicit in Clara's explanation of Swan's name. She says, " 'I saw in this magazine a man named Robin, he was a movie star, so handsome, so much money—that when I was pregnant—I thought of what I would call the baby if it was a boy. I would call him Swan,' " she decided then, " 'because I saw some swans once in a picture, those big white birds that swim around—they look real cold, they're not afraid of anything, their eyes are hard like glass. On a sign it said they are dangerous some times. So that's better than calling a kid Robin, I thought, because a Swan is better than a robin. So I call him that" (259). In time, the child does indeed become what his mother dreams he shall be, and what Lowry has predicted he will become: a swan-like man, cold, unafraid, and dangerous, his father's murderer. Nevertheless, as Teper Bender suggests, "Yeatsian metaphors serve as emblems of Swan's inner division, embodying the mysterious warring forces within his imagination" (*Joyce Carol Oates* 26). Swan is a Leda "struggling against winged assailants as vainly as Yeats's Leda," according to Teper Bender: "In his brain there was a bird fluttering to get out. He was aware of it in his most helpless, frantic moments, or when exhausted. Its wings beat against the walls of his head" (*Garden* 352; qtd. in Teper Bender, *Joyce Carol Oates* 27).

Clara's violent dream so transforms her son's gentle nature that, like Richard Everett in *Expensive People*, Swan concludes that suicide is his only escape from a script he did not write himself. After Swan's suicide Clara lives the remainder of her life watching violent television shows, as if she were only an innocent creature, a spectator to violence. As this plot suggests, Oates is sensitive to the politics of family life, but a psychoanalytic interpretation would obscure the novel's critique of Revere's devouring ego, just as it would obscure the novel's emphasis upon the larger issue of socioeconomic conflicts that divide the two families. An analysis of the daughter's part is useful in foregrounding socioeconomic issues, for Clara's decision to marry Revere, a man old enough to be her father, is the direct result of her poverty and his wealth. It is through this marriage, in fact, that both families become tragic figures in a ritual cultural of sacrifice. Revere's unmitigated agency, his devouring of what rightfully belongs to

others—including a woman who rightfully "belongs" to a younger man—
erupts in violence toward other members of the human family. Although
the Walpoles and the Reveres do not recognize themselves as participants
in a cultural drama, they are nevertheless actors in a tragedy.

What Oates says of Yeats, that his "tragic heroes are heroic because
they are gifted with the audacity to undertake certain actions; though they
fail, though they do not personally transcend their fates, they are heroic
in their ritualistic enactment of the common human dilemma" (*Edge of
Impossibility* 167), might be said of Revere, Clara, and Swan in *A Garden
of Earthly Delights:* "they are heroic in their ritualistic enactment of the
common human dilemma." Gifted with audacity, Clara ritually reenacts
"the common human dilemma," though she does not transcend the tragic
script and does not understand the forces that destroy her. The novel implies
that Clara has an alternative, that marriage to Lowry might have enabled
her to transcend destructive cultural forces, but Clara herself does not
understand this. Nevertheless, Clara does struggle, and she does choose.
Her choice occurs at the moment she rejects her passion for Lowry—
Swan's biological father—in order to marry Revere, using her son to claim
the socioeconomic power she has been denied. Although victimized by the
injustices of a competitive economic-political system, Clara finally rejects
the more expansive, spiritual consciousness she experiences while making
love to Lowry. Yet because Lowry had abandoned her earlier while unaware
of her pregnancy, Clara experiences this loss of self as a vulnerability too
perilous to allow, "as if a wound had been opened up in her, secret in her
body" (243). Nevertheless, even after Clara has become Revere's mistress,
it is with Lowry that she feels a loss of ego, with Lowry that she feels
"something heavy and close to death, like lying on the bottom of an ocean of
sweat, their bodies trembling from all the violence they had suffered" (243).

Though Lowry returns to offer himself to Clara, acknowledging his
mistake in leaving her, she chooses to remain Revere's mistress, acting a
part, an inauthentic part, in someone else's dream: "She knew she must have
the look of a woman in a picture who had everything decided for her, who
had never had to think, whose long complicated life had been simplified by
some artist when he chose one instant out of it to paint: after that to hell with
her" (245). Clara understands that after her service to the male artist, after
she has served as an object of his fantasy, the artist would not care what
happened to her. Thus, she only pretends to play the part of the passive
heroine, the part of "a woman in a picture who had everything decided for

her," while plotting to survive. Through this plotting, Clara develops her native intelligence into a kind of cunning, but she does so at the price of a potentially more expansive imagination. In a rare, vulnerable moment, she reveals this hunger to her son: " 'If I had a chance to learn things, to read all those books and study them . . .' " (360). When Swan smiles at her, Clara says, " 'I would give anything to be smart. . . . You think I like the way I am? All my life there were people around me who could see farther than I could and backwards farther too—I mean into the past. History, things that happened and get written down. And they could understand life. But I couldn't' " (360). Tragically, Clara never has the opportunity for an education that might have freed her from the tragic ritual of sacrifice in which she plays a part.

This sacrifice, the daughter's sacrifice, is evident in the tripartite structure of *A Garden of Earthly Delights*, each of which is given a man's name: Carleton, Lowry, and Swan. Clara's name does not appear; instead, she is sacrificed to a violent plot and becomes, in turn, an adult who sacrifices her child. The adolescent Clara had stolen an American flag from a middle-class yard; and after her marriage she always displays an American flag in her yard. However, possession of the flag does not mean that she has achieved the American dream, for Clara's dream could not be fulfilled with material possessions alone. She had once known another kind of hunger: upon first meeting Lowry, for example, she had felt "that the God the minister had talked of was present. He was this hot pressure that hung over her, this force lowering Himself into her body, squirming into her. That God was still hungry, the hamburgers hadn't done Him any good" (95). Clara had yearned to expand her consciousness and imagination, but finally she concluded that survival required her to marry the Father. Teper Bender concludes that Oates's "allusions to Yeats are subversive: his Leda is ravished by transhuman appetites; her Clara is seduced by tawdry advertisements. But her irony works both ways: the mythic weave of poetry unravels in the violent pull of ordinary existence" (*Joyce Carol Oates* 29). But I wonder: since it is Oates herself, rather than Clara, who is writing sacrificial plots, just how subversive are these allusions to Yeats?

As if to explore this very question, in *Expensive People* Clara is transformed into an educated mother who is also a writer. Yet Natashya Everett raises her son, just as Clara had raised her son to become a hard and competitive man like his "successful" father. This time, however, the outraged son kills his mother, not his father. Unfortunately, psychiatrists don't believe Richard's story because patricide, not matricide, is the crime in their interpretive model. Furthermore, in the Freudian version of the child's crime, the famous Oedipus complex, the focus is upon the son's unconscious hostility toward his father rather than upon the father's hostility toward the son. The fact that psychiatrists (and adults in general) don't believe Richard Everett's story leads to his dramatic confession, in the first sentence of his memoir, "I was a child murderer" (5). Richard, who was only eleven when he murdered his (childish) mother, explains that he doesn't mean "child-murderer, that is, a murderer who happens to be a child, or a child who happens to be a murderer"(5). He tells readers that after writing his autobiography, he intends to kill himself. The memoir itself is an act of verbal violence that Richard likens to "a hatchet to slash through my own heavy flesh and through the flesh of anyone else who happens to get in the way" (6). Explaining that his memoir "isn't well rounded or hemmed in by fate in the shape of novelistic architecture" (6), Richard mocks those formalist critics whose narrow attention to aesthetics makes them deaf to his confession, a story of painful hunger suffered in the midst of plenty.

Richard, like Clara before him, is hungry for something that "no hamburger could fill," and he consumes suicidal quantities of food as he writes his memoirs. Indeed, though the setting has changed from the country to the city, *Expensive People* parallels *A Garden of Earthly Delights* in a number of ways. For example, Natashya Romanow marries Elwood Everett, a man older than she, for the same reasons that Clara marries Revere: for his money. And like Clara, the discontented Natashya periodically leaves home, abandoning her husband and son as she attempts to escape "normal" life. In addition, both mothers commit infidelities which are observed by their intelligent sons, and both sons, afraid of losing their mothers, strive to win their love. Swan concludes that he can win Clara's love only by acting the part she has plotted for him, that is, by taking over his father's lands and business. Richard, the product of a more educated mother, does much the same thing, literally acting out a part outlined by his mother for a short story called "The Sniper." In both novels mothers fail their children, scripting them for violence; however, Oates seems to identify with both Clara and Nada even as she criticizes them.

The reason for this identification, I believe, is that a maternal ethic informs Oates's conception of her responsibilities as a writer. This maternal ethic, which is even more explicit in *Expensive People* than in *A Garden of Earthly Delights*, leads Oates to ask whether she, like Nada, is failing the young by writing violent plots for them to act out. Although the needs of children are a central concern in the trilogy, Oates feels anxious that she is failing as a mother/author. This anxiety becomes evident in her portrayal of Nada Everett, an indifferent mother who is also the author of essays and short stories that Oates herself has published. For example, in his mother's notebook Richard finds a reminder to "Revise 'Death and the Maiden' and change title" (116); Oates actually did change the title to "Where are you going, where have you been?". Richard also finds a story called "The Molestors" (161–79) that Oates had published earlier in *The Quarterly Review of Literature*. Most important, however, Richard finds and acts out one of Nada's ideas for a story called "The Sniper," an idea that appears in her notebook as follows: "Idea for a short novel: the young man (like J?) leads two lives, one public and the other secret, buys a gun. frightens people, doesn't hurt them" (117). This is the role that Richard himself chooses to enact. Yet his mother's journal entry considers the plot only in aesthetic terms: "I can stretch this out to three episodes but no more, find . . . then the fourth, when you've been conditioned to the others, results in the murder: planned all along though maybe he didn't know it. (Too corny? Should he know it, or not?) The sniper. 'The Sniper.' I'll think of a theme later" (117).

By acting out his mother's story, Richard derives a sense of power that his daylight self doesn't possess, primarily because his mother conceals both her past identity, her identity as the daughter of poor immigrants, and her present identity as a writer. Richard's secret relationship with his mother, his identity as a sniper, gives him a sense of power: he can begin as her character and then, by killing her, become an author himself. Like the sniper in his mother's outline, Richard first snipes without actually killing anyone, but he knows all along—or does he?—that he will finally shoot to kill. His victim will be his own mother. Since the real Richard is, in fact, a stranger to Nada, identifying the killer as an anonymous sniper adds yet another ironic twist. What makes the crime so "perfect," and thus difficult to solve, is that a motive cannot be established for what appears to be a random act of violence. Yet detection is exactly what Richard most desires. He wants to be taken seriously; he wants to be understood as having a motive, but having become a cynic, he expects that his readers, like his psychiatrists, will not believe him.

Given her sympathy for Richard and her satire of Nada, it comes as a surprise that Oates identifies her writing as Nada's. One explanation for this explicit identification with Nada might be that, in this way, Oates foregrounds her differences with a woman whose art does not serve the needs of children. In other words, though both Natashya Romanow Everett and Joyce Carol Oates write violent plots enacted by the young, this single similarity sharpens the profound differences between them: for example, Nada's naive worship of visible (material) power; her belief that she can erase her own history; and her indifference to her son, an attitude that makes her the "nada" or negative of Oates's ideal of the mother/writer. Implicit in the satire of Nada Everett is an ideal mother/author, a mature, honest, and caring writer who uses her considerable talents in the service of humanity, particularly on behalf of children. Such a writer would act as a medium for the voices of children—for example, "The Children of Freedom" in *Expensive People* (125) and "The Children of Silence" in *them* (7).[4] Because Nada is the negation (the nothing) of such an ideal, Richard tells us that he named his mother "Nada." In a footnote he says, "My mother had wanted me to call her 'Nadia' but, as a small child, I must have been able to manage only the infantile 'Nada.' Hence Nada—strange name" (12).

But will anyone believe Richard? Since he is only a child, and therefore by definition someone who is not to be taken seriously, Richard expects to be discredited, declared an "unreliable narrator" not only by psychiatrists but by literary critics as well. Richard begins his satire of such readerly expectations early in his narrative, in a chapter called "My Earliest Memory." In a footnote he remarks, "As I read this over, this rendition of infant impressions strikes me as very bad, but let it stand. The experience is there, the reality is there, but how to get at it? Everything I type out turns into a lie simply because it is not the truth" (31). Probably none of us has access to the truth of our memories, but that doesn't make Richard Everett a liar. Fiction is a lie, but that doesn't make it "not the truth." This play with "truth" is one example of how Richard participates in the competitive literary game. He anticipates every hostile move by his readers, even writing reviews of *Expensive People* which appear in literary journals and in the *New York Times Book Review*, *Time* magazine, and *The New Republic*. One article by "Hanley Stuart Hingham, a famous critic, writing in any one of the literary quarterlies," invokes Freud to attack the novel. After reducing the novel's eating images to sexual hunger, Hingham writes, "Those of us who have read Freud (I have read every book, essay, and scrap of paper written by Freud) will recognize easily the familiar domestic triangle here, of a son's homosexual and incestuous love for his father disguised by a humdrum Oedipal attachment to his mother" (135–36).

Richard tries desperately to confess his crime to overcome his lonely sense of freedom—the isolated freedom Nada had encouraged—but his therapist only says, "Richard, let me assure you of this: hallucinations are as vivid as reality, and I respect everything you say. I know that you are suffering just as much as if you had killed your mother" (254). No one believes Richard— not his father, not the detective that his father calls in on the case in an effort to humor his son, and not the series of psychiatrists Richard goes to for help. "My favorite was Dr. Saskatoon," Richard says, "who explained gently to me that I had loved my mother so much, indeed overmuch, that I could not accept the fact of her death being caused by anyone except myself; a familiar delusion, he assured me" (253). In other words, *Expensive People* satirizes psychiatrists and psychoanalytic literary critics because a Freudian conception of the family romance, focusing upon the son's hostility toward the father, ignores the hostility of fathers, such as Laius or Elwood Everett. Oates defines her fiction, not in Oedipal terms, but as an elaboration of the Cronus myth,[5] a drama in which the father's hostility cannot be overlooked. According to this plot, Cronus, fearing that his power will be usurped, orders his wife and sister, Rhea, to feed her newborn infants to him. Rhea finally rebels, hiding her infant son Zeus until he is old enough to conquer his father and claim his power. Rhea, like Clara Walpole, waits until her son is old enough and, in this way becomes complicit in the violent competition between father and son. Nada has the power to rewrite this ancient plot, but instead she writes violent plots herself.

Perhaps for this reason, Richard anticipates his failure, just as he had once failed to achieve the high IQ score that Nada expected of him. Furthermore, although Richard had taken the exam over again, raising his score from a mere 153 to 161, Nada had left him again. In his desperate effort to win his mother's admiration and love, Richard, like Swan Revere, felt that he must seek achievement beyond the merely human. He says, in a caricature of Yeats's swan: "I felt as if I were trying to fly with wings soaked in sweat, feathers torn and ragged, falling out, and on my shoulders Nada rode with triumphant, impatient enthusiasm, her high heels spurs in my ribs—me, the child, the shabby angel pumping his wings furiously and weeping with shame; Nada, the mother, digging in her heels and cursing me on. I kept struggling up into the sky, my eyes bloodshot and my heart just ordinarily shot, waiting for the end . . ." (Oates's ellipsis 48).[6] Like Clara, Nada uses her son in the service of her own egoistic designs, as a weapon in her plot to climb into an upper-class heaven, leaving behind her lower-class origins. Richard does not learn his mother's true identity, nor meet her actual parents, until after her death. It is very American, this dream, and therefore probably understandable, at least as the dream of an uneducated woman such as Clara Walpole. It is less understandable in a woman as highly intelligent and gifted as Natashya Romanow.

Little wonder, then, that when Richard reads "The Molestors," he feels that he has been abandoned by his mother. The story demonstrates that Nada has the capacity to imagine the feelings of a molested child, and this obvious imaginative ability makes her refusal to imagine the needs of her own son even more reprehensible. Yet it doesn't occur to Nada that it might make a difference to Richard if she took the time to imagine him. Why is an intelligent woman so obtuse when it comes to the needs of her own son? Richard tries desperately to find an answer to this question. One reason, he surmises, is that she sees no relationship between mothering and writing, thinking of her writing as a frivolous sideline to the serious business of being "normal," that is, pretending to be an unimaginative wife and mother in an expensive home. Because Nada was born poor, her desire to be accepted by expensive people makes her behave as if she's stupid. Nada doesn't recognize that many expensive people actually admire her writing ability, as Richard explains: "At the age of ten I could tell they were proud of Nada for being a 'writer,' but she never caught on. Even after the women chatted energetically about their ballet classes, sculpting classes, theater groups, Great Books Round Tables, Creative Writing Clinics, she never caught on; she had a certain opaqueness, a failure of vision common to people who see only minute things well" (57).

What makes Nada a failure as a mother, at least from her son's point of view, is her denial of her writing ability, her habit of minimizing her intelligence and talent. She keeps leaving home, Richard recognizes, because motherhood and writing exist in separate realms. Yet the ability to imagine a child is not dissimilar from the ability to imagine a character, and a character in a novel can become as independent of its author as a child born of a mother. In fact, what makes Richard so dependent upon his mother's approval—indeed, obsessed with a desire for her approval—is his need for her love. As Richard tells us, "Mothers who cringe and beg for love get nothing, and they deserve nothing, but mothers like Nada who are always backing out of the driveway draw every drop of love out of us" (183). This passage does not imply that a woman should not leave a loveless marriage, nor does it suggest that a mother should exist only for her children. In fact, Richard's pride in Nada's writing ability illustrates Oates's early resistance to conservative views of a mother's role; hence, I disagree with feminist critics such as Mary Allen who categorize her early work, along with the fiction of other women of the era, as "conservative in its views of women's work, birth control, and abortion, yet 'adamant as to the abuses of motherhood' " (Greene, *Changing the Story* 54). *Expensive People* implies, in its satire of Nada's attempt to act the part of the romantically isolated artist, a different conception of authorial power, a power analogous to a mother's ability to imagine the needs of her children and, as they mature, allow them freedom from her control.

In Oates's next novel, *them*, she once again portrays the young, rich or poor, as "struggling heroically to define personal identity in the face of incredible opposition, even in the face of death itself," as she says in the Preface to *Where are you going, Where have you been?* (9). Her focus is upon the children of the poor who struggle to make their lives meaningful in a society that denies "the democratic essence of divinity." Hence, the title points to the novel's most revolutionary theme: that "we" are "them," that the grammatical as well as the social boundaries separating us are illusory. In *them*, as in *A Garden of Earthly Delights*, a Yeatsian rhetoric marks those scenes of passion, those sacred moments when unions of I/you, portrayed as analogous with communions of us/them, are potentially the greatest. The failed romantic union of Jules and Nadine is imagined as tragic, not only because violence follows, but also because, as children of the rich and poor, they represent the hope of breaking down the walls that divide us, the walls that prevent the emergence of a genuinely democratic society. Despite antidemocratic forces in the United States, Jules still dreams of flowing out and into Nadine, of losing himself in her. Tragically, Nadine cannot allow such a flowing forth of passion. Certain icy beliefs enclose her in a bell jar that she cannot escape. What are these beliefs, and why is Nadine so incapable of passion? According to Oates, the "princess" is a prisoner in the tower of her "father's ethic of the cold, locked-in ego," a state that "dooms her to frigidity" (*New Heaven, New Earth* 278 n. 4).

This emotional frigidity, a kind of perpetual virginity, also characterizes Karen Herz in *With Shuddering Fall* and Sister Irene in "In the Region of Ice." In these women an internalized moral script that defines sexual passion as a "fall" has an economic parallel: the falling of the daughter of an upper-class father into the possession by a lower-class son. This moral/economic system of beliefs enables the wealthy father in a capitalistic system to retain the daughter for himself in an attempt to hoard his property.[7] It is not by accident that such "princesses" as Karen and Nadine are frequently associated with the stone-cold statues of the Virgin Mary, a daughter who brought forth a son without losing her status as a virgin. For psychologically, the "good" daughter remains virginal even after intercourse, unable to act upon her own desire but ever submissive to the desires of others. For example, though Nadine Green submits passively to Jules's embrace, as Karen submits to Shar's embrace in *With Shuddering Fall*, she remains self-contained, hermetically sealed inside her father's image of his "good" daughter.

The Yeatsian rhetoric appears in this novel when the lovers, Jules and Nadine, meet for a second time in a Detroit chophouse. A "Mr. Yates" is present in the restaurant's dark background; later, as the pair make love, Nadine is described as "desiring the divinity in him, so violently aroused . . . [she] could do nothing but claw at him, wanting it, hellish in agony" (370). Nadine's failure of imagination, her habit of seeing Jules as one of "them," as a representative of a fallen world, ensures her frigidity. Although Nadine sensed in Jules "a rich, violent power that should have been hers, since it came from her body," nevertheless, "somehow it was not hers—it was denied her, mysteriously" (371). Nadine resorts to violence—shooting Jules after their lovemaking fails—because she cannot escape the paternal logos that is inscribed in her body and mind. She remains a captive of the daughter's part, a daughter from the upper-class heaven of Grosse Point, scripted for her function as an object of exchange in a hierarchic homosocial order. Oates portrays Nadine as an icy, upper-class "enemy," not out of any hostility to women, but out of an effort to sanctify the lives of the poor, an effort to portray Jules and his sister Maureen not as a naturalistic case studies but as actors in a communal tragedy.

Oates acknowledged that while writing this novel, she "felt Nadine to be the enemy, since I was obviously on Jules' side" ("Transformations of Self" 48). Yet, having stated that, temporarily, her sympathy for Jules precluded sympathy for Nadine, Oates told the interviewer that she had also written a poem from the woman's point of view: "A poem of mine in *Love and Its Derangements*, called 'You/Your,' was written out of exactly the same maniacal stupor as certain parts of *them*; but it is from the woman's point of view, her befuddlement at her dependence upon a man, upon a man's loving her, from which she will get whatever identity she possesses" ("Transformations of Self" 48). The woman, it happens, was Jules's mistress, Nadine, who later tries to kill him. "And why not?" Oates asks. ("Transformations of Self" 48). The fact that Oates takes the side of Jules in the novel—a sympathy motivated more by class than by gender—does not prevent her from portraying Nadine sympathetically in a poem. Furthermore, the novel's negative portrayal of the upper-middle-class Nadine is effectively balanced by a sympathetic portrayal of Maureen. And since Maureen belongs to the same social class as well as the same generation as her brother Jules, certain gender differences become apparent in what Charlotte Goodman calls a "male-female double *Bildungsroman*" (30), differences not as evident in *A Garden of Earthly Delights* or *Expensive People*. According to Goodman, *them* is a novel that "describes the shared childhood experience of a male and a female protagonist who inhabit a place somewhat reminiscent of a prelapsarian mythic garden world where the male and female once existed as equals" (30).

Yet, through a separation of male and female, Goodman says, such a double bildungsroman "emphasizes the dichotomy of male and female experience in a patriarchal culture" (42), a doubling by which women writers have "radically altered or subverted the genre" (42). I do not see this doubling as a *radical* subversion of the genre; however, Oates's portrayal of the contrasting experiences of Jules and Maureen certainly demonstrates attentiveness to gender stereotypes: for example, both are victims of violence, but Jules is far more imaginative and assertive than his sister. Indeed, he is more imaginative and assertive than even the upper-class Nadine, who is presumably better educated. Tragically, as Goodman argues, though Jules is more active than his sister, Maureen, the lives of both are diminished. The title of Part Three, "Come, My Soul, That Hath Long Languished," emphasizes the fact that both Maureen and Jules awaken from spiritual death, but their imaginations are impoverished and their futures uncertain. As in *A Garden of Earthly Delights*, spirituality and imagination are closely linked: defining one's self as human means expanding the imagination, an expansion that occurs primarily through love, but also through reading and writing. Tragically, however, education fails to expand the imaginations of Jules and Maureen; rote learning in the over-crowded urban Catholic schools of Detroit only narrows their imaginations even more. The novel criticizes the way in which our society assigns worth to human beings based on gender or class, and it parodies the tendency of naturalistic novels to deny spiritual yearnings to the lower class. In contrast, this novel defines as "evil" those lacking the imaginative capacity for love, distinguishing between those with the audacity to risk the "I" through love from those who remain self-contained. Love is always an act of imagination in Oates's fiction, yet many of her characters view such passion not only as threatening but as criminal.

Hence, rather than judging the Wendalls from a moral position above and outside their world, Oates strives to passionately imagine their world, the world of "them," from within. As readers, we come to understand why, for example, Jules's imaginative capacity is eventually so stunted that he is able to kill. As a spirited child, when Jules accidentally sets fire to a barn while playing with fire—and uttering magic incantations to impress his sister— his angry grandmother, seeing only the child's destructiveness, predicts that he will end up in the electric chair. The nuns in his Catholic grade school make similar predictions. Yet Jules is not as easily defeated as his sister. For example, when he loses his English notebook and drops out of school, he quickly finds a substitute dream, a dream signified by the photograph of a girl that he manages to retrieve when the wind grabs it, dashing it into the mud of an expressway. Jules has seen enough movies to imagine himself as "a character in a book being written by himself" (99), the author of his own fate. Thus, despite repeated brutal defeats, the ever-optimistic Jules continues to think of himself as a hero, the Alan Ladd or Marlon Brando of a story he is authoring himself. He imagines that "so long as he owned his own car he could always be in control of his fate—he was fated to nothing. He was a true American. His car was like a shell he could maneuver around, at impressive speeds; he was a second generation to no one. He was his own ancestors" (335).

This romantic plot initially gives Jules a sense of freedom, but it is the kind of freedom that leads Jules, repeatedly, into dead ends. One such dead end is Nadine Greene herself. In love with Nadine, daughter of a wealthy family in Grosse Point, Jules presents himself as a romantic suitor. At the same time, though the romance plot provides Jules with a potentially liberating script, a model for self-definition, for Nadine this plot is oppressive, requiring a form of self-annihilation. As Du Plessis has noted, the romance plot defines heterosexuality in such a way as to deny subjectivity to women. The same plot, which defines the man as a subject, requires that Nadine act as an object who exists only for a man. Nadine says, " 'You know, Jules, a man's love creates a woman's love. You've made me the way I am' " (349); her romantic passivity destroys their potential love. For example, when Jules first sees Nadine, she seems "under an enchantment," as "the girl," as "someone's daughter, unassailable" (230–31). Dressed in white, she is like the fairy tale princess in the tower, and when Jules enters Nadine's home in Grosse Point, he longs to be "the carpet beneath her feet" (258). Her aloofness reminds Jules of a statue of the Virgin Mary and of an equally unattainable nun, Sister Mary Jerome, whom Jules had secretly loved as a boy. Despite the spiritual nature of Jules's quest, he discovers only the nullity of Nadine's innocence. Jules understands that "her sad, evil vision of purity kept him pure. He could not contaminate her with his lust; she seemed to feel nothing" (275).

In this criticism of Nadine's "perverse" and "obscene" purity, Oates defines her own moral vision: Jules's lust for Nadine is portrayed as spiritual, while Nadine's fear of his lust is described as a "sad evil vision of purity" (275). Nadine is acting out this vision of purity when she fires two shots into her lover's body and then turns the gun on herself. This act of violence ends Part Two, which, closing with the words, "The spirit of the Lord departed from Jules" (380), conveys the impression that Jules dies. Forty pages later, like Lazarus himself, Jules appears once again on the streets of Detroit. The surprise of this resurrection requires readers to confront the distinction between spiritual and biological death. Maureen's awakening, though somewhat less dramatic, is equally sudden and Lazarus-like. After lying mute in bed for more than a year, she suddenly speaks, asking whether a letter from Jules has arrived. Her uncle Brock, who has patiently and lovingly read Jules's letters to her, helps to resurrect Maureen. The ironic fact that Brock is also a killer (years ago he had killed his sister's lover) suggests the capacity of human beings for a great range of behavior. As in this instance, love of family may sometimes make a difference, but family love is not enough. A case in point: Jules sends letters that help to heal his sister, but this act of familial love does not change the fact that we live in a society that denies "we are all members of a single family," that denies Jules and Maureen a sense of participating in a larger family.

This novel satirizes the hierarchic moral code of the romance plot that assumes that the rich should be able to define themselves at the expense of the poor, or that man should be able to define himself at the expense of woman. More specifically, though Jules feels a sense of expansion, of "ballooning," as he acts out the quest plot, the same script provides no such possibilities for Nadine, for Maureen, or for any of Oates's heroines, from Karen Herz in *With Shuddering Fall* to Shelley in *Wonderland*. Although these young women leave home to escape being defined by others, they seem unable to become their own authors.[8] Even after many defeats, Jules continues to dream his romantic dream, and at the novel's end, he tells his sister that Nadine is still at the center of his yearning: " 'I want to marry her, anyway, that woman, the one who tried to kill me, I still love her and I'll make some money and come back and marry her, wait and see—when I come back, a little better off, we can see each other. All right?' " (478). Jules is still fired by the secular scripture, a quest plot often embedded in naturalistic novels, but this idea of himself, this form of self-authorship, is at best ambiguous. Still the questor, still imagining himself the author of his own story, Jules sets off for California, but he has become, to Maureen, just one of "them."

Maureen has survived, having had the initiative to act out the marriage plot, but she has sacrificed her family and imagination in order to escape the ghetto. Yet we understand why, as a lower-class child, Maureen concludes that the suffering of characters in most novels "was greater than her own. How could she or her people be raised to this level of suffering?" (166). We also understand why, although Maureen is attracted to the quiet order of libraries, she dares to dream only of becoming a secretary, never a teacher or writer herself. The closest Maureen comes to the act of writing is as the secretary of her class—a duty that requires neatness and accuracy, not imagination, as the nuns emphasize. Because of her training for submission and obedience, virtues appropriate to a future wife, Maureen's loss of the secretary's notebook makes her feel as if her life were coming "undone," an experience she likens to "that time her period had begun in school" (157). As a girl, it seems obvious, her "fate" is even more restricted than her brother's. Indeed, because Maureen's mother, Loretta Wendall, cannot imagine a fate different from her own for her daughter, she further victimizes Maureen. She belittles Maureen's efforts to read, accusing Maureen of lying about going to the library, and she conveys to Maureen her belief that only a woman's body can save her from poverty, preferably through marriage, but failing that, through prostitution. Loretta actually treats Maureen as a prostitute, turning her into the bait by which to keep her second husband, Furlong.

Finally, Maureen can no longer see how books might be relevant to her life; she cannot even imagine herself worthy of being portrayed in a novel. Acting out her mother's limited vision of a daughter's part, she turns to prostitution, storing her earnings in a book called *Poets of the New World,*

an allusion that signals Maureen's "fall" not from virginal innocence but
from the spiritual realm of imagination and love. After her stepfather,
who harbors incestuous desires for Maureen, discovers her with another
man, he nearly beats her to death. Betrayed and brutalized, Maureen goes
to bed from April 1956 to June 1957, where she lies in vegetable state,
unable to think or talk. Goodman argues that Maureen, like other Oates
women, retreats into a state of "cataleptic denial" (41), but she neglects to
point out that both brother and sister experience such a living death, and
both return from it. Strangely, despite Oates's Yeatsian passion to imagine
"them," Maureen expresses antagonism toward a woman named "Joyce
Carol Oates." In a note to her former teacher, she says, "You failed me"
(314). Maureen doesn't write, "You gave me an F," but makes the more
ambiguous accusation, "You failed me." The implication is clear: "Joyce
Carol Oates," the teacher, has failed Maureen, her female student. Although
Joanne Creighton thinks that most readers will find the author of the
Note "indistinguishable in any way from the 'real' author" (*Joyce Carol
Oates* 65), the distinction is important, for author Oates sees what "Miss
Oates," the teacher of Maureen, fails to see: her kinship with a woman
student.

Nevertheless, in an interview with Linda Kuehl in 1969, Oates admitted
that "she identified more with the aggressive Jules than with the passive
Maureen" (Goodman 41). Not until some years later did Oates acknowledge
her identification with Maureen: "I see shadowy aspects of myself in her,
and recognize my voice in her in ways I would not have understood when I
wrote the novel. I was troubled in writing it, for indeed the Wendall's lives
became my own and their souls entered mine" ([*Woman*] *Writer* 368). As if
after completing the novel she could see the gender problem more clearly,
Oates calls attention to the issue of authorial power in the "Author's Note"
to *them*. Ironically—for surely it is intended as irony—Oates implies that
Jules might write a better novel than she. As if merely providing an account
of the fates of her major characters, she says: "We have all left Detroit—
Maureen is now a housewife in Dearborn, Michigan; I am teaching in
another university; and Jules Wendall, that strange young man, is probably
still in California. One day he will probably write his own version of this
novel, to which he will not give the rather disdainful and timorous title
them" (n.p.). It is highly improbable that Jules, a high school dropout, will
write a novel with a title which is superior to Oates's "rather disdainful and
timorous *them*"; of course, it is even less probable that Maureen could write

a novel with the revolutionary moral vision implied in the title *them* since, in the novel's final scene, Maureen refers to her brother as one of "them."

The fact that daughters, whether rich or poor, cannot imagine themselves as teachers or writers is the consequence, not of their lack of innate intelligence, but of society's scripting—its constricting—of their imaginations. Otherwise, why would middle-class women, those wealthy enough to attend college and imagine themselves as writers, remain mute instruments of the paternal voice and will, incapable of asserting their own desires?[9] However, acts of verbal or behavioral self-assertion on the part of the young, regardless of their social class, are generally viewed as "criminal" by adults, regardless of their social class. At the same time, this moral code—a romantic code that idealizes innocence—is gendered so that a woman's loss of innocence often is judged more harshly than a man's, even when the crime itself is the same. Readers may, for example, judge Clara far more harshly than her husband, for it is she who trains Swan to compete against his stepbrothers, killing them if necessary in order to claim all of Revere's wealth for himself. Yet Revere has far more power over this competitive code than does Clara. The same double standard, not the author's but society's, is also evident in *them*: it may be "heroic" for Jules Wendall to steal Nadine Greene (whose passivity is considered "virginal") from her family or to liberate himself from rage through violence, but when Maureen sells sex or steals another woman's husband, she is judged a "whore" or a "fallen woman." Author Oates strives to revise such unjust moral judgments, entangled as they are in class and gender constructs, not only in the novel, but in her criticism.

Although acts of imagination—through artistic sublimation—provide alternatives to violence, this option is not available to Jules or Maureen because of the economic and social injustices of our society. "We are all part of a single human family," Jules reads aloud, repeating the words of Vinoba Bhave, who is pictured on the cover of *Time* magazine. "Fire burns and does its duty" (95) reads Jules, whose spiritual yearnings are fired by Bhave's words: "My object is to transform the whole of society. Fire merely burns. . . . Fire burns and does its duty. It is for others to do theirs" (95). As a child Jules had associated fire with magic; now he understands fire only in the most literal terms—as the kind of fires set during the Detroit riots. During these riots, Jules himself finally finds a way to express his spiritual passion, which by then had turned to rage: he kills a man. For a society such as ours, Yeats's "Leda and the Swan" may be an appropriate image of the violence of social change; however, as Oates became increasingly attentive to gender, she also became increasingly ambivalent toward the tragic vision in Yeats's poem. Furthermore, as I demonstrate in the next chapter, it was Oates's sympathy with a fictional daughter—a young woman named Shelley—that led her to revise the tragic conclusion of her fifth novel, *Wonderland*, and, at the same time, move beyond the too-powerful influence of writers such as Yeats and Shakespeare.

3

"The Central Nervous System of America": The Writer in/as the Crowd in Wonderland

As crowds of protesters converged in the streets to protest United States involvement in Vietnam during late 1969 and the early 1970s, Joyce Carol Oates was writing her fifth novel, *Wonderland*. This novel was published with two different endings. The first version, the 1971 hardcover edition, conforms to the practice of aesthetic unity, looping back to its point of origin, an act of patriarchal closure. This tragically closed circle illustrates a textual practice that mirrors a concept of the self—the self as an isolated, enclosed, competitive ego—in which such violence originates. Julia Kristeva describes such texts—those that mirror the bounded self—as "bounded texts" (*Desire in Language* 36–63); in such works, regardless of genre, textual boundaries demarcate a romantic ego, tragically isolated from community. Such a tragic/romantic close describes the ending of Oates's initial edition of *Wonderland*, an ending in which the adolescent heroine is sacrificed to maintain textual unity and social stasis. Shelley represents an entire generation of young Americans sacrificed to a war maintained by official or "monologic" consciousness (Bakhtin, *The Dialogic Imagination* 3–40). Jesse Vogel, Shelley's father and a famous brain surgeon, represents this monologic consciousness—he knows only one language, science—and Oates's first ending depicts Jesse as a contemporary King Lear carrying the dead body of his daughter as he grieves for this sacrifice to the (male) ego. In Oates's 1973 paperback edition of this novel, she rejects tragic closure, refusing to sacrifice the body (writing) to maintain the illusion of (vocal) unity. She replaces univocal tragic closure with the ambivalence of dialogue. " 'I think you are the devil,' " says Shelley to her father, and he answers, " 'Am I?' "[1]

In Oates's revision of this transitional novel, she resists subordinating the voice of her adolescent heroine to achieve a unitary authorial voice, a voice usually assumed to be masculine. In *Wonderland*, the monologic voice is identified with the hero, Jesse. In at least one respect, Jesse is a typical American male since his consciousness has been narrowed by his faith in scientific objectivity. However, as Oates portrays Jesse, his objectivity is actually "realism," an anthropocentric illusion that denies the existence of the self, a self mistakenly defined as merely subjective. It is this self, Jesse's ghost self, that awakens him at night, this self that circles obsessively around the body of his daughter Shelley. In *Wonderland*, then, Oates explores the boundaries between "objective" and "subjective" modes of discourse—between science and romance—as they define personality and as they construct categories of gender. Through her hero's obsession with the theory of homeostasis, Oates examines those discourses that have shaped American culture, a culture that, while claiming to be democratic, has silenced the voices of women, children, and the poor. The novel begins on December 14, 1939, at the end of the Great Depression, moves through the period of the assassination of John Kennedy, and ends with protests against the war through the summer of 1970.

While Jesse remains deaf to the "Other," censoring the voices of music and poetry, the voices of women and children, the voices of memory and body, Oates herself was struggling with the contending voices and texts in U.S. culture, attempting to achieve a harmony, a unity, that would not censor such voices. The author's voice is located on the margins of discourse—epic, historic, literary and scientific—and it illustrates how the novel struggles, as Bakhtin says in *The Dialogic Imagination*, with itself and with other genres. In the first edition of *Wonderland*, Oates had—as "Author, Man"—sacrificed the body of an adolescent girl to maintain traditional boundaries of text and self. Her revision makes a different argument, insisting upon a democratic chorus of voices rather than a single, monologic consciousness. Rejecting the convention of aesthetic unity, Oates resists a false unity; she also recognizes that hierarchies of gender as well as class are maintained by univocal closure. Although Oates does not explain her revision in these terms, she did say, during an interview with *Newsweek* in

1972: "With *Wonderland* I came to the end of a phase of my life, though I didn't know it," and she added that her collection, *Marriages and Infidelities*, published in 1972, "was a step in that direction" (Clemons, "Joyce Carol Oates" 77).

This latter title, of course, suggests the logic of the double: both marriages and infidelities. *Wonderland* illustrates Oates's transition from monologic to dialogic authorial consciousness, as she struggles to synthesize colliding voices and texts in a period of violent social change. Explaining her revision of *Wonderland*, she added this footnote to an essay published in 1973, "Art: Therapy and Magic": "Only once in my entire life did I very consciously— very intellectually—resist my intuition regarding something I wrote (the conclusion of one of my novels, *Wonderland*); with the result that, in deepest humility, I had to revise it after its appearance in the United States—causing the kind of confusion and inconvenience I dread" (20). In fact, this change has created critical confusion, but at the same time the "mistake" has been instructive. In her revised ending, Oates obeys the logic of dreams rather than the logic of the intellect, where monologic consciousness sometimes functions as tyrant. Instead, she moves toward dialogism—a consciousness that has its roots in carnival, in folk festival, in crowds. In the grotesque realism of *Wonderland*, elements of carnival emerge in images of carnival, tricksters, and doubles.

Oates's resistance to epic and scientific monologism is embodied in a trickster figure named Trick Monk, a scientist turned poet, an image of the double. Oates's voice is located in the rivalry between Trick (romantic poetry) and Jesse (science), both medical students. Their homosocial rivalry intensifies as the men compete for "the hand of" (body) Helene, the daughter of a doctor whom both men worship. In this struggle of voices, of genres, Oates attempts to find a method of composition and characterization that will illustrate her thesis: a "Song of Myself" at once individual and communal, a female equally with the male, the brain equally with the body. Individuality, as she says in her *Newsweek* interview with Walter Clemons, is a myth: " 'I absolutely don't believe there is very much originality. I just see myself as standing in a very strong tradition and my debt to other writers is very obvious. I couldn't exist without them. I don't have much autonomous existence, nor does anyone. We are interconnected—it seems we are individual and separate, whereas in fact we're not' "(73–74). Tragically, Jesse does not understand his kinship with others, especially with women—though he has, all of his life, struggled with the question.

Jesse first began to explore this question on December 14, 1939, when only a boy of fourteen. Nauseated by a quarrel between his pregnant mother and his worried father, Jesse had excused himself from a Christmas assembly. The voices of the school choir singing "Hark the Herald Angels Sing" echo in the background as Jesse glances above a vomit-filled toilet. There he sees this drawing: "A woman's body seen from the bottom up, the legs muscular and very long, spread apart, the head at the far end of the body small as a pea, with eyelashes nevertheless drawn in very carefully so that they look real. Someone has added to the drawing with another, blunter pencil, making the body boxlike, the space between the legs shaded in to a hard black rectangle like a door. The arms have been changed to walls and even the suggestion of brick added to them . . . It is a mysterious drawing, two mysterious drawings, one on top of the other like a dream that fades into another dream, a nightmare conquered by another" (30–31). This drawing graphically depicts the nightmarish underside—the repressed—of epic, or monologic, consciousness.

Epic consciousness, by claiming that "man" is not of woman born, forgets the body, and the law of the father—a disembodied voice—inscribes itself as a trace: one dream fades into another as woman becomes the building material of culture. Jesse's initiation into this social order is violent: he almost becomes yet another son sacrificed to the father. He bears the wound, from his father's gun, for the rest of his life. The end of the novel foregrounds this same sacrificial morality as it recurs in the 1960s, when American children—whom Oates names "Angel," "St. John," and "Noel"—become victims of a war-torn culture. Victimized as a child, Jesse becomes, in his turn, a victimizer. Jesse develops, from a series of father surrogates, from "men of science," what Susan Griffin in *Pornography and Silence* calls "the pornographic mind of our culture." Like the graffiti artist, he learns to master his fear of "the enlarged space between the woman's legs," a space which, at the age of fourteen, he thinks of as "something you could walk into and lose yourself in, all that empty blackness" (31). Through his mastery the graffiti artist enacts his revenge upon woman's power. Compulsively, binding his hysteria, the "masculine" mind denies the power of woman's womb by giving her a brain the size of a "pea." He views her body from outside, rather than from within, aggressively, distorting the body with his pen. The second male artist, with his "blunter pencil," superimposes a building upon her body, establishing himself as woman's architect. Her body becomes his building material, his property, his text. This widely shared view of woman denies her equality, denies her voice.

As a scientist, Jesse learns to share this view of woman-as-nature, as desacralized matter under man's dominion. Despite its desacralization of matter, scientific discourse, Julia Kristeva argues, accepts epic logic: "Epic logic assumes a hierarchy within the structure of substance. Epic logic is therefore causal, that is, theological; it is a belief in the literal sense of the word" (*Desire and Language* 78). Insisting on unity, the binary mind simply shifts its monotheism from God to the scientist, to the scientific "mind of man." Oates gives Mary Shelley's "Frankenstein" an American identity, transforming her hero, during a specific thirty-year period, from a monster created by Frankenstein into a duplicate of his creator. In Book One, Jesse, the only survivor of his father's murder-suicide, moves from his grandfather's home to an orphanage and, next, to the Pedersens. Adopted by Karl Pedersen, a doctor, Jesse takes on a new identity, this time becoming the son of a "mad-scientist" who wants to create Jesse in his own image. In this way Oates portrays the epic consciousness of Willard Harte and Karl Pedersen, fathers who, regardless of differences in class, share a belief in their rightful authority over their families. Both fathers also believe in the American myth of individualism. Thus, despite widespread economic failure, Willard Harte takes personal responsibility for his business failures, killing his entire family—as if their fate must be determined by him alone.

The many allusions to Whitman in *Wonderland* emphasize Oates's belief in the democratic essence of divinity, her desire to transform epic hierarchies and to sing the body equally with the mind, the female equally with the male. Official discourses have silenced this American dream, a dream that has fallen between the cracks of monologic discourses, epic, scientific, and romantic. The title of the opening book of the novel, "Variations on an American Hymn," suggests Oates's desire to transform a sacrificial morality—like that practiced by Dr. Pedersen—into a celebration of the dreaming body, a consciousness that has been repressed, distorted into pornographic fantasies, in our culture. As the son of Willard Harte and, later, Karl Pedersen, Jesse learns nothing about a democratic dream; instead he sees the mutilated bodies of the Hartes and the obese bodies of the Pedersens, victims of political/economic hierarchies. And in the flesh of Mrs. Pedersen, he also sees the nightmarish consequences of Dr. Pedersen's pornographic fantasies, a man who is "the head" of his family, as well as his community.

Dr. Pedersen literally holds the fate of the Pedersen family in his hands when, during their Christmas, the "good" man opens "The Book of Fates," the family photo album. Throughout the years of her marriage, the album reveals, the once-slender Mary Shirer—a doctor's daughter—has grown increasingly obese, as have her children, Hilda and Frederich. Oates's descriptions illustrate ambivalence; she is both satirical and sympathetic or—as Kristeva says is characteristic of novels in the tradition of Menippean satire—*Wonderland* is "both comic and tragic, or rather, it is *serious* in the same sense as the carnivalesque; through the status of words, it is politically and socially disturbing" (*Desire in Language* 83). Mrs. Pedersen appears in Jesse's doorway, a kindly woman "who filled the doorway in a huge mint-green cotton house dress; on her feet were straw shoes with orange tassels and small brass mock bells on the toes" (161). And Dr. Pedersen appears, in a photo taken at an Elk's Club Halloween Party for the Crippled, "enormous in a harlequin outfit, all rags and bells, holding a kind of scepter" (119). This carnivalesque description of the obese Pedersens identifies their religion: eating, consuming. It was "a ritual," complete with a table cloth "gleaming white, like an altar cloth" (91).

The balloon bodies of the Pedersens mirror the inflated ego of Dr. Pedersen, a man whose benevolent public persona disguises a secretly pornographic philosophy. Mrs. Pedersen exposes her husband's secrets to Jesse, in her words, but even more graphically, with her body. In despair, Mrs. Pedersen drinks. On one occasion, when she locks herself in the bathroom, Jesse helps to remove the door. He sees her body lying naked, an enormous body with "the head at the far end . . . too small for it" (157). Mary Pedersen tells Jesse that, shortly after their marriage, her husband had locked her in the bedroom, forcing her to shave the hair off her body and to look at photos of dismembered bodies with pornographic captions. She also tells Jesse: " 'He talks all the time about his public philosophy, but what about his secret one? Once a patient has come to him, he believes the patient is *his*. He owns the patient, he owns the disease, he owns everything. Oh, he's crazy" (171). Pedersen is a man so admired that he is invited to give sermons at the Lutheran Church, yet his wife tells Jesse, " 'The great Dr. Pedersen has made mistakes . . . but he would rather he watches them die and won't bring in anyone else . . . right until the end he thinks he's right, he's unable to believe he might be wrong' " (171).

Pedersen adopts Jesse because, as an orphan, he will be more submissive to his will than his own children, who have grown ill from passive resistance to their father. At every meal they must report on their intellectual achievements to their father, meanwhile filling their love-starved bodies with increasing quantities of food. Hilda feels her father's questions as "the body being addressed at its uppermost part, the head," and "she noticed how meekly the head nodded at the top of its squat stem and the torso of the body leaned forward, eager and obedient, as if prepared right now" to do her father's bidding (122). Having been forced to become an extension of her father's ego, a human computer, Hilda finally screams at him: "*You want to stuff me inside your mouth. I know you . . . You want to press me into a ball and pop me into your mouth, back where I came from. You want to eat us all up. Father wants to kill me. Eat me*" (140). According to medical or psychoanalytic definition, Hilda would be considered hysterical, but Pedersen had earlier comforted her with these monomaniacal words: "You will have me inside you, in a way, even after I am gone—inside you, carried around inside you" (133). Hilda recognizes that there is no escape from her father's voice: "He knew about the tiny sac inside her, that elastic, magical emptiness that could never be filled no matter how much she ate. It was the size of the universe" (131).

As a scientist, Jesse learns to share Dr. Pedersen's disdain for the merely physical, an attitude disguising his fear and hatred of the body, particularly the female body. Music or poetry—the rhythmic discourses of the body—remain mysterious to Jesse, who has learned that they are not essential to his survival. Yet, at different points in the narrative, Jesse has twin brothers, doubles who represent the voice of music, the voice of poetry: first it is Frederich, described in "monkish" terms, as having a face "small for the rest of his body, prematurely lined, with a mouth like his father, small and monkish" (92); and later it is Trick Monk. It does not occur to Jesse to wonder, as his sister Hilda does, "Is there a part of the soul that is not male or female?" (141). Even history is bunk, unimportant to a man of science, according to Dr. Pedersen: " 'If you make claims about history and death and sickness and chaos I have no time for you. What can history tell us? It is all a joke! Manure! We are not to be dragged down by the stupidities of the past' " (109). He explains to Jesse that, instead " 'we have the health of the living organism that strives to be God. I am striving, straining—' "(109). Arrogantly, Dr. Pedersen argues that other people, "stupid crowds and herds, like animals" are meant to die in wars that stimulate economic growth: " 'What is war, Jesse? Is it death? Never! It is the very heartbeat of life—the last resource of life's energies!' " (109). From Mrs. Pedersen, Jesse learns that the "good" doctor is working to design a germ bomb for the government of the United States.

Jesse learns his hatred of crowds from the egocentric Pedersen. Later, when Jesse encounters crowds of protesters as he searches for his daughter, Oates describes him as a man who "hated this formlessness. He was seized with a sudden hatred for it, almost nausea. He hated it, hated them. Hated the crowd in its joy in being trampled. Hated the noise. The communion." To Jesse, the crowd is "anonymous garbage" (449). From this "mass consciousness" Jesse desires "a single figure, a truth. Wasn't there a truth, a single truth, a single human being at the center of this mob? A single eye that would see everyone, everything, and pronounce judgment upon it?" (449). The question Oates has posed here is the same question that, according to Michael Holquist, is always the "obsessive question at the heart of Bakhtin's thought" (307). It is "the mystery of the one and the many." Bakhtin would describe Jesse's mind as "monologic." Oates portrays Jesse's "monologic" yearning as a search for a father figure that, in this era, is manifest in a collective deification of science. Presumably a scientist free of social conflicts, amoral and objective, Jesse refuses to acknowledge self-doubt or confusion. He remains rigidly self-contained, making science his "single truth" and worshipping a series of scientists, his unacknowledged fathers: Drs. Pedersen, Cady, Perrault.

Oates portrays Jesse's consciousness as monologic, fearful of crowds, while at the same time she strives to transform the rhythms of the crowd into music. The tension becomes apparent as Jesse confronts the "communion" of the crowd, "its strange mass consciousness." He thinks of crowds as "cancerous protoplasm": "He had seen it many times through a microscope, eating away its own boundaries, no limits to it, an inflammation seeding everywhere—to the spinal fluid, to the brain. How they surged in the chill open air of Chicago, roused as if by godly chimes—the bells of sunken churches, pealing and pulsating in a rhythm that people like Jesse could feel only remotely, being too old" (448–49). In contrast to the rhythms of the crowd, this "rhythm that beat in the loins," Oates gives us the voice of Dr. Pedersen, an arrogant individualist who sees crowds as fodder for war. Human beings, he has told Jesse, are fated to repeat war, and war is "the very heartbeat of life." One might ask, as Pedersen does not, what point there is in healing individual bodies destined for dissolution in war. Pedersen's answer, of course, would be: for profit. This is not the "wisdom of the body" speaking, for the body has no "instinct" for death, but rather for life, for eros. It is rather the mind, narrowly defined as individual—as an isolated ego—that silences the body's wisdom.

In Book Two, "The Finite Passing of an Infinite Passion," Oates explores Pedersen's pornographic mind as it evolves during the turbulent period of the late 1950s and into the 1960s protests against social injustice. During these years—which include the assassination of President Kennedy, race riots, and the Vietnam War—Jesse completes medical school and marries. His marriage and work seem to him apolitical, although the news of Kennedy's death reaches him as he presents a paper on brain research. Those who lived through this period in American history will recall the image of Kennedy's shattered brain, a brain Jesse regards as "individual." Yet at this time Jesse buys a gun, a gun that he later comes close to using against a young man. In 1963, his daughters are very young, and he wants to protect them. Jesse not only denies the sacredness of matter, however; he also ignores the promptings of his own body. Little dialogue occurs between his brain and body, and no dialogue occurs between Jesse and his wife. Like Dr. Pedersen, he marries a doctor through the body of his daughter, a courtship mocked by Trick Monk. Both men are seeking the love of Dr. Cady—an eminent scientist, a Nobel Prize winner—through the courtship of his daughter. Jesse is to win this contest, but it is a marriage without love that leads him to fantasize about adultery and later to sexualize his love for his daughter, Shelley. To dramatize Jesse's flight from the body— the hole in his consciousness—Oates introduces Trick Monk, a brilliant young medical student described in carnival terms, as "a young king and court jester, a clown with license to say anything" (206).

At the time of Trick's appearance, Jesse is engaged to a young woman, a nurse named Anne-Marie. Initially Jesse wants to tell her about his feelings, his arguments with professors; "however, he knew that she would not understand. He had no right to force her to understand. If he loved her he would guard her from such thoughts; if he loved her he would not bring her into himself, into his consciousness, but would allow her to remain herself" (196). Where has he learned to expect such mindless love? "He had learned from the few novels he had read in his lifetime that love demanded rescue. . . . The story demanded that a male rescue a female from danger and he would be punished if he failed" (196). As he joins the medical priesthood, he learns to share Trick Monk's preference for distance from the female body and, finally, he abandons Anne-Marie. Trick, who voices thoughts for which Jesse has no vocabulary, "affected a horror of the body that was lyric and heavy, whimsical and grave: 'We in medicine,' he says, 'should go after the ultimate cure—the separation of the spirit from the flesh. Everything else is unsanitary nonsense' " (208). He mocks Jesse's desire to be of service to humanity.

Gradually, Jesse develops a similar disdain for the flesh although, for a time, he listens in horror as Trick shares his philosophy, beliefs remarkably similar to those of the monkish Dr. Pedersen. " 'Did I ever tell you, Jesse, about my secret hopes for a career?' " Trick asks Jesse. " 'It's a little late now, but I'm thinking of switching to ob. work; I'd like to be a great gynecologist; I'd like to take loving, gentle smears from the bodies of women, and examine them like this, in the solitude of the laboratory. I would be a most devoted and discreet of lovers and I would keep every secret' " (210). A man's body might fail him (surges of desire in a man's body make him vulnerable to failure) whereas the scientist may exercise complete control, entering a woman from a safe distance. Trick voices Jesse's fears: " 'I too would like to be invisible in this race of men, an instrument, a metallic model of an organ—for the real thing, the real organ, is apt to be disappointing, eh? Disappointing to a woman' " (210). Finally, Trick tells Jesse that he dreams of becoming a poet: " 'One kind of elimination is as good as another. Don't be a snob,' " he says, " 'because you're in love. Discharging in your beloved's body, discharging in her brain—which is more rewarding after all? I have a horror of germs' " (211). The scientist, like the lyric poet, writes the bodies of women from an anaesthetic, ascetic distance. Straining to become an omniscient, disembodied voice, Jesse sacrifices his body on the altar of his monkish profession. Jesse learns to fear "woman," for he might lose his power in "the center of her being, a socket of pure power that would suck him into it and charge him with its strength—asking nothing of him but the surrender and collapse of all his bones, the blacking-out of his consciousness" (215).

Jesse does not share Helene's recognition that, in the bodies of animals, one can see "how we can live and die." When Helene expresses her fears of our "animal" fate, "Jesse was astonished. He had wanted to comfort her, but how could he comfort such words?" (246). He doesn't want Helene to think independent thoughts: "It hurt him to think that she should contemplate suffering like that, moving restlessly and independently of him, of his love for her. . . . Did she really think they must suffer like those animals? Her flesh and his flesh, flesh no more divine than that of the animals, doomed to the same bawdy fates" (246). Jesse refuses to acknowledge what is self-evident to Helene: that we must all die. Instead, he has censored his memory of the body, just as he has repressed the memory of his biological family, the

Hartes. Having erased from consciousness his personal history, he doesn't recognize the communal, the tragic implications of the death of the Harte family. Since he doesn't share this memory with Helene, she never knows him intimately, nor does he know her in this way. In fact, his love for her is nothing personal; rather, it signifies his love for Helene's father, Dr. Cady, a man who occasionally uses "unscientific words like destiny, beauty, creation" (191). Marriage to Helene answers Jesse's desire for paternal love, answers his question: "How to be that man without debasing himself" (228).

Ambivalently, Oates both pities and parodies Jesse's childish father-worship. " 'A superior personality reduces him to Jell-O,' " Trick says, in a painful parody of Jesse's naive love for Cady, his god: " 'In the presence of the great Benjamin Cady I provide an ashtray for him with my hands, automatically unconsciously, and he taps his ashes out in my hands just as automatically, accepting me as an ashtray without even thinking about it" (202). Jesse's "romantic" courtship of Helene, as Oates portrays it, makes explicit his addiction to father-worship. Trick echoes the word "Jell-O" in a poem—a debased version of Whitman's "Song of Myself"—that he sends to Helene. Having been abandoned by his fathers—by Willard Harte, his grandfather Vogel, and Dr. Pedersen—Jesse will seek fulfillment of his communal yearnings, which have been perverted into a father-worship, through the body of Helene. Trick's poem demonstrates the loss of a democratic sense of community in the crevice between scientific and romantic discourse. The poem acknowledges what Jesse censors, his flight from his body, his hatred and fear of the vulnerable flesh. Trick's "SONG OF MYSELF," is a poem of self-hatred that distorts Whitman's celebration of the body; it begins "*I am a vile jelly / that grew wings / and a bumpy facial structure*" (250). The phrase "vile jelly"—which echoes Cornwall's words as he stamps out Gloucester's eyes in the third act of *Lear*—illustrates the tragic hatred of the body. The poem, though sent to Helene Cady, actually speaks of Trick's struggle with his love/hate for the "great" Dr. Cady. The struggle between Trick and Jesse, like the struggle between Cornwall and Gloucester, alludes to the competition for the father's love, for the attention of a man who "automatically" uses Trick as an ashtray. The poem continues: "*beneath your bare feet / I would subside again / to jelly / to joy*" (250–51).

Sending his poem to Helene, Trick makes a pathetic though indirect appeal for Cady's love, but this romantic distortion of Whitman's "Song of Myself" emphasizes the individual, the ego, rather than the sacred body of the crowd. Since Jesse sees his marriage to Helene as apolitical and views his scientific romanticism as "objective," it is Trick Monk who voices his inarticulate philosophy. When Helene and Jesse finally agree to a farewell dinner with Trick—whose courtship of Helene has enraged Jesse— their struggle over the body of Cady's daughter erupts in violence. Trick's confession of having eaten a piece of a female body triggers Jesse's rage. Trick says, " 'I cut out of a female about your age, Helene, a uterus that was not at all damaged, and took it home with me in a brown paper bag and kept it in the refrigerator for a while . . . and then I did a very strange thing, I tried to broil it . . . I wanted to broil it and eat it like chicken, which it resembles to some extent' " (257). Yet Trick is merely voicing Jesse's own view of the body and of women. As Helene soon learns, marriage to Jesse effectively reduces her to her reproductive organs, for he does not regard her as possessing a mind, a consciousness like his. Jesse regards her primarily as a vessel for his seed.

Because Jesse hasn't the time to "imagine" his wife, Helene, she functions, as Pedersen's wife Mary had, as a point of contact between her father and her husband. "She floated between them, her father and her husband. They seemed to have no real consciousness of her except as a point of contact, an object, a beloved object" (264). Like Mary Shirer Pedersen, she finds that her father and her husband "did not seem to listen to her. They talked at her" (265–66). Years earlier, Jesse's adoptive mother had told him that her sanity was being destroyed by male deafness to her voice. Yet Jesse had learned the harsh consequences of listening to a woman when Pedersen, in his anger, had abandoned him. Mrs. Pedersen had told Jesse that her husband would be angry at her departure, " 'But for years I've known I would have to leave him. It's a question of survival. My sanity. I tried to explain this to my father and to Reverend Wieden but they didn't understand; men don't understand, they don't see that I am a human being of my own. I am Mary Shirer. . . . I am still Mary Shirer' " (164–65). Jesse, too, learns a practiced deafness to women, a practice that nearly destroys his wife and daughter.

And just as women have no voices, the body has no wisdom, according to Dr. Perrault, another father figure to Jesse. People would be better off without the distractions of the senses, Perrault believes. Panels of scientists will select the brains of brilliant men, and "resurrection" will become a fact in Perrault's heaven. Creation by male brains will replace creation in the womb. Like a contemporary Frankenstein, Perrault explains his vision during a dinner conversation: " 'We could not tolerate a prodigious brain losing its health because of a sentimental attachment to its body. We cling to our bodies even when they are diseased because they are all we have known' " (339). Perrault explains this terror as " 'like the old terror of leaving one world and going to the next world. But, unlike that old cosmology, the new world—the new body—would always be superior to the old. Guaranteed' " (339). This time, he adds, " 'resurrection would be real; you would wake up in paradise. The old body, the old earth: cast away for a true heaven. But first we must educate people out of the vicious sentimentality of loving the body, loving the personality, the personal self, the *soul*, that old illusion' " (339). Perrault undoubtedly believes that his brain-children, like disembodied angels, would provide a more satisfactory progeny. Jesse doesn't seem to understand that, in Perrault's puritanical heaven, women would simply be eradicated and, perhaps, children too. However, Helene responds by calling Perrault a "killer."

Oates describes the nightmarish landscape of America as a mirror image of the consciousness of men like Perrault in Book Three of *Wonderland*, "Dreaming America." Like a contemporary Mary Shelley, Oates is strugg-ling to rewrite Perrault's *Paradise Lost*, a paradise in which Jesse's daughter, Shelley, becomes a projection screen for Jesse's ghost self—his body, his memories, his passion—a self that rises in the night to circle obsessively, incestuously, about the body of his daughter. Epic discourses—scientific, historic, and literary—have shaped Jesse into a typical American male whose inflated ego does not question its urge toward mastery. Although the flight from the body is not exclusively a male problem—and Oates portrays Helene as frightened of motherhood and the body's music—the problem is far more severe for her husband. Oates describes Helene's fear of her body during the early years of her marriage: "She has been afraid to think about love, about loving a man, because it had seemed impossible, ugly, brutish. She had resisted thinking about death. It was too ugly. She had grown up with a dislike of being touched, even by her parents. . . . Always she had feared her body" (267–68). She stays in her loveless marriage not, as some women do, for economic reasons (she has an independent source of income) but out of a fear of living in her body. The experience of having children, initially so frightening that she considers an abortion, gives Helene some bodily sense of the wisdom of the body.

Jesse, however, has little experience of the body's wisdom. Finally, his oppressed, armored body rebels. He meets a woman called "Reva Denk," and in pursuit of her he feels "a lust that radiated out from his loins to make everything glow, the more distant muscle, the bony structures behind his ears, the smallest toes—everything, a festival of parts—glowing with certainty, with lust, with love for that woman" (377). Jesse does not, however, act upon this love-lust, for he assumes—as Oates does not—that "lust" is evil, that he must control himself. In an act of masochistic self-containment, he cuts into his flesh with a razor that is like a "surgical instrument": "He held the razor in place against his left cheek, and felt up and down the length of his body a sharp thrill of lust, so keen that he nearly doubled over . . . but he did not drop the razor blade again; instead he held it firmly and stretched the skin of his left cheek downward with one hand . . . And then lightly, timidly, he scraped the blade against his skin and blood spurted out at once" (378). Finally, he digs the blade into "the tangle of pubic hair," and frees himself. It is a bizarre but perfect fulfillment of Dr. Perrault's puritanical belief: "Life is pain. Pain is life" (312). Jesse's attempt to live a "pure" and impersonal existence, a life free of Reva Denk, whose name sounded "airy and then heavy as dirt" (316), leads him to sexualize his love for his daughter.

Out of resistance to her father's incestuous desires, Shelley runs away from home. In a letter to Jesse, she tries to explain why his love drove her away: "You were never home but when you came home you would sit at the edge of the pool and watch me swim,—*oh I burned in the sunshine in the glare of your watching me; walking naked in front of any man now is not a risk for me, not after you*" (404). However, having been so conditioned to being the object of the male gaze, Shelley readily becomes the property of a young man named "Noel," a man who parades her on a beach wearing only a sign: "The Fetish." Noel takes economic advantage of this male desire for ownership. In Shelley's new "family"—a community of war resisters, drug addicts, and other "criminals"—men generously share "the fetish," their communal property. By contrast, Jesse is a "good" man, a man who could not bear the thought that other men "could get at his daughter through the orifices of her body," and he pursues her like a lover "sick with yearning . . . heartsick, lovesick" (437). While bringing her home from a detention center in Toledo (where her V.D. test was negative) Jesse's "other self had sprung out. . . . It had taken hold of Shelley and shaken her violently" (433). Afterward, lying in bed beside his wife, "He felt the agitation of that other Dr. Vogel who prowled the house in the dark. He had to get up to join him. The other self, the ghost self, tugged at him and insisted that he get out of bed and come downstairs, where he could sit in the dark of the large, long living room, thinking of the night and of his daughter sleeping in a room almost

directly above him" (433). Shelley's flight is a form of resistance to the law
of the father, to fathers who seek to fill a hole in their consciousness with
the bodies of women.

Later, in Book Three, "Dreaming America," the voices of Shelley and
Helene struggle to be heard, to intervene in Jesse's incestuous quest. In the
hardcover edition of *Wonderland,* Jesse does not hear their voices; however,
in the revised, paperback edition Jesse begins—though very tentatively—
to listen to Shelley. Oates's departure from the conventions of univocal
composition marks a break with the bounded text. Oates's argument with
the weight of tradition may also be inferred in the poetry of Trick Monk and
in Shelley's letters. Shelley articulates the experience of a woman reading.
In a letter dated December 1970, she writes: "When I was nine years old
Grandfather Cady gave me a large illustrated copy of *Alice in Wonderland*
and *Alice's Adventures Through the Looking-Glass.* I sat with it up on the table
before me, a big heavy book, reading the paragraphs one by one and trying
not to fall into them and lose myself, trying not to feel terror, *it's only a book"*
(401). She tells her father that when Noel asks her what her worst fear is,
she answers: "A book falls down from a library shelf and comes open. It
is a very large book with a heavy binding. It falls onto me, knocking me
down, and then everything is very still—no ones knows about it, the book
is not alive and has no will, it means no evil against me and I am lying there,
paralyzed" (401).

The weight of tradition, of books, paralyzes a woman's will. "It's only
a book," Shelley writes. It's only reading. Yet a woman learns the shape
of her body from books that empty a woman of the right of authority,
forcing her to mediate her experience through the male mind. For example,
in a letter from Shelley to Jesse dated December 1970, she asks, "How
would you know the shape of your own body then, if you couldn't read
about other bodies?" (402). The shape of Hilda Pedersen's body, of her
mother Mary Shirer's body, of Helene's body, of Shelley's body—these are
the results of woman's function as an object of exchange, a possession, a
fetish. This male logos, or monotheism, which Freud regarded as evidence
of spiritual progress, negates female creativity. As Christine Froula argues
in "When Eve Reads Milton," "Milton's silencing and voiding of female
creativity recall the anxiety about female independence allegorized in the
nativities. . . . The male Logos called upon to articulate the cosmos against
an abyss of female silence overcomes the anxieties generated by the tension
between visible maternity and invisible paternity by appropriating female

power to itself in a parody of parthenogenesis" (308). Twice, Jesse himself has been a sacrifice to this logic: first, when his biological father tried to kill him and again when Mr. Pedersen punished him for helping Mrs. Pedersen escape his house. "With this check and with this letter," Pedersen had written to Jesse, "I pronounce you dead to me. You have no existence. You are nothing" (183–84).

Thus, the Christmas music that Jesse hears in the background as he looks at the pornographic image of a woman's body over a toilet is an appropriate joining of the sounds and images that void the creative minds and independence of women. *Wonderland* argues for a transformation of "the cosmos" as defined by men like Vogel, Pedersen, Perrault, Cady and, by implication, Milton and Freud. It argues for a culture that listens to the voices of the Hartes—the poor—and to the voices of women and children. It also argues that in the "abyss of female silence" is meaning, the beauty of the body, male and female. In the body of Jesse's daughter, Oates illustrates the tragic consequences of patriarchy's oppression of women. When Jesse finds Shelley, he sees her "face wasted, yellow, the lips caked with a stale dried substance," a sick child whom he initially mistakes for a boy. Shelley explains that the shape of her body is meant to protect her from him, from his possessive mind. "Shelley babbled, 'Noel is my husband here— not you—never you—when I have a baby it will be for all of them here, and not you—Why did you come after me? I can't go back. I'm all dried out. Look—'" (475). She tells Jesse: "'I'm all shut off, there's a curse on me to shut me off, my body, I don't know what happened—there is no blood and no baby either—the police have a radar machine that dries us all up—'" (475). As these children perceive it, they are being destroyed by their society, by a "radar machine that dries us all up."

It would be easy to dismiss this accusation, particularly this exaggerated— this "hysterical"—view of the power of police. Yet these children have been forced to flee from their fathers, whether to avoid being sacrificed to war or sacrificed to sexual abuse, like Shelley, to their fathers. "I am thinking of Christmas 1967," Shelley begins her December 1970 letter to Jesse, a letter that ends with this plea: "You walked out on us that night, Christmas night. You were gone all night. I don't want to think about where you walked, or why you left us like that, or why I sat at the top of the stairs waiting for you to come back, in secret, in the dark, afraid to go to bed. I want to be free. Love, Shelley" (407). Helene also remembers the Christmas Jesse had walked out on them, but she can't put together the fragmented pieces of her husband's history. He has never told her this history, a history he assumes to be merely personal, "subjective." The voices of Shelley and Helene call to Jesse to share this pain, to free himself and them. However, Jesse has no vocabulary for his feelings, as if his brain—and the brains of his patients—have no connection to their bodies or to the social body.

Oates places Jesse's consciousness in a social context, the tragic event of November 22, 1963, the death of President Kennedy: "Before two o'clock it had all happened and had become history: the motorcade in Dallas fired at, the President struck in the head, the President pronounced dead" (395). Jesse experiences the president's death almost viscerally, as if "again and again the impact of those bullets [were] in his own body; the head, the vulnerable head, the precious brain. . . . Why was it always this way, men dying, men dead? Why the exploded skull, the burst brain, why so many men in a procession that led to death?" (395). This is also the night that Jesse, trying not to think of Reva, wanting to protect his family from death—wanting to have dominion over death—turns the glare of his passion upon his innocent daughter, Shelley. The censorship of public passion— the romanticizing of desire—characterizes the various discourses Oates has examined in *Wonderland.* Jesse, having no vocabulary for these realities, is a typically "innocent" American male. Is this the reason, the novel asks, that men become killers? Is this denial of the body what motivates the impulse toward mastery, a mastery aggressively imposed upon the bodies of women by the phallic pen? The second boy had drawn the women's body—with her tiny head and giant body—as a house, the building material of culture. Between her legs was a door, leading into an empty blackness, an abyss.

In Jesse's search for his daughter, the novel implies, he may find the meaning in this hole in his consciousness, a puzzle he had tracked on the night of Christmas, 1969, thirty years after his escape from a gun-toting father. He had left because "he had to hunt out something" (434). Circling the house like "an animal, a hunting animal," his "panic faded as his strength faded. He found that he had circled around his house, a circle that must have taken him five miles, the house remaining in its center, in the very center of his consciousness, his wife and daughter sleeping in the center, while snow fell in their sleep" (434). At the center of this house is his daughter, whose body he wants to contain, as Pedersen had contained his wife and children. Unless Jesse remembers his past, he will not find a way out of his circle, he will not hear the voices of women and children. For behind this nightmare of the wrath of fathers, whose love he seeks, is a memory of life in the womb, a nativity scene that reminds us of dependency, death, and organic identity. Jesse's search for Shelley leads him back to his old friend, Trick Monk. Trick has become a poet of the body, having retitled a poem about the central nervous system "Vietnam."

Again, it is a woman's body that brings them together; this time, however, it is Shelley's body. "Remember the man you almost killed?" Shelley writes in a letter to Jesse (451). When Jesse finds Trick, the poet begs to be treated as an equal, " 'not in the world of reality, only in the world of poetry' " (456). He shows Jesse a review of his poetry that describes "the increasing irony of the distance between the object *perceived* and the object *conceived* in American society" (456). In this increasing distance between science and poetry—between Jesse's "objective" and Trick's "subjective" perception—Shelley functions as an object of exchange, a shell empty of meaning, a currency. Jesse begs Trick to listen to him, but Trick fears him: " 'Dr. Vogel, my dear Jesse, you don't understand. You want to kill us. Don't kill us. Don't look at us like that,' Monk said. He had begun to cry. 'I can feel it in you, the desire to do something—to dissect us, or operate on us—to snip our nerves—to clean us out with a scouring pad' " (457). Jesse protests that he hadn't intended to kill Trick, that science doesn't ask the death of poetry. However, perhaps to defend himself from the charge that his poetry may be political, Trick says that Nixon "is a kind of hero to me . . . he is a cult down here actually, America's attempt to create the *Ubermensch*" (456). In this pathetic appeal to Jesse, Trick claims contradictorily that poetry does not exist "in the world of reality." These two discourses, old "enemies," are aspects of the same brain, a feeling-thinking brain, a brain that is part of the body. Yet neither Jesse nor Trick recognizes the relationship of their discourses to the communal body: "The Central Nervous System of America."[2] They do not hear each other, and no dialogue occurs between them.

However, *Wonderland* does suggest the possibility of a transformation in consciousness in its evocation of Whitman's "En-Masse." One crowd scene suggests, for example, that the articulated anger of unfulfilled women— the "object" misconceived or misperceived—might transform public consciousness. For example, Helene ends a potentially romantic interlude with a man called "Mannie" when, leaving a shopping center called "Wonderland East," she hears the angry voices of a crowd of protestors. " 'Take your fucking war and shove it!' " shouts an angry girl, at which point Helene, walking into the crowd of young people, had slapped the girl, who seemed to be saying, "*It is over for you . . . it is over, over, over for you!*" (424). This violence temporarily frees Helene from a romantic obsession, but her freedom is not permanent—only "The Finite Passing of an Infinite Passion." Nevertheless, the novel points to the need for passion to come out of the "romantic" rooms of private, personal history and into the street. Despite Oates's depiction of such anger—anger with the potential to change society—the unity of her first conclusion (1971) mirrors Jesse's effort to contain himself. Jesse/Oates's desire to contain himself is premised upon belief in a unified "I"—the "I" of the romantic ego, a denial of interrelatedness that requires the subordination of women upon whose bodies/texts he projects his "feminine" aspects.

This confusion of boundaries—Jesse's desire to keep inside himself what belongs outside—shapes the political realities of Yonge (young/Jung) Street, the nightmarish landscape that he enters in his search for his daughter. When Jesse leaves the United States to enter Canada, he gradually discards his individual identity. He buys new clothes that will give him anonymity in the crowd, leaving his old clothes, along with his identification papers, in a trash can. Then he buys an underground newspaper, THE HOLE WITH A VOICE: "The biggest headline was in black: NIXON PLANS MASS CONCENTRATION CAMPS. Other stories dealt with FBI narcotics agents' activities, the 'Most Wanted' list in the United States, a communal picnic of draft dodgers and 'freaks'. . . . Inside, a smudgy cartoon showed a middle-aged, flabby man holding a gun to the head of a long-haired child, presumably his own son. *We all die for our country*, the caption said" (my italics 467). In this "hysterical" language (the language of the communal body), the political unconscious speaks. Oates must decide whether Jesse will resist his compulsion to control, especially to control his daughter, or will finally break this homeostatic pattern.

In order to resist this compulsion, Jesse must learn to read dialogically, that is, poetically. At decisive moment in his life, Jesse sees, once again, a womb drawn on a wall over a toilet. This time, however, "At the very center of the little womb was an eye, elaborately inked in" (466). In contrast to the graffiti artists at the beginning of the novel, this artist places the "I"— the eye—within the womb. Does this shift in vision suggest that the artist recognizes himself in/as the body of the crowd? Or does it imply that Jesse seeks control even over the womb, as do other father figures in this novel? The image allows for either interpretation, the one tragic, the other open: after all, "hole with a voice" may be a womb out of which children and our future emerge. The future depends, in part, on Jesse, who must move beyond emotional paralysis. Jesse's education, however, has not prepared him to explore the body/brain, or the central nervous system that connects them, within the context of language and culture. Oates herself believes that " 'wherever one encounters the Aristotelian-Freudian ideal of homeostasis, in opposition to the Oriental or Jungian ideals of integration of opposites, one is likely to encounter a secret detestation of the feminine' " (Teper Bender, *Joyce Carol Oates* 55). But Jesse, highly intelligent, a neurosurgeon, regards the complex relationships of mind and matter, self and society, culture and consciousness, as outside his field of inquiry.

Years earlier, Jesse had concluded his recitation of the history of the theory of homeostasis at the Pedersen family dinner table: "In *The Wisdom of the Body*, the American physiologist, Walter Cannon, quotes the French physiologist Charles Richet: *'The living being is stable. It must be so in order not to be destroyed, dissolved, or disintegrated by the colossal forces, often adverse, which surround it. . . . It is stable because it is modifiable—the slight instability is the necessary condition for the true stability of the organism.' "* (my ellipsis 107). Although such family "homeostasis" is ultimately violent, as Teper Bender points out, the Pedersens live according to this static model. The family is controlled by Pedersen, the "head," the monologic intellect. As Jesse learns the theory of homeostasis, he also acquires Dr. Pedersen's desire for control, as well as his contempt for women. Only once, while in medical school, does Jesse question this lesson. After hearing one of Dr. Cady's lectures, Jesse asks himself, "Isn't the great lesson of science *control?* The lesson of homeostasis and cybernetics: *control?*" (195). Not recognized as contrary to genuine objectivity, this desire for control impedes scientific investigation. "So long as thought has not become conscious of itself," argues Evelyn Fox Keller, "it is prey to perpetual confusions between objective and subjective, between the real and the ostensible" ("Feminism and Science" 118).[3]

Shelley Vogel, like many other youngsters in this novel, is leaving home to escape such control; nevertheless, in the first edition of *Wonderland*, Oates herself struggles to maintain control of the text, just as Jesse struggles to maintain control of his daughter. Violence is engendered by those patriarchs who, like Jesse, want to maintain control of the social body: the Vietnam War is one symptom of this desire for control; father-daughter incest is another. In the Preface to the 1971 edition, Oates states, "The fence will not give," words that unite the beginning of the novel with its final scene. In this final scene, Jesse has tracked his daughter to a fence where she is too weak to escape him. Unlike the younger Jesse—who was strong enough to leap a fence in order to escape his violent father—Shelley dies as Cordelia dies, in the arms of her incestuous father. In the 1973 edition, however, the fence finally gives way. Oates marks this change with a prefatory poem called, "Wonderland" signed (though it had been published elsewhere under her own name) by Trick Monk. The double-voiced poet, Oates/Trick, images the future as a child developing in the womb: "the eye widens/ the iris becomes an eye/ intestines shape themselves fine as silk/ I make my way up through marrow/ through my own heavy blood/ entering my own history like a tear/ balanced on the outermost edge/ of the eyelid" (10). Neither scientist nor artist controls this mysterious process, a process envisioned here as an evolution of consciousness—within the womb, within the communal body.

PART 2

Dialogic Authorship in the 1970s: Marriages and Infidelities

In the fiction of the 1960s and early 1970s, the daughters in Joyce Carol Oates's fiction rarely escape victimization. When young women attempt to take control of their own lives—as we see in daughters of the poor such as Clara Walpole, Nada Everett, and Maureen Wendall, as well as daughters of the rich such as Karen Herz and Shelley Vogel—they generally fail to become self-narrating women. Helplessly, they become characters in someone else's plot rather than authors of their own lives. With Oates's revision of the conclusion of *Wonderland* in 1973, however, her daughters gradually begin to take more effective control of their lives. As evident in the case of Shelley Vogel in *Wonderland*, in order to claim the right of self-narration, a daughter must confront paternal law both within the institution of the family and beyond. Jesse Vogel, as both father and doctor, stands at the border between private and public life, as do other fathers in the fiction of the 1970s, who represent the power of institutions such as law, politics, psychiatry, religion, education, and business. In fact, throughout the 1970s, Oates locates her investigation of daughter-father relationships on this border between public and private spheres, and, especially in her woman-centered novels of this decade—*Do with Me What You Will* (1973), *The Assassins* (1975), *Childwold* (1976), and *Unholy Loves* (1979)—exposes those beliefs and practices that perpetuate injustice and violence against women. In the 1970s, as I illustrate in the chapters that follow, Oates deliberately violates novelistic conventions in order to exploit what Mikhail Bakhtin identifies as the novel's inherent plasticity, its capacity to change even its own conventions.

As Oates has frequently stated, she does not write to maintain social and literary conventions that serve the status quo—a violent status quo; she writes to transform an unjust society. When she revises the conventional hierarchies of monologic discourses—both literary and extraliterary—her revisions are not accidental, not the result of haste and careless editing, but evidence of a deliberate authorial strategy, an effort to locate the voices of narrator(s) and characters on *the same plane*, democratically. In these novels, Oates rejects the romantic assumption that the authorial self can be "alone and independent of anyone else" (Todorov 105). Instead, authorial utterance anticipates a response, a strategy Bakhtin has named "dialogic." Frequently, as in both *Do with Me What You Will* and *Childwold*, the author/narrator openly engages in dialogue with her characters, characters who gradually become their own authors. This practice does not indicate the author's loss of control; it suggests instead a different conception of authorial power. Yet, when Oates remarks that her characters "have the autonomy of characters in a dream," some critics infer that she has lost artistic control. For example, Samuel Coles suggests, "It is as if exorcism replaces fiction. Confession overpowers literary container" (119). But Oates is not confessional, nor is she practicing automatic writing, as if she were Yeats's wife. Although the unconscious surely plays a part in the writing process, the structural design of a novel requires conscious decision making, and Oates's dialogic strategies are built, quite consciously, into the very structure of her novels.

As evident from the title of her short story collection, *Marriages and Infidelities*, by the early 1970s Oates was well aware of the power of dialogic (the logic of two, of both/and) as a strategy for revisioning the work of literary fathers. Even the titles of many of her short stories— "The Dead," "The Turn of the Screw," "Metamorphosis," and others— illustrate the theme announced in her title: her desire *both* to honor certain dead writers, such as Joyce, James, and Kafka, *and* to commit carefully crafted acts of literary infidelity, as if her imaginative marriages to these "masters" were governed by a vow to love, honor, and *disobey*. In the short story, as in the novel, once its dialogic nature is identified, it can become "an emancipatory form useful to the woman writer because of its multi-voicedness," as Patricia Yaeger suggests in *Honey-Mad Women* (30). Yaeger points out, for example, that "male bodies and texts can be made to circulate through women's texts—breaking that circuit of meaning in which women have been the objects of circulation" (161). This is Oates's explicit strategy in "The Sacred Marriage," as in many of the stories in *Marriages and Infidelities*, as Showalter and others have recognized. The same emancipatory metaphors—and revisionary intentions—shape her aesthetic practice in novels published in the 1970s, as I demonstrate in the three chapters that follow.

Oates announced in 1972, "We achieve our salvation, or our ruin, by the marriages we contract" (Clemons, "Joyce Carol Oates" 77). Two years later, responding in a letter to a review of *Do with Me What You Will*, she explained: "Some marriages are stifling, and thwart the individual's natural growth; but there are other marriages, healthy marriages, that allow both individuals fulfillment" ("Oates on Marriage" 12). She had in mind, she said, not just marriages between men and women, but "marriages—in another sense—with a phase of art, with something that transcends the limitations of the ego" (Clemons, "Joyce Carol Oates" 77). At this time, Oates herself was ending one "phase of art" to begin a different kind of "marriage," a different kind of commitment, in her fiction: "I am trying to move toward a more articulate moral position," she said, "not just dramatizing nightmarish problems but trying to show possible ways of transcending them" (77). This change is most immediately evident in Oates's collection *Marriages and Infidelities*. While wedding her vision to that of James or Kafka or Chekhov, Oates commits loving infidelities, as Teper Bender explains, often by shifting the point of view from male to female, from father to son, or from victim to victimizer ("Autonomy and Influence" 54–56).

In Oates's re-visioning of Joyce's story "The Dead," for instance, she depicts a woman named Ilena, a woman with a different kind of marriage: a commitment to a certain kind of art. In this auto-graphic story, as Oates explained to interviewer Sally Quinn, she imagined Ilena as "a projection of what her life could have become, which is the main reason she has avoided the pitfalls of the media 'circus.'" She said, "'I anticipated what it might be like in terms of my private life, in terms of my marriage'" (6). The protagonist, Ilena Williams, is twenty-nine. Like Oates, who was pictured on the cover of *Newsweek* in 1972 after winning the National Book Award for *them*, Ilena is a writer who has recently appeared on the cover of a national magazine after being nominated for The National Book Award. (Unlike Oates, Ilena had not won the award.) Since her nomination, Ilena has received countless invitations to speak, invitations that (unlike Oates during the 1970s) she generally accepts. While Ilena's novel *Death Dance* has been a best-seller for weeks, she herself is dying. A teacher at a small university in Detroit (like Oates, who taught at the University of Detroit during the 1970s) Ilena had married an instructor in radiology at Wayne Medical School (Oates's own husband was then a professor of English with a specialty in eighteenth-century British literature) and later divorced him (Oates has remained happily married now almost thirty years). Ilena takes drugs frequently (Oates refuses even caffeine), has ceased menstruating, and is indifferent to her body. She is suffering from depression, insomnia, exhaustion, and drug addiction, but as a recent divorcee she feels "virginal" again, and she continues to write suicidal fiction. According to Joanne Creighton, "Joyce Carol Oates does admit to one period of personal crisis, in 1971, when she felt bogged down with social commitments and close to collapse" (*Joyce Carol Oates* [1979] 18).

Her solution was to accompany her husband to England on his sabbatical, a decision that gave her the time and space to imagine a marriage to a different kind of art. In "The Dead," however, Ilena's marriage to a conventionally romantic kind of art, as well as to a certain kind of man—a man who feels "unmanned" by her success—is deadly. Ilena's first novel had, in fact, been based on stories of young girls at the University of Michigan, girls who had belonged to a "suicide club" (456). Ilena herself secretly belongs to this suicide club (as Sylvia Plath and Ann Sexton once had their own suicide club), a commitment to death disguised by romantic fantasies. Although Ilena has many love affairs, she has become so "intellectualized" that her "entire body" has become "passive and observant and cynical" (473). Thus, it is not only Ilena's "marriage" to a certain kind of art but also her lack of a genuine marriage of mind and body that leads to her death. In the story's final scene, reminiscent of Joyce's "The Dead" but with a shift in point of view, Emmett's face haunts her: "Far inside her, too deep for any man to reach and stir into sensation, a dull, dim lust began for Emmett. Hardly more than a faint throbbing. Emmett, who was dead. She wanted to hold him, now, instead of this man" (488). Finally, like Joyce's hero, she hears only "the gentle breathing of the snow, falling shapelessly upon them" (488).

As Elaine Showalter says, although Ilena's behavior is evidence of a form of "self-enacted punishment for writing well," if we are to understand the story in its entirety, we must attend to its dialogue with the male literary tradition ("*The Dead* and Feminist Criticism" 17). Through such re-visionary fiction, as Showalter argues, Oates is "re-imagining the male literary tradition" (18). Oates's strategy is similar in novels of this decade. Like Ilena in "The Dead," Elena in *Do with Me What You Will* remains virginal in her marriage. Her older husband, who worships her—in his mind, she is like a statue of the virgin, the child-woman—cannot reach the place deep inside her that might stir her into sensation. But to Marvin Howe, a man old enough to be Elena's father, Elena's role is not primarily sexual— he has many other women for that—but rather the role of a daughter- wife. Thus, it is evident that in this fiction of the early 1970s (and, in fact, throughout the 1970s and 1980s) that Oates is often writing as a "resisting" reader, to use Judith Fetterley's term. Through her marriages with the "masters," Oates intends, with a turn of the screw, to tell old stories from a new point of view: that of the disobedient daughter or wife. In this way, she is revising the cultural story, usually imagined as a story of sons who inherit the father's authority—whether religious, legal, scientific, or literary—by mothering her literary daughters, giving them the strength to voice their self-assertion, their resistance to the father-lover.

The short story collection *Marriages and Infidelities* opens with a story that might be considered an announcement of Oates's dialogic authorship of the 1970s: her marriages and infidelities to paternal discourses, literary as well as extraliterary. Entitled "The Sacred Marriage," the story honors Henry James even as it commits carefully crafted "infidelities" to James's "The Aspern Papers." The great writer in Oates's story, Connell Pearce, has plotted his ritual worship before his death. He writes: "Let us imagine X, the famous Spanish novelist, a nobleman. Born 1899. . . . X is handsome, aging, elegant, a dandy, something of a phony (his exaggerated Catholicism, his loyalty to Franco, etc.). Totally dedicated to his art" (34). To claim immortality, Pearce chooses his language carefully—"The language of this parable must suggest that—the transformation of a man into his art"—but he also marries a young woman whose body will enable him to touch the future: "Yes, X is about to die and wants to write the novel of his own life. In Madrid he selects a certain woman. He is a noble, dying old man, she is a very beautiful young woman. *She* is worthy of being his wife" (34). The daughter-wife not only "nurses him through his last illness, [and] buries him," she also "blesses all the admirers of his art who come to her, for she alone retains X's divinity. *Her body. Her consecration.* A multitude of lovers come to her, lovers of X, and she blesses them without exception, in her constant virginity" (Oates's italics 34).

Oates's revision of James's "The Aspern Papers" parodies the male artist's dream of immortality. When the critic-son, Howard Dean, comes across this "parable" by the great father-creator, he has already acted out most of the master's plot. He has come to Mouth-of-Lowmoor to the Pearce house, ascending the mountain to be welcomed by Pearce's widow, a woman young enough to be his daughter. Howard recalls that Pearce has been known for "using" women, but he rationalizes that " 'he had loved each one of them deeply' " (19). When Pearce's widow shows him the house, Howard feels that he has come to a sacred place, a temple. Emilia takes Howard into the bed of the great Connell Pearce and, since "she alone retains X's divinity," she "blesses" Howard, uniting him with the great father through her ever-virginal body. In this bed, as in Pearce's study, Howard loses himself in a marriage in which "the boundaries between the three of them become hazy" (28). Howard had not expected, however, that Emilia would entertain other critic-sons; thus, when she warmly welcomes a Felix Fraser from the University of California, Riverside, Howard feels betrayed. Following this betrayal, he comes upon a fragment left behind by Connell Pearce, the summary of the plot in which he has played his part. Despite his depression as he descends the mountain, son Howard regains his enthusiasm for his homosocial marriage to the father. After all, he has his work.

By contrast, as Oates demonstrates in *Marriages and Infidelities*, a daughter's fidelity to the father condemns her to perpetual virginity, to a world of ice. Through obedience to the father, the daughter may become a mute vessel, as does Emilia in "The Sacred Marriage," or Yvonne in *The Assassins*, a body/text uniting warring fathers and sons. In novels of the 1970s, Oates begins to transform such obedient, ventriloquated daughters into lovingly disobedient daughters who claim their own voices, and make their own marriages. As a dialogic daughter, Oates herself "honors" the fathers—James, Joyce, or Chekhov—but asserts her own right to create, her right to claim cultural authority. Such disobedience "implies denial of patriarchal rule," as Nelly Furman says in "The Politics of Language" (70). Furman argues that by refusing "to abide by the critical contract which privileges the author, the textual reader joins the ranks of the disloyal and the unfaithful" (71). Furman compares the reader's contract with the author to the marital contract of a wife/mother that "guarantees paternal origin and hegemony" (71). As Furman notes, Jane Gallop employs the same analogy in *The Daughter's Seduction* when she says: "Infidelity then is a feminist practice of undermining the Name-of-the-Father. The unfaithful reading strays from the author, the authorized, reproduces that which does not hold as a reproduction, as a representation. Infidelity is *not* outside the system of marriage, the symbolic, patriarchy, but hollows it out, ruins it, from within" (Gallop 48; qtd. in Furman 71).

By giving her stories famous titles, Oates establishes herself as a resisting reader who has joined "the disloyal and the unfaithful." By imagining herself a daughter who (incestuously) weds the fathers who control American institutions—the lawyers, politicians, artists, clergymen, psychiatrists, and businessmen—Oates commits "infidelities" that hollow out, from within, their unjust social/textual practices. Although I examine only those novels in which the experiences of daughters are central, every Oates novel published in the 1970s illustrates another of the author's "marriages and infidelities" to male-dominated institutions: science, as represented by Jesse Vogel in *Wonderland*; law by Marvin Howe in *Do with Me What You Will*; politics and philosophy by Andrew Petrie, the visual arts by Hugh Petrie, and religion by Stephen Petrie in *The Assassins*; literature by Fitz John Kasch in *Childwold*; Christian faith (of a fundamentalist kind) by Nathan Vickery and academic skepticism by Japheth Sproul in *Son of the Morning* (1978); literary interpretation by Lewis Seidel and music by Alexis Kessler in *Unholy Loves*; and business by Edwin Locke in *Cybele* (1979). Oates's novellas, *The Triumph of the Spider Monkey* (1976) and *A Sentimental Education* (first published in 1979), also sharply criticize American institutions—social welfare and penal institutions and the military-industrial complex, respectively. "I am writing a number of novels, one after another, that deal with the complex distribution of power in the United States" Oates told interviewers Michael and Ariane Batterberry in 1973 (42).

As is evident from Oates's focus on the daughter's marriages and in-fidelities to (the discourses of) the fathers, most of her novels in this decade continue to marginalize/silence the mothers. The mother-daughter relationship does not become central in Oates's fiction until the 1980s; however, it figures prominently in certain novels of the 1970s, particularly in *Childwold*. During the 1970s, Oates may be conceived, not as a daughter, but as a mother-author who, while nurturing the autonomy of all her characters, gradually began shifting her attention to daughter-heroes. Although it may be true that "the hero is her author's daughter" (Gardiner 79), it remains necessary, as Oates's novels illustrate, to redefine the heroic. Thus, as Oates strives to give her daughter-heroes the power of self-narration, of authorship, she critiques and transforms conventional notions of the heroic, as well as conventions of narration and plot. For example, in *Childwold*, Laney's first menstrual period, an important event in a woman's maturation, is given a central place in the narrative, while "heroic" images of bloodshed, always the result of violence, are rendered as comic. Significantly, in both *Childwold* and *Unholy Loves*, women emancipate themselves from destructive relationships with men, as the marriage plot is transformed into an emancipatory metaphor for other kinds of commitments.

In short, in these novels Oates begins to transform traditional Oedipal (father-son) plots, while also subverting literary conventions that perpetuate a masculine, individualistic conception of the author. For example, she began to devise strategies to portray the author not as "monologic," not as an isolated unity, but as a site permeated and altered by contending voices and texts. In *The Assassins*, for example, Oates stages a scene in which the figurative dismemberment of the narrative "I"—embodied in a (woman) writer named Yvonne Petrie—dramatizes what is often invisible to readers: the woman novelist's "lavish" self-division into all her characters, all her voices. This dismemberment scene marks the end of Oates's tragic conception of American society. Indeed, one of the characters/voices in her next novel, *Childwold*, explicitly criticizes the tragic vision, particularly in terms of its encoded hierarchies of class. Thematically and structurally— in the fluid movement from voice to voice—both *Childwold* and *Unholy Loves* are fictive elaborations of Oates's belief in the "democratic essence of divinity": all the voices in these novels, including the author's, occupy *the same plane*.[1]

Marriage as Novel: Beyond the Conventions of Romance and Law in Do with Me What You Will

Feminists may disagree about how to interpret *Do with Me What You Will*, but Elena's leave-taking, her refusal to be a plaything to her husband, as some critics have noted, is comparable to Nora's decision in Ibsen's play, *A Doll House*. Unlike Nora, however, Elena has a life—and a marriage—beyond the final pages of the novel. For in this work, Oates is "writing beyond the ending" of the romance plot. As we have seen, such plots, if tragic, end in the heroine's death; if comic, they end in the heroine's marriage. According to the traditional romance plot, a woman must choose; she cannot have both marriage and a career, as Du Plessis reminds us in *Writing Beyond the Ending*. In *Do with Me What You Will*, because Elena leaves her marriage to go in quest of Jack, the married man she loves, readers have not always recognized that Oates is writing beyond the ending of the romance plot. Yet Oates has not confined her heroine to the conventions of traditional comic or tragic plots; that is, she has not condemned her heroine to either marry or die. Such monologic closure, as Julia Kristeva argues, actually disguises the inherently dialogic or double-voiced character of the novel as a genre, for ideologic, not merely aesthetic, purposes: to deny women equality. As Kristeva says, the "bounded text" signifies "the idealization of woman (of the Other)" in order to give itself a "permutative center" by maintaining woman as "an object of exchange among members of the Same" (*Desire in Language* 50).

This "permutative center," this object of exchange among members of the same sex is, of course, the daughter. Once the daughter becomes someone's wife—the mother to "his" children—she becomes the bounded center, but an unmarried daughter threatens the order of society, especially its hierarchies of gender and often class. Thus, Oates frequently exposes the daughter as a site of the contest between men of different generations, as well as men of different social classes: Karen Herz leaves the house of her middle-class father to go with a younger man from the lower class; Clara Walpole in *A Garden of Earthly Delights* leaves her lower-class father to marry a middle-class farmer old enough to be her father; and Nada in *Expensive People* disguises her lower-class origins to marry a rich businessman. Maureen Wendall in *them*, a child of the lower class, marries for similar, economic reasons. Nadine Greene, also a daughter in *them*, leaves her upper-class home in a Detroit suburb, having been abducted by her lower-class lover, Jules Wendall; psychologically, however, she remains a princess in her father's tower. With Shelley, a middle-class daughter in *Wonderland*, Oates again employs this pattern of enclosure: a daughter locked in the tower, in the plot, of the father's incestuous desire. Again and again, Oates tries to solve the riddle of daughterhood, resurrecting Shelley, her Cordelia figure, in the short story, "How I Contemplated the World from the Detroit House of Correction," in a play, *Ontological Proof of My Existence*, and in a revision of the ending of *Wonderland*.

Not until *Do with Me What You Will* does Oates find a way of writing beyond the ending of the textual/cultural boundary that encloses a daughter in the father's script, his bounded text. *Do with Me What You Will* opens with an image—the image of a fence—that recalls the Preface to the first edition of *Wonderland*: before the daughter can "leap over a fence to escape him," her father "grabs hold" of her, and her eyes "snap shut, obedient as a doll's" (16). Oates's choice of a fence as the image of the daughter's confinement works on at least two levels, for, as Lynda Boose says, the fence is "a double one: one of its markers defines the father's control over inner family space; the other, his authority in the space of the outside, cultural world" (46–47). *Do with Me What You Will* opens at this fence, just at the point where *Wonderland* ends. Like Shelley, Elena is an obedient child whose eyes snap shut or stay open, obedient as a doll's, according to the commands of her father and her male-identified mother. The parental commands are in fact contradictory since Elena is a pawn in her parents' divorce. Standing at the fence surrounding Elena's school, her father, who has lost custody, orders her to "Crawl under,

Elena. Hurry. Now" (10). While he hides her, Elena's father commands Elena to be silent, but when Elena's mother finally finds her daughter, she commands that she speak. Whether the command is for silence or speech, the ventriloquated Elena obeys. Thus, when Elena's mother commands her to marry a man old enough to be her father, she obediently marries Marvin Howe.[1] However, although Elena is at first a "Sleeping Beauty," a woman who is hypnotized by commanding adults, she finally asserts her desire, and, by making her own choices, escapes the bounded text.

By committing adultery, Elena betrays the husband-father. However, this transgression alone is not enough to free her from the romance plot, a plot in which the daughter-wife, such as a Guinevere, is unfaithful to the father-king. Such romantic plots, which Northrop Frye calls the "secular scripture," are often accompanied by "the theme of incest, very often father and daughter" (44), yet Frye argues that "this shows us nothing at all about the relation of fiction to reality: what it shows us is that some conventions of storytelling are more obsessive than others" (44). His assertion is, of course, premised upon the formalist assumption that literature has nothing to do with life. In fact, historical changes in the daughter's part—on the social plane—are reflected in changing themes in the romance, in particular the theme of virginity. According to Lynda Boose, with a historical shift in kinship structures—a shift that proved disastrous for daughters—virginity became more important in the romance. Boose quotes Julian Pitt-Rivers: " 'From the moment that the notion of honour is attached to female purity, kinship loses its basis of reciprocity and becomes political and ego centered, a competition in which the winners are those who keep their daughters and take the women of other groups in addition' " (Pitt-Rivers 166, as quoted in Boose 60). At this historical moment, father-daughter incest became far more common in the romance. From the perspective of the daughter-novelist, the novel's capacity for parody would be especially useful for calling attention to the fact that father-daughter incest is, in fact, a paradigm for heterosexual romance.

In *Do with Me What You Will*, Oates parodies the romance plot, especially the father-daughter as a paradigm for heterosexism. In this novel Oates's relationship to romantic convention, as well as to the law (a monologic discourse), is consistently dialogic, or parodic. For example, the title of the novel illustrates a double-voiced use of legal language: at the novel's end, Elena refuses a plea of *nolo contendere*, and she refuses to allow her husband to do with her what he wills. She rejects the passivity of *nolo contendere*, a legal plea for mercy, in order to claim the right to her own judgment, her own desires, her own will. As Eileen Teper Bender has noted, "Despite the misreadings of this novel by some feminists, Oates shares the outrage which lies at the heart of the contemporary feminist critique" (*Joyce Carol Oates* 74). As Teper Bender says, readers who view the end of the novel "as part of a masculine fantasy: a seeming capitulation to the romantic ideal," criticize Elena's quest for Jack because it damages Jack's wife and child. Yet Jack and Rachel's marriage is stifling both of them; it exists in word only. Furthermore, as Teper Bender says, it is Elena's refusal of passive obedience—her transgression of boundaries—that frees her from the part of a sleeping beauty: "The very word 'transgression' thus recovers its roots; the act of passing through ordinary limits opens new territory for the self" (Teper Bender 80). As Oates's narrator says, "Never in her life had she conquered any territory, achieved any victories. Never" (546); thus, Elena's transgression actually reverses mythical and romantic archetypes—that is, if her quest for Morrissey is recognized as a "hunt," as "the masculine erotic" (Frye 104).

Furthermore, together Elena and Jack create a marriage that is not the same as their previous marriages: it consists of an intimate dialogue, embedded in the romantic plot and in the trial framework of the novel. Most important, as indicated by a shift in tense in certain italicized passages, their marital dialogue occurs *after* the end of the novel. Their dialogic marriage moves beyond cultural/textual boundaries of monologic discourses. The very presence of Elena's voice, a voice to which Jack listens much more carefully than he had during their adulterous courtship, accentuates the absence of her voice earlier in the first plot/scripture. According to this scripture, Elena is "good" if she remains a virginal daughter and an obedient wife, but "bad" when she asserts her own desires. Such a willful, sexual daughter, as Eve in the Old Testament, must be punished by expulsion from the garden; for, like Guinevere, she brings death to the father's kingdom. In contrast to these plots, as Teper Bender says, Elena and Jack have a life beyond this ending: "Running along with the more conventional plot is a curious 'sound track,' an evolving discourse which Oates presents in italicized dialogue between two lovers. Telling the tale, reviewing and arguing over the accumulated evidence, sifting through the memory of their difficult and problematic passage, they also attest to their union and survival" (*Joyce Carol Oates* 77).

As co-narrators of their lives, and as co-creators of a healthier marriage, both Elena and Jack illustrate their liberation from external authors. They are not being scripted or plotted by internalized parents, by the "giant gods" of their childhoods. Their sexual passion leads, not to punishment, but to an awakening of their bodies that, in the daughter's case, finally awakens her mind as well.[2] This awakening begins at the center of the city, where the lovers meet beneath a statue called, "The Spirit of Detroit." With emphasis upon Jack's need for new glasses, Oates parodies the romantic notion of "love at first sight," for neither Jack nor Elena really sees the other. Their eyes are focused instead upon internalized and fossilized fathers whom they worship, though without full consciousness of their internalized religion. The Alger monument represents this fossilized patriarchal worship whose ideal family structure has been so damaging to Elena and Jack. As Ellen Friedman notes, the trial structure of the novel builds its "case" by first presenting Elena's story, then leaving her in a state of paralysis beneath the monument, then presenting Jack's story, which ends just as he sees Elena staring at the statue.

Each of them has, as Friedman says, been brought to this space, this moment, by the same giant. Elena feels she has been "*Hurtled across the landscape, picked up in one place and set down in another*" by the godlike Howe (139), and Jack feels "*as if an ordinary man were seized by a whirlwind, picked up and flung a great distance, and then left,*" his own words echoing Howe's (200). Friedman argues that what undercuts the sense of fatality— the notion that these are "star crossed lovers"—is the "metaphor of crime" (121). While the next part of the novel is called "Crime," however, the title simply calls attention to yet another convention of the romance. One recalls, for example, that the crime of such star-crossed lovers as Lancelot or Guinevere is an act of adultery, an act defined as a crime against the law of the father/king. Therefore, this convention must also be transformed, a transformation that occurs only when Elena and Jack break the father's law while at the same time recognizing this transgression as the price of becoming an adult. Friedman does not identify lawyer Marvin Howe as the novel's father-god; however, Howe plays the role of "savior" to Elena, whom he "saved" by marriage, and to Jack, who imagines Howe as a father-savior, a powerful substitute for his weak father. For both Elena and Jack, Marvin Howe represents the Law of the Father; he constitutes the petrified boundary, the fence, of their imaginations.

Yet the father-god limits the development of daughters and sons in different ways, as the novel emphasizes in its depiction of the meeting of Elena and Jack at the statue, "The Spirit of Detroit." As if hypnotized, Elena studies the figure of a man, "immense, godly," who is holding in one hand "an object meant to be the sun," and in the other, "a small couple, a man and a woman, the woman holding an infant" (162). Biblical words, from II Corinthians 3:17, are inscribed on the monument's base: " 'Now the Lord is that spirit and where the spirit of the Lord is, there is liberty.' " At this moment Elena is far from liberty; as if drugged, she continues reading the inscribed explanation: "God, through the Spirit of Man, is manifested in the family, the noblest human relationship" (162–63). It may be a noble institution, but within their families both Jack and Elena have experienced paternal neglect and, indirectly, paternal violence. Each has emerged from a "family romance" that has locked them into stereotypical gender roles— aggressive Jack, passive Elena—and each has, as a consequence, made an unsuitable marriage. As in "The Sacred Marriage," Elena has become a mute child-bride, a perpetually virginal daughter-wife to the wealthy lawyer, Marvin Howe. Her stillness, as she stares at the "immense, godly" man, is a mirror image of her role in marriage. By contrast, Jack is like the son in "The Sacred Marriage" or in "Extraordinary Popular Delusions" who is too obsessed with his quest for father-love to fully imagine a woman's existence. Jack only glances at the statue; what he sees at its base is not Elena, but the wife of Marvin Howe, property of his "father" and "savior."

Here we have the configuration of "The Sacred Marriage" once again: father, son, and holy ghost. The holy ghost suggests the possibility of an erasure of the mother; however, there is not even a trace of the daughter in this trinity.[3] According to the father-son cultural story, whether sacred or secular, the daughter is not an individual with desires and dreams and a voice of her own, but a point of contact between alienated fathers and sons. Jack, who has experienced such alienation, says of Marvin Howe, the man who defended his father in a murder trial, "One day he'd known more about my father and the rest of us, the pathetic Morrisseys, than we knew about ourselves, he had absorbed us completely, as if he'd created us—like a novelist writing a big crowded novel" (210). However, as Jack recalls, once Howe had won the case, this father-author had become indifferent. What Jack does not recognize is that he is seeking this indifferent "father" through the body of the father's daughter-wife, Elena. Hence, Jack's quest for Elena is also a quest for secular salvation from the father. As a reviewer in the *Harvard Law Record* says, "The incursions of the legal conceptions of guilt and innocence into the morality of those whose lives are inextricably involved with the combative advocacy of the courtroom are portrayed in the struggle for Elena; each lawyer envisions her as the ultimate verdict of innocence, of not guilty; as if, by winning her, they would somehow be granted an acquittal from all their myriad depredations, their spiritual rapine" (Flanders 14).

In this patriarchal script, the daughter becomes again the sacred property, whereas the son can at least hope to become, like the father, a man in possession of secrets. Jack himself, recalling the women in Kafka's *The Trial* who seem to know secrets, "half-believed [Elena] knew secrets" (418). Jack had actually become a lawyer, like Marvin Howe, in order to possess such secrets. Although Jack appears unlike Howe—Jack defends liberal causes while Howe is politically conservative—they both play the same game: a game of winning and losing, a game of legal power largely indifferent to principles of truth and justice. As a "son" to the great Marvin Howe, Jack wants to emulate Howe's power to absorb his clients, to speak for them, and to win in court. Jack's wife Rachel, who detects this game and its cynicism, accuses her husband of preferring guilty clients, of preferring those "pawns" more easily manipulated in the "sport" of legal competition. She says, "You believe in the law. You really do. It's like any arena where a game takes place—a football game, a baseball game—and when the game is in session you believe in all the rules . . . all the tedious crap of the law, English law, precedents, whatever you people claim to worship . . . I think it's because you believe only in yourself, you're just an isolated person, Jack, a cynic" (293). Rachel is right. As Jack demonstrates in his cynical defense of a confessed rapist—"innocent until proven guilty"—even when a client admits his guilt, Jack manipulates the legal game in order to "win" even when it requires making the rape victim herself appear guilty.

For example, when Jack's client, a black man, confesses that he has raped a white woman, explaining that it made him feel "like a general or somebody in a movie, where things go right" (267), Jack tries to win the case by proving the rape victim guilty. Despite the client's confession of guilt, the game requires that Jack defend his "innocence"; therefore, Jack begins by manipulating his client (as Howe had once so masterfully manipulated Jack himself) using statements such as: "She identified you absolutely, in spite of her hysterical state?" (272). Jack questions the client in a manner that will prove the victim guilty of her own rape: "This woman was behaving in a way that was provocative?" (272–73). He also makes an issue of the victim's class and prior loss of virginity: "She's been on and off Welfare since 1964 . . . she's been unemployed since September of last year, but without any visible means of support" (273). He suggests to his client that to "save" him, he'll prove the rape victim guilty—guilty of being a "fallen" woman who "has to convince a jury that she didn't deserve to be followed by you, that she didn't entice you, she didn't smile at you. She has to convince a jury that she didn't deserve whatever happened to her" (273). However, the rapist, who wants his victim to know and remember him despite his indifference to her, argues that she "must of seen my face." He tells Jack, "I saw hers but didn't take it in" (277), adding: "Gave her a good look at my face. My face is important to me" (277). Here is the spirit of Detroit, and, as a lawyer, Jack is party to the rape.

Like a machine, rather than a human being with a conscience, Jack serves the law. Like Marvin Howe, Jack believes that the law is "what's left of divinity" (124). What is truly criminal, as portrayed in *Do with Me What You Will*, is this cynical manipulation of a presumably democratic legal system for egocentric purposes. The novel underscores the fact that the law is frequently used to do violence to women, children, and the poor. Jack's defense of a genuinely innocent man, Mered Dawe, is especially effective in illustrating how paternal violence is perpetuated by the law's "Old Testament" principles. Dawe is arrested ostensibly for passing on a marijuana cigarette to a minor. He has obviously been framed for this "crime" by a police informant; Dawe's real crime is that his vision of love threatens the Old Testament morality of the court. In a lecture to a large audience, an audience that includes Elena, Mered Dawe explains his vision of "light and heavy love": "Light love draws us up into the galaxy, which is ninety percent personality-free . . . but heavy love drags us down into the mud of the self and the great mud of wars, of which all U.S. wars including the present war are merely temporal phenomena. Down in the mud we fight one another, compete from birth till death; in the galaxy we are free of that tragic struggle" (420–21). But this son's gentle protest against the Old Testament law brings down the father's wrath: Mered Dawe, who is brutally beaten and imprisoned following this lecture, becomes yet another son sacrificed to maintain a patriarchal society.

In her critique of the boundaries of the father-son cultural story, Oates emphasizes that if the son resists the father, like Mered Dawe, he becomes a sacrifice, and if the son *obeys* the father, like Jack Morrissey, he becomes a sacrifice. As Jack tells Elena, he sometimes feels, "half-joking, half-serious," that his life is a reenactment of an ancient Aztec ritual he has read about: "a religious ritual, Aztec Indians, the past . . . these Aztec youths were evidently allowed to become gods for a short period . . . or maybe they were selected, I don't know . . . on the understanding that they would eventually have their hearts cut out at the altar in some kind of religious ceremony" (444). Trying to explain himself to Elena, he continues, "They agreed to be gods, and then they agreed to have their hearts cut out. I wonder if the godliness is worth it?" (444). As Jack's story suggests, whether one obeys or disobeys, the result is the same. With a Buddhist parable, a riddle Mered Dawe cites in his last letter to the judge from whom he pleads for mercy, Oates makes this point: "The Zen Master holds a stick over the pupil's head and says to him fiercely, 'If you say this stick is real, I will strike you with it. If you say this stick is not real, I will strike you with it. If you say nothing, I will strike you with it' " (494). There's no escape from this Kafkaesque "trial" of life, at least not in terms of the logic of the father-son scripts, sacred or secular. According to the logic of the parable, pain cannot be avoided.

Nor can death be avoided. The life of the body cannot be avoided. As Elena and Jack experience passion, this awareness of their mortality breaks through their socially constructed egos. Both realize that they are not gods and goddesses but ordinary human beings. As Ellen Friedman argues so persuasively, this loss of romantic innocence "permeates" the novel. "Oates's dominant method of characterization is deflation," says Friedman: "Those characters who begin as romantic figures, who have a sense of themselves as limitless, are at the end reduced to more realistic proportions" (*Joyce Carol Oates* 117). Marvin Howe, of course, has this romantic sense of himself. As he tells an interviewer: "I can see into the future. . . . I am never wrong. . . . I know not only that I have won but how well I have won, how deeply I have pushed myself into the imagination of other people, how powerfully I have guided their wills" (ellipses mine 120). The novel parodies, and transforms, this notion of godlike author/ing, even though Howe himself remains convinced of his godlike powers. Another man, Howe believes, would not achieve his victories; such victories "would elude him because after all he would be only human," but Howe believes that he is "different." He doesn't fear "mortality" because, with his clients, he has "triumphed in so many lives . . . bringing them back to life again" (121). Like a novelist, he can live "a multitude of lives" (121).

Such transcendence constitutes a denial of mortality, a repression of the life of his body, as Howe finally discovers at the moment Elena tells him she must leave. His life, Howe argues, depends upon her staying. In fact, as long as Elena plays the daughter part, she functions as a mirror in which

Howe sees himself as youthful, as transcending death itself. This desire becomes apparent as Howe, in an attempt to persuade Elena to stay with him, tells her about a stag party he had once attended. At this carnivalesque party, he says, "the bottom had fallen out of the universe," for he had recognized—in the body of an old woman—that he would die. He says, "The master of ceremonies had been building up to this. He made us all believe that something truly amazing was going to come on stage. . . . And then . . . two bicyclists pedaled out, and they were women, naked, but then it became obvious that there was something wrong with them: they were very old women" (554). As if still shocked, he repeats, "They were *elderly women*. But of course they were made up with bright make-up and lipstick and feathers and sequins and all the usual junk, and . . . and . . . and they were so old . . . God, their faces were wrinkles, masses of wrinkles! They were very skinny," and yet, he says, "they were riding these bicycles, like circus bicycles, decorated with balloons and paper flowers" (554). First the shock of surprise—"The audience was surprised, of course, and then after the first few seconds of shock every one started to laugh" (554)—then, one old woman's fall reminds him of his own aging mother, and "the bottom had fallen out of the universe" (554).

Howe tells Elena that he believes she has saved him from this knowledge of impending death and that she will—if he pleads for mercy—save him again. What Elena has discovered is that, just as she cannot save Howe, he cannot save her. She must claim her own life. Elena's decision to leave her stifling marriage, her recognition that she must claim her life, comes to her through memories that have been repressed for years. Childhood memories—of her mother's voice, of her trip to a wooded area as well as to California with her father—activate Elena's imagination, awakening her desire, just as the image of the aging woman had awakened Howe's consciousness of mortality. For Elena and Jack, passion finally transforms them, bringing them to an awareness of their mortality. This awakening does not occur in the early stages of their adulterous love, for they begin their affair in a period of self-delusion, with Jack seeking to unite with "father" Howe through the body of his wife, and Elena seeking something she could not name. In fact, when Elena makes love to Jack for the first time, she has no specific man in mind; her desire is "*confused with the rocks at the edge of the ocean, the chilly salty odor*" (346). Elena is also aware that her lover is "in a kind of combat," and so "couldn't notice anything she did" (346). At this first meeting with Jack, Elena has little consciousness of her own will, and their meeting is more his idea than hers. Elena is responding to Jack's desire, for it was he who had written his phone number on a card, pushing it through the mail slot of the door to Marvin Howe's house. Oates makes a point at once serious and comic with this card, which is a reminder of Jack's appointment with an ophthalmologist: Jack doesn't *see* Elena.

Elena understands this point. She knows that Mered Dawe can imagine her—"Dream me," she asks him (459)—but Jack Morrissey is too caught up in the male contest to think of her, to imagine her. Jack's element is "heavy love," which is the real spirit of Detroit: "Sometimes he could almost taste it, the air of fighting, of combative sizing-up and measuring and testing, constant testing; not just in the courts but out on the street . . . human contact gone wild" (229). For both Marvin Howe and Jack Morrissey, who are "married" to this homosocial game, Elena represents what is outside this struggle. In fact, whether her body is the object of rape, "it" is contested territory in their homosocial struggle. The excitement of theft, of conquest, stimulates Jack's initial interest in an affair with Elena. On one occasion, he becomes so obsessed with being discovered in a rented hotel room that he takes Elena to a wooded area. Jack associates their affair with private rooms, but in this wooded area where "the forest opened to receive them and then closed in silence," Elena experiences her first orgasm. Memories of her father, as well as Jack's unusual tenderness and her growing intimacy with him, stimulate her desire. As Elena *actively* helped Jack, "something drew itself up in her, suddenly, effortless and concise as raising of a hand in an intimate gesture so graceful she experienced it in utter disbelief" (383). Then she experiences a force from outside her socially defined self, a sacred force that grips her body until "it fell back upon her, localized and urgent, muscular, terrible" (384).

This description of a woman's orgasm is not likely to appear in romances out of the courtly love tradition; furthermore, Elena's imaginative, visceral experience of the sacred contrasts sharply with the fossilized figures depicted in the Alger monument. According to biblical scripture, the daughter's body acts as a passive vessel for the male seed, not for her own experience of the divine. Like Eve, Elena has now tasted the forbidden fruit; she has direct experience of a power beyond the law. Jack's worship of the stony principles of the law had made him into a word machine; finally he "had had to give up Elena because the *Machine*, with its sanity and rigorous morality, had been unable to control her" (520). Elena, too, had tried to give up Jack. Once her husband had discovered their "crime," Elena had tried to deny what she experienced with Jack. She had felt "pregnant" with Jack's love even while she occupied the social space designated for her as "Mrs. Marvin Howe," but when Jack had confronted her with the choice, Elena had reverted to the helpless behavior that, during her childhood abduction, had protected her from an angry father. She sees herself as "a child . . . on a bed, one eye crusted over, under a pile of blankets waiting, watching the door, frightened also but not showing fear" (462). Finally, to rouse Elena from the passivity induced by such fear, Jack threatens to kill them both: "Now I know how holy you are, how dead and empty you are, you thing, you dead empty thing—you *thing*, you *thing*" (466).

What Jack recognizes is that this object he has stolen from the father-king is not a real woman: "You're so deadly, you're so virginal," he shouts. Yet Elena clings to her role, as if only by being a "sacred object" in this masculine game does she have any "ontological proof" of her existence. Thus, in exchange for the supposed security of the father's definition, Elena accepts her status as a "thing." This point is underscored by a sudden shift from the scene in which Jack makes this accusation—just after he has nearly killed them both—to the scene in which Elena's husband confronts her with the evidence of her crime: legal papers, photographs, tapes, rolls of film. As Elena sees herself through these legal documents, evidence of her betrayal of her father-husband, she feels endangered. However, when she faints, her husband burns the documents, "as if performing a sacred ritual before her" (467). Both scenes show how self-deluding it is for Elena to imagine herself safe from the violence of men, but she attempts to do just this. When Marvin later takes her to one of his many houses—houses that once belonged to murderers Howe has "saved"—Elena cannot shut out the danger. She recognizes herself as a "thing," as one of the spoils of masculine warfare among different classes and races.

This realization strikes her as she takes her daily walk along an isolated beach into a nearby town. Out of the corner of her eye she sees two men watching her, sizing her up as a potential rape victim, seeing her as some man's expensive property. She feels her excitement, and the excitement of the men—the excitement of the hunt, of the masculine erotic, in which she is the prey. As she turns onto Howe's property, she notes the signs: "Warning. No Trespassing. Private Land" (535). But she hides in the house, and nothing happens, not this time. She explains to her husband, "I would be careless of my life if I stayed here. Because I might let something happen to me" (536). She adds, "I don't want to make someone into a killer." What she recognizes is that victims may act as accomplices in their own victimization. Of course, as a child, Elena had little choice, but as an adult she has the power to choose. Certainly her physical awakening, the orgasmic experience that temporarily frees her of a limiting social identity, prepares her for this moment, but what releases her, finally, from childhood sleep is the decision to claim her own life.

At this moment her self-authoring has begun. Once Elena leaves the house of the father—not because another man claims her, but to claim her own life—she moves beyond the ending—"The Summing Up," as Oates calls it—of convention: romantic, legal, and religious. Oates does cite a precedent for such a heroine. At one point Elena reads "a water stained copy of *Middlemarch*" (350), an allusion suggesting that, just as Dorothea's second marriage is a compromise, so is Elena's. Neither Oates's Jack Morrissey nor Eliot's Will Ladislaw is the "perfect" husband, and marriage does not completely satisfy the yearnings of either Elena or Dorothea; nevertheless, each woman has a voice in these second marriages. The conclusion of *Middlemarch* implies such a coming-to-voice for Dorothea; but we actually hear Elena speaking to Jack, and Jack listening, beyond the ending of *Do with Me What You Will*. In this italicized and embedded dialogue, Jack tells Elena his "theory about marriage," that it is "*a long conversation where you relive your life, remembering things, maybe inventing a few things . . . you don't really live alone, because after you fall in love you tell it all, it's like a book two people create together, a novel*" (409). In this conversation, which takes place in a time beyond the plot of the novel, Oates offers a redefinition of marriage: "It's like a book two people create together, a novel." This definition differs from patriarchal laws that historically gave only a husband a voice (a monologic voice) in defining marital rights. The sacred and secular scriptures historically have given man his rights by denying the rights of woman.

By leaving the house of her father-husband, Elena disobeys this law to claim her status as a subject with her own voice and authority. Analogously, Oates claims her own authority as a novelist, choosing the dialogic potential of the genre. The novel actually offers two models of the novelist. According to one model, only the father-author has power, like the power of a lawyer who, as Jack described Marvin Howe, "had absorbed us completely, as if he'd created us—like a novelist writing a big crowded novel" (210). Bakhtin gives the name "monologic" to this type of novel. Kristeva argues that this kind of novel, "the bounded text," mirrors the cultural text in which the daughter is the site of struggle between the father and son. George Eliot imitated the father-author model in *Middlemarch;* in *Do with Me What You Will* Oates resists the father-author model in order to emancipate her characters. As the characters in this novel grow and develop, they acquire their own capacity for self-authoring. In this respect, Oates's characters are like us; as Tzvetan Todorov says of Dostoevsky's characters, they are "like us; incomplete, they are like so many *authors*, rather than the characters of ancient authors" (103). Such characters are not used as the author's mouthpiece, nor does the author assume the self to be "alone and independent of anyone else" (Todorov 105). Oates "marries" the character Marvin Howe to commit "infidelities" to this romantic conception of authorship. *Do with Me What You Will* offers instead a revisionary conception of authorship and a revision of the romance-marriage plot: according to the dialogic (law of two), a woman does not become "one" with her husband, nor does he become her "author."

5

Wedding a (Woman) Writer's Voices: Dis-membering the "I" in The Assassins, Re-membering "Us" in Childwold

In "Feminist Fiction and the Uses of Memory," Gayle Greene asserts that memory became important in feminist fiction during the 1970s. A return to the past—a return to our "mothers' gardens"—became necessary, because without this journey, women cannot change. As Greene says, "We search for our mother's gardens, in Alice Walker's terms; we search for our mothers—and this search (which is at times not easily distinguishable from nostalgia) figures prominently in contemporary women's fiction" ("Feminist Fiction" 300). During the 1970s, this search for her mother's garden became a prominent feature of Joyce Carol Oates's fiction, beginning with *Childwold* (1976), a novel that also marks a dramatic shift in her vision. In sharp contrast to all of her earlier novels, including *The Assassins* (1975), which immediately precedes it, *Childwold* begins the process (a process even more pronounced in the 1980s) of moving the mother-daughter plot from the margins of culture to its center. If read together, auto-graphically, these two novels illustrate how the dis-membered daughter-writer of *The Assassins* is healed by re-membering the mother-land in *Childwold*. More specifically, *The Assassins* dramatizes a (woman) writer's violent dismemberment into the (male) voices of her characters, while *Childwold* lyrically weds voices past and present, male and female. From this point forward, the mother-daughter story will figure in a more central way in Oates's novels, informing and sustaining her comic vision throughout the 1980s.

Childwold is a revisionary novel that retells the story of the daughter's seduction of the father by rewriting the parts of both the "Seductive Daughter" and the absent mother.[1] As Judith Lewis Herman reminds us in *Father-Daughter Incest*, the myth of the "Seductive Daughter" can be found in the biblical story of Lot, as well as in Nabokov's popular novel, *Lolita*. Humbert Humbert, the narrator of *Lolita*, actually expects readers to believe that a twelve-year-old "nymphet" named Lolita has seduced him. Psychoanalytic literature tells a similar story in which Freud finally concluded that the daughters who came to him with stories of sexual abuse were telling lies, presumably out of their own desire for their fathers. The psychiatric myth is that hysterics fantasize sexual abuse by their fathers.[2] In contrast to *Lolita*, *Childwold* dramatizes the aging father's desire to possess the daughter, but the daughter manages to escape and claim her own voice, a voice that Nabokov had silenced. As Ellen Friedman says, "Laney, as her given name, Evangeline, implies, is the inchoate evangelist of Oates's vision" (*Joyce Carol Oates* 184). Eileen Teper Bender agrees, describing Laney as the author's "youthful alter-ego" and noting that Laney begins to tell her own story at the end of the novel. Using words from the novel, Teper Bender describes this act of self-narration as a process of " 'dreaming back,' " a process that begins when Laney "senses her own power to restore Kasch [Oates's Humbert Humbert] to life through the artistic imagination" (*Joyce Carol Oates* 91).

Childwold, according to Teper Bender, is Laney's narrative, and Laney makes it her story by "raising her voice above that of the perverse lover, the promiscuous mother, the autocratic and loveless English teacher, the twisted criminal, and the maddened fierce old man" (91)—in short, *above* all the characters in *Childwold*. I submit, rather, that although Laney does acquire a voice, and although we imagine her as a narrator, she is only one of a crowd of voices, all of which exist, more democratically, *on the same plane* as the author-narrator's voice. Just as Elena and Jack become coauthors of their love story and come to occupy the same plane as the author of *Do with Me What You Will*, all the characters in *Childwold* exist on the same democratic plane as the author-narrator, regardless of gender or class. As in Virginia Woolf's *The Wave*, the voices in *Childwold* mingle and collide; therefore, as critics have pointed out, the novel makes great demands upon readers. To readers accustomed to the conventions of the monologic novel—conventions Bakhtin associates with Tolstoy, but which we also know from Thackeray and Eliot—the dialogic novel, as practiced by Dostoevsky, Woolf and Faulkner, is more demanding. But as Julia Kristeva explains, the dialogic novel simply obeys another logic (*Desire in Language* 64–91). This logic was certainly not obvious to early reviewers, who found *Childwold* incoherent and repetitive. Yet, as Gary Waller emphasizes, *Childwold* marks Oates's shift to a more complex aesthetic practice. It also marks a shift to a more subversive—that is, to a feminist—aesthetic practice: it subverts hierarchies of gender and class; it parodies the tragic vision; and it rewrites *Lolita*, transforming Humbert Humbert, a monologic narrator, into a man named Kasch who fantasizes but does not act upon his "paedomorphic" lust.[3]

Significantly, Oates does not simply reverse the gender/class of Nabokov's narrator, making Laney a narrator of the kind who deprives others of their powers of self-authoring. Instead, she resists the romantic conception of the author as a god who determines which characters or "realities" have value and which do not. Some writers, Oates says in a critique of *Lolita*, see "divinity everywhere—literally everywhere—like the American Transcendentalists, like Dostoevsky, like all mystics," while others "deny it flatly, and believe that they, as isolated individuals, possess all that is sacred or at least important, in themselves, and who truly do not need any sense of communion or kinship with other people" ("Postscript" 106). Oates's strong resistance to Nabokov's authorial stance—particularly his "loathing" of most people—the same creatures upon whom Dostoevsky "lavished love—prostitutes, drunkards, bullies, saints, the mad, the diseased, *even* those who might have been hilarious targets for satire" ("Postscript" 107)[4]—fueled her democratic vision in *Childwold*. These are the very people Oates honors in *Childwold*, marrying her voice to Laney's illiterate mother, on welfare with her variously fathered children; to Laney's brother Vale, blown up in Vietnam, an attendant in a car wash who assaults those who have what he desires; to Laney's grandfather Hurley who lost almost all his land during the Great Depression; and to many others, including the wealthy Fitz John Kasch—a tragically isolated Humbert Humbert who marries Laney's mother only to kill a man in her defense, after which he condemns himself to death.

Art is political, as Oates herself emphasizes in her comments upon *Lolita;* that is, novelistic conventions mirror authorial assumptions that may or may not be democratic. In order to illustrate this point, it is necessary to reconsider the novel Oates published just prior to *Childwold*, the explicitly political *The Assassins* (1975). In this complex novel, Oates also challenges monologic conventions in order to dramatize an author's democratic kinship with her fellow creatures. As Joanne Creighton remarks, Oates may

not have provided most readers with enough textual clues to interpret
The Assassins, but this novel deserves attention from those who wish to
understand her departures from conventional practices of characterization,
plot, and closure. Moreover, if *The Assassins* is recognized as dramatizing the
(woman) writer's lavish self-division during the creative process, *Childwold*
may be understood as celebrating the (woman) writer's democratically plural
voices. Oates has described *Childwold* as "poetic," because it focuses more
upon image than upon narrative, but it also transforms the lyrical "I" into
the communal "we." The narrative moves along, as Childwold's river does,
in waves of interior monologue that shift into dialogue, as the desires of
one character are perceived by another, and as the voices of one person
are interiorized by someone else. This portrayal of the self as plural is
consistent with a view articulated in Oates's essay, "Stories That Define
Me," which assumes that this self, composed by stories, is plural. All Oates's
characters can, for example, be considered aspects of her story, and in *Childwold* she makes this kinship visible, addressing Laney as "you," imagining
Kasch's obsessive "I," conceiving of herself, through the character Kasch,
as marrying not just Laney's mother, but the entire family and its place:
Childwold.

By contrast, in *The Assassins* the author's "marriage" to her characters
is portrayed as a violent dismemberment of the (woman) writer. Oates
explained her intentions in an interview with Robert Phillips: "My effort
to wed myself with a fictional character and our synthesis in turn with a
larger, almost allegorical condition resulted in a novel that was difficult
to write and also, I suspect, difficult to read" ("Joyce Carol Oates" 37).
Reviewers and scholars quickly confirmed Oates's suspicions, with Peter
Prescott charging that the novel was "very bad, nearly incoherent" and
Judith Thurman asking, "Is she insulting us—is this a joke? Or has the
meal been catered completely from her unconscious?" (*Ms.* 43). "Certain
rules must be observed," Thurman says, if a writer wishes to take risks
with style.[5] Although Thurman assumes that Oates arrogantly disregards
the needs of readers, it might be argued just as easily that Oates regards
readers with great respect. Her sensitivity to readers is evident, for example,
when she tells Robert Phillips that she tries "to write books that can be
read in one way by a literal-minded reader, and in quite another way by
a reader alert to symbolic abbreviation and parodistic elements" (373).
Nevertheless, even critics ordinarily alert to symbolic abbreviation and
parody interpreted the dismemberment of Yvonne Petrie in literal terms.

For example, both Gary Waller and Ellen Friedman interpret Yvonne's murder—a violent scene in which her body is chopped up by hunters—as an actual event. Only Teper Bender argues that Yvonne "endures an imaginary assassination, envisioning her dismemberment at the hands of strangely familiar but nameless assailants," but Teper Bender nevertheless continues to see Yvonne solely as a victim, a woman "lacking the lover who might save her from the dark vortex of hallucination" (*Joyce Carol Oates* 84).

But Yvonne is not necessarily looking to a man to save her. Indeed, the novel implies that, while the Petrie men look to Yvonne for salvation, Yvonne's salvation can be found in her own imagination. Lacking the ability to imagine Yvonne, the Petrie men see only her physical being, not as someone with an imagination and an identity of her own. To them, she is an "invisible woman." As the widow of Andrew, they see her primarily as the object of their homosocial conquests. However, Yvonne is depicted as a (woman) writer whose own artistic hallucinations[6] have the power to free her from masculine projections. Yvonne's mind is invisible to the Petrie men, but the dismemberment scene makes violently visible the imaginative process by which the (woman) writer divides herself "lavishly" into all her characters. If she subordinates herself completely to the views in her husband's writings, it is she who will become the literal sacrifice, but if she rejects her husband's concept of the godlike writer, she will experience a loss of ego, a kind of figurative dis-memberment, during the writing process. As Teper Bender says, at first Yvonne's dead husband "exerts a ventriloquist's influence over her work, language and thought so powerful that it is she who seems the victim" (83). However, though Yvonne is initially ventriloquated by the writings of her megalomaniacal husband, her figurative dis-memberment transforms the homosocial center of *The Assassins*.

According to Waller, the novel's parts—Hugh, Yvonne, Stephen—"are held together by three structural concepts through which the book's intellectual patterns emerge—the world, the flesh, and the spirit" (186). But such a petrified "trinity," with Yvonne at the center, identifies Yvonne as "the flesh," thereby conflating her with the archetypal "Woman," with "Nature." In fact, Yvonne's dismemberment into the (woman) writer dramatically challenges this structure, violently re-figuring her relationship to the homosocial order, an order represented by the men who compete for her. In *The Assassins*, in one of the most violent scenes in her fiction, Oates attacks the archetype "Woman" in an attempt to dislodge a pattern of beliefs deeply lodged in our collective unconscious—a belief perpetuated by political, religious, legal, and artistic practices. To the homosocial Petrie men, seeking their dead brother through Yvonne's body,[7] the widow exists only as a point of contact between them, only as "Woman." An individual woman has no authentic existence for such men; she is invisible. Each isolated member of the Petrie family, locked in the prison house of his (male) ego, is a microcosm of America's "stunted body politic" (Teper Bender, *Joyce Carol Oates* 86). Fearing death, the Petries project the burdens of the flesh onto "Woman," thereby perpetuating petrified artistic, political, and religious beliefs that threaten the survival of our democratic culture.

Our beliefs can kill us, as Oates states in an essay on Sylvia Plath. "The moral assumptions behind Plath's poetry condemned her to death," she says. "Let us assume," Oates says, "that Sylvia Plath acted out in her poetry the deadliness of an old consciousness, the old corrupting hell of the Renaissance ideal and its 'I'-ness, separate and distinct from all other fields of consciousness, which exist only to be conquered or to inflict pain upon the 'I' " (*New Heaven, New Earth* 115). Such a belief may once have been necessary in order to "wrench man from the hermetic contemplation of a God-centered universe and get him into action," she says, but it has now become "pathological" (115). This pathology pervades the body politic in *The Assassins*, as each member of the Petrie family imagines himself competing for the role of family hero, a role that Andrew Petrie once occupied and that finally killed him. By striving to replace her dead husband, Yvonne becomes as competitive as her Petrie-fied rivals, the artist Hugh and the saint Stephen. Oates herself has objected to a competitive notion of writing: "I can't even grasp what Hemingway and the epigonic Mailer mean by battling it out with the other talent in the ring. A work of art has never, to my knowledge, displaced another work of art. The living are no more in competition with the dead than they are with the living" she told Robert Phillips, adding, "Being a woman allows me a certain invisibility" ("Joyce Carol Oates" 383). Although Oates does not cast the problem of the competitive "I" in gender terms, this conception of the subject—which she defines as "a once-vital Renaissance ideal of subject/object antagonism"—certainly has gender implications. As Oates herself says in the same essay, "If life really is a struggle for survival, even in a relatively advanced civilization, then very few individuals will win; most will lose (and nearly all women are fated to lose); something is rotten in the very fabric of the universe" (*New Heaven, New Earth* 119).

Thus, even if Yvonne Petrie claims a masculine role for herself, attempting to write as a man, according to this conception of identity, a woman cannot escape victimization. It may be that because *The Assassins* challenges our assumptions about the nature of identity (and not because it is incoherent or unedited) that many readers, myself included, find it difficult to read. In addition, *The Assassins* is a parody of the tragic vision. Oates considered the possibility that tragedy may be a genre in need of revision in an essay on D. H. Lawrence first published in 1972—three years before publication of *The Assassins*. In Lawrence's mind Oates finds "a curious and probably unique equation between the exalted pretensions of tragedy and the rationalizing, desacralizing process he sensed in operation everywhere around him: in scientific method, in education, in industry, in the financial network of nations, even in new methods of war that resulted not in killing but in commonplace murder" (*New Heaven, New Earth* 58). The Joyce Carol Oates who wrote *The Assassins* seems to agree with Lawrence, seeing tragedy as "representative of a distorted claim to prominence in the universe, a usurpation of the sacredness of the Other, the Infinite" (*New Heaven, New Earth* 58). The scene of Yvonne's dismemberment parodies the (woman) writer's own distorted claim to prominence in the universe, her claim to be a godlike author.

The strangely familiar assassins who chop up Yvonne's body as she watches all claim prominence in the universe. Though unidentified, the Petrie brothers, all of whom are competing for the role of hero and who, therefore, want a piece of Andrew's "bride" Yvonne, might be assailants. The scene, depicted as follows, initially appears to be realistically rendered:

> Gigantic, a willow tree with innumerable trunks. She stared at it. She would not turn to face them.
> The first shot struck her in the shoulder, near the neck.
> She fell. She had already fallen. There was another shot and one of them ran to where she lay, bent over her. She could make out the fresh mud splashed over the dry, encrusted mud on his boots. She was dying but she could see that sharply.

At this point, readers might assume that, yes, a dying person could actually watch and observe her own murder, but as the narration continues, attentive readers will discover that a realistic interpretation of this scene is impossible to sustain: "*That's it*, someone said. *That did it*. The others ran forward. One of them was carrying an ax. He was big-shouldered, squat. He wore a hunting cap and a plaid wool shirt. She could see him clearly but she could not scream because she was paralyzed: she was already dead. She died, but was still there. *That did it*, one of them said" (439). If the scene is intended as a realistic depiction of Yvonne's murder, how can she be reporting her own death?

Even after announcing, "She died, but was still there," the narrator continues, providing specific details, as follows: "The man with the ax stood squarely, his feet apart. He raised the ax, he grimaced, brought it down hard on her wrist—in one stroke it cut through the bone and severed the hand. She could not scream. Everything slipped from her, was mute" (439). Yet the narrator speaks, calmly and dispassionately, of her own dismemberment: "She felt the blow as if it were a terrible vibration of the earth itself, or of the water; there was no pain, no sensation, only the terrible weight falling, crashing upon her. He raised the ax again. Again he grunted. He brought it down this time at her shoulder, where the shoulder and the arm joined. The others had turned aside. They were not watching" (439). Careful attention to detail indicates that this scene, though a figurative rather than literal dismemberment, is structurally parallel to a newspaper report of a fourteen-year-old girl's actual death and dismemberment. The point is, surely, that figurative language—in this case, the language of archetypes—shapes collectively shared beliefs that, in turn, determine human actions.

The scene is also structurally parallel to the scene in which Yvonne becomes an object of sexual conquest by a Petrie cousin with political aspirations, one of the now-dead Andrew's competitors. In words echoing the description of the squat hunter, Harvey Petrie "straddled" Yvonne, "panting and struggling with her . . . frantically, gripping both her shoulders" (412). Yvonne feels Harvey's weight above her, just as she feels (imagines) the weight of the hunter above her and his terrible will to possess her, "The terrible weight falling, crashing upon her . . . he grunted . . . the ax straddled her . . . his timing off. . . . He tried again" (439). Still competing with the dead Andrew, Harvey Petrie is indifferent to Yvonne even as he acts the part of her lover. These instances of narrative parallelism are transformed yet again in the art of Andrew's artist brother. The satirist, Hugh Petrie, imagines the dismemberment as a "copulation-crucifixion" (203). In Hugh's drawing, the upside-down body of the woman is the cross, the willow tree, "a ludicrous fleshy cross" for the crucified one, the martyr, "Man." It is a role that any of the Petrie men, with their penchant for heroic martyrdom, might play, including the saintly Stephen Petrie whose denial of the life of the body is, Yvonne recalls, a kind of arrogance. "She remembered him as gentle, almost timid, self-effacing and at the same time strangely presumptuous, even arrogant. He did not need her, he did not need anyone" (436). Sensing Stephen's arrogance, Andrew says, "*Perhaps you shouldn't mistake yourself for Christ*, my boy" (529). But Andrew himself, as well as Hugh, seeks martyrdom in an effort to become more than human, *to transcend* the world of the flesh.

In their presumed superiority to the physical world, the Petrie men become intellectual assassins, and, in her flight from life of the body, Yvonne imagines herself as one of them. However, the figurative violence—the writer's lavish self-division into multiple voices—puts into question the artistic, political, and religious beliefs of the Petrie family: their belief in woman-as-flesh and in man-as-hero. Nevertheless, Yvonne is represented not as the dismembered Orpheus or the crucified Christ but simply as a woman writing, a woman imagining herself as "Other." Oates confirmed this interpretation of the novel during an interview with Robert Phillips. When Phillips said that Andrew's wife "was never really attacked outside the country house; she never left it. Her maiming was all confined within her head," Oates replied, "What a surprise! You read the scene exactly as it was meant to be read" ("Joyce Carol Oates" 371). Why do readers miss the textual clues that point to this event as figurative, as a parody of the tragic vision? It may be, as Creighton says, that Oates does not provide enough clues; however, some of the difficulty comes from the fact that *The Assassins* is written as a deliberate challenge to the deeply held beliefs of her readers.

For example, the novel parodies so-called realistic depictions of political assassinations. Conventional novels of assassination provide clues for detecting enemies "out there," but fail to examine the enemy within, that is, society's beliefs or myths. Hence, this novel is certain to be a disappointment for those readers who expect it to depict an investigation—an investigation of physical rather than metaphysical evidence—in order to establish the identity of the "assassins." *The Assassins*, written in the aftermath of the assassinations of John F. Kennedy, Martin Luther King, and Robert Kennedy, at a time when conspiracy theories flourished, actually repudiates such a method of hunting for assassins. According to this novel, the object of the hunt is not to identify a particular assassin, but to recognize that, in the very American struggle for dominion over others, we all become assassins. As *The Assassins* points out, though Americans take pride in our supposed democracy, widely shared aristocratic beliefs, such as those held by the Petrie family, are responsible for the violence in our culture. In his speeches and essays, Andrew Petrie openly expresses the cruel and anachronistic beliefs, the petrified hierarchies of class and gender, that our society maintains at the cost of authentic democracy. The public wants to perceive Andrew as "heroic," and he acts the part, Yvonne notes, with a "god's sense of omnipotence" (275), but in private he is often weary and exhausted. After his death, she finds a blood-spattered page from his incomplete book with the chapter title "The United States of America: The Experiment That Failed" (266). As Hugh Petrie remarks, quoting Nietzsche, "Around the hero everything turns to tragedy" (160). In short, a collective belief in the hero—or, more important, the egoistic desire to be the hero—leads to competition and violence.

It may also lead critics to interpret Yvonne's dismemberment as tragic. But if we interpret her death as heroic, as the sacrifice of (a female) Orpheus, such a reading ignores textual clues that identify her as both a woman *and* a writer—clues such as the fact that she overhears conversations: she "listened without appearing to listen" (250), or "she had overheard on a telephone call" (251), or "she overheard two postmen talking" (251). We are also told that Yvonne constantly observes and interprets other people's actions, that she makes an effort to comprehend the attitudes of those who speak to her but do not really see *her*. Yvonne is an intelligent woman who understands that "they did not see her. She was invisible. Had never existed. There was a phantom in her place, a near-transparent creature. She watched this creature and she watched and listened to the others in the creature's presence and felt only a dim, sullen contempt for the masquerade" (258). Oates explains Yvonne's dilemma—the dilemma of any thoughtful woman—in the "Afterword" to *Invisible Woman*: "A Woman often feels 'invisible' in a public sense precisely because her physical being—her 'visibility'—figures so prominently in her identity. She is judged as a body, she is 'attractive,' or 'unattractive,' while knowing that her deepest self is inward, and secret" (99). But invisibility is no protection and, during the scene of her dismemberment, Yvonne felt as if "the bride herself had been effaced, defaced. Her face lost. It had begun then. It continued still. Someday they would kill her as they had killed Andrew: face and body brutally assaulted. Torn inside out. Mangled. Mutilated. . . . they would shake their heads and say she had brought it upon herself, she had willed it, she had *unconsciously*" (my ellipsis 258). The (woman) writer who lives according to the archetypes of our "man-centered" society is likely to become a sacrifice, a suicide; therefore, in order to survive, Yvonne must commit infidelities to beliefs that define her simply as an archetype of "nature."

These are, however, the undemocratic beliefs of the "aristocratic" Petrie family: monarchical, monotheistic, monologic. The aging Mr Petrie has a gaze like a "magnified sun, like a spotlight" (161), as if he were a contemporary sun king, and it is his father's "great man" theory of history that son Andrew, the first-born son, articulates in his political speeches and writings. The Petrie mother, as invisible as Yvonne, is necessary only to bring forth a son. Actual women—representatives of the flesh, the unconscious, the maternal—are treated with contempt, not only by the Petrie family, but by the contemporary "priests" to whom Hugh appeals for a cure, the psychiatrists.[8] Both Dr. Wynand, Hugh's Freudian analyst, and Dr. Swan, his Jungian psychiatrist, are less interested in Hugh than in making his "case" an illustration of their particular theories. Although Hugh has fallen in love with Yvonne and thinks, "I need not a cure but a love potion" (192), Hugh's psychiatrists dismiss love; it does not fit their theories. Dr. Swan, a Jungian, argues, " 'The female who appears in your dreams, Mr. Petrie, the giantess who threatens and disgusts you—you dare to imagine that *that* creature is a mere mortal woman, a woman of your acquaintance?' " (192), while the Freudian Dr. Wynand simply reduces Hugh's desires to the biological. Hugh comes to prefer "the simple-minded reductivist game of Dr. Wynand—where all mysteries are biological, are solved in terms of biology, genitals belonging to one 'individual' merely yearning for the genitals belonging to 'another' " (191).

According to one psychological theory, "Woman" is inflated, a goddess who is more-than-mortal woman, and not to be confused with Yvonne; according to another theory, woman is reduced to something-less-than-human, a dismembered body, a genital organ, a vagina. If she is a "goddess," she presumably does not exist in the flesh, as an actual historical woman; if she is not a goddess, then she is only a biological organ, certainly not a thinking, desiring creature who is more like "man" than not like him. The scene of Yvonne Petrie's dismemberment, at the dynamic structural center of the novel, re-visions the petrified terms "God, man, and nature." Such a revisioning, according to Susan Griffin, is necessary for the survival of this planet. "What is required," says Griffin, "is a revolution in thought, a deconstruction and reconstruction of both theology and language" ("Curves Along the Road" 62). This revolution will occur through what Oates calls "the farther reaches of man's [and woman's] hallucinations," for as Griffin says, "Hallucinations are like the ghosts of forgotten thoughts. They speak to us of whatever we have repressed" (92). The return of the repressed occurs in the scene of Yvonne's dismemberment: we are reminded of the reality, for example, that "nature" is not outside us, but within. In this respect, we occupy the same plane as the sacred willow tree, however much the death-denying intellect (ego) forgets this obvious fact. Because the Petries struggle against bodily consciousness, Hugh ends up as a mind caged inside a machine, a suicide like his brother Andrew. The saintly Stephen, whom Yvonne imagines holding a set of shears, is similarly cut off from his body, a separation (a dualism) inherited from Judeo-Christian religion.

As long as Yvonne Petrie remains dedicated to publishing her dead husband's writing, she shares his view of nature, seeing it as "pointless" because it is mute; she "resents it for imposing such muteness upon her; she is verbal, quick-minded, aware of herself as a performer" (253). This awareness of one's self as a performer is identified as the ego, a self-consciousness that disappears when, during the intense creative process, consciousness moves beyond the boundaries of the self. The artist, the dreamer, must confront this loss of self, Oates says, for "the absolute dream, if dreamed, must deal with death, and the only way toward death that we understand is the way of violence" (*The Edge of Impossibility* 6–7). If read literally, Yvonne's violent death is a ritual sacrifice through which participants (readers) regain their communal identity through sharing their terror and pity. For those who read the scene figuratively, the ego is lost, and the repressed communal identity regained, through the writer's (and reader's) self-division into all the voices in the novel, including the voice of the mute willow tree. Although the scene might also be understood as illustrating a native American view of nature—"Our mother, in her form known as Sophia, was long ago said to be a tree, the great tree of life" (Paula Gunn Allen 57)—it is problematic to refer to nature as "mother" because, as Ynestra King says, "Women have been culture's sacrifice to nature" (113). As long as men claim dominion over nature, the sacrifice of both nature and women will continue.

To transform the dualistic (monologic) system of thought that presumes nature is "fallen" and without meaning, the system of thought that perceives "Woman" as nature, the dismemberment scene in *The Assassins* divides our attention between Yvonne-as-sacrifice and Yvonne-as-observer of her assassins: thus, dialogically, she is both the sacrificed "Woman" (the archetype) and the self-divided (woman) writer. Read figuratively, Yvonne's self-dismemberment re-visions the Greek myth of Orpheus, a myth that, according to Joseph Campbell, was later incorporated into the Christian crucifixion. The divine character of the god, Campbell says, "must have symbolized that coming to us of the personified transcendent 'ground of Being,' through whose willing self-dismemberment . . . that which *there* is one becomes these many *here*—'like a felled tree, cut up into logs'" (25). By contrast, Yvonne's death does not make her a goddess; instead, as a writer she partakes in a creative communion with her characters and her readers. As her co-creators, though ordinary readers, we participate in the sacred. And since such creativity is "natural," the mute world represented by the willow tree, the realm beyond words, also participates in the sacred. Indeed, Yvonne's dismemberment makes sacred what, in the world of tragedy, is "lower": the realm of voiceless nature; the realm of the historically silenced "feminine"; the realm of illiterate humanity, the "masses."

What remains background in *The Assassins*—the mute natural world brought violently to the foreground with Yvonne's dismemberment—becomes central in *Childwold*. The family of Laney Bartlett, the so-called "masses," become the beloved of upper-class John Fitz Kasch. This time the author divides herself lyrically into the "I" of Kasch (cash), yearning for the "you" of Laney, but finally marrying into the "we" of Childwold when he takes Arlene Bartlett as his bride. Voices flow into each other like a river, including the voices of birds and animals, men and women, rich and poor, all on the same plane. The flow of blood in *Childwold*, Laney's first menstrual flow, is likened to the flow of the river, thereby displacing the flow of blood that signals the hero's violent death in tragedy. Although Oates had stated in 1971 that "the only way toward death that we understand is the way of violence," *Childwold* offers an alternative vision, a celebration of the fecundity of nature and of the female body. The knowledge that we are "of woman born" reminds us that we must die, and in *Childwold* this shared recognition of mortality becomes the basis for a redefinition of community.

Hugh Petrie appears again in *Childwold*, this time transformed into an intellectual named John Fitz Kasch, a stand-in for Nabokov's Humbert Humbert. Unlike Humbert Humbert, who views his impending death as punishment for his own actions, John Fitz Kasch comes to see death as part of life, as natural and inevitable. Dialogically, wedding her vision to Nabokov's to create Kasch as a Humbert Humbert, Oates commits infidelities to his *Lolita*. For example, though both Kasch and Humbert seek immortality through a child-woman, Humbert's murder of his alter-ego,

Quilty, is portrayed as tragic, while Kasch's murder of his antagonist is portrayed as a childish accident. In addition, the novel transforms Humbert's monologic confessional mode into a polyphony of voices, voices lyrically communal rather than individual. Within this larger context, the hero's actions lose their centrality; they become instead part of a natural cycle of birth, growth, and death. Change is seen, not as tragic, but as inevitable. For example, Kasch himself changes: the Kasch recollecting his past as a pedophile is not the same man. The new Kasch, it seems, has finally lost his romantic ego.

At various points in *Childwold*, as Kasch is "dreaming back" over the events that led him to marry Arlene Bartlett and, in defense of her, to accidentally murder her former suitor, Earl Tuller, he voices the author-narrator's dialogic vision: "Kierkegaard was a cripple like me, a vengeful dwarf, ugly, wizened, never a day without pain (like Pascal also: why is there so much pain in us, in genius?) which explains the cruelty of his pronouncement: Either/Or. But it must be Both/And! BOTH/AND! Both the girl and God, both time and eternity, both beloved and daughter, wife and sister, beauty and goodness. Both! Both!" (192). This logic is poetic, the logic of dreams; it refuses to obey the monologic either/or. At yet another point in the narrative, Kasch speaks as author-narrator, explaining why the tragic vision is false: He thinks, "Such a confusion of voices, of thoughts. They are all mine and yet they are not unified. I want no unity, no false unity. I want no forced chronology, no lying emphasis upon one fact at the price of excluding others, I want nothing hypocritical and synthetic" (137). He rejects the dramatic model as well: "In drama there are great events that bring about insight, insights, wisdom, pity and terror and purgation (or so it is said). These revelations are always in the fifth act and they are always expressed in fine, careful language, in poetry" (137). But his tone is increasingly ironic: "The past is illuminated by such magic, and the future is—the future is comprehended. Sometimes there is no future. But that, too, is part of the revelation" (137).

For the same reason, Kasch rejects psychoanalysis, which is also based upon this theatrical model of personality. Personality is too complex to be apprehended as a unity, he argues, even though the intellect may wish to impose such order upon it. Personality, as Kasch explains, is more like a river: "Reality is what I am thinking, what is thinking through me, using me as a means, a vessel, a reed, even, streaming through me with or without my consent; the interior life is continuous, unhurried, almost undirected, unheralded. Flow of thoughts, feelings, emotions, observations. Broken reflections. The glittering, winking look of the river . . . I want no false unity in my life, in my temporal life, because it would be a lie" (Oates's ellipsis 138). Not events, as represented by plots, but the flow of consciousness is the greater reality. And this consciousness is embodied. Even in sleep, our bodies dream, and without dreams, generally associated with the "feminine," we would have no works of art. *Childwold* takes us back to the realm of dreams, desires, and play:

Childwold
Childwood
Childwide
Childworld
Childmold
Childwould
Childtold (49)

The image of the child-woman evokes in Kasch this "litany, a sacred chant" (49). And though Kasch's desires are perverse, as were Humbert Humbert's, the novel transforms the hero rather than sentencing him to death as Nabokov does after Humbert kills his double, Quilty. To imagine the self as double, or even as multiple, does not necessarily indicate madness.

Oates regards the belief in the singular self, the "I," as pathological, for it is this belief that leads to a repression of the "feminine" aspects of the self—the unconscious, the body—and this repression, in turn, develops into perversions such as pedophilia. Laney is an image of Kasch's "anima," to use the Jungian term, just as Lolita is an image of Humbert's despised and cast off "feminine" inner life. The repressed "double" is also the realm of the "masses," or the "political unconscious," as Jameson calls it.[9] Kasch himself immediately genders Laney's home in Childwold, seeing it as "big flopping ungainly place, like a slovenly woman, ill-proportioned, blatant, uncanny" (63). The home and yard he describes as "a universe of trash, of beauty" (64), a beautiful/ugly place, both/and. The Law of the Father, the Rule of One, does not govern in Childwold: many of Arlene's children cannot name their fathers. It is a place where the power of fathers appears to be waning: Grandfather Hurley has lost ownership of the land, and he will soon die; Arlene's husband is dead, and her various lovers either disappear or, like Earl Tuller, die. But none of these deaths is viewed as tragic; instead, they are understood as "natural," obedient to the laws of growth, procreation, and death. In Laney's experience of her first menstrual period, she recognizes this law: the law of flux, change, metamorphosis. When she hears her mother use the word "period" in front of a doctor, she thinks "how dare she, how dare they, it was secret, it was sacred" (194). Seeking privacy, she rides her cousin's horse to the river where she feels "the vibrations . . . water pounding downstream, downstream, the deep-chested breathing of the mare, the beat of the sun and the seeping blood" (197).

In this sacred place, a realm of "nochrist, nogod, dark earthy-wet rivulets, secret, sleep" (198), she hears "strange singing words, not to be understood," and she wonders: "What does it mean, why did you come here, what led you here?—a place, another of the sacred places you will remember all your life. . . . Here everything is living, everything is alive . . . . you lean forward to ease the pain" (ellipses mine 197). Here Oates portrays an experience marginalized in tragedy, a young girl's coming of age. Even in "Romeo and Juliet," there would be no place for a Laney, a child of the "lower class," much less the depiction of a young woman's first menstrual period. Yet what Laney learns from this flow of blood is important: "it's normal, it's beautiful, it's alive, it's living, you don't own your body, you don't own the creek, you can't control it, you mustn't try, you must float with the current . . . everything is spilling toward you, around you, inside you, through you, your blood flows with it, you are rivers and streams and creeks, there is a heartbeat inside you, around you" (my ellipsis 197). In tragedy, by contrast, the flow of blood is brought about by acts of violence—often by the father's refusal to let go, his refusal to acknowledge loss of control through the natural process of aging. Yet Laney's mother faces the reality of her daughter's growth. Reading a passage from one of Laney's books, loaned to her by Kasch, Arlene discovers that she cannot understand the passage Laney had marked: "In that instant Arlene felt that she would never be young again: not only would Laney outlive her, and live a life she could not control, but Laney was already grown from her, slipped far from her, beyond Childwold" (89).

While Nabokov portrays Lolita's mother as jealous of her daughter, Oates depicts Arlene as angry and hurt. As a mother, Arlene feels a genuine sense of estrangement and loss, yet she also fears that Laney's growth may be too rapid, especially given her involvement with a much older man. For this as well as for financial reasons, Arlene offers herself to Kasch, a marriage more appropriate since Kasch is forty-one and Arlene is forty, while Laney is only fourteen. Intellectually, however, Arlene and Kasch have little in common. Arlene cannot comprehend the passage her daughter has been reading from Kasch's book: " 'I only know myself as a human entity; the scene, so to speak, of thoughts and affections; and am sensible of a certain doubleness by which I can stand as remote from myself as from another. However intense the experience, I am conscious of the presence of and criticism of a part of me, which, as it were, is not a part of me, but spectator, sharing no experience, but taking note of it; and that is no more I than it is you. When the play, it may be the tragedy, of life is over, the spectator goes his way. It was a kind of fiction, a work of the imagination only' " (89).

Here again Oates identifies the doubleness—that sense of being a spectator—from which Kasch and his counterpart, Humbert Humbert, suffer. The "spectator" (the ego) comes to believe it has created life, and fantasizes that when the fiction is over, the author can walk away, as if he does not live a life of the body. What Laney learns at the time of her first menstrual period Kasch will learn, much later, through an act of violence: that his consciousness is embodied. In a violent encounter with Earl Tuller, Kasch learns that he too is mortal and will perish. From the author's angle of vision in *Childwold*, however, the violent encounter of two assassins looks like this:

A rock dropped in the midst of struggle, clumsy grunting
sobbing cries,
graceless, adults stumbling like giant children, oh give it
here! Here! Give it
here! And then—
                    A M E L O N F O R B R E A K F A S T
Scent so powerful, my head The shape, the odor, the several
snapped forward—muskmelon—clinging seeds, slimy-slick, a
little
taste & eat—senses filled to the soft, bruised—these
fruits, these
brim—beauty, beauty, beauty—head-shells—skulls—Can it
be!
springing out of the earth, these What! I! He! This!
fruits, these souls. Taste. Eat. My Where—? What has—?
eyeballs rolled in my head—oh
love, love!
When will—? When will—?
                                        Never.
How fell, this fall; but how, how so rudely fallen? All
innocent. Innocent, all.
The three of us wedded but innocent; must be forgiven. (287)

Thus does Kasch remember his fall—the death of Earl Tuller and the end of the "Bridegroom's" innocence—and the weight of guilt. Arlene had picked up the rock, he recalls, but he had struck the fatal blows. He wishes to be executed immediately, a martyr who alone assumes the burden of guilt; like Humbert he declares himself guilty (Quilty) and attempts to face his execution nobly. Yet Arlene, who had taunted her former suitor's impotence, must share in the guilt, as must Earl Tuller, the victim. This sharing of guilt requires, however, that individuals acknowledge their doubleness, a loss of innocence graphically represented in Kasch's double-entry journal. Kasch is no longer one, no longer a heroic figure, but a creature of flesh and blood. He notes, for example, that a skull, like a melon, is easily bruised, pulpy; that he and Earl behave like "giant children"; that their communion is violent: "Taste. Eat." Dreaming back over his life, his vision married to Laney's, Kasch sees himself as neither hero nor martyr, as neither great nor small, neither all nor nothing. He is simply an aspect of Childwold, part of nature's profusion, an abundance the novel celebrates in Whitmanesque lists.

The novel ends and begins again as Laney calls to Kasch, who has imprisoned himself in Laney's attic bedroom. She stands amidst "starlings, grackles, cowbirds. Crows. The high shrill screaming of insects. Great battalions of clouds, like chunks of rock, of ice, blowing down from the mountains" (294), waiting for a sign from Kasch. Although he had been shut up in a mental institution after killing Earl, Kasch now lives alone in the abandoned farmhouse. In this place, waiting to hear Kasch's voice, Laney hears a profusion of voices, not human: "Something is crying, whimpering. The wind. The birds. The insects" (295). She also sees the mute world: "Buttercups, Queen Anne's lace, heal-all, goldenrod, blue chicory flowers, insect-riddled blossoms. Eating. Devouring. Cloud into cloud, bud into blossoms into ragged shredded petals, bagworms in the apple orchard, in the pear orchard, half the trees marked with their ugly gray tents—why doesn't someone burn them down?" (295). Laney thinks she can hear it, "Here it's silence: you can hear the silence pulsing beneath the noise of the insects. . . . Kasch? Is it really you?" (295). In this moment at the novel's close, a new Laney, no longer the child Kasch once loved, attempts to reopen a dialogue with Kasch, her former mentor. At the same time, Laney has grown beyond Kasch's vision of her.

Laney returns to Childwold, as Oates does, understanding that memory enables us to define and redefine ourselves. As Greene says, "Memory is our means of connecting past and present, and constructing a self and versions of experience we can live with. To doubt it is to doubt ourselves, to lose it is to lose ourselves; yet doubt it we must, for it is treacherous" ("Feminist Fiction" 293). Laney is no longer contained by Kasch's vision of her, just as Lolita could not be contained by Humbert Humbert's imagination. Indeed, Kasch is not Laney's creator any more than Humbert Humbert is Lolita's, though Quilty tries to imagine himself her creator. Quilty writes a play in which Lolita is but a figment of his imagination, but Kasch learns that he is not *the* creator; both he and Laney exist beyond the boundaries of words, beyond the boundaries of the ego. Yet they need each other. Human beings become cocreators in an organically creative universe—the same creative force that brings forth flowers and insects, chickens and dogs—through their participation in language, in dialogue. We cannot exist in isolation, even though we may need such isolation, temporarily, in the process of maturation—Laney in her attic bedroom, Kasch in his self-defined exile. At the end of *Childwold*, Laney is calling to Kasch, yet in the process of reading the novel, it isn't always possible to separate his voice from hers, her memories from his, their experiences from those of their families. The river of words respects no boundaries. As we enter into this flowing river of words, we too become creators of a region known as Childwold.

6

Self-Narrating Woman: Marriage as Emancipatory Metaphor in Unholy Loves

If *Childwold* is Joyce Carol Oates's "portrait of the artist as a young woman," as Eileen Teper Bender suggests, then *Unholy Loves* may be understood as its sequel: a portrait of the artist as a maturing woman. Like Oates herself, Brigit Stott is a college professor and a novelist who, at the end of *Unholy Loves* is almost thirty-nine, close to Oates's own age at the time she wrote this academic novel. Unlike her fictional predecessors, Brigit survives the unhealthy effects of academic life—the armoring of the body required by the fiercely competitive game of intellectual warriors—to reclaim her emotions, her community, and her narrative authority. Brigit finds that writing may serve as a kind of "therapy";[1] more specifically, she finds that the process of writing an autobiographical novel, during which she mourns her losses, enables her to stop reenacting destructive romantic scripts. Brigit comes close to the despair of Ilena, the suicidal woman teacher/writer in "The Dead," but she survives. What accounts for the difference is that Brigit learns to value her membership in an academic community, however flawed, and, listening to the voices of personal memory, grieves for all those she has lost. Thus, *Unholy Loves* marks an important moment in Oates's development as a (woman) writer.

Many of these changes, especially as they affect women, are portrayed in Oates's short stories and novels. In the 1960s, for example, Oates wrote stories of guilt-ridden and powerless teachers, most of them daughters of the church, and most of which take place in Michigan where she was "in residence" at the University of Detroit. Both Sister Irene of "In the Region of Ice" and Ilena in "The Dead" work at Catholic universities in Detroit, as does the night-school teacher in *them* whose name is "Joyce Carol Oates." During the 1970s, most of Oates's women teachers—the "intellectual warriors" and the "romantic handmaidens" in stories from *The Hungry Ghosts* (1974)—are trying to find jobs and earn tenure in a Canadian school called Hilsberry, a place similar to Windsor University where Oates taught at this time. These stories record the turbulent campus protests of the era as well as the harsh realities of shrinking job possibilities in English departments in the United States. Although the stories in *The Hungry Ghosts* are darkly satirical, just five years later, in *Unholy Loves* (1979), Oates depicts an academic woman who is tenured and has published two novels. In addition, Brigit Stott's growing ability to see the value of her own life—the value of personal memories—enables her to begin writing again. The change of setting—a liberal arts college in upstate New York—reflects Oates's return to the U.S. to become writer-in-residence at Princeton. Women teachers are also central characters in the contemporary novels, *Solstice* (1985) and *Marya, a Life* (1986), both set in New England. As women struggle to redefine themselves in these novels, they find it necessary to reconcile conflicts not only with the male-defined academic community but within an emerging women's community.

As Elaine Showalter has noted, the presence of a women's community is perhaps the greatest difference between Oates's "The Dead," published in 1971, and *A Bloodsmoor Romance* (1982). However, *Unholy Loves* (1979) provides compelling evidence that this change in Oates's oeuvre did not occur as abruptly as Showalter's comment might suggest. In fact, *Unholy Loves* appears to resurrect Ilena Williams from "The Dead" in order to re-vision her story. Like Ilena, Brigit is an academic and a novelist who, after a failed marriage and a failed romance is suicidally depressed. As Showalter says of Ilena, she has a "troubled relation to the male institutions of the university, marriage, and literature" that leads her to believe that she must "fail at something," until finally she feels that she has "failed at being a woman" ("*The Dead* and Feminist Fiction" 16–17). In *Unholy Loves* Oates writes beyond the ending of her own short story by providing Brigit a powerful alternative to the heterosexual romance or marriage plot: Brigit survives because, in contrast to Ilena, she continues to teach and to participate in an academic community. The emotional support of this community, though far from ideal, provides Brigit with a substitute for the romance plot: her "marriage" to teaching and writing, her commitment to something beyond herself that saves her from destruction by romantic myths—"the myth of the isolated artist" especially.[2]

At the close of the novel, Brigit also has an incipient desire to become part of an emerging feminist community. Although, as Showalter says, Ilena has "no women friends, no female precursors, no women's community of love and ritual from which to gain nurturance," in the late 1970s the strength of the women's movement was growing just as Oates began to explore the possibilities of women-centered communities, first in *Childwold* and then in *Unholy Loves*. Like her predecessor Laney, Brigit differs from Oates in important ways, but she can be described as auto-graphic. In other words, Brigit does not live out all of Oates's life experiences (for example, in contrast to Brigit, Oates has been happily married for many years) but Oates draws upon her own experiences as a writer and teacher, as well as her certain knowledge of the feminist community in academe,[3] to create her protagonist. For example, during the mid-1970s Oates herself was testifying openly about her love for teaching. "I love my students," she told interviewer Sally Quinn in 1975; "I get so involved with them. It's like a little family" (6).[4] She also told interviewer Jo Ann Levine in 1976, "I have been teaching what seems like all my life. What I love about teaching is becoming involved with my students. . . . It is very important emotionally, psychologically, and intellectually. Writers, if they live in isolation, can become increasingly cut off from other people!" (14). By contrast, Brigit never talks about teaching, even though she genuinely cares for her students.

Yet Brigit learns the importance of community—the importance of her love for students and faculty—and this saves her from Ilena's tragic fate, isolation and death. What has changed is that during the late 1970s Oates found more positive, but still psychologically valid, solutions to the problems of a female academic. It should be noted, however, that feminist themes in *Unholy Loves* are present in her fiction from the outset. As I shall illustrate, a number of her short stories focus specifically on the problems of women who attempt to gain admittance to academe and, once there, to maintain their physical, emotional, and mental well-being. Like religion and science, higher education is premised upon the usually unstated, often unconscious binarism: "man" = mind, "woman" = body; therefore, even the presence of women in academe is transgressive. Oates dramatizes the consequences of this mind/body binarism in a short story called "At the Seminary," first published in 1965. As Ellen Friedman says, this story illustrates "the threat [that] women's biology poses to male institutions and the denial of natural processes on which these institutions depend" ("Joyce Carol Oates" 233). In this story, in the company of her parents, daughter Sally visits her brother, Peter, at the seminary where he is privileged to receive an education that, despite her obvious intelligence, she is denied. Just as Father Greer, who is giving the family a tour of the seminary, points to an off-limits cloistered area, Sally "felt the faithful blood inside her, seeping, easing downward" (105). To protest her exclusion from a life of the mind, Sally suddenly "took a hard, brutal step forward, bringing her flat heel down hard on the floor" (105).[5] Both Ilena and Brigit find, as Sally does, that the presence of a mind in a female body poses a serious threat to the illusion, cherished by intellectuals, of the mind's transcendence. However, Oates resolves the mind/body problem much more positively in *Unholy Loves*.

A second, related problem is that some women attempt to survive by adapting to the unhealthy competitive ethic that governs academic life. As Friedman says, Oates's fiction illustrates "that a woman's participation in the academy depends on her adoption of patriarchal language, forms, and rituals, on 'aping' males" ("Joyce Carol Oates" 239). But in *Unholy Loves*, Brigit begins to resist rather than ape males. In Oates's early fiction, however, women are often so preoccupied by rituals of competition that, like their male counterparts, they frequently fail to adequately care for their students. For example, Sister Irene in "In the Region of Ice" (1965) cannot protect a male student, Allen Weinstein, from his wealthy and abusive father, just as "Miss Oates" in *them* (1969)[6] cannot adequately protect a female student, Maureen Wendall, from her poor and abusive stepfather. In accordance with the male-defined and male-controlled structures of their respective educational institutions, Sister Irene and Miss Oates behave more like daughters obedient to powerful father rather than like nurturing mothers. As Madeleine Grumet argues in *Bitter Milk*, the father-daughter relationship repeats itself in an institution where authority is imagined as male. A daughter-teacher, one who is preoccupied with a need for recognition and love from the father, will inevitably fail to nurture the young. But what is the alternative for academic woman? That is, how are women teachers to care for other people's children without, at the same time, suffering from a loss of power in an institution still controlled by men, most of whom not only lack maternal skills but do not respect them in others? The authors of *Women's Ways of Knowing*, who reject the "domination of feeling by thought," find in Sara Ruddick's *Maternal Thinking* a method for transforming classroom practice and, potentially, institutional practices as well.

Although the charge of "essentialism" is invariably raised whenever one employs the term "maternal," Ruddick is, in fact, careful to point out that both men and women have the capacity to learn maternal thought and practice. Maternal thought is not innate or instinctive, Ruddick argues, but, like any discipline, has certain constitutive goals and practices. According to Ruddick, maternal thinking is constituted by the demand for the child's *preservation, growth,* and *social acceptability.* Ruddick believes that a major goal for feminists should be to bring "a *transformed* maternal thought into the public realm" (226), such as in higher education. A transformed maternal thinking—by which Ruddick means a feminist transformation— should not be confused with the mothering of (male) adults, but should be understood as clearly recognizing the power differentials in human relationships. In addition, maternal thinkers understand that they must always nurture themselves, rather than sacrifice themselves to the needs of others. Brigit, for example, finally refuses to sacrifice her creativity to either her childish lover or to a neurotic student. During one lonely Christmas season Brigit had allowed an "alarmingly infantile" nineteen-year-old girl to move into her apartment (175). The young woman had manipulated Brigit by claiming she "was afraid she would kill herself if she remained in the girls' residence hall" (176). Noisy and intrusive, the young woman had driven Brigit out of her own apartment to her office or the library where, "homeless herself," she rehearsed the ways she could ask the girl to leave. One day Brigit found this note: "*Dear B., Hate to run out on you like this just before Christmas without even a personal good-by & thanks but I got a chance for a ride all the way to Ft. Lauderdale & he's leaving right now. Thanx a Million for Everything. Love, Kim*" (176). Women who deny their own needs and emotions, as Brigit does in this instance or as Ilena does in "The Dead," suffer a range of consequences, from the comic to the tragic.

However, neither Brigit nor Ilena have children who suffer, as does Dennis, the eleven-year-old son of Nora Drexler, a woman professor in the short story, "Magna Mater." Nora, a divorced mother, also inflicts the academy's competitive beliefs and practices—including a belief in the mind's transcendence over the body and emotions—upon her only child. A forty-five-year-old professor at an eastern university, Nora has defined herself, though not consciously, as a daughter seeking to please an indifferent father, a former professor of philosophy at Harvard. In recent years Nora's life has become disordered, untidy: her husband has divorced her to marry a younger woman, her father is dying slowly, and her son, she feels, is "trying to drive her mad as his father had tried to drive her mad" (*Goddess and Other Women* 189). Nora's problem becomes apparent when colleagues, the Colebrooks, bring Nora greetings from a former student—now a published poet—named Benjamin Edwards. Nora recalls only that "Edwards had done graduate work with her some time ago; he had attempted an ambitious, heroic study of the poetics of Pound, but the dissertation had never really taken shape and so he'd drifted onto another topic, with another professor, and finally he had been asked to leave the program" (203). But Edwards, who has been invited back by the creative writing department, has struck back at his overly "rigorous" professor with a satirical poem called, "How Leda Got the Swan" (203). With this gendered inversion of Yeats's image, Edwards portrays the Zeus-like power of his former magna mater. Nora rationalizes her competitiveness as a practice based upon "a consciousness freed of the body, of all temporal limitations," a belief stated in a five-hundred-page dissertation on Eliot's poetics, "which had as its thesis the vision of the poet as transcendent—triumphing over personality, over the limits of the body itself" (205).

By contrast, in the final pages of *Unholy Loves*, Brigit draws upon personal memories to write an autobiographical novel, an act of resistance to Eliot's poetics. Another difference is that Brigit, in contrast to Nora, is kind to her students, even, on occasion, overgenerous with her time. Nora, who is cruel and judgmental of her students, seems to overcompensate when dealing with her own son. Her son watches closely as his mother rationalizes her "at times rather cruel" review-essays "defending the Church against outsiders," preserving poetry as "the possession of a very few" (205). Always governed by her intellect, always under control, Nora has never complained about the exhausting demands of being a mother, a teacher, and a scholar, not even about her divorce and her husband's marriage to a younger woman. Nora is never angry. She has striven instead for perfection, and only once, when she noticed that her father had not bothered to read her latest book, had a "terrible thought flooded her: *None of this will save us*" (186). Brigit finally acknowledges not only feelings of anger and grief but also fears of her own mortality. Because Nora denies thoughts of mortality, loss, and abandonment, her son has nightmares about "*a mouth chewing and grinding and making wet noises*" (197), making visible what Nora's belief in poetic transcendence forces her to repress. As Dennis becomes increasingly fearful, Nora calls a psychiatrist who tells her, carefully, that "there are actually no disturbed *individuals* as such. And never any disturbed children, of course. There are only disturbed households" (197). Vulnerable to any criticism from paternal authority, Nora makes no appointment, and her son becomes increasingly disturbed. In a perfect echo of his mother's feelings, Dennis says, "I hate that man, I hate the woman too. I hate all of them, don't you? . . . I don't like living people" (209).

Like Ilena's reverence only for dead lovers, Nora's reverence for dead poets has its consequences for the living. Brigit Stott struggles with similar problems in *Unholy Loves*, but she comes to value the living as much as the dead, the personal as well as the impersonal, the emotional as well as the intellectual. As the novel closes, she claims the right to resist the narrative voices—and the structures of authority—that have come close to defeating her. As Elizabeth Meese says, "If we seek to transform the structures of authority, we must first name them, and in so doing, unmask and expose them for all to see" (16). This task of unmasking and exposing the structures of authority shapes the structure, the narrative technique, and the ending of *Unholy Loves*. The novel identifies the competitive ethic that prevents academic men and women from achieving a more ideal community, a community that nurtures its faculty and students. As I shall illustrate, Oates employs a communal structure in this academic novel, a structure that—though it appears linear or sequential—turns out to be something like a song cycle. The ideal of community, sometimes stated explicitly by the characters themselves, organizes the five-part structure of the novel. With the exception of Part IV, "Hour of Lead," with its clear reference to Emily Dickinson's poem of near-suicidal despair, all five parts of the novel focus upon faculty parties: I, "At the Byrnes' "; II, "At the Seidels' "; III, "At Albert St. Dennis's and at the Housleys' "; and V, "In the Founders' Room." Each occasion honors the "great man," the father-poet, Albert St. Dennis, who is visiting Woodslee.

The hosts of these parties—Byrnes, who is the dean, and Seidel, a powerful member of the English department—are engaged in a power struggle that masks their desire for the father's love. In the end, Albert St. Dennis, who is too old even to acknowledge the identities of these combatants, dies by setting himself on fire. After St. Dennis falls into a drunken sleep, his own smoldering cigarette creates the blaze. Both Dean Byrnes and Lewis Seidel are, however, undone by this event: Byrnes because he is held responsible for having brought St. Dennis to Woodslee and having arranged his accommodations, and Seidel because his own conscience condemns him for having left St. Dennis in a drunken state with a still-burning cigarette. Seidel and Byrnes had become enemies, we learn, over the issue of the color of the college stationery. Oliver Byrnes had triumphed, the pale blue had been chosen despite Seidel's public ridicule: " 'Sky-blue! Powder-blue! Ladies' lingerie-blue!' " (277). However, beginning in Part III, the voices of women arranged in sequential chapters—in particular the voices of Brigit, a professor, and Sandra Jaeger, a faculty wife—function as counterpoints to those of Seidel and Byrnes. Gradually the narrative focus shifts, identifying structural parallels between Brigit and Sandra, despite differences in their status. For example, both attend holiday parties, one at Albert St. Dennis's, the other at the Housleys'.

The Woodslee parties are attended by circles of people—circles constituted by relationships of friendship, power, or romance—that are subject to various kinds of change: by promotion and tenure, hirings and firings, divorces and betrayals, illnesses and deaths. Although men tend to have more public power, Oates also depicts men at private moments when they have taken off their armor; for example, we see Byrnes happily tidying the house after his party honoring St. Dennis and Seidel close to tears as he waits for a word of blessing from St. Dennis. Thus, we come to understand that these men are driven to competition by their desire for love and recognition from the father; however, each man's "marriage" to the father, a father embodied by St. Dennis, leads not to salvation but to self-destruction. For example, Byrnes's wife, recognizing that she doesn't exist for her sexually impotent husband, suffers a breakdown, and Byrnes, weakened by this crack in his armor and by the death of St. Dennis on his watch, is forced to leave Woodslee. His fierce competitor, Seidel, who happens to smoke, becomes a victim of emphysema, partly because he has been weakened by guilt over St. Dennis's death and over his exploitation of others, especially women. He has, for example, committed adultery, most recently with the young wife of a new assistant professor, Ernest Jaeger, with the unspoken agreement that Sandra Jaeger's husband will be reappointed at Woodslee. To keep this promise, Seidel arranges to force sixty-three-year-old Gladys Fetler, a more popular teacher than he, into early retirement. Furthermore, although both Byrnes and Seidel egocentrically credit themselves with having brought Brigit to Woodslee, affirmative action has, in fact, forced them to do so.

Ironically, neither Byrnes nor Seidel is present at the novel's final party, held in the newly named Albert St. Dennis Founders' Room. The poet, St. Dennis, is dead, just as the illustrious founding fathers are dead or destroyed. Despite the college's glorification of men, a member of the faculty remarks to Sandra Jaeger, "Woodslee is infused with the spirit of democracy" (206), obviously unaware that Sandra has just learned that her husband's contract won't be renewed. Because of her husband's desperate struggle to retain his position at Woodslee, the twenty-four-year-old Sandra has already been forced to learn the truth of what St. Dennis says to Brigit at a different party that same night: "Life conspires to cut us off from one another." Referring to his own work, *The Explorers*, St. Dennis says, "The Explorers begin as lusty ignorant boys, vessels of flesh, and though they throw themselves into the farthest reaches of the universe it never occurs to them to explore themselves. . . . It never occurs to them to love themselves" (Oates's ellipsis 229). Brigit hears this and comes to understand it, but none of the lusty boys, now in their fifties, hears it. "*We must love one another while we have one another,*" says faculty wife Charlotte Haas at the Seidel party for St. Dennis, but Lewis Seidel doesn't hear her. He is too busy listening for the doorbell to ring, announcing St. Dennis's arrival, to hear the words of a faculty wife or to enjoy his other guests. Again, no one listens when, at Gladys Fetler's retirement party, Leslie Cullendon proposes a toast from his wheelchair, not to "another 'great man,' " but to "just us" (320). Everyone leaves hurriedly, unable to publicly confront Leslie's imminent death.

Our collective repression of individual mortality, the novel's structure implies, presents the greatest obstacle to achieving the ideal of community. Suicides by faculty and students provide gruesome evidence of the isolation and despair at Woodslee and in society at large, but the competitive game continues. As the "lusty ignorant boys," the intellectual warriors, seek through conquest to win the father's love, they fail to truly love themselves, their families, and their communities. Brigit Stott participates in this "masquerade"—"this ceaseless task of presenting a self to a circle of selves" (300)—until, finally, a failed romance exhausts her. Her romance with Alexis Kessler begins after the first party of the year "at the Byrnes'," when St. Dennis himself joins the hands of Brigit and Alexis as they sit on either side of him. Yet neither Brigit nor Alexis truly sees the other; they see only undeveloped aspects of their own personalities. For example, though Brigit has shown no concern for her appearance, Alexis begins to remake her, dressing her, applying her makeup, creating her public persona. And, although Kessler has been blocked as a composer, what Brigit seeks from him is her own lost music, the semiotic dimensions of language, the frozen melody of her emotions.

Ironically, it is the loss of both Kessler and St. Dennis that enables Brigit to recover this music. Finally Brigit can no longer separate her public and her private lives. A painful and disturbing dream, in which the private memory of her aging grandfather merges with her public grief at the loss of St. Dennis, weaves together these experiences of loss: "Remembering, she wept with the pain of it: the sense of irreparable loss; the knowledge that she had stayed away from a dying man [her grandfather] who had loved her in his own way; she had been selfish and cowardly and despicable" (306). Weeping for all those she has lost, she heard, at last, her own voice, "Let them go, let them die, let them be lost," and, returning to her writing with this new-found voice, "she forgot about herself entirely" (307). In the flowing of tears, in the "letting go," as in Dickinson's poem, she finds the creative rhythm once again. In the meantime, however, Brigit's commitment to teaching had kept her alive. Teaching had provided her at least a semblance of community, even if it is "a world of marriages" (35) in which Brigit leads a "near monastic life" (45). This community is important because Brigit's family sees her as "just Brigit," as a woman who has failed at marriage, while Woodslee at least validates her worth as a professor and novelist. However, although the teaching community is important to her, "she flinches from discussions of teaching and nervously brushes aside all compliments—for if one speaks of something treasured, might it not be lost?" (23). Brigit's reserve on this topic appears to be a defensive tactic made necessary by the competitive code of the academy. Perhaps this reserve—or the tendency to speak only ironically, satirically—is also the reason that the academic novel remains a minor genre by most estimations. Armored with irony, we imply by inversion what it is that we hold sacred.[7]

Lewis Seidel imagines that what he most values is conquest. As a graduate student, "he had conquered Marx to his own satisfaction," and "as he had conquered, one by one, book by book, every important writer of the modern era" (66), he had abandoned his "boyish enthusiasm" in order to see himself as a "scholar-critic who not only comprehends his material but, in a sense, overcomes it" (66). Simple pleasure and love vanish, rejected as mere child's play; the sacred text becomes the object of attack, as with jokes. What Seidel does not see is that he himself, from a certain perspective, is becoming a joke. With the coming of St. Dennis, Seidel fantasizes himself as a critic-poet who will practice, though he is fifty-one years old, an "experimental metacriticism of the sort being done by younger men who are scornful of the old-fashioned structures and value judgments." To establish himself as one of the "younger men," he will joust with the great father himself. He imagines a "dialogue, a duet," with "his own voice and that of a representative artist of the old order locked together in ferocious combat" (65). In other words, Seidel's romantic fantasy—the father-son competition identified by the Bloomian model of literary criticism—is as preposterous as Brigit's fantasy of "marriage" to St. Dennis. The aging poet has already been seriously weakened by far stronger adversaries, to which St. Dennis gives the name, "the Mothers." As he tells Brigit and Alexis: "Yeats knew, Auden knew, St. Dennis knows, he can smell them and taste them, hadn't he written of the plunge of life in *The Explorers*, which must, alas, lose its energy and its sacred, proud beauty and come to rest . . . come to rest as the Explorer-heroes come to rest, ultimately, in the arms of the Mothers . . . hadn't he written of it already . . . must he live it out now in the flesh?" (Oates's ellipses 63).

St. Dennis may write of it, imagine it, and yet resist living it out, just as Lewis Seidel resists recognizing himself as no longer a son but an aging man, a father himself. It may be, however, that a fleeting awareness of his own mortality inspires Seidel's passionate quest for St. Dennis's blessing. If Byrnes has brought St. Dennis to Woodslee, earning himself favorite-son status, Seidel will win the father for himself. Thus, Seidel offers to provide a ride home for the poet—who has drunk too much and thrown up on the Byrneses' living room carpet. In the privacy of the poet's apartment, Seidel says to his wife, "Stupid cow. Get out of the way," as he removes a lit cigarette from St. Dennis and tucks him in for the night. "Amazing," he thinks, "that this person is Albert St. Dennis! *This* person" (80). This childish idolizing of the poet reveals his love for the father: "Shut up," he says to his wife when she interrupts his reveries, but he is "blinking tears out of his eyes" (8). If Seidel were to acknowledge this love, it might free him to genuinely love his wife, but as an intellectual warrior, one who worships the father, he masks feelings of tenderness. He imagines himself locked in a "death-combat" with the father-poet—a struggle from which a "timeless truth" will emerge—and in the war zone of his imagination, both young and old women, such as Gladys Fetler and Sandra Jaeger, become victims. Seidel never truly listens to women, but he doesn't quite hear St. Dennis either.

Because of Seidel's fantasies of power, his monologic maiming, he is deaf to the truth of shared mortality. Instead, it is Brigit who hears St. Dennis tell his truth about dying. In St. Dennis's dirty kitchen, where he is searching for one of the dishes he has prepared for his guests, the tattered old man says, "New Year's Eve is no time to be alone," for at such times, he explains, "The planet is about to plunge into darkness and our souls are frightfully sensitive at such times" (226). He continues, "The Explorers, don't you know, set forth with such joy upon their voyages. . . . But all along the Mothers were waiting. Observing, don't you know, in absolute silence. . . . *There is no language to the body!* The Mothers, the Weavers, content to bring all exploration to an end; content to embrace their sons in the end. What they weave they then unweave" (226). And so it is for Brigit and others in Woodslee. Individual lives, as in St. Dennis's death, are "unwoven"; love affairs, such as Brigit and Alexis's, begin unraveling; a student commits suicide, fortunately not someone Brigit knows; Sandra Jaeger commits adultery; Gladys Fetler is forced into early retirement; assistant professors are given termination notices. The circles at Woodslee break apart: circles of friendship among assistant professors, when a few are retained and others are terminated; circles of power of deans and department chairs, as some are demoted and leave while others acquire new status. When St. Dennis dies, for example, a scapegoat must be found; as a result, Dean Byrnes is forced to leave Woodslee.

Gladys Fetler is also forced to leave Woodslee, and Brigit does nothing to help her. Brigit, who had once remarked cynically "I can't bear good people" (34), watches as Gladys Fetler becomes herself the victim of "Machiavellian political maneuvers" (293). Despite the fact that Dr. Fetler has been "magnanimous about promotions and tenure and raises, always wishing to see the positive side of a colleague's record" (202), this nurturant attitude does nothing to save her. Indeed, it cannot become effective, this novel implies, unless faculty work collectively to transform the politics of paternity—the separation of intellect and nurturance—into a sense of community in which individual agency is mitigated by "maternal thinking." Tragically, when Gladys Fetler learns of her betrayal and appeals to Brigit, the younger woman listens but takes no effective action. At Fetler's retirement party, Brigit recalls, "It was a most embarrassing clumsy half-hour, that session in Brigit's office some weeks ago when Gladys Fetler first received notice from the administration that her early retirement was strongly advised" (292). Brigit tells Gladys she knows nothing of department politics and, though she does make an appointment with the department chair to inquire, she accepts at face value his claim that the move came from "higher up," and his expression of sympathy, " 'It's a pity, yes' " (294), that such an excellent teacher has been forced out.

No community, no religious or social order exists to support Gladys Fetler, and unlike her namesake, Brigit does not found one. She has even rejected Gladys Fetler's gestures of friendship. Dr. Fetler was "sixty-three years old and gracious and ladylike and kindly and youthful, and from the start she'd been extremely friendly to Brigit—who had drawn back from her, not wanting intimacy, not wanting maternal compassion" (33). Instead, guilty and ashamed, Brigit only admires Gladys Fetler, who is a good teacher who is still publishing—"her most recent publication is a note on the staging of Webster's *White Devil*, in *PMLA*"—and still active physically and socially (33–34). But if Brigit has failed to support Gladys Fetler, she has failed even more to support Sandra Jaeger, a faculty wife. Apparently, it does not occur to Brigit to think of a faculty wife as a potential member of a feminist community. The structure of the novel serves as a counterpoint, suggesting a parallel between the two women, not only in Part III but again in parts IV and V of *Unholy Loves*. In Part III, as stated above, each woman attends a different New Year's Eve party, but both have been dealt severe blows: Brigit because she quarrels with Alexis, Sandra because her husband has received notice of nonrenewal. In Part IV, "The Hour of Lead," Sandra loses her romantic "innocence" when she saves her husband's academic position by having an affair with Lewis Seidel. Meanwhile Brigit ends her romance with Alexis and, following the death of St. Dennis, falls into a deep depression.

Yet each woman's "hour of lead" has very different consequences, especially in terms of their development as writers: Brigit, a published novelist, finds that writing an autobiographical novel is therapeutic and liberating, but Sandra, a private diarist, finds little comfort in writing about her affair with Seidel. Indeed, because she fears discovery, she decides to burn her diary and never write again. But with one last hope for honesty in her marriage, Sandra invites her husband to read her diary before she destroys it. He refuses. His reason, he says, is respect for her privacy, but he may actually be afraid of finding out about her "infidelity" which, at some level, he must know about. Had he read his wife's diary, he might have learned that her body, not his mind, is responsible for securing his position in the department. Tragically, Lewis Seidel creates a place for Sandra Jaeger's husband by sacrificing Gladys Fetler. Always a realist, however, Oates creates a woman teacher who has advantages that other academic women lack. For example, Brigit is relatively young, she is tenured, and she has already published two novels, *Worlds Elsewhere* and *Melodies*. In addition, the power of women, as a collective, to transform academe is suggested in the novel's structure. Even though the name "Brigit" alludes to St. Bridget, a widow who founded an order critical of civil and ecclesiastical authorities in fourteenth-century Sweden, Brigit's sense of kinship with other women emerges only in her guilt at the end of the novel. Nevertheless, like the Bridgettine order, *Unholy Loves* is dedicated to reforming the vision of authority that governs the "unholy loves" of the academic community.

Moreover, in the novel's final scene Brigit demonstrates that she has found strength enough, from her "marriage" to community and writing, to reject a destructive romance. When her lover hits her, Brigit actually strikes back and draws blood. This scene provides a sharp contrast to the Brigit who, at the outset of the novel, actually fantasizes giving up her own writing career to marry the godlike Albert St. Dennis, who is "second only to Yeats." Ironically, although Brigit and others worship St. Dennis, imagining him as the great man personified, the tattered old man himself does not articulate such a vision, nor does he embody it. When St. Dennis turns out to be a mortal man, like her own grandfather, Brigit recognizes that her romantic idealizations of the poet have prevented her from recognizing the value of her own life and memories. In this way *Unholy Loves* develops the theme that "we achieve our salvation, or our ruin, by the marriages we contract" (Clemons, "Joyce Carol Oates" 77), which Oates identifies as central to "The Dead" and other stories in *Marriages and Infidelities*. She had in mind, Oates explained, not just ordinary marriages, but also commitments of other kinds—to teaching, for example, or to art.

In contrast to the isolated Ilena, Brigit Stott shows how a woman teacher's salvation may come from her "marriage" to the ideal of communal love, her commitment to the holy love of both teaching *and* writing. Though Brigit comes close to sacrificing herself on the altar of romance, she discovers that her true commitment is not to Albert St. Dennis or Alexis Kessler, but to a higher self represented by their commitment to poetry and music. Brigit learns that she must nurture these gifts in herself and in her students. The danger of isolation has taught her the value of community. As St. Dennis says, the winter solstice is no time to be alone, for the isolated are much more vulnerable to the Mothers, that is, to the presence of death felt so strongly in "the hour of lead." Yet, paradoxically, it is during "the hour of lead" that Brigit finally undergoes a profound change. Initially, she feels that "she cannot fight the narrators, cannot compete with them, she hears them distinctly at times and would isolate them from her but she is too tired, she is deathly tired" (266).

Finally, however, her flowing tears thaw her frozen emotions. The death of St. Dennis, which calls forth a flood of repressed memories—the death of her grandfather, the loss of her friend Louellen and her husband Stanley—releases her from the emotional paralysis that has blocked her writing. Brigit recognizes that only through language can she free herself from the powerful narrators that would claim her, that would still her voice. She now understands that a consciousness "permeates language and is somehow given birth by it, and is always with us, we are never free. From birth onward we are surrounded by it . . . a cocoon of words . . . a living web of language. The world is filtered through it. There is no world except what is filtered through it. A living web" (Oates's ellipses 267). We know ourselves only through this "living web," and thus we must all become narrators of our lives. Brigit accepts this responsibility. At the end of *Unholy Loves*, she tells Alexis, " 'It's so difficult to explain. But whatever happens to me for the rest of my life . . . won't be inevitable' " (my ellipsis 335).

PART 3

Communal Authorship in the 1980s: The (M)other in Us

Joyce Carol Oates's concern with establishing and maintaining a sense of community governs many of her aesthetic innovations—innovations in plot, structure, imagery, and narrative technique—in novels of the 1980s. Although the dream of a democratic community is central in Oates's fiction from the outset of her career, in novels of the 1980s and early 1990s her strategies for representing that dream have changed. During this decade, for example, Oates employs what Marianne Hirsch calls "postmodern plots" in order to write beyond the ending of the heterosexual romance; in addition, Oates creates unusual communal narrators, women who speak for a feminist "we." In these novels of the 1980s, the daughters in Oates's fiction have also changed: in sharp contrast to the daughters in most of her early novels (with the exception of *Childwold*) many of these daughters return, usually in midlife, to establish relationships with their devalued mothers. In almost every novel of this decade, a female protagonist finds that in order to redefine herself in relationship to a community, she must return to the past, especially her maternal past. This pattern persists whether the novel is set in the nineteenth century or the twentieth. In this respect, Oates's plots are similar to those of other contemporary women writers in whose novels, according to Marianne Hirsch, "The process of subject-formation has become a major preoccupation for the narrator/protagonist who sees herself as part of a newly emerging feminist generation" (138–39). As I have illustrated in chapter 6, *Unholy Loves* ends just as Brigit Stott begins this process: a return to the past that will enable her to redefine, in feminist terms, herself and her community.

As depicted in much of contemporary women's fiction, the daughter's desire to reclaim her matrilineal past marks her break with the misogyny of culture. For in order to ally herself with the mother, the daughter must transgress the patriarchal imperative, "Away from the mother," an injunction that, as Oates argues in an analysis of *King Lear*, is dangerous not only for daughters, but for society as a whole. "The patriarch's unspoken imperative, *Away from the unconscious, away from the mother*, is dangerous precisely because it is unspoken, unarticulated, kept below the threshold of consciousness itself" (*Contraries* 75). This imperative is rooted, Hirsch argues, in the fear and discomfort with the body that comes from entanglements with "pregnancy, birth, lactation, miscarriage, or the inability to conceive" (166), all of which are associated with female victimization. Even feminists, Hirsch notes, have a profound ambivalence toward the body, especially toward the maternal body, an ambivalence that often impedes the daughter's quest in these novels. Because daughters associate mothers with the vulnerabilities of the body, during adolescence they often disavow them, choosing to ally themselves with fathers who are associated with the supposedly superior aspects of "culture." Inevitably, however, these same daughters discover the need to reclaim their matrilineal inheritance.

According to Kim Chernin, daughters continue to face a dilemma that society as a whole has not resolved: the question of how the daughter is "to become the mother without taking on her sacrifice?" (200). This dilemma, which daughters confront in much of contemporary women's fiction, has prompted Hirsch to ask, "What plots become speakable between mothers and daughters, what developmental paradigms emerge for fictional heroines and for women writers, and how is female subject-formation represented?" (127). The answer, Hirsch suggests, can be found in "postmodern plots" that are "structured around the motif of return, the process of memory, and the desire to come to terms with the past by integrating it with the protagonists' present self-representation" (139). As I shall demonstrate in Part 3, Oates employs such plots in both her postmodern novels, set in the nineteenth century, as well as the realistic novels set in the twentieth. In addition to the motif of return, these novels share certain recurring images—images of the repressed (m)other in the political unconscious—that daughters share with the culture as a whole. For, in a misogynist culture, daughters generally devalue and repress any identification with their mothers, even if they are feminists. The daughterly perspective in feminist narratives and scholarship, Hirsch says, "can be said to collude with patriarchy in placing mothers into the position of object—thereby keeping mothering outside of representation, and maternal discourse a theoretical impossibility" (16).

Thus, the voice of the mother continues to be silenced, not only in psychoanalytic theory, but in much feminist literary theory: "Feminist theorizing glosses over the stories that mothers are perhaps trying to tell, the stories that the psychoanalytic frame in which we have been thinking has made us unable to hear" (Hirsch 174). Even feminist psychologists such as Nancy Chodorow, who emphasize the importance of the pre-Oedipal phase for daughters, continue to employ an Oedipal model. Yet an Oedipal psychology not only silences the mother, according to psychologist Ellyn Kaschak, it leaves intact a theory that requires daughters to see themselves through paternal eyes. If we are to move beyond an Oedipal psychology, Kaschak argues, we must take into account the perspectives of both mothers and daughters, points of view missing or subsumed in Freud's conception of the Oedipus complex. In her reexamination of Freud's interpretation of Sophocles' drama, Kaschak finds that Freud focuses on a single play, *Oedipus Rex*, ignoring two plays in Sophocles' trilogy in which daughters play important roles. In *Antigone*, the pivotal play in the trilogy (which was written first but is performed last), the daughter's part is central, and in the second play, *Oedipus at Colonus*, Antigone and her sister Ismene serve as the eyes of their blind father. Freud's theory not only ignores the daughter's part, it also ignores the fact that in two of the three plays, Oedipus is not a son but a father. "The father of psychology all but ignored the psychology of fathers" (60), as Kaschak says.

Because of this failure to examine the psychology of fathers, the father's desire for his daughter has been denied by psychoanalysts as well as by literary critics. Since Freud's repudiation of the seduction theory, psycho-analysts have argued that actual incest does not (or rarely) occurs; instead, the daughter is presumed to fantasize (to desire) an incestuous relationship with the father. In this way, the father projects his desire onto the daughter: "The deeds of the father are replaced by the desires of the daughter (or son)" (Kaschak 59). Now that feminists have "conclusively established and documented the prevalence of molestation by fathers and other adult male relatives" (59), Kaschak argues, a new model of female development must be formulated. She proposes a feminist model of female development in which the daughter refuses to see (or desire) with the father's eyes. Rather than viewing her self through the eyes of an indeterminate male, the daughter must reintegrate aspects of the self that have been fragmented by the male gaze. In this struggle to reintegrate the self, to see herself with her own eyes, Kaschak argues that the daughter must acknowledge her kinship with her mother, as well as other women. Oates explores this process of reintegration, as well as relations with sisters and mothers, in almost all the novels of this decade. In addition, female friendships are central in at least three novels of this decade: *Marya, a Life, Solstice,* and *Foxfire, Confessions of a Girl Gang.*

In order to value female friendships, as I suggest above, daughters must first overthrow the patriarchal injunction, "Away from the mother." Unfortunately, as illustrated in many Oates novels of this period, Oedipal fathers continue to obstruct such alliances, often through incestuous or seductive behavior toward women younger than their wives, including their own daughters. Such immature behavior is motivated, according to Jessica Benjamin, by the father's fear of acknowledging his dependency and mortality.[1] The fathers/husbands in these novels who cannot admit dependency—especially dependency upon a woman—transform their denial into the need to dominate. At the same time, Oedipal fathers feel entitled not only to emotional support from their wives, but also from their daughters—just as both Lear and Oedipus expect their daughters to provide the emotional support that ordinarily comes from wives. Why do fathers demand "all" of their daughters? In most of these novels, as in much of Oates's earlier fiction, the departure of the daughter, especially the youngest daughter, signals the aging father's impending death. Since the father equates the departure of his last and youngest daughter with the threat of death, he wards off this fear by demanding that his daughter love him "all."

The father's sense of entitlement to his daughter, evident in the frequency with which fathers overcome the incest taboo, arises from the fact that historically she has been defined as his property. As a result, says Kaschak, "The oedipal father cannot tell, in a deep psychological sense, where his psychological/physical self ends and that of his daughter begins" (67). To avoid engulfing his daughter in incestuous fantasies, the father must experience his own boundaries and directly confront his aloneness and mortality. He must discover, as Kaschak says, that "he is not king, just a human being in a world of other humans" (73). In short, the father must relinquish his grandiosity. Only one novel depicts a father who succeeds at this Oedipal task, a task that requires the father to overcome romantic innocence: Lyle Stevick in *You Must Remember This*. However, as Kaschak points out, "Neither the antigonal nor the oedipal complex is a purely personal or familial drama, but each includes an interplay with those aspects of experience with the socio-cultural" (87). This interplay between the personal and the political, the familial and the cultural, is particularly visible in Oates's depiction of daughters in novels of the 1980s.

One example of the change in Oates's fictional daughters, according to Elaine Showalter, is the contrast between "The Dead," published in the early 1970s, and *A Bloodsmoor Romance*, published in 1982. In "The Dead," Showalter says, Ilena's "infidelity, her betrayal of the male tradition is an isolated cultural act. Significantly, she has no women friends, no female precursors, no women's community of love and ritual from which to gain nurturance" ("*The Dead* and Feminist Criticism" 18). A different pattern emerges in *A Bloodsmoor Romance*. This novel stages a return to the mother, a return in which the five Zinn sisters also seek kinship with their sisters. At the same time, author Oates stages a similar return by illustrating her kinship, not only with her literary forefathers, but also with her foremothers. As Showalter says, "*A Bloodsmoor Romance* merges the female and the male literary tradition, the female Gothic romance with *The Blithedale Romance* of Hawthorne ("*The Dead* and Feminist Criticism" 18). These plots, in which transgressive daughters return to the mother (biological and literary), move us beyond the theory of "failed community" that Dale Bauer posits in *Feminist Dialogics*—and that she illustrates in the suicides of Zenobia in *The Blithedale Romance*, Edna in Kate Chopin's *The Awakening*, and Lily in Edith Wharton's *The House of Mirth*.

A failure of community is evident in Oates's "The Dead," as Showalter notes; however, all of the postmodern novels—*Bellefleur*, *A Bloodsmoor Romance*, and *Mysteries of Winterthurn*—as well as many of her realistic novels stage a return to the mother, a pattern that suggests a feminist alternative to a failed patriarchal community. It must be emphasized, however, that this feminist alternative is possible only within certain historical contexts; in other words, the return to the mother appears to be an option only at those historical moments when women share collective political strength. Not surprisingly, then, during the second wave of the women's movement in the 1970s, women began to write what Adrienne Rich has described as the "great unwritten story" (*Of Woman Born* 225), the story of mothers and daughters. To tell this story, women novelists had to break out of suicidal "closed circles" of the prefeminist 1960s, according to Gayle Greene.

Greene argues, for example, that although Sylvia Plath may have written *The Bell Jar* (1963) "to free herself from the past, the novel seems, rather, to have reaffirmed the hold of the past" (67). *The Bell Jar* was published in the U.S. in 1971, the same year that Oates's "The Dead" first appeared. Since that time, Showalter emphasizes, Oates's protagonists have moved beyond their isolation from other women; they have begun to understand that their survival depends not only on a return to the maternal past but on their ability to forge alliances with other women, past and present.

In other words, the return to the maternal past must also re-revision the past if it is to make possible a rewriting of the narrative of female development. As Hirsch argues, "The story of female development, both in fiction and theory, needs to be written in the voice of mothers as well as in that of daughters. It needs to cease mystifying maternal stories, to cease making them objects of a 'sustained quest'" (161). Marya Knauer makes this discovery in *Marya, a Life*, as do many of the female protagonists in Oates's novels of this period. In my view, then, Oates's novels, along with Kaschak's theory of female development, answer Hirsch's call for stories "written in the voices of mothers as well as in that of daughters." If most women novelists were, during the 1980s, engaged in "the privatization and depoliticization of their concerns, the sentimentalization of the family, the resignation to things as they are" (Greene, *Changing the Story* 200), it should be noted that Oates politicizes the family in her nineteenth-century novels, as well as those set in the McCarthy, Kennedy, and Watergate eras. As I argue in the chapters that follow, Oates re-visions the family romance, employing techniques that foreground the porous boundaries between daughters, families, and the body politic.

In short, despite the backlash against feminism in the 1980s, Oates's vision is explicitly feminist in this decade. This change is especially evident in *Marya, a Life* (1986), a novel that provides an auto-graphic record of Oates's shift in focus from father-identified to mother-identified daughters in the mid-1970s. Oates herself says, "Whether Marya Knauer's story is in any way my own 'story,' it became my story during the writing of the novel" (*[Woman] Writer* 378). In auto-graphic terms, the novel "became" Oates's story because it returns, in its structure, to the moment in Oates's oeuvre when she began to divide herself up differently, that is, when the father-identified Yvonne Petrie in *The Assassins* (1975) became the mother-identified Evangeline Bartlett in *Childwold* (1976).[2] Marya Knauer is, in fact, quite similar to Yvonne. For example, after the death of their lovers, both

Marya and Yvonne imagine something deathly growing in their wombs. Both repeat the phrase "*Death without, death within* . . ." like an incantation, as if their bodies/minds have absorbed the deathliness of their culture. While attending international conferences, both women faint when they try to speak for (and as) their dead lovers. In contrast to Yvonne, however, the death of Marya's lover impels her to undertake the mother-quest, to explore the shadowy land of her personal past. Just as the novel ends, Marya is preparing to return to the land of childhood memories, seeking answers to the mystery of her maternal heritage, as Laney does in *Childwold*.

This pattern is a salient feature of most of Oates's novels of the 1980s. In *Marya, a Life*, for example, Marya at first denies her female body, identifying instead with the "male" mind; however, when she looks at a photograph of her mother at the end of the novel, her attention shifts radically to the mother-daughter relationship. At this point in the novel, if not earlier, it becomes evident that, though the novel is written in the third person, it can be read as a memoir in which Marya recalls her pride in a "masculine" ability to win and, in the winning, to damage others. Among Marya's confessions she includes a number of competitions in which her own "winning" injured others, almost all of them in academic settings: as an undergraduate scholarship student, a graduate student, and an untenured professor. However, Marya's fierce competitiveness must be understood in the context of her desperate struggle to survive in a world dominated by men. After her father's death, when abandoned by her impoverished mother, Marya grows up in the home of her paternal uncle, where she always feels like an outsider. Marya wards off feelings of vulnerability through her academic achievement. Nevertheless, after graduation from high school, when she walks away with most of the honors, Marya's defeated male competitors force her to identify as female, and to recall her status as the "flesh," by shearing off her long hair. "She remembers, afterward, one of them prying her legs apart—she remembers him prodding and jabbing at her—trying to enter her—trying to force his penis in her—but she might have squirmed free, arching her back, or one of the others hauled him away" (129).

Yes, women know violence, but more often from the position of loser, from the place of the vanquished. It is this place that Marya—along with many other female protagonists from this decade—is determined *not* to occupy. As an undergraduate, Marya concentrates fiercely on the struggle for high grades—if she wishes to stay in college, she must earn honors—

and she makes little effort to develop friendships with other women. Marya lives in isolation in an attic room at the top of an old house that she shares with other poor women on scholarships. Since they perceive other women only as competitors, the scholarship students do not break out of their isolation; instead, they resort to stealing from each other. In retrospect, Marya sees these thefts as symptomatic of a desire for friendships absent in the distrustful atmosphere of the academy. Marya's own competitive armor is so formidable that only one woman, Imogene Skillman, dares to enter Marya's attic room, her inner sanctum. Competition destroys the potential friendship between the two women, the upper-class Imogene and the working-class Marya. The sign of Marya's victory is her possession of a pair of earrings she has stolen from Imogene. Some years later, while a graduate student, Marya again emerges as the victor, her status partly the result of her sexual liaison with a much admired professor. Later still, Marya wins the competition for a tenure-line position, but her competitor, who is also the man who might marry her, punishes her by withdrawing his love.

As in other novels of the 1980s, a sporting activity functions as a code for those homosocial competitions in which Oates's female protagonists actively and often successfully participate. The novel's description of Marya's "friendly" bicycle ride with Gregory Hemstock dramatizes the fierceness of their competition for the same academic position. Marya, "an Amazon of a sort, a warrior woman," remains clear-sighted about her disadvantages in this competition, disadvantages of both gender and class. For example, although she agrees to a thirty-mile bicycle ride with Gregory, she can see her disadvantages from the start: Gregory owns a "handsome ten-speed English racing bike with smart blue reflectors that spun about, affixed to the spokes of the wheels; Marya's was a fairly shameful old thing—a mere three-speed with a worn seat, slightly rusted pedals, a frayed wicker basket into which she usually stuffed her books and papers" (252). Given Marya's obvious gender and class disadvantages, for which Gregory offers no allowances, it is not surprising that she ends up battered, suffering from lacerations and bruises incurred during a near-suicidal plunge down a steep hill. Surprisingly, however, Marya wins the tenure-line position— once again at a considerable loss, the loss of Gregory's affection. Perhaps because she fears such losses, Marya replaces Gregory with a married man, Eric Nichols, whom she mistakenly assumes she cannot "lose" since their love for one another is never openly acknowledged.

As in other novels of the 1980s, Marya's shadow[3] story—which will become the novel's mother/daughter plot—remains marginal while, for many years, she struggles for survival in the male-dominated professional world. Unfortunately, until midlife, Marya values only men, usually men old enough to be her father. These men become Marya's "lovers," each man seeing in her something lost or absent in his own life, as Marya sees in them the life of the mind. For Father Shearer, a dying Catholic priest, Marya represents the life of the body that he had formerly rejected; for Marya the priest represents the life of the mind from which women have been excluded. Later, for Maximilian Fein, a medieval scholar, Marya becomes a surrogate for a daughter who had died in childhood; once again, what Marya desires is the life of the mind that has usually excluded women. As Professor Fein's protégé, and as his mistress, Marya nevertheless loses something far more valuable than her academic prizes. During the drive to the hospital to see Professor Fein, who has suffered a cerebral hemorrhage, Marya feels in "Else Fein's sudden intimacy, even the pressure of her strong fingers," a yearning she hadn't understood (231). This maternal touch awakens in Marya a yearning for the mother she had lost in childhood. The older, wiser Marya, writer of this third-person autobiography, describes her ride with Elsa Fein in romantic diction: "The two of them making their way through the twilight of a winter morning, in a sleigh of some kind, or was it a boat, a little blue boat, pushing its way bravely forward" (231–32).

Marya, a Life also illustrates how matrophobia gives birth to sororophobia. As Helena Michie says, "Sororophobia . . . has much in common with, owes it very existence to, is even we might say a daughter of 'matrophobia'" (9). Oates does not sentimentalize relationships between mothers and daughters. For example, Marya finally experiences a crisis that forces her to undertake the quest for her lost mother: the death of her lover, Eric Nichols. Since Marya never marries Nichols (who is already married) their affair recreates Marya's painful outsider experience, the position she occupied while growing up in her uncle's household, along with their biological children. The death of Nichols forces Marya to recall the past, even as she acknowledges that her consciousness is embodied: that she was born of woman. As a child, after viewing her father's corpse, Marya recalls feeling terribly hungry: "Marya was so hungry her hand trembled holding the peanut stick; she felt a tiny trickle of saliva run down the side of her chin" (13). Yet for years she has repressed associations of death, food, and the maternal, as well as all desire for the maternal. Too much pain is associated with her yearnings to be mothered. After Marya's widowed mother had left her with her father's relatives, Marya had competed with her cousin, Alice, for her Aunt Wilma's attentions. However, on the "terrible Saturday morning" that Marya overhears her aunt tell a friend, "*She's not my kin, she's my husband's niece*" (21), she gives up the dream of being mothered. From this moment on, Marya's distrust and hatred of the mother—both Vera and Wilma had abandoned her—is disguised by a disdain for women.

Competition and envy among women are portrayed, not only in *Marya, a Life* but also in *A Bloodsmoor Romance, Mysteries of Winterthurn*, and *Solstice*. Although some feminists have criticized such portrayals of women, "why," as Michie asks, "should the concept of sisterliness not include, among other elements, competition and envy?" (9). According to Oates, her own "feelings toward Marya are sisterly, if at times ambivalent" ([*Woman*] *Writer* 376). She also says, "I don't believe that Marya represents me any more than do several other of my female characters of recent novels—Sheila Trask, for instance, of *Solstice*, or Deirdre of the Spirits of *A Bloodsmoor Romance*; or even the unregenerate murderess Perdita of *Mysteries of Winterthurn*" ([*Woman*] *Writer* 376). Each of these female protagonists—Sheila, Deirdre, and Perdita—is an artist, and each experiences conflicts with other women, conflicts as fierce, or fiercer, than those with men. As Showalter says, "Oates never idealizes the process by which Marya comes to the decision that at mid-life she must reclaim a matrilineal past. The community of women is not idyllic, but torn by rage, competition, primal jealousies, ambiguous desire, and emotional violence, just like the world in which women seem subordinate to and victimized by men" (*Ms.* 50).

Although these communities of women are not idyllic, they make it possible for Oates to re-vision the very nature of authority and author-ing. To re-vision fictional authority, as Susan Lanser and Rachel Blau Du Plessis have argued, women must transform heterosexual plots, as well as "conventions of narration that have kept women's voices separate and individualized" (Lanser 224). Oates redefines the very nature of community as well as the concept of narrative authority in many novels of the 1980s. As I shall demonstrate in chapter 7, each of the feminist narrators in Oates's postmodern novels speaks from a place of authority, an authority made possible by a feminist community. In addition, like Marya, each of these narrators rediscovers the value of her mother and sisters and, in the process, challenges the heterosexual romance plot. In chapter 8, I illustrate how Oates, while appearing to write realistic novels, actually challenges representational practices that perpetuate unjust social practices. Through the use of fluid point of view and recurring images, for example, Oates emphasizes the intimate relationship between familial and national politics. Finally, as I argue in chapter 9, in *Foxfire, Confessions of a Girl Gang*, Oates creates a narrator, an "I" that speaks for a "we," while at the same time acknowledging that no author speaks the truth for all times, places, or peoples.

Daughters of the American Revolution: "Idiosyncratic" Narrators in Three Postmodern Novels

Joyce Carol Oates has announced as the "on-going theme" of her postmodern quartet "the wrongs perpetrated against women . . . and the vicious class and race warfare that has constituted much of America's domestic history" ([*Woman*] *Writer* 374). Although these themes are central to all three postmodern novels completed during the 1980s—*Bellefleur, A Bloodsmoor Romance*, and *Mysteries of Winterthurn*—many feminist critics remain suspicious of any project defined as "postmodernist in conception." The reason is, as Teresa Ebert explains, that feminists view male postmodernists as "dismantling the notion of politics itself" (887). Oblivious to gender issues, male postmodernists have also announced the "Death of the Subject" just at the moment women have claimed the right to become subjects.[1] Such a death, claims Linda Hutcheonson in *The Politics of Postmodernism*, destroys agency, thereby rendering political action impossible. Hutcheonson maintains that "postmodernism manipulates, but does not transform signification; it disperses but does not (re)construct the structures of subjectivity. Feminisms must" (168). Nevertheless, Ebert believes that, if we make a distinction between "ludic" and "resistance" postmodernism, it is possible to "reunderstand it in more social and political terms" (886). This distinction is critical to an understanding of Oates's feminist politics in these postmodern novels.

Ebert bases her distinction between "ludic" and "resistance" postmodernism on a Bakhtinian theory of language "that views the relation between word and world, language and social reality or, in short, 'difference,' not as the result of textuality but as the effect of social struggles" (887). Resistance postmodernism, she explains, "draws its linguistic theory not from Saussure but from Bakhtin and Voloshinov, who argued that the 'sign becomes an arena of the class struggle' or, more generally, of social struggle" (887). "The question for feminism," Ebert says, "is how can it build a transformative politics on a postmodern difference that throws out certainty and destabilizes identity?" (892). Feminists are concerned that such a destabilizing of identity may hinder a feminist agenda, but as Oates's postmodern novels illustrate, it is possible to destabilize identity in the service of feminist goals. As feminist critics have frequently noted, women writers tend to perceive the self not as a coherent, well-bounded unity, but as a self-in-relationship, a subject-in-process, a subject whose agency is embedded in community. "Central to feminism," Bonnie Zimmerman argues in "Feminist Fiction and the Postmodern Challenge," "is the definition of a communal, not just individual, self: the connection of one woman to her mother or foremothers, her sisters, her historical or literary role models" (178).

Oates has long promoted a communal concept of the self. For example, in 1973 she argued in "The Myth of the Isolated Artist" that belief in a unified and autonomous self is "totally erroneous" and dangerous, for "as long as the myth of separate and competitive 'selves' endures," she explains, "we will have a society obsessed with adolescent ideas of being superior, of conquering, of destroying. The pronoun 'I' is as much a metaphor as 'schizophrenia' " (75). The illusion of an autonomous and unified self has resulted in a form of white, masculine agency that has tyrannically denied public agency to women of all races. Agentic and communal consciousness have been split off from each other in Western culture, according to psychologist David Bakan, with increasingly dangerous consequences for human survival. It should be noted that this split is gendered: women are expected to bear the burden of communal consciousness while at the same time they have been denied agency in the public realm. For this reason, feminist postmodernists, including Oates, are now engaged in writing beyond the ending of such a subject in order to formulate a new subject: a self-in-communal-relationship. According to Patricia Waugh, "Much women's writing can, in fact, be seen not as an attempt to define an isolated ego but to discover a collective concept of subjectivity which foregrounds the construction of identity *in relationship*" (10).[2] As Waugh says, " 'I' [is] also a 'you' in the eyes of others" (13).

However, since women's responsibility for kinship relationships—for the remnants of community—has resulted in oppression, Oates's postmodern, historical novels demonstrate that only by first claiming a public "I" can women begin to transform sociolinguistic norms. By claiming agency in the public sphere, women participate in reconstructing subjectivity, a transformation that may, in time, enable all women to develop both modes of consciousness, both agency and community. These novels make the point that one must first have a self, an "I," not in order to sacrifice it to the family but rather to transform the gothic family, and eventually the society, that reproduces sadomasochistic gender identities. In what is an explicitly feminist critical essay, Oates illustrates the lack of agency in the stereotypical nineteenth-century "feminine" role by citing the following passage from "A Woman's Thoughts about Women" (1857): "Dependence is in itself an easy and pleasant thing: dependence upon one we love perhaps the very sweetest thing in the world. To resign oneself totally and contentedly into the hand of another; to have no longer any need of asserting one's rights or one's personality . . . how delicious this all is."[3] Some twentieth-century readers of gothic romances may still feel that such a surrender of agency to their "Heathcliffs" is "delicious," but feminists certainly do not.[4]

Oates's postmodern novels parody the restrictive gender codes of such popular fiction as the family saga, the gothic romance, the detective and the horror story (in the forthcoming *A Crosswicks Horror*). Aware of how the privileging of "classical" fiction mirrors the privileging of male modes of consciousness, she disrupts the boundaries between popular and canonical fiction in order to expose the gender codes that both share. For example, the postmodern trilogy parodies gender stereotypes represented in both Hawthorne's canonical romances and Susan Warner's domestic romances. At the same time, Oates emphasizes that the value of domestic romances can be found not in their structure—which demands death or marriage for the heroine—but in "descriptions of female domestic life, including conversations between women (with no men present); descriptions of church activities, quilting bees, blackberry-picking excursions, passages of rigorous self-examination and prayer" ([*Woman*] *Writer* 192–93). As she says, these areas of experience are frequently absent—and devalued—in male-authored romances.

Oates has a problematic relationship to historical texts and fictional tradition, as do most male postmodernists, but her response to this inheritance is complicated by gender. For example, she shares the postmodern concern with exposing the codes of popular and classical tradition—a concern with representation, with the disruption of boundaries, and with subjectivity. However, she shares, primarily with other feminist postmodernists, a concern for women's historic sacrifice of public agency in the private maintenance of human relationships—the very dependencies denied by the construction of a so-called "autonomous" masculine subjectivity. As Zimmerman points out, feminist postmodernists often focus upon the gothic family because it is the family that produces sadomasochistic gender relationships—inequalities also reproduced in public institutions. At the same time, Oates does not assume that the irony of a twentieth-century feminist is necessarily superior to the faith of her nineteenth-century foremothers. She says, "My vision is postmodernist, and therefore predisposed to irony; as a woman, however, an inhabitant of the 1980s, I don't feel at all superior to these puzzling heroines of a bygone world. I simply feel different. Very different" (197). Oates's postmodern novels, all set at the end of the nineteenth century, record this difference just as it is about to disappear into the twentieth century.

In Oates's postmodern novels, the family is a site of both critique and transformation. Oates explains that she is striving "to 'see' the world in terms of heredity and family destiny and the vicissitudes of Time (for all four of the novels are secretly fables of the American family)" ([*Woman*] *Writer* 372–75). These are definitely comic fables, for all the daughters escape from the gothic enclosure of the family in order to pursue their own public quests. However, once a daughter has established an agentic identity, she tells her own story as *one narrative among many*, thereby acknowledging an "I"-in-relationship. In acts of narrative resistance, all three narrators reveal that their fathers have committed crimes, not only against the poor and other races, but also (secretly) against their wives and children. Hence, the very act of narration, the act of exposing these crimes, becomes a feminist strategy of resistance. By violating nineteenth-century literary and social codes, which prohibited women from speaking in public, each narrator acquires an identity, a singular and idiosyncratic "I." However, this "I" turns out to be a "positional I," a communal "I," shifting in its dialogue with a variety of voices within and beyond the family. Through this process of postmodern narration, the family is transformed. This transformation is especially evident in the family saga *Bellefleur*, which expands the definition of *family* to include, as do some native Americans, not only human beings but living creatures of all species.

The hermaphrodite Germaine Bellefleur tells her tale in such a way that readers become aware that she is related not only to her family but also to her readers. Germaine, a liminal creature, has an intersubjective identity that moves beyond categories of time and space, beyond genres and species. The narrators of Oates's next two postmodern novels, the spinster-psychic Deirdre in *A Bloodsmoor Romance* and the editor and ax-murderer Perdita in *Mysteries of Winterthurn*, are equally complex and intersubjective. For example, Deirdre begins as an orphan of unknown parentage, but she becomes a psychic who possesses the mysterious power of channeling voices; she is also, by implication, the novel's narrator. Just as remarkably, it is Perdita, the ax-murderer of her minister-husband, who becomes editor of her (second) detective-husband's most famous "cases" in *Mysteries of Winterthurn*. Yet these narrators cannot be defined merely as "personal"; instead, each challenges the concept of individualism. In fact, the identities of these narrators—whom Oates describes as "idiosyncratic but not distracting" ([*Woman*] *Writer* 372)—are posed as puzzles for readers to solve.

What makes these narrators "idiosyncratic"? It is not only that each narrator is unique—though certainly a hermaphrodite, a psychic, and an ax-murderer can be described as unique—but that each narrator's identity is presented as a mystery. Whose voice is this, we ask, who is narrating? Yet, ironically, once readers identify the supposedly anonymous narrators as characters in the novels, their authority is diminished. In contrast to an anonymous authorial narrator, a narrator godlike in his omniscience, the authority of the "I" narrator is always contingent on her position in the story. If, as Zimmerman says, "the task of feminist fiction is to create an authoritative voice, not to undermine an already existing one" (176), it is important to address the question of narrative authority posed by Oates's postmodern novels. How, specifically, is the authority of these idiosyncratic narrators constructed? The answer is, as I shall illustrate, that their authority comes from their membership in communities. The voices of "place"—communities called Bellefleur, Bloodsmoor, and Winterthurn—speak in these polyphonic novels, and "all the narrators," as Oates says of Joyce's *Ulysses*, "are aspects of this single voice."[5] At the same time, each multivocal narrator identifies herself as doubly parented, as heir to maternal as well as paternal stories. In Susan Lanser's terms, then, these narrators are "communal," for they speak as "either a collective voice or a collective of voices that share narrative authority" (21). My analysis of communal narration begins with *Bellefleur*.

"What happens when women come to power and identify with it?" Julia Kristeva asks in "Women's Time" (44). The women in *Bellefleur* may be taken as Oates's intergenerational response to this question. Leah Bellefleur represents what Kristeva describes as the first moment (or generation) of women's entry into history, an entry marked by an admiration for masculine values, a desire for revenge and mastery, and a rejection of traditional feminine or maternal values that conflict with the desire for public power. However, Leah begins her quest for revenge and mastery only after giving birth to a hermaphrodite child, Germaine, who signifies a second moment in women's time. According to Kristeva, this moment is defined by a rejection of a unitary image of self-identity and an emphasis upon female subjectivity. Germaine, who is born with male genitalia, shatters essentialist and unitary notions of identity. Even the child's name—the same as her eighteenth-century foremother's—emphasizes the fact that female subjectivities change over time. As Germaine develops into one of the novel's narrative voices, she comes to signify a third moment in women's time, a moment characterized by awareness of differences of class, race, or sexuality and by a criticism of the sacrificial violence engendered by such hierarchies.

At the same time, Germaine is a member of the wealthy Bellefleur family whose violent history is quintessentially American. Yet even the concept of "family" undergoes a transformation in this complex novel. Oates describes *Bellefleur* as a "family saga," but she has given notice that her project in the postmodern quartet is "a radical revisioning of the world and the craft of fiction" ([*Woman*] *Writer* 372–75). It is not surprising, then, that *Bellefleur* radically revises conventional definitions of family. For example, though the Bellefleur name refers to generations of fathers and sons, it is transformed—through poetic association with the "belles" of the family—into a name for generations of mothers and daughters whose voices have often been silenced and whose stories the novel tells. However, the novel's definition of "family" is even more radical, offering an ecofeminist re-visioning[6] of family that includes the voices of all forms of life: birds, plants, ponds, animals, all. The novel's complex narrative techniques point to the fact that many of the stories we tell about "family" actually obscure our kinship to other races, genders, and species. To make this point, rather than telling the story of a single family, Oates seams together a variety of "stories" in *Bellefleur* and, as always, subjects them to careful scrutiny. One of the novel's tropes for this quilting together of stories is Aunt Mathilda Bellefleur's "The Celestial Time Piece."

Beginning with the "Author's Note," Oates employs a variety of strategies in *Bellefleur* to critique an individualistic conception of the "author," especially the author who plays "god." At the same time, the novel demonstrates that it makes a difference who is narrating. *Bellefleur* answers Cheryl Wall's call for "a new concept of authorship that does not naively assert that the writer is an originating genius, creating aesthetic objectives outside of history, but does not diminish the importance of difference and agency in the responses of women writers to historical formations" ("Feminist Literary Criticism" 560). As Oates explains in the "Author's Note," she is not the "originating genius," for she obeys "imagination's laws" (n.p.), including, for example, the laws of genres.[7] In addition, through her allusions and in her critical essays, she pays tribute to many writers who have taught her the craft of fiction. For example, she reveals much about her own complex strategy in *Bellefleur* when, in a description of the "structural complexities" of *Wuthering Heights*, she says that "the novel's tales-within-tales are employed for artistic ends: the ostensible fracturing of time yields a rich poetic significance; characters grow and change like people we have come to know" ("Frankenstein's Fallen Angels" 549). *Bellefleur* achieves a similar "fracturing of time" and "yields a rich poetic significance" through its quilting together of multiple tales in a wide range of genres. Though the novel may be described as "epic" in scope, the epic concept of time, in which the future is predicated upon the past, does not prevail in *Bellefleur*; rather, the novel envisions an indeterminate future. A variety of discourses are quilted together in the novel, foregrounding the temporal and spatial dimensions of genres, or "chronotopes" as Bakhtin calls them.[8]

As in *Wuthering Heights*, the physical details of life are presented in an ambivalent space in *Bellefleur*, a space that should not be confused with "realism." The space in which *Bellefleur*'s characters grow and change, like the space in *Wuthering Heights*, is governed by the logic *of becoming*, in obedience, as Kristeva says, to the logic of "*analogy* and nonexclusive opposition, opposed to monological levels of causality and identifying determination." (*Desire in Language* 70–71). The novel is, therefore, dialogic, rather than monologic.[9] Metamorphosis governs the movement of characters from one genre to another, as well as their organic changes through time. For example, tragedy is transformed into comedy with the marriage of Germaine, sole survivor of the historic massacre of Bellefleurs in 1825, to Jedediah, brother to her dead husband. The novel parodies family sagas by transforming the genre's larger-than-life romantic characters into human beings of more ordinary proportions. For example, as Leah and Gideon age, they actually shrink, and as Germaine matures, those gigantic figures of childhood—parental figures that appear in myth, legend, fairy tale, romantic, gothic, and tragic fantasy—lose their hold upon her imagination. Moreover, as Germaine reads American history, with its stories of lynchings and massacres, she perceives the relationship of language, of the Symbolic, to social injustice and bloodshed. Beginning in 1744, with Jean-Pierre Bellefleur's acquisition of Indian lands and, in the present era, with Leah's attempt to reclaim these lands, the Bellefleur history is literally written upon the bodies of their victims: the bodies of Bellefleur wives and mistresses; the bodies of Bellefleur children, many of them maimed or sexually abused; and the bodies of the poor, including the native American, African, and Mexican races—all of whom are exploited by wealthy Bellefleurs.

However, even though the Bellefleurs would rule over the land and other people, they eventually become part of what they desire to control. Through metamorphoses, organic and linguistic, miraculous and ordinary, the shape-shifting Bellefleurs become part of the landscape. The "Author's Note" explains: "That the implausible is granted an authority and honored with a complexity usually reserved for realistic fiction: the author has intended." Unfortunately, not all of Oates's critics recognize the logic that governs *Bellefleur.* For example, in a review of *Bellefleur,* "The Strange Real World," John Gardner argues that Oates is attempting "to transmute the almost inherently goofy tradition of the gothic (ghosts, shape-shifters, vampires and all that) into serious art" (Bloom 9). Though Gardner describes Oates as "one of the great writers of our time," he believes that she is "essentially a realist," and so when she writes of "a man who is really a bear, vampires or mountain gnomes," she ceases to be persuasive. However, when characters shift visibly from one genre to another or from one life form into another, they are certainly not obeying realistic conventions. There is, for example, no attempt at realism when Raphael Bellefleur disappears into his beloved pond, having been transformed into a fish or, for that matter, when "Mink Pond" itself disappears, having been transformed into air (by organic process?) or, perhaps, having been transformed into a painting with that title by Winslow Homer.

Gardner also criticizes other violations of realistic conventions, such as the introduction of a minor character named "Rasche" without an explanation of her motives for accompanying Gideon on his suicidal mission. According to Gardner, "the end of a novel is a bad place to sacrifice convincingness for the sake of larger meaning" (101), but in fact the "Author's Note" announces that *Bellefleur* quite deliberately sacrifices "convincingness" to imagination's laws. Gardner criticizes the novel's unanswered questions, such as, "Why does Gideon give the dwarf Nightshade to his wife Leah?", failing to recognize that the refusal to answer all questions is a deliberate strategy—borrowed from Joyce's *Ulysses*. Oates reveals her indebtedness to *Ulysses* when she says, "We come away from the novel as we are likely to come away from life itself, with numerous teasing, maddening, unanswerable questions" (*Contraries* 187). As Perry Nodelman has noted, *Bellefleur* deliberately thwarts reader efforts at mastery by leaving unanswered such questions as "Whatever happened to Yolande after she left Bellefleur?" (Friedman and Fuchs 262). According to the logic governing *Bellefleur*, the hermaphrodite Germaine embodies, not Gardner's "goofy Gothic," but rather the language of metamorphosis, the logic of becoming, the desire for a future not predicated upon the past. The logic of metamorphosis governs nature—the transformation of matter—just as it governs the imagination.

The mind's myth-making propensities are evident, for example, in the linguistic joining of "Hermes" to "Aphrodite" in *herm-aphrodite*;[10] Germaine, as herm-aphrodite, obeys not the law of one but the law of the double. One of Germaine's hermeneutic functions is to make visible the language of one, to foreground the violence of a socio-symbolic contract that scars her body immediately after birth. When the doctor faints at the sight of Germaine's double genitalia, it is her grandmother Della who scars the infant's abdomen by removing the male genitalia: "with one, two, *three* skillful chops of the knife, [she] solved the problem, once and for all" (105). For years Della had been angry at the Bellefleur men, and now she announces, "triumphantly": " 'Now it's what it was meant to be, what God intended. Now it's one, not two; now it's a she and not a he. I've had enough of *he*, I don't want anything more to do with *he*, here's what I think—' and with a sudden majestic swipe of her arm she knocked the bloody mutilated parts, what remained of the little legs, and the little penis and testicles and scrotum, onto the floor— 'what I think of *he!*' " (106). Ironically, however, Della's preference for the female genitalia, a reversal of patriarchal hierarchies, remains obedient to the law of one, the monologic law of realism. Germaine, however, is not governed by the law of one; she is a trickster figure, a shape-shifter, whose true kinship is to other liminal figures in the novel—the spider "Love," the cat "Mahalaleel," or the dwarf "Nightshade." The law of these shape-shifters is the poetic law of the double rather than hierarchical law of one. Germaine's genesis is both poetic/organic genesis; s/he germinates in womb and words.

As hermaphroditic interpreter, Germaine is described as "heir to weighty volumes" that she will remember (as she herself ages) "with disturbing clarity, for though she had not been capable of understanding more than a few sentences here and there she had pored over these books at length, turning the stiff yellowed pages reverently, reading aloud in a shy, faltering whisper" (538–39). Germaine, then, is described as a reader of history and a most likely narrator (though not the only narrator) of the Bellefleur family history. The novel transforms romance—which is only one version of the family's history—into social satire by weaving together generations of Bellefleur wives who are described in floral terms and given floral names, such as Violet and Lily. We learn, for example, that on the very night of Germaine's birth, in a gothic chapter called "Nocturne," Gideon begins the first of many romantic infidelities with his conquest of Garnet, a poor relative and a servant in Bellefleur Manor. Garnet is a pale substitute for Leah, a "lush, plump, darkly red multifoliate rose, spoiled by years of careful nurturing in fertile, manure-rich soil"; by contrast, Garnet is a "straggly wild rose, one of those stunted anemic, but still pretty blossoms whose petals are, almost at once, blown; such wild roses are usually white, or pale pink, and their pistils are frail and powdery as a moth's wings; even their thorns are meekly dull beneath one's exploratory thumb" (102). Like his forefathers, including Jean-Pierre, Gideon takes revenge upon his wife—whose powers of reproduction remind him of his own mortality—through conquest of a succession of women, including a little girl. Action is Gideon's substitute for introspection, a way of arranging his life to avoid awareness of death, a flight from the responsibilities of fatherhood. And yet another chapter in the family history is written.

Nevertheless, *Bellefleur* illustrates an attitude toward time and change that "might even be called optimistic," as Oates says of *Wuthering Heights*. As alternatives to the apocalyptic visions of Gideon and some of his fore-fathers, we are offered visions of metamorphoses, visions of a future not predicated upon the past but flowering out of its bloodshed. One vision of the future is embodied in Germaine, who was named for her nineteenth-century foremother, the Germaine who escaped the bloody massacre at

Bushkill Ferry in 1825. Since Leah's daughter, Germaine, is only four
years old when the novel ends, a gap of many years (between the end of
the novel and its beginning) must be inferred to imagine Germaine as a
narrator of the Bellefleur history. A similar gap occurs in the narrative
of Germaine's foremother, Germaine O'Hagen Bellefleur, whose history
seems to end with her marriage to Louis Bellefleur. But both Germaines
are to become storytellers. Since they are women, however, their stories may
not be believed. Are women actually credible witnesses? The narratives of
both women, Germaine-past and Germaine-present, put language itself
on trial. As Germaine tells the story of her foremother's victimization, she
illustrates a heightened awareness of the violence engendered by hierarchies
of difference. Her narrative makes visible the sacrificial foundations of the
symbolic contract.

The narrator's satire of language is especially apparent in the trial that
follows the bloody massacre at Bushkill Ferry in 1825. The testimony of the
victim, Germaine Bellefleur, is discredited as she becomes a scapegoat for
a community that, in an effort to preserve its "innocence," projects its guilt
upon an innocent woman. In a chapter called "Revenge," the community
has its revenge upon the wealthy Bellefleurs by making Germaine, the
family's sole survivor, guilty of the crime. The defense attorney, in his
role as defender of community "morals," mocks Germaine's testimony in
order to win a verdict of "not guilty" for his clients. He appeals to the
jury's fear and hatred of others—other races, other beliefs, other voices—to
win the case. Although Germaine's assailants had disguised themselves by
dressing in women's apparel, she had recognized them by their voices—
voices familiar to her. "With a mocking hesitancy," the defense attorney
attacks her claim, making repeated racist allusions to "an *intimate* friend . . .
who had shared the Bellefleurs' household for years . . . ?" (500). "Might the
killings, the attorney asked, have had anything to do with the Onondagan
woman? With the fact that she was living common-law with Jean Pierre
Bellefleur . . ." (500).

In a satire of what is considered relevant—or germane—in a court of law,
the novel portrays the aggressive legal tactics used to discredit the testimony
of a woman: her supposed *lack* of business knowledge, her *lack* of objectivity
in "her deranged state," her *lack* of masculine logic. "Hysterical" women,
of course, make unreliable witnesses, a point the attorney makes again and
again: "*You ask us to take seriously, Mrs. Bellefleur, an accusation that by your
own account must be judged as frankly dubious . . .*" (500). Sexism and racism

are evident in the defense attorney's summing up: "In the other wing of the house Jean-Pierre Bellefleur and the Onondagan woman had been killed, quite some distance away; and in the parlor and kitchen the children. So she hadn't witnessed those murders" (501).

In this way, the community maintains its innocence, projecting upon whatever is "alien"—the Onondagan woman, the Negress behind the mirror—the shadow of "evil." This frozen binary ethic allows white men to maintain a society that sacrifices women, children, the poor, and ultimately even the planet. By contrast, in the fluid motion of dream images—in metamorphosis—the body recognizes its eventual dissolution, its partic-ipation in substance. This is the language of eros that, under the control of comic plots, ends in marriage, and under the control of tragic plots, ends in death. In *Bellefleur* such beginnings and endings undergo transformation. Germaine O'Hagan Bellefleur's life does not end with the tragic massacre at Bushkill Ferry; instead, she marries Jedediah. They continue the family, and Jedediah, we are told, dies at the age of 101. In the final chapter of *Bellefleur*, "Angel," Jedediah learns of the massacre from a young Indian, a friend of the family, who tells him, "You believe in nothing," and insists that he must marry Germaine (556). "You must return and marry her: you must continue the Bellefleur line: and you must exact revenge on your enemies" (556), he says. But Jedediah no longer believes in revenge. "Do you believe, then, at least," says the Indian messenger, "in *marriage?*—in *children?* In your Bellefleur blood?" (557). In the final sentence of the novel, Jedediah cries, "I don't know what to believe," but readers know that he did come down from Mont Blanc to marry Germaine.

Beginning in her opening chapter, "The Arrival of Mahalaleel," the novel parodies mythical (or cyclical) time reenacted in the conventional endings of realistic novels. Neither the beginnings nor the ends of various books of *Bellefleur* coincide with human desire. With the unpredictable arrival of Mahalaleel—whose coming awakens the large, sleeping family—the novel opens a space for their quarreling voices, relativizing "truth" and parodying the family "romance." The Bellefleur "family romance" is not a private affair, for it is constituted by a family of genres whose anthropocentric illusions constitute a denial of the non-coincidence of organic and linguistic beginnings. The experience of reading *Bellefleur* allows readers to become conscious of the desire to create a unity of its fragmented narratives; nevertheless, reader efforts to unify the quilted narratives may lead to the realization that no single time—and certainly no single voice—has dominion in the novel. Whatever theoretical unity one posits, the novel's plenitude of "meanings" always escapes such formulations. For example, the novel's opening sentence fragments the narrative of romance—the story of human desires—since the arrival of Mahalaleel does not coincide with Gideon and Leah's desire for a child.

The arrival of Mahalaleel is rendered in poetic language, as metamorphosis. The creature first appears outside the house when Gideon, from an upstairs window of the manor, sees what at first appears to be "a gigantic water spider," quickly transformed into "a large slovenly wisteria tree . . . buffeted by the wind so that it gave the appearance of moving toward the house" (8–9). Gideon wants the creature outside, but Leah desires to keep it inside, but neither of them will control Mahalaleel's freedom to move inside and outside the manor. Having named the creature, Leah assumes that she owns it, and thus "mastery"—in a kind of reversal of cultural norms that equate maleness with mastery—appears to shift to her.[11] In their oversized passions Leah and Gideon are like Catherine and Heathcliff in *Wuthering Heights*, whose egocentricity Oates describes as "the seductive and deathly centripetal forces we all carry within us" ("The Magnanimity of *Wuthering Heights*" 438). Yet the coming of a cat, a creature known for its indifference to human desires, violates romantic conventions, points to the adolescent egotism of Leah and Gideon who, in their struggle for dominion, compulsively reenact the history of their forefathers.[12] This novel prevents reader identification with Leah or Gideon by violating the conventions of romance. Not only do the swollen passions of the couple, who first appear in the "enormous" bed, become the passions of ordinary human beings, both Leah and Gideon also shrink and age rapidly. Once they have aged, the couple's romantic nostalgia suddenly appears unattractive, a childish denial of time that demonstrates a lack of concern for the future and for children.

The death of Leah and Gideon is not the tragedy of *Bellefleur*; the tragedy is, as Oates says of *Wuthering Heights*, "the passage of time itself" (440). A denial of biological time is apparent in Gideon's irresponsible romantic conquests and in Leah's attempt to restore Bellefleur Manor and its lands. The novel parodies romantic convention by describing the physical details of aging: Gideon becomes "Old Skin and Bones," and Leah notes with horror how her skin is wrinkling and her hair is thinning. Their efforts to stop time, to return to a once "glorious" past, lead to acts of violence, both private and public. The reader is prompted to ask why, during a period of only five years (of "novel" time) Gideon and Leah age so rapidly. One wonders how characters who appear, initially, as characters in a romance become "realistic" individuals who suddenly do things impossible within the constraints of the realistic novel. Almost simultaneously, then, questions of time and genre arise. Bakhtin's theory of chronotopes, which identifies genres in terms of their space-time coordinates, provides a method for analyzing this complex dimension of *Bellefleur*. The "Author's Note" suggests that "time twists and coils," a process that becomes apparent as characters move from one genre to another, their transformations calling attention to the spatial-temporal boundaries of various genres. In this way, dialogue occurs, not only between characters but between the genres in which they appear.

Examples of chronotopes,[13] foregrounded as characters move from one genre into another, include Jedediah's movement from epic time—"distanced, finished and closed like a circle"—by way of travesty (an attack of diarrhea) into a reality of " 'lower' order in comparison with the epic past" (*The Dialogic Imagination* 19). The transformation of tragedy—where confrontation with time occurs through violence, death—into comedy occurs by way of marriage when Germaine Bellefleur, sole survivor of the Massacre at Bushkill Ferry in 1825, marries Jedediah, brother of her dead husband Louis. Thus, despite a severed limb, the family tree continues. The transformation of romance into satire becomes visible when lyric poet Vernon Bellefleur, who had dedicated his "Lara" (lyric) poems to Leah, the unattainable and idealized object, is transformed into a social critic who is murdered by an angry mob. Later, Vernon is transformed into a text when a collection of his poems called "Query" are published by Anubis Press. The poems are again transformed when Vernon's father, Hiram, burns them. A more commonplace transformation of romance into gothic occurs when Garnet, Gideon's first "romantic" conquest, runs from the manor to attempt death by drowning, only to be rescued by a nobleman. In another satire of the gothic romance, Veronica, the victim of her lover Count Norst, lives on to become a plump, aging aunt who only appears to have no appetite. Romance becomes fable when Hepatica Bellefleur marries a lower-class laborer to find herself transformed into the wife of a bear who gives birth to a bear-cub. The transformation of Leah and Gideon's twins, who represent the gendered division of science and romance, occurs through rebellion: physicist Bromwell writes his "Hypothesis Concerning Anti-Matter," and Christabel refuses to remain an object of exchange in the service of her mother's dynastic project.

Like the movement of the eye required by the patchwork patterns in Aunt Mathilda's quilt, the chapters of *Bellefleur* require readers to move backward and forward, from one genre to another, to actively piece together the family's history. An occasional chapter, bringing together in a synchronic composition the historical obsessions of Bellefleur men with horses, planes, and cars, suggests that objects may change rapidly in historical time but that attitudes change very little. Because the novel does not unify its many narratives, readers become co-narrators, seaming together the many patches in the quilt. For example, although it is only one of many possible "endings," I prefer to imagine the novel ending with the chapter in which Germaine, safe at Aunt Mathilda's, helps to quilt "The Celestial Time Piece," which is still a work-in-progress. In ideal terms, quilting is a domestic art, a community activity that allowed women to share their feelings and their artistry. The process of quilting, in which something new is made of something old, also suggests a future made out of the past. Such a transformation of the old into the new affirms the hope of a future for Germaine. The child is celebrating her fourth birthday on the day that Gideon leaves her at Aunt Mathilda's, giving her his watch to compensate for his failure to take her on an airplane ride. Later, in a chapter called "The Broken Promise," she has her revenge on her father, angrily destroying the watch even though "she knew she would never see him again, and it would do no good to cry, to scream, to throw the watch down into the dust and stamp on it: she knew" (543). All the chapters in Book Five, "Revenge," might be considered variations on this theme: the desire to even the score with an old enemy, time.

Throughout the novel, Germaine's foreknowledge—she has, presumably, an "uncanny" ability to predict the future—signifies the writer's desire for mastery, the desire to control time, however temporary. In its epigraph from Heraclitus ("Time is a child playing a game of draughts; the kingship is in the hands of a child") the novel emphasizes that the desire for mastery is always, inevitably overcome by the passage of time. Book One, "Mahalaleel," explores the various kinds of games through which the Bellefleurs attempt to gain mastery, particularly the relationship of such desires to the child Leah is carrying. The novel also makes visible a process that has often been conspicuously invisible in fiction: the "canny" details of pregnancy. Remarking on the omission of the details of Catherine's pregnancy in *Wuthering Heights*, Oates suggested that perhaps there was "no vocabulary" for "so blatant a fact of physical life" (447). By contrast, *Bellefleur* provides a vocabulary for this "pregnant" point. The desire for transcendence or mastery takes root, *Bellefleur* suggests, where procreation and death remind us of our similarity to other substances. The placement of a chapter called "The Pregnancy" just before a chapter called "The Curse" is highly suggestive. Although some women call menstruation "the curse," menstrual blood makes the future possible. Germaine, for example, a child nourished in her mother's womb, her menstrual blood, survives a bloody battle between her parents in order to become narrator of her family's stories.

Yet Germaine's mother, who is increasingly alienated from her body and from Gideon, wants only mastery. The silent competition between Leah and Gideon, in which Germaine becomes a pawn, takes a variety of shadowy forms. In her struggle for mastery, Leah resists the Bellefleur men who attempt to define her not as a creature of intelligence but as "Other." For example, when Bromwell calculates how many times his pregnant mother wins at cards, he describes it as "uncanny" because it defies his scientific logic. Bromwell is as awed by Leah as the family's lyric poet, Vernon Bellefleur. When Vernon dedicates his "Lara" poems to Leah, she grows angry, frightening her worshiper. The attribution of "uncanny" abilities to Leah—whether by Bromwell or Vernon—seems to be motivated by their perception of her awesome reproductive power, and by a desire to contain this power through scientific or poetic mastery. Gideon too feels intimidated by Leah, whose body now seems "colossal" to him. He feels weak when she expresses sexual desire and when, during pregnancy, her body stretches "tight as a drum, *tighter* than a drum" (54). In a chapter called "The Uncanny Premonition Out of the Womb," Leah summons Gideon "as if she were royalty, and he one of her subjects," and he yearns for a return to the past when she had needed his love: "Now the woman was so wonderfully, so arrogantly pregnant, what need had she for him?—what need had she for a husband?" (78) Of course, they do not speak of such feelings; instead they quarrel. Because Gideon's paternity is invisible, he insists "brokenly," and only in silence, "I am the father. *I* am the father" (81). Paradoxically, it is their lover's quarrel that generates the contraries of the novel. In the chapter called "The Curse," family members quarrel, as usual, over what *it* might be. Hiram, a sleepwalker since childhood who carries a secret vial of poison, defines "it" as "just chance," for although he does believe in God, it is a god, "comically limited, and near worm out." Bromwell, who wants nothing to do with superstition, says it may be "genetic"; Gideon says it is the simple fact that "Bellefleur men die interesting deaths. They rarely die in bed." It was Jedediah, who died in bed at the age of 101, who said, *"The jaws devour, the jaws are devoured,"* his last words, according to family legend. It is Emmanuel, mapmaker and lover of Indian culture, who explains the curse in native American words: "Natauganaggonautaughaunnagaungawauggataunagauta —which meant . . . a space-in-which-you-paddle-to-your-side-and-I-pad-dle-to-mine-and-Death-paddles-between-us" (30–32). Earlier, however, Hiram had said, "you can embody a curse without being able to articulate it" (29). Members of the family speculate about this mystery, asking repeatedly what the curse upon their family might be. The novel suggests that "perhaps the curse had something to do with silence" (31). Discussion of the body is taboo, however, perhaps because "it" embodies the curse of mortality. Avoidance of the intimate details of sexuality, procreation, and death is, of course, symptomatic of a death-denying culture.

Also out of this desire for transcendence come fantasies of revenge against nature. Book Five, which is called "Revenge," suggests that the very notion of an "ending" may be a form of culture taking revenge against nature. For example, in one possible ending, the epic figure, Jedediah, has apocalyptic visions, a fantasy of revenge against nature. As Susan Griffin says, our culture has "a long tradition in which the separation of the body and mind and a bleak notion of an apocalyptic future have been mingled" ("Curves along the Road" 129). In this apocalyptic vision of the future, there is no place for children. To transform revenge into love and apocalypse into regeneration we must move down the mountain, as Jedediah does. Another possible ending, this one depicting the twentieth century, shows Gideon leaving Germaine at Aunt Mathilda's where she will be safe from his own apocalyptic fantasy of revenge against Leah. Gideon's final act will be to dive his plane into Bellefleur Manor,[14] killing all inhabitants. In this episode, Germaine is an actual child torn between her quarreling parents. For example, when Leah asks, " 'Suppose you had to choose, Germaine, between your father and your mother' " (488), Germaine refuses to answer, preferring to remain on both sides of the question, for, though a child, she is also an image of the double, of dialogic consciousness.

In "Women's Time" Kristeva remarks that the artistic productions of women have been "a reiteration of a more or less euphoric or depressed romanticism and always an explosion of an ego lacking narcissistic grati-fication" (43), but *Bellefleur* criticizes the depressed romanticism of Leah and Gideon, illustrating its destructive consequences: Gideon's sexual assaults on Little Goldie and Bellefleur Manor, and Leah's exploitation of her children and, indirectly, the slaughter of migrant workers. Despite their efforts, neither Leah nor Gideon is "master," neither is author, of Bellefleur. Who, then, is the "author" of *Bellefleur*/Bellefleur? The answer is that "we" are, though we are all subject to "imagination's laws." If we imagine Germaine as the novel's narrator, she is "our" creation. She cannot exist without a community of readers, just as she cannot exist without family and community. As readers, we become co-narrators, shifting from one genre to another. This reading activity demonstrates the relativity of time—and space: on the top of Mont Blanc, the epic; near Lake Noir, the romance; in the woods, the fable; and inside Bellefleur Manor, the gothic. Through its dialogue with these many genres, *Bellefleur* makes visible the spatial-temporal dimension of language. As Bakhtin says, the novel speculates in time; Germaine is an image of such writerly/readerly speculations: she represents the unpredictable future, the time of becoming.

Joyce Carol Oates creates an equally "idiosyncratic" narrative voice in *A Bloodsmoor Romance*. The novel opens in a voice, Diane Johnson says, "from which it will be seen that we are in the hands of a garrulous narrator possessed of a 19th-century style, complete with sententious sayings, extra commas and italics and with no compunction about leaping ahead of her story" (15). This narrator also has no compunctions about interrupting her chronicle in order to "limn" (6), or paint at great length, the diverse personages in her romance. Although an abduction takes place in the novel's opening sentence, the narrator does not return to this mysterious event for seventy-five pages, not until after introducing Miss Deirdre Louisa Zinn and each of her four sisters, as well as her adoptive parents and Kiddemaster relatives. Even at the end of the novel twenty years later the narrator does not reveal the outcome of this abduction, nor does she reveal her own identity. The narrator's strategy of narrative "interruptus" raises a number of questions. For example, why, since a conventional romance novel usually has only one heroine, does this novel have five? And why are we never told who pilots Deirdre away in the hot air balloon? According to romantic convention, an abduction—whether by horse, carriage, or balloon—is a male-initiated action to which a female often submits, but the novel does not confirm this gender-based assumption. Most important, why does the narrator choose anonymity, leaving readers to puzzle out her identity?

Much of the controversy over *A Bloodsmoor Romance*, a novel that Elaine Showalter calls "a feminist romance,"[15] centers on the puzzle of narrative voice. Female critics generally praise the narrator's "feminine" voice, whereas most male critics consistently criticize it. Since gender politics shape the debate over the narrative "voice" of *A Bloodsmoor Romance*, one wonders what difference it would have made if the author of this romance novel were a man, not a woman. Inevitably, this concern over authorial identity returns us to Michel Foucault's familiar question, "What does it matter who is speaking?" Foucault answers that the authorial presence has disappeared, that the author is effaced, that the personal author is absent, having written him- or herself out of the text. What remains is not the subjective presence of an author but, according to Foucault, "the author function," or signature. Yet reports of the author's death may have been "greatly exaggerated," for few critics of *A Bloodsmoor Romance*, whether feminist or misogynist, have heeded the news. Only Eileen Teper Bender, who describes the narrator—the author's persona—as "appropriately anonymous" (*Joyce Carol Oates* 132) may have in mind Foucault's impersonal "author"; however, Teper Bender doesn't explain why anonymity is appropriate. Does she mean that, in the wake of poststructuralism, such authorial anonymity is appropriate, or does she mean that anonymity is appropriate for a nineteenth-century "feminine" narrator, who would have wished to avoid public exposure? She might also mean that the narrator's anonymity is appropriate because women's voices historically have been excluded from the canon of American literature.

By making narrative voice a puzzle for readers to solve, *A Bloodsmoor Romance* resists such erasure of women's voices and texts, even as it prompts critics to examine the relationship of gender to the problem of narrative authority. The novel opens in what may at first seem to be the voice of an authorial narrator (Lanser's term)—that is, a narrator who exists on a plane above the characters and who, while commenting upon their actions, speaks directly to the public. However, the illusion of gender-neutrality so necessary for an authorial narrator is swiftly destroyed when, in the novel's second sentence, the narrator uses nineteenth-century "feminine" language: "Well may you blink and draw back in alarm at that crude word *abducted*: and yet, I fear, there is no other, to be employed with any honesty" (3). The loss of the gender-neutral voice characteristic of the "authorial" narrator immediately raises questions about the identity of the narrator; by remaining anonymous, however, she does retain some of the authority accorded an authorial narrator. Some of this power comes from the fact that her anonymity invites readers to conflate her voice with the author's.[16]

In fact, a number of critics have come close to identifying "Joyce Carol Oates" as the narrative voice of *A Bloodsmoor Romance*. Johnson says, for example, "This narrator is not, of course, to be confused with the author; yet so successful is the characterization, it is tempting to believe that, Victorian postures and archaic diction apart, the voice is really the voice of Joyce Carol Oates" (16); while Showalter says, "A woman medium, 'Deirdre of the Shadows,' possessed by voices from the spirit world which she must translate, is Oates's representation of her own creative process" ("My Friend, Joyce Carol Oates" 46). James Wolcott also suggests that "Deirdre seems to be the author's stand-in, not only because she's such a pale wisp of injured feelings—a classic spurned duckling—but because she turns out to be a seeress, a psychic whose head is full of unruly voices. (Oates, as we shall see, often describes the creative process as an invasion of voices)" (68). Wolcott mocks such a conception of authorial consciousness, while Denis Donoghue concludes, "It is not clear from Oates's account of it what she means by voice." He speculates that she "might mean a writer's achieved style," or she might consider voice "the only form of existence, in which she is willing to have her essence manifested"; but he concludes, "If that is what she means, why is she willing to lend her voice to . . . anyone who happens to come along?" (16).[17]

Oates's concept of authorial voice, which represents a radical departure from romantic notions of a writer's "achieved style" or "essence," must be analyzed not according to a romantic aesthetic but according to what Mikhail Bakhtin calls a "sociological poetics" (Medvedev and Bakhtin 30). Lanser's argument—that questions of narrative voice must be understood in political as well as aesthetic terms—is abundantly evident in the highly charged critical responses to the narrative "voice" of *A Bloodsmoor Romance*. The most negative male critic, James Wolcott, describes the narrator as "a flustered old biddy" whose "coyness [is] not to be endured" (68) while Denis Donoghue complains that her "many ofts, nays, and alases" impede the narrative. "Even as a joke," he says, "it's very long" ("Wonder Woman" 16). Anatole Broyard praises the novel, but he too grows impatient with the narrator's voice: "One forgets now and again," he says, "that this is a parody and fidgets a bit as the voice of the narrator goes on fussing and adjusting her stays, so to speak" (15G). By contrast, Diane Johnson describes the narrator as "female, clever, facetious and mischievous" (16) while Elaine Showalter says that, although the narrator "pretends to be timid, incompetent, and conventionally feminine, she is in fact resourceful, eloquent, and brilliant" (*"The Dead* and Feminist Criticism" 19). Apparently, because women readers enjoy what Broyard calls the novel's "in-joke," they praise the narrator. By contrast, because men see themselves as targets of many of the narrator's jokes, they criticize her. Wolcott is particularly outraged when Mark Twain becomes the butt of a joke. "What is truly disagreeable," he says, "is Oates's shameless zeal—her willingness to do anything to tart up her book, even turn a writer as great as Twain into a pornographic buffoon" (69).

In short, critical response to *A Bloodsmoor Romance* illustrates Lanser's point that "discursive authority . . . the intellectual credibility, ideological validity, and aesthetic value claimed by or conferred upon a work, author, narrator, character, or textual practice—is produced interactively; it must therefore be characterized with respect to specific receiving communities" (6). Lanser's argument, that a narrator's interaction with specific receiving communities is gendered, is well illustrated by the critical reception of this novel: feminists generally praise the narrator's voice, while most male critics criticize it; however, even though critical response to the novel appears to divide sharply along gender lines, it is more accurate to argue that response is determined by a critic's gender politics. Yet the issue of narrative voice, already complicated by the issue of interaction with receiving communities, turns out to be even more complicated. As Showalter points out, this storyteller "pretends to be timid, incompetent, and conventionally feminine but . . . is in fact resourceful, eloquent, and brilliant" (*"The Dead* and Feminist Criticism" 19). In other words, not only has a woman author created the voice of a nineteenth-century "feminine"[18] narrator, she has also demonstrated, through her parody of that voice, her "masculine" resourcefulness, eloquence, and brilliance. To "parody" a voice is to double (echo) it; hence the voice cannot be described as singular. Furthermore, if irony is defined as an attribute of "male" speech, the narrator's identity is, in fact, doubly gendered.

However, critics have yet to analyze the novel's challenge to the romantic concept of a unique or individual narrative voice. Undoubtedly that is because, as Lanser points out, both authorial (omniscient) and personal (first-person) narrators "are invested in singularity—in the presupposition that narration is individual" (21). Communal narration "has not even been named in contemporary narratology" (21), according to Lanser, both because it works against the notion of individualism encoded in the novel's generic features, and because it has more often been a phenomenon of marginalized groups. However, despite this history of the "individualization of narrative," at least since the eighteenth century women writers have, Lanser illustrates, attempted to create communal narrators—that is, "either a collective voice or a collective of voices that share narrative authority" (21).[19] Such efforts to create communal narrators are also evident in contemporary feminist postmodern fiction, according to Lanser and Zimmerman. Oates participates in this feminist effort by creating a multivocal concept of narration in *A Bloodsmoor Romance*, as in other novels in the quartet, which challenges the individuality of both authorial and personal narrators.

But if Oates means to challenge the gendered conventions of narrative authority, why does she preserve her narrator's anonymity? Oates is certainly not original in her use of an anonymous authorial narrator. According to Lanser, many women writers—George Eliot being the most prominent example—have employed anonymous authorial narrators in order to create the illusion of godlike authority, even though it has required the wearing of a presumably "gender-neutral mask" (19). As Lanser points out, the status of authorial narrators derives from the illusion that they speak from "a separate ontological plane from the characters" (16), that they have the capacity for "reflections, judgments, and generalizations about the world 'beyond' the fiction" (17), and that they speak to a public audience. Since historically women have not had the right to public voices, it has been assumed—despite their presumed gender-neutrality—that authorial narrators are male.

As in George Eliot's *Middlemarch*, the anonymous narrator of *A Bloodsmoor Romance* retains the impersonal status of an authorial narrator but, in contrast to Eliot, Oates has marked her narrator's diction as "feminine," deliberately violating the assumption that an unmarked public voice is masculine. The narrator's feminine discourse suggests that she may in fact be one of the Zinn sisters. But once Deirdre's voice is identified as piloting the novel, she must immediately be redefined as a personal narrator, because—unlike an authorial narrator—she also participates in the action. Unfortunately, such a solution to the mystery of narrative voice results in a loss of narrative authority because, as Lanser points out, the authority of a personal narrator is always contingent. "Paradoxically," as she says, "authorial narrative is understood as fictive yet its voice is accorded a superior reliability, while personal narrative may pass for autobiography but the authority of its voice is always qualified" (20). However, since the power of authorial narration can be acquired, as Lanser says, only "by separating the narrating 'I' from the female body" (18), the use of a personal narrator has one clear advantage: it enables a (woman) writer to reunite the narrating "I" with the female body. *Jane Eyre* is probably the best known example of such a feminist claim to narrative voice.

Readers are sure to recognize Brontë's orphan-narrator, Jane, as a predecessor to Deirdre, the orphan-narrator of *A Bloodsmoor Romance*. However, as Lanser points out, *Jane Eyre* has left a troubling legacy, for such an emphasis upon the singularity of one's own voice, above all others, may also mean that the narrator's "energies are necessarily bent upon keeping others—perhaps especially her 'dear Reader'—from creating versions of her that might entrap her or threaten her representation of herself" (185). Initially, Deirdre appears to exercise her powers primarily for this purpose. She keeps readers preoccupied with her identity while also eluding reader representations of her, not only by cloaking herself in a veil of anonymity but also by making direct appeals for the reader's sympathy. For example, without revealing her identity, Deirdre says: "The reader is free to infer, with no demurral from me" (6); "O Reader, you may well imagine, and pity, the ensuing sleepless night" (96); "Consider, O Reader, how far—how tragically far" (482). However, an even more troubling legacy of *Jane Eyre* is that the protagonist claims her "I" at the expense of an imagined rival, her famous double, Bertha Mason, the mad woman in the attic. Like Jane Eyre before her, Deirdre also attempts to claim an imperial "I" at the expense of imagined rivals—rivals such as her sisters, as well as the spiritualist Madame Blavatsky and the scientists who dare to doubt her power over voices from the spirit world.

However, just as the narrative voice of *A Bloodsmoor Romance* is, in fact, a parody of feminine language, Deirdre turns out to be a parody of the author-narrator of *Jane Eyre*. For eventually, unlike the triumphant Jane, Deirdre learns the limits of the imperial "I." Initially, however, as both a female protagonist and a narrator, Deirdre demonstrates her superior capacity to manipulate voices from the spirit world. For example, she triumphs over her mentor and rival, Madame Blavatsky, when she agrees—as Blavatsky herself never agreed[20]—to appear before the Society for Psychical Research. In this test of her powers, the psychic easily overcomes her masculine inquisitors, eminent men of science who have dared to trivialize her sensitivity to the spirit world. Although warned by Blavatsky that "the infamous Society for Psychical Research, the onetime English Phasmatalogorical Society, had not Deirdre's welfare in mind, nor even the welfare of her future clients, but wanted to persecute; to hound; to pillory, to *crucify"* (297), Deirdre nevertheless agrees to the examination. " 'Remember,' Blavatsky warns, 'that this is the country, these are the people, who burnt witches not so very long ago, and who harbor a fierce hatred for those of us who would bring them salvation—those of us, I cannot but observe, who are of the female gender" (298). Despite Blavatsky's warnings, Deirdre risks her reputation to prove *her* superior powers, and to assert her Imperial Ego. In a comic scene in Part VI, "Ivory-Black; or, The Spirit World," Deirdre defeats the all-male Society. Ironically, however, this test of Deirdre's psychic powers leads to a decline in public interest in spiritualism for, after her famous triumph, it was thought that *"one must never tempt the spirits to 'prove' themselves"*; therefore, mediums no longer received as many requests for seances, and "were not being paid" (469). Consequently, though Deirdre is described by her clients as "ordained by God Himself to help bring about a revolution in human awareness, as to the fluidity of the barrier betwixt the two worlds!" (468), she is forced to earn a living in Europe.

Later, like Jane Eyre, Deirdre faces an even greater temptation: the temptation of a marriage that would, in the nineteenth century, usually result in the loss of her public voice and her autonomy. Such a temptation occurs for the first time when Deirdre meets with the new president of the Society, a Dr. Stoughton, who tries to persuade her to abandon her career as a medium, "for it is not suited for any young lady" (470). However, Dr. Stoughton proposes marriage in language so veiled—" 'It would be contrary to my own interests, as to the Society's, to suggest that you put all this behind you, and retire to another mode of life altogether' " (471)— that the wily Deirdre can easily pretend not to understand his intentions. She evades Stoughton's proposal by explaining that she has been " '*chosen* from birth' " for her public work as a medium; she is sorry that he finds her public life " 'so very disagreeable' " (471).[21] Smitten with Deirdre's visible self, Stoughton replies that he finds her " 'hardly disagreeable, in any of your selves,' " a statement referring, it would seem, to the various spirits, or voices—Bianca, Mrs. Dodd, the Raging Captain—who do her bidding. The "unmistakable irony" in Deirdre's voice, when she asks Stoughton if he would like to share his "sacred mission" with her, forces him to acknowledge that he has asked her to give up her sacred mission, though he would himself be unwilling to relinquish his scientific work. He argues that her public career is "accidental" to her "essence" and might one day exhaust her:

" 'Answering always to the demands of others, whether deceased spirits, or living clients,' he warns, 'may drain away your life's blood' " (474). But since his proffered alternative to public life is marriage—" 'the sacred duties of beloved wife, helpmeet and mother' " that would only drain away her life's blood in his service—she replies, in heavily ironic tones, that she prefers "intercourse with the Spirits" (475). So much for romance, at least with the living!

A Bloodsmoor Romance scrutinizes the theme of the orphan girl, a theme common in nineteenth-century domestic romances such as *The Wide, Wide World.* "It is the story," according to Nina Baym, "of a young girl who is deprived of the supports she had rightly or wrongly depended on to sustain her throughout life and is faced with the necessity of winning her own way in the world" (11). According to Madonne Miner, this theme is still common in twentieth-century domestic romances (187–211).[22] Some readers may, then, identify with a suicidally depressed Deirdre, who, having been hired by the wealthy Fairbanks to rid the estate of a ghost, finally meets her own double, the victimized orphan-child she thought she had left behind. Because Deirdre arrives at the Fairbanks estate in Fishkill, New York, feeling exhausted and isolated by fame, her heart bitter from perceived insults from her sisters, she comes to regard the ghost, Florette, as a "sister" in spirit. For like Deirdre, she had found it painful to live as a "Cinderella" in a wealthy family. Florette had become a ghost when, following her seduction and abandonment by a Fairbanks son, she had drowned herself in a pond on the estate. The narrator tells us, in ironic tones, of her "repugnance for so extreme a sinner, and for so shameless a liar (it being quite questionable that a scion of the great Fairbanks family should behave in an ungentlemanly fashion, or even consort with a female of the servant class in this wise)" (494).

In a feminist twist upon a favorite gothic theme of Hawthorne's, and with a reference to "the woodlandish ghouls" of Poe, the narrator depicts Deirdre's triumphant removal of Florette to the realm of the spirits. Primarily because of her strong identification with Florette, Deirdre grows exhausted during the ordeal of listening patiently to the ghost. Florette makes "a gesture of spontaneous sisterly affection—extending her arms toward Deirdre, across the pond—and Deirdre responded at once, with no prudent hesitation"; it was at this moment that "Florette managed to snatch off Deirdre's little golden Locket" (498–99), the very locket containing images presumed to be those of her long-dead parents. Although Deirdre had hoped to transcend her lowly origins (like any heroine of a romance) through her genius, not marriage (unlike most heroines of romances), she remains haunted by the voices of those she has left behind. Thus, another supposed triumph turns into a sharp satire of the female "imperial ego"— an ego fueled by memories of victimization. After Deirdre's near-death experience with her orphan sister, her thoughts return to the insults (real and imagined) she has suffered from her adoptive sisters, especially their cruel reminders that she was not a "blood" sister but only adopted and certainly not "high born."

A Bloodsmoor Romance satirizes the competition among daughters who, as a result of their conditioning within patriarchal families, have difficulty establishing trusting relationships with other women. In the novel's opening scene, for example, as they sit together in their Grandfather Kiddemaster's gazebo, a major source of conflict among the sisters is their competition for the father's love. Each sister imagines herself John Quincy's "favorite," and each imagines herself as the "star" in the family constellation. This striving for privilege, which is especially pronounced in Deirdre and Malvinia, does not win the father's love; John Quincy turns out to be indifferent to almost everything except his latest invention. But it does lead to hostilities among the Zinn sisters, a psycho-political reality that the narrator brilliantly "limns" as the "little women" sit decorously in the gazebo. From a distance the sisters appear to be lovely young women, conventional in dress and behavior, but in their hearts they harbor "outlaw" desires and antagonisms. These unstated hostilities, represented in the text by italics, jar the reader, as if Louisa May Alcott's diary entries, which reveal feelings of jealousy toward her sisters, had been inserted into the "sentimental" narrative of *Little Women.* In prose echoing Alcott's diary, the narrator recalls her feelings at the age of sixteen: *"O Father I dreamt that my sisters stood over my bed as I slept and though I was asleep I saw them clearly and heard their cruel whisperings and gigglings O"* (18).[23]

Like the orphan Jane, Deirdre is reunited with her sisters when the terms of an inheritance—in this case, Aunt Edwina's will—disclose the biological nature of their sisterhood: Deirdre, we learn, is related to the Zinns by "blood," not merely by adoption. With another feminist twist, Deirdre's inheritance comes, not from an uncle, as in *Jane Eyre,* but from an aunt, as in *Little Women.* The reading of Aunt Edwina's will in a comic scene near the close of the novel actually dramatizes a serious message: the indebtedness of twentieth-century readers and writers to their nineteenth-century foremothers. The will discloses that Aunt Edwina Kiddemaster, an "authoress" of conduct books who is presumed to be a "spinster," was actually Deirdre's biological mother. Blessed with this inheritance, Deirdre chooses, like Jane Eyre before her, not to hoard her wealth, but to share it—and, by analogy, her literary talent—by distributing it among members of her family, with the "radical" stipulation that each parent count as *one* person. As Edwina's daughter, of course, Deirdre is heir to her aunt's entire estate; she is also, by analogy, heir to her aunt's writing ability. Because, like Blavatsky, Deirdre has considerable skill in channeling voices, it is reasonable to assume that she acts as the narrator, or chronicler, of her story as well as the stories of her sisters. However, this analogy of a literary inheritance—shared among sisters—is not, by itself, enough to redefine Deirdre as a communal narrator.

As Lanser argues, such a narrator must have a definable community for which she speaks: "Because the structures of plot and narration in the Western novel are individualist and androcentric, the articulation of a communal female voice is not simply a question of discourse but almost always one of story and world" (22). The problem of story, or plot, is solved by depicting the lives of all the Zinn sisters as well as their mother, each of whom manages to transgress the romance plot. In other words, although Donoghue has declared that "the chief quality of Oates's imagination is obedience, and what it obeys is not nature or circumstance but other fiction" ("Wonder Woman" 12), the author's "outlaw" imagination is abundantly evident in these stories of a mother and five disobedient daughters. Each story overturns the traditional romance plot in a different, often hilarious, manner. The novel accomplishes its feminist transformations, the fulfill-ment of female desires, by exploiting a potentially radical feature of the romance novel: its habit of privileging the fluid subject of dreams over the more static, social defined subject of realism. As each sister pursues her own desires rather than submitting to social convention, feminist "romances" occur: Constance Philippa becomes Philippe Fox, who returns from travels in the West to rescue his childhood sweetheart from an attic; Malvinia becomes a famous stage actress with many lovers; Samantha becomes a scientist; Octavia, the most traditional of the sisters, becomes a marriageable widow; and, as stated above, Deirdre becomes a spiritualist whose abilities rival the great Blavatsky's. Finally, in the most radical transgressions of the traditional romance, the figure of the mother becomes a subject in her own right: Prudence Kiddemaster Zinn joins the suffrage movement.[24]

And, just as the novel has overturned the sex/gender system that might have prevented the elopement of Delphine Martineau Ormond and Philippe Fox, it overturns the financial system that forces women into marriages for the sole purpose of economic survival. It is Aunt Edwina Kiddemaster's wealth, which her daughter Deirdre generously shares with the Zinn family, that finally brings about a reunion of Zinn women and gives them the economic freedom to pursue romances with a decidedly feminist slant. Like Jane Eyre before her, Deirdre's wishes are granted: her wish to be part of a family *and* her wish for economic freedom. At the same time, the novel's many endings also satisfy fantasies of romantic union: Philippe Fox rescues his beloved Delphine, Malvinia marries her childhood sweetheart Malcolm Kennicott, Octavia marries Sean McInnes (now a lawyer, though once deemed an unsuitable match) and, as we know, the already happily married Samantha is freed from poverty and able to continue her scientific work. Even Mrs. Zinn, who finally recognizes that good things do not necessarily come to ladies who wait, joins the suffragists to campaign for the vote.

As Showalter has argued, these multiple endings illustrate a movement beyond the isolated heroines of Oates's earlier fiction. This point is particularly evident in Deirdre's belated recognition of her identity not as an isolated and romantic outlaw but as part of a family and a community (as readers learn, she, too, has a widow's peak). This community is, however, far from idyllic; in fact, the novel opens with a scene in which the Zinn sisters come close to openly stating their antagonisms, despite rules of maidenly propriety. Of course, this conflict is the reason that sixteen-year-old Deirdre leaves the gazebo on that fateful autumn day in 1879, not to return until twenty years later. Constance Philippa and Malvinia soon follow Deirdre's example, escaping from the octagon house[25] of their childhood to the "wide, wide world" of public life. In this respect, the novel rewrites Susan Warner's domestic romance, *The Wide, Wide World*, which concludes with a single heroine's submission to a husband within an enclosed domestic space. Unlike Warner's Ellen Montgomery, Oates's heroines are reunited with their mothers at the close of the novel. This reunion is especially true in the case of Deirdre, an "orphan" daughter who, after years of yearning for the love of her mother, is transformed into an assertive narrator. Furthermore, it is knowledge of a biological and literary mother that frees her from temptations of victimization[26]—the habits of self-punishment and surrender to romantic love. In time, all the Zinn sisters realize their dreams for both love and work, both private and public lives, as well as their desire for both spiritual and material riches.

Through the granting of such feminist desires in *A Bloodsmoor Romance*, Oates illustrates her participation in what Rachel Blau Du Plessis describes in *Writing Beyond the Ending* as a "project shared by twentieth-century women writers" who wish "to solve the contradictions between love and quest and to replace the alternate endings in marriage and death that is their cultural legacy from nineteenth-century life and letters by offering a differ-ent set of choices" (4). By "writing beyond the ending" of the romance plot not once but five times the novel creates a different set of choices for each Zinn sister as well as for each Zinn parent. As Showalter says, *A Bloodsmoor Romance* closes "in a triumphant note of feminist vision" (*"The Dead* and Feminist Criticism"* 19). At the close of the novel, which coincides with the close of the nineteenth century, only Deirdre's romantic "fate" is unknown: will she marry? and which of her two suitors will she choose? Although the narrator reports that it is the Indian suitor, Hassan Agha, that Deirdre chooses—"*this* is the suitor Deirdre could not bring herself to reject, tho' her heart, I am certain, resided with the Christian Dr. Stoughton" (581)—a few pages later we learn that Deirdre remains undecided. In a voice heavy with irony, the narrator tells us that while entering her father's workshop to erase her father's formula for destroying the world, "Deirdre was beleaguered, even at this crucial moment, by recollections of Dr. Stoughton's earnest continence, and Hassan Agha's smold'ring black eyes" (613). Such distrac-tion does not seem likely; this time, however, the ironic narrator chooses not to "o'rleap" strict chronology, instead revealing only what takes place as the nineteenth century turns—just beyond the last page of the novel, which ends at the stroke of midnight in 1899—into the twentieth.

The novel provides numerous clues, such as this ironic moment, that suggest that Deirdre chooses, metaphorically, to "marry" science and ro-mance by way of her spinster pen rather than marrying either of the men who propose to her. Of course, it may well be that, like Jane Eyre before her, she chooses both. And why not? In contrast to her mother, Deirdre's writing/narrating is motivated neither by unhappiness[27] nor by a desire to hide family secrets behind the rules of sociolinguistic convention. Deirdre uses her powers, not in the service of her father's will but to disobey him. Moreover, once the family's wealth shifts from Grandfather Kiddemaster to Aunt Edwina, power relationships in the family are radically altered. In addition, once Deirdre's desire for maternal nourishment is satisfied, the nightmarish structure of familial oppression—a staple of the gothic romance—is transformed into a feminist comedy. Despite their will-to-power, none of the Kidde- "masters" survives into the twentieth century. Finally, then, the central "voice" in *A Bloodsmoor Romance* is the community's rather than the voice of a single individual's—not even Deirdre's, whose voice appears to pilot the narrative.

But does Deirdre's voice pilot the narrative? If so, Deirdre must be defined as a communal narrator of the "singular" type. Politically, of course, it is problematic for a single narrator to speak for a plurality; however, if Deirdre is recognized, like Blavatsky, as a medium or a "channel" for many voices, she cannot be described as speaking in a single voice.[28] The mysterious nature of this plurality is, in fact, introduced in the Dickinson poem prefacing the novel, in which "twain" is transformed into a multitude when six damsels appear like blossoms on a tree. Undoubtedly, Oates had this Dickinson poem in mind when writing Part I of *A Bloodsmoor Romance*. The title of Part I, "The Outlaw Balloon," actually alludes to another of Dickinson's poems, #505. The analogy in this poem, between time travel[29] and the mysteries of artistic collaboration, is recreated in Part I of *A Bloodsmoor Romance*, which opens with Deirdre's "abduction" in a hot air balloon. As in the poem, the identity of the pilot-abductor is never discovered; hence, the motion of the balloon serves as a metaphor for the "outlaw" novelist who, as she writes, is simultaneously carried away by what Dickinson describes as the music of voices, by "bolts of melody." In other words, this communal narrator is not of the "singular" type, but rather a "simultaneous" communal narrator who listens and speaks (reads and writes) at the same time. This type of communal narration is represented, according to Lanser, "through formal strategies that allow the plurality to speak" (256).

If Dickinson's poem #505 guides our interpretation of Deirdre's abduction, the "outlaw balloon," like Aunt Mathilda's quilt "The Celestial Time Piece," is recognizable as such a formal strategy—or, to use Patricia Yaeger's phrase, an emancipatory metaphor. Beginning with the poem's opening line, "I would not paint—a picture—/I'd rather be the One/ Its bright impossibility/ To dwell delicious—on—," the narrator disavows her desire to create, claiming instead to wish to play the part of reader or listener: "I would not talk, like Cornets—/ I'd rather be the One/ Raised softly to the Ceilings—/ And out, and easy on—/ Through Villages of Ether/ Myself endured Balloon." Even while Dickinson pilots us through her poem, she states her desire to be the one piloted, the one abducted, the one carried away by the music of the poetry. It is a paradox, as Adrienne Rich says: "The images of the poem rise to a climax (like the Balloon she evokes) but the climax happens as she describes, not what it is like to be the receiver, but the maker and receiver at once" ("Vesuvius at Home" 169). This complex vision of artistry suggests how Oates imagines herself in relationship to writing: she is in the position of both the maker and receiver at once. On the one hand, she is the voice of the novel; on the other hand, she is the receiver of an inheritance, a tradition the novel portrays as an inheritance of texts/voices: the voices of Deirdre's foremothers, as figured by Aunt Edwina, as well as by her forefathers, as figured in the Raging Captain (Melville's Ahab). In this way, as Showalter says, Oates's feminist romance "merges the female and the male literary tradition, the female Gothic romance with *The Blithedale Romance* of Hawthorne" (*"The Dead* and Feminist Criticism" 18).

Oates's narrative voice is equally complex, and mysterious, in *Mysteries of Winterthurn* (1984), as evident from reviews. For example, Patricia Craig said she couldn't determine whether Oates was "reproducing a 19th-century detective novel, overturning it, expanding it, or sending it up" (7). On the surface, such genre play seems to contradict the feminist goal that Oates has announced in her Preface: to depict "historically authentic crimes against women, children and the poor, in the guise of entertainment." Why, for example, if Oates's purpose is to expose crimes against women, children, and the poor, would she reproduce a genre only to deliberately transgress its conventions? But that is precisely the point: Oates is reproducing the crime novel and, at the same time, transgressing its conventions in order to expose the ways in which this conservative genre has mirrored the very social conventions that perpetuate crimes against women, children, and the poor.[30] Anticipating questions about genre, Oates states in her Preface that "the formal discipline of genre forces us inevitably to a radical revisioning of the world and the craft of fiction" ([*Woman*] *Writer* 372). The detective novel, like the family saga and the romance novel, are particular ways of seeing the world that compel the (feminist) writer to transform the genre. In short, Oates's desire to radically re-vision both the world and the craft of fiction explains why, in the postmodern novels, she is organizing the "voluminous materials" of American history in patterns that she describes as "alien to my customary way of thinking and writing" ([*Woman*] *Writer* 372–73).

Exactly what are these patterns? In *Sisters in Crime*, Maureen Reddy argues that the traditional crime novel upholds the "masculine" value of an "objective" rationality, a way of knowing that *Mysteries of Winterthurn* exposes as "criminal" in itself. For example, detective Xavier Kilgarvan begins his career by upholding the standard of "objective" rationality, but he learns the limits and the dangers of such a stance. Optimistic about eradicating crime, Xavier shares nineteenth-century America's dream of progress, but by the end of the novel he has lost his commitment to the profession of detection. When he decides to marry Perdita Kilgarvan rather than expose his cousin as the ax-murderer of her minister-husband, he violates one of the detective's most important codes. Oates's transformation of Xavier from a detective into a husband and father is perhaps the novel's most explicitly feminist re-vision.[31] Such transgressions are deliberate, as the Editor states in the Prefaces preceding each case; therefore, attentive readers will anticipate violations of conventions of realism. In each of these violations (in the first case these violations especially evident in chapters called "Trompe L'Oeil" and "Slaughtered Lambs"; in the second case in a chapter called "Quicksand"; and in the third case in a chapter called "Hotel Paradise") Xavier makes a figurative journey during which he encounters his own shadow, his criminal self. These encounters violate the distance between the guilty criminal and the presumably innocent public that readers of the genre usually expect.

The novel violates this assumption to expose the fact that crimes against women, though they may be committed by a single person, are actually rooted in social injustice. Even murderers guilty of the most heinous crimes turn out to be acting in collusion with the unstated beliefs of the society. For example, in "The Virgin in the Rose Bower" the community accepts the father's complete authority over his daughter, authority that allows the father to sexually violate his daughter. By contrast, if Georgina Kilgarvan were to confess that she has killed infants born of the incestuous assaults, the community would severely punish her. In the second case, "The Devil's Half-Acre," the community also tolerates, even admires, the crimes of the "cruel suitor," a serial murderer who rapes and tortures his lower-class female victims. Although Valentine Westergaard is a Byronic hero—aristocratic, brutal, and well dressed—his female victims delude themselves with the fantasy (a fantasy still a staple of women's romance novels, according to Janice Radway) that their love has the power to transform the rapist into a loving husband. This fantasy proves to be deadly for those who "love" Valentine Westergaard.

Xavier Kilgarvan, who is himself a suitor in love with Perdita, solves the case of "The Devil's Half-Acre" by recognizing Westergaard as his shadow, his "twin." Likewise, in the last case, "The Bloodstained Bridal Gown," detective Xavier descends into a Dantesque realm of the "Paradise Hotel" where he encounters grotesque reflections of himself and the unjust society in which he lives. Perdita leads Xavier, as Beatrice leads Dante, in romantic patterns of ascent and descent (from bedroom to attic and dungeon or from church to brothel) that reveal, finally, how detectives and their readers participate in "criminal" fantasies of mastery. Like Oates herself, who enjoys assuming a variety of personas, or "voices,"[32] her detective-hero takes pleasure in wearing disguises in order to investigate crime. For example, in the final tale of *Mysteries of Winterthurn*, Xavier wears a disguise, a curly red wig, that identifies him as a "twin" to one of the murder suspects, Jabez Dovekie. The twinning of characters, a strategy Oates also frequently employs in her Rosamond Smith novels, points to the mystery of personality: behind our social personas, we are many different selves, with different "voices."

Although detective fiction generally portrays the detective as isolated and autonomous, Oates consistently challenges this belief in the isolated ego. In this respect, Oates is similar to other feminist writers of detective fiction who, according to Reddy, undermine the isolation and alienation of the detective-hero by portraying their detectives with connection to others. As Reddy notes, however, since the crime novel is as much mothered as fathered, Oates and other feminists are not revising a male-defined genre. Historically, however, as science gained ascendancy, a split occurred during the nineteenth century, and the "sensational" novel, which allowed for the solution of mysteries by means other than the "realistic" or scientifically verifiable, was relegated to an inferior status. The use of "feminine in-tuition" was strictly outlawed, despite the fact that poetic intuition was a characteristic of Poe's detective. One can detect, in this history of the genre's exclusion of "feminine" ways of knowing—a way of knowing in which the knower partakes of the known—the gradual "masculinization" of the genre's aesthetic practice.

Despite the fact that women writers helped to shape the genre, the detective story enacts the masculine assumptions of Western civilization. As William Spanos argues in "The Detective and the Boundary: Some Notes on the Postmodern Literary Imagination," the genre privileges "the pursuit of knowledge to the (mind's) radiant eye over the other bodily senses," and this eye is an "omniscient, omnipresent hidden deity out of reach of free play which looks down indifferently on his creation from a distanced vantage point in the sky" (196). Some women, in particular writers and readers of mystery stories, may share this "impulse to omnipotence," but the "distanced vantage point" of the genre does greater damage to women who, because they are identified with the physical, are more often its victims. As Spanos states: "Behind the metaphysical eye, in other words, lies the impulse to omnipotence, the Will to Power over *physis* not simply for the sake of understanding its anxiety-provoking mystery, of transcending the uncertainties and dread of existence—the dread (angst) that, unlike fear, has *no thing* or Nothing (das Nichts) as its object" (197). It is this dread of "no thing," the void associated with "Woman," that motivates male crimes in Winterthurn, a place that is as much a region of our contemporary souls as an actual spot on a map. It is, for example, the dread of "no thing," or mortality, which provokes Judge Kilgarvan's brutal treatment of his wives and daughters, just as this dread inspires Valentine Westergaard's brutal murders of five young women.

By contrast, when women commit crimes in Winterthurn, they are usually attempting to resist brutality and oppression. For example, Georgina Kilgarvan has killed four or five infants (the Editor counts four, the detective five), but only to prevent the community, once it discovers that she is an incest victim, from punishing her for her father's crime. Only in Georgina's poetry, where she tells it "slant," does she voice her resistance to the "Law of the Father." Likewise, although Perdita kills her minister-husband and his lover, her crime is an act of resistance—and revenge—against the socially sanctioned oppression of wives. Perdita's cruel husband, the "good" Reverend Mr. Bunting, has not only denied Perdita the opportunity to mother an orphaned child (insisting instead that the infant be allowed to die a "natural" death), he has also taken his wife's inheritance, the proceeds from the sale of Georgina's poetry. Therefore, as the Editor of her husband's cases, Perdita employs textual, in lieu of literal, violence. In this respect, the (woman) writer and her readers are "sisters in crime," their acts of resistance affirming their sympathies with the oppressed. By engaging in the pleasure of such resistance, readers become accomplices in Oates's project: "the radical revisioning of the world and the craft of fiction." Another pleasure of *Mysteries of Winterthurn* is that it allows the feminist to acknowledge her (or his) own will-to-power.

Critics who do not become Oates's accomplices in this feminist project—especially those who fail to identify Perdita either as the murderer of her minister-husband or as the Editor of her detective-husband's most famous cases—often charge the author with the failure to edit her writing.[33] However, even though feminist critic Cara Chell mistakenly assumes that the narrator is male—she argues that Oates "sets the much-vaunted 'reality' of her pompous, presumably masculine, narrator on its head" (8)—she recognizes that *Mysteries of Winterthurn* "makes visible . . . the historical, stereotypical absurdities about women still believed as 'true' by twentieth-century male novelists and their culture" (8). Like the narrator of Charlotte Perkins Gilman's "The Yellow Wallpaper," the narrator of *Mysteries of Winterthurn* exposes the absurd "ratiocinative" claims of scientific men in a variety of professions: judges, detectives, doctors, philosophers, business-men, clergy, educators. Once it is understood that the Editor is not speaking in the voice of an authorial narrator—who has godlike omniscience—but as a participant-observer, readers will recognize that Perdita's insights come from her ability to reflect intelligently upon her experiences as a woman in a misogynistic society. Very often, as a result of this experience, Perdita's insights are superior to those of Xavier, the supposedly "rational" and "objective" male detective.

While the cases in *Mysteries of Winterthurn* illustrate Xavier's "rational" intelligence and skill in detection, they portray a man forced to acknowledge his "Will to Power" as potentially dangerous. Xavier solves each case, but his brilliance leads not to personal triumph but to a recognition of the limits of his authority. Xavier's solutions always present a dilemma: if he triumphantly solves the case, he will at the same time betray those he loves by exposing their complicity in crime. For example, to solve his first case, Xavier must expose Georgina as the "criminal," a betrayal of Perdita as well as the entire Kilgarvan family; to solve the second case, Xavier must identify the serial killer as Valentine Westergaard, which means betraying his own brothers, who are Valentine's accomplices; and to solve the final case, he must identify the woman he still loves as the ax-murderer. Hence, even though Xavier is not "innocent" of Perdita's possible motives for killing her minister-husband, it takes some time before he can acknowledge that she—and no one else—has, with Lizzie Borden fury, killed her minister-husband, his mistress, and her mother-in-law. Perdita's cover story is that she has been raped by a murderer, an intruder; however, the true story is that she has been victimized by a husband who denies her love, children, and an inheritance from the estate of her poet-sister, Georgina. Following the murder, Perdita has blood stains on her bridal gown—which she has worn with comic appropriateness—but the community cannot believe that

Perdita, like Lizzie Borden, could be guilty of such unladylike behavior. Xavier, too, resists knowing what the clues tell him, not only because he loves Perdita, but because he may be implicated in the murder.

However, since the conclusion is not a tidy one, it is impossible to determine to what degree Xavier has participated in a cover-up. Xavier had returned to Winterthurn wearing a disguise, a wig of curly red-hair, and almost every witness reported having seen a " 'red-haired specter' " running from the rectory shortly after the murder. One witness reported seeing Xavier "carrying in his arms the *limp and flimsily clad body of a comely young woman,*—the rector's wife, Perdita," while a ten-year-old boy who was playing near Jewett Pond described a "red-haired giant" carrying "*a bloodied ax cradled in his arms,*" which he threw into the pond (360–62). Based on these reports, it is probable that Perdita had called Xavier to ask for his help. He had arrived, in disguise, just in time to dispose of the murder weapon and, possibly, to help his beloved to prepare her alibi. Readers may base such inferences on the fact that Xavier had received a message from a "veiled lady" (probably Perdita) on September 10th, a message that asked that he come to Winterthurn. However, Xavier had not received the message until twenty hours later, just ninety minutes before the murders took place, at which time he was "some two hundred and thirty miles away" (344). Therefore he probably did not help commit the murder. Yet, because Xavier wears a red wig, he must also be considered a murder suspect.

As in any well-written mystery, a number of plausible leads turn out to be false. Besides Xavier, another plausible suspect, who also happens to have red hair and a strong motive for murdering Reverend Bunting, is Jabez Dovekie, a local "ice man" and a foreigner. Although police and others saw this as a "tidy" conclusion to the mystery, Xavier continued his search, not only because Dovekie's bloody footprints "were to be found only within a radius of a few feet, just inside the door" (398), but because Xavier believes the narrative of the murder too complex for an uneducated man to have perpetrated it. A more plausible suspect, Xavier believes, is Ellery Poindexter, who may have believed himself "cuckolded" by his wife Amanda (who was having an affair with Bunting). Because, perhaps unconsciously, he is protecting his beloved Perdita, Xavier is desperate to prove Poindexter the guilty party.

Xavier's suspicion of Poindexter becomes, however, not a search for physical clues but an occasion for the detective to examine his own "lust after death." Wearing his red-wig disguise, Xavier follows Poindexter to Paradise

Hotel, a known brothel, where, it turns out, the suspect has been leading a double life. Paradise Hotel is a place where, as Xavier learns, women are brutalized by men, many of them using false names. While in the bar of the hotel, Xavier hears Poindexter confess to a vague crime—though one committed five years before—for which he continues to feel guilty. But when Xavier tracks his suspect to his "honeymoon cottage," he learns that Poindexter feels guilty, not because he had murdered his wife but because he has afflicted his own child with syphilis. Xavier, who has forgotten his binoculars, is touched by the pathos of Poindexter's secret household, his mulatto mistress and their sick child. Having violated the code of intellectual distance, signified by the binoculars, Xavier must confront his own desire for a family. Such a desire is the result of Xavier's heightened awareness, as he ages, of his own mortality. In fantasy, of course, the detective has control over death. Dr. Holyrod Wilts, whom Xavier meets in the Paradise Hotel, identifies this detective fantasy in the code of one who "was pledged to seek out the cause of its *literal agent*: for common belief required that a murdered person necessitated a murder: that this murderer be wicked, and must be removed from the community: and that, once he was removed, the community would reside again in health, and justice, and good cheer, and whatever,—*the agent of Death being conquered*" (444).

However, it is not only the destruction of this illusion but the loss of the illusion of Perdita's innocence that leads to Xavier's nervous breakdown. The crisis comes at the moment Xavier must ask: if Poindexter did not kill Bunting, who did? Furthermore, who wrote the obscene letters to Reverend Bunting's female parishioners? Is it possible that the identity of murderer, letter writer, and Editor are the same? Again and again, Xavier reads drafts of obscene letters enclosed in *The Collected Sermons of Harmon Atticus Bunting* until he hears a familiar voice. " 'Whose voice?—whose voice do I hear?' the stricken man cried aloud" (455), after which he falls into an even more despondent mood. Finally, Xavier burns the notes, confessing that he, himself, is the murderer. The question is: who is Xavier trying to protect? The answer can only be that he is protecting Perdita, whose voice he recognizes in the letters, just as, in solving his first case, he had recognized the pseudonymous voice of "authoress" Iphigenia as the voice of Georgina. Perdita's voice, along with her feminist irony, can be heard in an "anonymous" letter addressed to her minister-husband's lover, Amanda. This letter, in which Perdita accuses Amanda of hypocritical adultery, reads as follows: "Tis the Devil's very own delicacy you are, tho' chastely professing otherwise! . . . like many another wife of this quaint region in whose mouth (as the naughty expression would have it) *butter would not melt*. Nay" (455). The letter also parodies the church's own misogyny: "It is no secret to me, that Woman is but a gilded & primped sepulcher,—a chasm of sickly heat,—a bunghole, as St. Augustine would have it, into which Man falls to his damnation. Such frailties can be attributed to the Moon's tide, tho' I (who know the wicked heart of Woman well) should attribute them to a *volition diseased and spiteful & mischievous & wanton*" (455).

It strikes this reader—as it must have struck Xavier—that the voice in this letter, which is not only furious but also ironic, is wondrously similar to that of the coolly ironic "Editor."[34] This solution seems reasonable since, after becoming Xavier's wife, it is plausible that Perdita would assume the task of editing his cases. It is also plausible that a female with the intelligence of the Editor would have been capable of planning the ax-murder and leaving behind an ironic touch: a "mocking array of *hearts*" (367) placed on the bodies of Reverend Bunting and Amanda Poindexter.[35] But the question remains: how can the singular voice of the Editor, Perdita Kilgarvan, be described as "communal"? The solution to this mystery is that, like Perdita and Xavier, we are all, in varying degrees, implicated in crimes perpetuated by the conventions of our unjust society, conventions mirrored in genre of crime fiction. To resist these "criminal" conventions, we must join the community of feminist, resisting readers. Readers of *Mysteries of Winterthurn* must engage in such a feminist questioning of conventional authority if they are finally to "solve" the murder mystery, as well as the mystery of narrative voice.

As Reddy suggests, "Women writers, and especially feminist women, might be expected to play around with the issue of narrative authority, and to be at least somewhat distrustful of authority generally" (10). Readers who fail to identify Perdita as the ax-murderer will not recognize her as the Editor of her detective husband's most famous cases. Yet the solution to both mysteries—who commits the ax-murder and who tells us about it—gives the novel its most powerful feminist punch. Hypothetically, the novel seems to ask: what would Lizzie Borden have told us if she could have spoken or written to us from behind the veil of a "lady"? Even feminist critics such as Cara Chell and Eileen Teper Bender assume that the narrator is male. Yet it is Perdita who teaches us, as she teaches Xavier, to distrust patriarchal authority. However, only those readers who identify Perdita as the Editor will understand that the woman who has taught Xavier to read as a feminist is also teaching readers of *The Mysteries of Winterthurn* to read women's writing. To read women's writing it is necessary, for example, to learn to recognize "clues" exposing institutionalized crimes against women. Some of the best clues are provided by way of the novel's allusions to nineteenth-century fiction. In the first mystery, for example, feminist readers will recognize that the mural "The Virgin in the Rose Bower" recreates the drama of Charlotte Perkins Gilman's "The Yellow Wallpaper."[36] In the second mystery, the author's infidelities to certain canonical works, such as Hawthorne's *Blithedale Romance*, alerts feminist readers to the author's critique of the politics of the "masculine" aesthetics.[37] And the third mystery invites readers to act as a "jury of her peers," as in Susan Glaspell's story by that title.

The first case, carefully edited by Perdita, begins with an allusion to the opening chapter of *Wuthering Heights* that is to guide our readings, our interpretations, of Glen Mawr Manor. We are warned, for example, not to assume that Georgina is an "angel in the house," nor to assume that men are gentle or that dogs are obedient—mistakes that Lockwood makes when he enters Thrushcross Grange. In fact, during her visit to Glen Mawr Manor, Abigail Whimbrel finds that her cousin Georgina is barely civil—she does not meet Abigail at the train and does not share her bed—though tea is politely served in the drawing room. A portrait of "the late Chief Justice in his judicial robes" hangs above the mantel, and Georgina sits, in seeming domestic tranquillity, in a chair near "a somewhat untidy stack of books" as "the inert though wheezing form of a large mastiff,—Jupiter his name" (13) sleeps by Abigail's feet.

When philosopher Simon Esdras, brother of the late Judge Kilgarvan, accuses poor Jupiter of killing Abigail's infant, we know immediately that Simon Esdras is incompetent (as is Hawthorne's Clifford Pyncheon). Simon, who fancies himself a philosopher, has been blind for years to the suffering of women who, in the very house where he has been writing his "A Treatise on the Probable 'Existence' of the World," have been physically and sexually abused. Equally as blind is Dr. Colney Hatch, who has for years been treating the Kilgarvan wives and daughters. The good doctor, like his counterpart in "The Yellow Wallpaper," conveniently assumes that his female patients suffer from innate or self-inflicted injuries and ailments. Colney Hatch never imagines, never guesses, that men might abuse women; instead, he assumes that women suffer from being born women, a curse "naturally" more pronounced after marriage. The Editor informs us: "As an aside, I should mention here that Dr. Colney Hatch, the physician most frequently employed by the leading families of Winterthurn,—the Kilgarvans, the Westergaards, the Von Goelers, the De Forrests, the Peregrines, etc.—had oft expressed the intention of publishing a scientific study on this troublesome subject, closely investigating female incapacities as they are exposed in diverse stages: childhood, puberty, early marriage and motherhood, menopause, and senility" (39). The doctor hasn't a clue about crimes against women, probably because he commits them himself. For example, in his scientific treatises, "He had hoped to establish an actual correlation betwixt the *anatomy* of the sex and its social, moral, and intellectual *destiny*" (39). So much for scientific objectivity!

Another occasion for the complicity of feminist readers is provided by the novel's transformation of the old "locked room" convention of detective fiction into a scene of women's reading and writing. Two "soul murders" take place in the Honeymoon Room at Glen Mawr Manor, but the solution to the crime cannot be found in an overlooked physical detail, such as a secret passage or window, in the locked room. Instead, as in "The Yellow Wallpaper," the clue to maternal madness can be found in the mural, wallpaper that signifies the imprisonment of nineteenth-century women within the enclosures of patriarchal writing. If we return to the scene of the crime—the locked room of matrimony—we find that, though Abigail has locked the door, she cannot protect herself from scripture *except*, perhaps, by writing herself. In fact, as she reads the Bible, Abigail's mind wanders, and she begins writing in her diary. While writing, she notices certain odd details in the "trompe l'oeil mural by Fairfax Eakins." She sees that "the Virgin, for instance, held the Christ Child somewhat awkwardly on her knee" (12), as if wishing to drop him. Earlier, while showing the room to Abigail, Georgina had commented on the mural. As if forgetting Abigail's presence, she repeated the mysterious words of St. Therese: "An angel with a flaming golden arrow pierced my heart repeatedly. The pain was so great that I screamed aloud, but simultaneously felt such infinite sweetness that I wished the pain to last eternally" (24). At this moment, Georgina could hardly keep from coughing uncontrollably, probably because the mural sentimentalizes the sadomasochism of gender inequities. Why doesn't Georgina speak out? The answer is clear: Judge Kilgarvan, Georgina's "virtuous" father, has sent women to the gallows for infanticide, even in cases where the pregnancy has resulted from rape. Winterthurn is a place where the power of "truth" and "virtue" reside in male-defined institutions and their discourses, whether law, medicine, or religion.

Nevertheless, as Abigail writes in her diary, aspects of religious discourse, as represented by the mural, are transformed. "Angels *may* turn demon, with the passage of time,—if starved of the love that is their sustenance" (99), Perdita tells Xavier. Here she is teaching the detective—along with readers—to recognize clues to female oppression. A similar moment occurs in the first case when, some years earlier, an angry and impatient Perdita had slammed the door of the dungeon at Glen Mawr Manor, locking Xavier inside, where he is forced to read women's writing. From writings on the walls of this dungeon, Xavier learns of Judge Kilgarvan's violence, not only toward his wives, but also his daughters. He finds, for example, this poem (an obvious parody of Dickinson)[38] written in the style of Iphigenia: "Herein, a broken Sinner—/ Ah, engorged in Shame!—/ Godly Husband & Father—/ Blessed be Thy name!/ If—You will forgive—/ & I rise to Your bosom— again—" (104). Since Georgina's Master is her Father-Husband, release from the dungeon means only that she must submit again to sexual violence: "I rise to your bosom—again—."

When Xavier asks Perdita[39] "if the language did not suggest to her that of her own sister Georgina," she responds "irritably, in a voice of uncharacteristic harshness" that it dated back to " 'ancient times,' " and that, according to her father, "Indians, slaves, and servants had been sequestered in the cellar of Glen Mawr" (104). Perdita's somewhat evasive remark links the oppression of women to other oppressed groups, calling attention to the fact that the oppressed have often been found guilty of crimes committed against them. For example, the righteous Brothers of Jericho, who identify the killer as Georgina's black servant Pride, execute him. By branding his body with the letter B (repeated in a pattern across his chest), they indicate, of course, that his only crime is being "Black." By way of such ironic commentary, the Editor directs us to question the testimony of a number of "respectable" white men: a male philosopher, Simon Esdras (who kills Jupiter, presumably for the vicious crime of infanticide); a man of science, Dr. Colney Hatch (who blames his victims for the abuse they suffer); and the highly respectable Judge Erasmus Kilgarvan (who sexually abuses his wives and daughters). In this feminist novel, most professional white men are guilty of crimes against women.

In all three cases, the true mystery is not a question of "who?" but the question of "why?"—a question that inevitably implicates the community in the crime. The Editor attributes the genre's preference for the question "who?" rather than the more complicated social question "why?" to the reader's habit of identifying, at least in nineteenth-century crime novels, with a conventionally upper-class detective hero. As the Editor says in her second note: "The conservative mystery lover will object that the case fails to conform to the purest standards of the genre (the question of *who* committed the several murders being, for the most part, ancillary to whether he will be exposed—which is to say, whether the ambitious young detective Xavier Kilgarvan will get his man, or suffer professional humiliation)." Hence, the second case is designed to prompt such questions as, "Why is the 'cruel suitor' acquitted, even though he is known to be guilty?" or "Why does the community so deceive itself as to the identity of the serial murderer—even to the point of hanging an innocent man?" or "Why does even Xavier's mother blame him, rather than Valentine Westergaard, for exposing the participation of Wolf and Colin Kilgarvan in the murders of young women?" Part of the answer comes from the fact that, as the Editor predicts, Valentine's victims, "mere factory-girls of the lowest social caste," often "fail to excite interest in themselves" (149). According to convention, the Editor implies, the genre mirrors society's tolerance—its boredom—with the slaying of lower-class women.

By identifying the killer early in the case, the Editor tries to direct reader attention to just such "boring" questions. This case prompts readers to ask, for example, why the community tolerates the fact that poor children who work in factories are regularly victimized, their bones broken or their hair torn out by machines, and also tolerates the fact that girls who work in the homes of wealthy citizens are often seduced, impregnated, and sometimes killed. "The Devil's Half Acre" also dramatizes the willingness of the community to scapegoat a Jewish male, one Isaac Jacobson, rather than acknowledging its complicity in crimes committed by aristocrat "Valentine" Westergaard and his "friends." In violation of the genre's customary separation between public and private, the community's complicity with the killer is fully established in "Devil's Half Acre." The comfortable distance that readers expect from detective fiction breaks down when Xavier discovers that his brothers have aided Valentine in the brutal slayings of five women. Although the idealistic Xavier proves that Valentine is guilty of heinous crimes, however, his own mother takes the stand to defend Valentine, a friend of her sons. The self-deluded Mrs. Kilgarvan prefers to view her sons as "little angels" who are entitled to "devilish" behavior. In her view, Valentine Westergaard was only acting out romantic fantasies.

Valentine actually began his life of crime in the bosom of his own family, first by killing his assertive sister and, shortly afterward, killing a young chambermaid. These early successes embolden him to murder five more women. Even after he confesses to these murders, he is acquitted, and he marries the "Veiled Lady" who had attended his trial. This Veiled Lady (a figure reminiscent of Hawthorne's Veiled Lady) had apparently fallen victim to the same romantic fantasy as the lower-class women Valentine had murdered: the fantasy of transforming a "cruel suitor," a Byronic hero, into a protective father-husband. Despite early warnings—such as the suitor's volatile temper, his "unpredictable" jealousies that lead to slapping and then to punching—women continue to see Valentine as a "gentleman." However, rather than blaming the deluded victims, the Editor directs reader attention to our society's misogynistic beliefs, beliefs that sanction violence against women. Besides providing gruesome details of the murders, Valentine's trial spells out these beliefs. Colin Kilgarvan's testimony parrots his master's beliefs: " 'Nature is a very pox to be overcome,' says Master, *'but she must be overcome.'* Therefore much scrubbing will be required. It is far worse than other times. For Master says she is particularly unclean. She is filthy says he and must be punished" (Oates's italics 313–14). The audience is spellbound by Valentine, who begins his Dimmesdale-like confession by declaring that *"all Colin Kilgarvan had said of him, was true"* (317).

In time, Xavier comes to understand that even the science of detection is not immune to such beliefs. For example, the "Editor's Note" to "The Bloodstained Bridal Gown" warns us that this final case will transgress yet another code of detective fiction—"the inevitable *tidiness* of the conclusion"—the kind of ending that "boldly upholds the principle, *in defiance of contemporary sentiment*, that infinite Mystery, beyond that of the finite, may yield to human ratiocination" (340). This widely shared belief is signified by the Emersonian eye: "An unblinking eye that sees all, absorbs all, comprehends all, each and every baffling clue, and binds all multifariousness together, in a divine unity" (340–41). Xavier had wished, probably no more than many of his reader-accomplices, to emulate such a masterful "eye," but he finally accepts his failure *"to be divine."* Only after he acknowledges the limits of his powers of ratiocination does Xavier win Perdita's love, and only after Perdita acknowledges her "guilty" desire for Xavier can she return his love. As the novel ends, the voices of Perdita and Xavier, joined in matrimony, become part of the voices of the place, a place called Winterthurn.

Porous Boundaries: Daughters, Families, and the Body Politic in Realistic Novels of the 1980s

"Whatever happened to feminist fiction?" asks Gayle Greene (*Changing the Story* 193). During the 1980s, she answers, feminist fiction has retreated to a focus on the family in a manner "reminiscent of the fifties" (195), a retreat brought about by a backlash from both outside and inside the feminist movement. To support her claim, Greene lists more than a dozen women writers whose novels illustrate "the privatization and depoliticization of their concerns, the sentimentalization of the family, the resignation to things as they are" (200). If Greene is correct, feminists have reason to value Oates's novels of the 1980s, for they accent the interplay between the personal and the political, with persistent emphasis upon gender as it intersects with race and class. All art is political, as Oates illustrates in her short story "Detente," because it seeks to alter consciousness. In "Detente," set at an international conference, a Russian writer named Vassily explains through a translator, "My books are political . . . as all art," to which Antonia, an American writer, responds, "In essence art isn't political, it's above politics, it refers only to itself" (*Last Days* 123). Vassily insists: "Art seeks to alter consciousness, hence it is a political act. A mere glass of water is an occasion for politics," he adds, explaining that he has in mind "an article about the poisons that have drained into the mountain lakes in this area" (124–25).

According to this definition—that "art seeks to alter consciousness, hence it is a political act"—Oates's fiction is most certainly political. She has stated, for example, that she writes, always, with "enormous hope of altering the world" ("Stories That Define Me" 1). Through an analysis of three "realistic" novels of the 1980s, this chapter explores Oates's hope—which she shares with other feminist writers—of altering reader consciousness: *Angel of Light* (1980), a portrayal of the upper-middle-class Halleck family, set in Washington, D.C., during the Watergate period; *You Must Remember This* (1987), a depiction of the working class Stevick family, set in upstate New York during the McCarthy era; and *Because It Is Bitter, Because It Is My Heart* (1990), a portrayal of four different families of different races and classes set in the era of John F. Kennedy's assassination. I use the term "feminist realism" to define these novels—as well as *Solstice* (1985), *Marya, A Life* (1986), and *American Appetites* (1989), which I do not discuss here[1]—because, while Oates appears to obey the conventions of realism, she actually uses a variety of re-visionary, feminist techniques: complex structures that shift center and margin, a fluid point of view that challenges the masculine construct of the self, and images that call attention to the political unconscious, to the (m)other in us all. Oates's revisionary strategies are apparent to some feminist critics. For example, Sally Robinson has noted that Oates's fiction "raises questions about the politics of representations" ("Heat and Cold" 401), and Lorna Sage argues that even in *Marya, A Life*, a novel modeled on the realistic bildungsroman, "Marya's representative status (a self-made woman of our time) is slewed by the book's doubtful representational status" (186). By contrast, most male critics—Thomas Edwards, Paul Gray, Greg Johnson, John Skow, Victor Strandberg, and John Updike—describe Oates as a realistic writer, rarely calling attention to her feminist politics. Henry Louis Gates is the striking exception.

Gates has also noted "the canny modulation between different points of view [in *Because It Is Bitter*], which makes it impossible to distinguish indirect discourse from interstitial narrative." He adds, "In Oates's craft the boundaries of character are so porous as to subsume every thing else" (27–28). As I shall illustrate, in addition to employing a narrative technique that illustrates the porous boundaries between "us" and "them," Oates creates an innovative structure, a moving center, in *Because It Is Bitter, Because It Is My Heart* in order to challenge traditional "realistic" novels, which, when they fail to challenge hierarchies of difference, perpetuate injustices. Oates also employs patterns of images in these novels that emphasize the porous boundaries between the individual and the social body. Recurring images associated with the (m)other—images of the body, of birth and death, of wombs and tombs, of food and sexuality—call reader attention to the repressed (m)other in America's political unconscious. These same novels use competitive sports—tennis, boxing, horse racing, or racquetball—to represent the homosocial (Oedipal) order. These games encode the male-created rules and practices that govern the institutions through which men—repressing the (m)other in themselves—dominate women and children.

What daughters need, these novels demonstrate, is a truly democratic society in which mothers have equal power not only within the family but beyond it. Tragically, as long as the family reproduces gender hierarchies, social injustice will continue. According to Jessica Benjamin, "The groundwork for this [hierarchical gender] division is laid in the mother's renunciation of her own will, in her consequent lack of subjectivity for her children, and particularly the male child's repudiation of his commonality with her" (82). Despite the fact that the mother's renunciation of her own subjectivity continues to be enforced by institutions—religious, legal, political, and scientific—both the plots and imagery in these novels suggest that, despite powerful opposition, mothers must attempt to claim their own subjectivity. Benjamin makes a similar argument when she says, "Only a mother who feels entitled to be a person in her own right can ever be seen as such by her child, and only such a mother can appreciate and set limits to the inevitable aggression and anxiety that accompany a child's growing independence" (82). Despite societal limits imposed upon maternal power, these novels demonstrate that mothers who struggle to assert their own desires and rights leave their daughters a powerful legacy. By contrast, in families where mothers cannot or will not assert their rights, daughters become vulnerable to paternal seduction or rape.

As Judith Lewis Herman argues in *Father-Daughter Incest*, where fathers are most tyrannical and mothers most submissive, daughters are most vulnerable to actual incest, while paternal seduction—psychological incest—occurs more often in families where mothers have some sense of their own identity. However, as these novels illustrate, the mother-daughter bond is not likely to be strong in either the incestuous or seductive father–headed household. As a result, most of Oates's daughters defer the mother-quest until late in adolescence or, in some cases, until their mid-thirties or later. In early adolescence, in an inevitable effort to separate from their mothers, daughters identify with their fathers, or father-surrogates, sometimes to the point of hating their mothers. Kirsten Halleck in *Angel of Light*, the most extreme example, actually plots the death of her mother, whom she blames for the suicide of her father.[2] In *You Must Remember This,* "Daddy's sweetheart" (43), Enid Stevick, also becomes her mother's deadly rival, but Enid's opposition to her mother takes a different form: at age fifteen, in a secret act of rebellion, she begins an incestuous relationship with her uncle. The alliance of father and daughter—"Daddy and his littlest girl have a secret understanding [from which] Momma is excluded" (26–27)—prepares Enid for an affair with an uncle twice her age. Yet when Enid has an abortion at age seventeen, she begins to value her mother. And in *Because It Is Bitter, Because It Is My Heart* Iris Courtney actually marries a man not for love of him but for love of his mother.

I begin my analysis with *Angel of Light,* a story of personal and political betrayal set in the Watergate era in Washington, D.C., that re-visions the plot of *The Oresteia.* From a feminist standpoint, as Hirsch says, such paradigms of the mother/daughter plot as *The Oresteia* are "seriously insufficient," but they do provide "frames of reference" that may be "modified, reconstructed, and transformed" (29). *The Oresteia* provides such a frame of reference for the plot of *Angel of Light:* the murder of Isabel (Clytemnestra),[3] the passionate and sexual wife of political leader Maurice Halleck, by her children, Kirsten and Owen (Electra and Orestes). Such a mother-murder, and not a father-murder, as Freud asserts in *Totem and Taboo,* is the foundation of the patriarchal order. As Luce Irigaray argues, the murder of Clytemnestra "is the mythic representation of the mother's exclusion from culture and the symbolic order" (qtd. in Hirsch 30). Froma I. Zeitlin makes a similar point in her analysis of *The Oresteia.* Zeitlin says, "If Aeschylus is concerned with world-building, the cornerstone of his architecture is the control of woman, the social and cultural prerequisite for the construction of civilization. *The Oresteia* stands squarely within the misogynistic tradition which pervades Greek thought, a bias which both projects a combative dialogue in male-female interactions and which relates the mastery of the female to higher social goals" (48).

Oates historicizes the plot of *The Oresteia* by making Kirsten and Owen descendants of John Brown, the abolitionist whose attack on Harper's Ferry became a famous episode in American history. Like their forefather, Owen and Kirsten are motivated by a desire for righteous vengeance against evil. However, they fail to understand that, in the very act of killing those they presume guilty of evil, they become agents of evil themselves. Oates's title, "The Angel of Light," makes this point since "angel of light," Thoreau's biblical name for John Brown, conveys a double meaning: on the one hand, like Satan himself, the "innocent" Halleck children bring "light" into the "dark" corruption of Washington politics; on the other hand, Owen and Kirsten become angels of darkness, angels of violence and death. As I shall illustrate, Oates's feminist critique of the misogynistic architecture of American political life is also evident in a motif of bird images which links the personal and the political. Through the use of this motif of bird images, an allusion to *The Oresteia*, Oates re-visions Aeschylus's drama, first performed in 458 B.C. The novel opens as Owen and Kirsten become angels of wrath who plot the murder of their mother, Isabel, and her former lover, Nick Martens. The novel, like *The Oresteia*, closes with matricide, Owen's murder of his mother; however, Oates has added an epilogue in which Nick Martens, in exile on the Maine seacoast where he is recovering from near-fatal injuries inflicted by Kirsten, reflects upon his life. Nick sees his own predatory political and personal morality mirrored in certain birds: "The predatory birds draw his attention, he feels a certain kinship with them, a bleak consolation that has something to do with their crude calls and their hooked bills and their evidently insatiable appetites" (427).

Because Kirsten has chosen not to kill Nick, not to exercise the law of *lex talionis*, he now questions the very political order so firmly established at the conclusion of *The Oresteia*. In short, the plot of *Angel of Light* doesn't simply repeat the mythical past but re-visions it. However, when the novel opens, Kirsten is very much a "Daddy's girl," and food-rejection is one symptom of the hatred she feels toward her mother. Following her father's death, Kirsten loses weight rapidly, refuses to bathe, and behaves like a manic-depressive. Self-righteously, although Kirsten herself has cheated on exams and has broken into other girls' rooms at her boarding school, she is "militantly idealistic"—a "*grieving* un*forgiving* daughter" (32). When Owen visits Kirsten at school, he discovers that his sister is "insomniac, anorexic, gay and chattering nonstop, mute for days, not showering, not changing clothes, rude to her roommate, weeping in her roommate's arms"; in other words, "playing it for all it's worth, Owen thinks sullenly. Daddy's girl" (32). Readers may be more sympathetic to Kirsten than Owen is, but he is exactly right: Kirsten is a father-identified daughter who hates her mother. Her rejection of food—an enactment of that ancient injunction: "Away from the mother!"—is not simply a "personal" problem; instead, Kirsten embodies a cultural disorder precipitated by a life-hating denial of the (maternal) body.

The novel complicates ethical issues by gradually subverting Kirsten's father-identified moral judgments. For example, although some readers may applaud Kirsten/Electra for idealizing her presumably saintly father and taking revenge on her adulterous mother, Isabel/Clytemnestra, the novel provides details intended to prompt readers to qualify their sympathy for Maurice and to soften their harsh judgments of Isabel. Our sympathy for Isabel comes from the knowledge that a male art teacher, jealous of the originality of Isabel's sculpting, had falsely accused her of plagiarism, as well as from the knowledge that her status-hungry father had forced her into marrying a man of wealth and prominence. As a result, the beautiful Isabel—whose beauty men have defined as her only power—concludes that an affair with Nick Martens, the man she genuinely loves even though he is her husband's best friend, is her only avenue of escape from a loveless marriage. When Nick rejects Isabel's love, not out of loyalty to Maurice, but out of loyalty to the homosocial game, Isabel exercises her limited power through a succession of infidelities. As a result of these infidelities, daughter Kirsten, who does not understand the psycho-political context that governs Isabel's destructive behavior, self-righteously blames her mother for her father's suicide.

Furthermore, although Maurice appears to be saintly in comparison to Isabel and Nick, who betray his trust, he is actually implicated in the violent plot, for it is Maurice's suicide—his grandiose effort to take upon himself all the guilt for a scandal originating in his Washington office—that inspires his children to plot the murder of Isabel/Clytemnestra. Some critics view Maurice as a saintly man—Colakis describes Maurice as "gentle . . . earnest, idealistic, and deeply troubled" (126)—but the novel depicts his suicide as egocentric martyrdom, an act designed to prove his moral superiority to his betrayers. Maurice's failure to acknowledge his anger—his desire for revenge—leaves his children to enact a burdensome emotional inheritance. In this respect, Maurice fails as a father: he thinks only of himself, not of the children he abandons. Moreover, despite his idealism, Maurice is blind to the privileges he enjoys as a wealthy, white male in a sexist, racist, and classist society. Hence, he also fails as a husband, for he views his wife primarily as a prize he has won in the homosocial game he plays with other men. The homosocial code requires loyalty to other male players of the game and to the game itself rather than to a woman. Committed to this game, Maurice remains obtusely innocent of his wife's true character, while Nick eventually abandons Isabel because, according to the rules of the homosocial game, he cannot act upon his genuine passion for her.

June Martens spells out the rules of this homosocial order in her feminist commentary on a tennis game between her husband, Nick, and Maurice Halleck. Remarking that the tennis game is reminiscent of the Greek story of rape and war, "The Judgment of Paris," June says that, although such stories are "crude and merciless," they "tell us implacable truths about ourselves, truths that don't seem to change across the centuries" (274). Part IV of *Angel of Light*, called "The Game, Bitterfeld Lake, July 1967," gives a precise historical setting for the novel's reenactment of the Trojan War. Isabel, who has married the richer man, is the "queen" that Nick Martens wants to steal from his prep school friend, Maurice. June reminds the wives watching the match—a game she recognizes as a contest for the lovely Isabel—that according to Greek legend it was a beauty contest that started the Trojan War when Eris "threw an apple 'for the fairest' in front of three goddesses—Hera, Aphrodite, and Athena" (277). The competing goddesses try to bribe Eris and, finally, when Aphrodite offers Helen of Troy as a bribe, the Trojan War begins. June's retelling of the myth reveals her understanding of the subordinate place of women in the homosocial order. As June concludes, "Nothing [in a woman] seems to matter except physical beauty, not even wisdom, not even *power*. Just physical beauty" (277–78). June's allusion to myth establishes a causal link between violence—war, politics, scandal, murder—and the personal rivalries between public men. In this rivalry, the rich have considerable advantage over the poor, just as men have a clear advantage over women. June points out the injustice of gender hierarchies when she says, "Paris is the judge. He's only a mortal but he has the power to judge goddesses because he's a man. Because they give him power. It doesn't say why they give him the power" (278). Though highly prized by men, Isabel's beauty becomes a disadvantage, marking her as the prized object of masculine competition. The body of a beautiful woman is simply the "X" that locates the site of male competition and violence.

Even in a sexist society, however, mothers retain some freedom of choice: they may accept their devalued place, or they may resist society's devaluation of the maternal. For example, in *Angel of Light* June Martens finally exercises the limited power she has by divorcing Nick and leaving the game behind. By contrast, Isabel—"the fairest of them all"—stays in Washington, where she dies a violent death. By portraying this capacity for choice, these novels avoid a problem that Jessica Benjamin describes as "a major tendency in feminism [which] has constructed the problem of domination as a drama of female vulnerability victimized by male aggression" (9). Feminists have not adequately analyzed the submission of women, according to Benjamin, because once it is admitted that women participate in relationships of domination, women will be forced—in a victory for men—to assume responsibility for the problem. Adult women in these novels do participate, to varying degrees, in relationships of domination, but these relationships are always placed within the sociopolitical context of male control. For example, although Isabel Halleck engages in extramarital affairs, readers are encouraged to interpret her infidelities as acts of revenge against a husband who expects her to sacrifice her subjectivity and artistic potential. Because Isabel fails to develop her talent as a sculptor, choosing instead to expend her energy in adulterous affairs, Kirsten comes to hate her.

Nevertheless, the novel provides details of Isabel's childhood, associated with the image of the dove, that are designed to elicit reader sympathy. For example, we learn that, because Isabel's mother had moved to Minnesota after divorcing Isabel's father, the child had rarely seen her mother. This lack of maternal support may be one reason Isabel had acquiesced to the wishes of her tyrannical, status-seeking father that she marry a man she does not love in order to become an upper-class socialite, a "Washington" wife. In fact, as readers learn later, Isabel's passion for Nick is genuine, her love for Maurice feigned. At one point Isabel comes close to admitting that her father has "bullied her" into dating Maurice, that he listened to her phone conversations and read her letters, that he asked questions about the prestigious Halleck family. "What does your father want?" Maurice had asked during their courtship, but Isabel had only wept in reply. Secretly, however, Maurice knew "he didn't deserve her. He didn't deserve her beauty" (196). Secretly, Isabel agrees. Isabel commits her first infidelity immediately after their engagement is announced—a betrayal marked by the loss of a dove-barrette, a gift from her fiance. With Maurice's blessing, Nick and Isabel had gone off alone for a walk along the Maine coastline to get to know each other. During passionate lovemaking, Isabel had lost the barrette, a loss discovered only after she and Nick returned to Maurice: "She bites her lip, she is vexed, almost tearful. She says suddenly, patting her head, Oh, it's gone—the dove—is it gone? Did I lose It? Or wasn't I wearing it? I can't remember—Oh hell—" (198).

The consequence of Isabel's loss—not a loss of virginity but a loss of integrity, the integrity of her own desires—is tragic. Rather than fulfilling her own desires as a woman and an artist, Isabel has learned, as Kaschak would phrase it, to see herself through the eyes of the father; as a result, Kirsten inherits what Sandra Gilbert describes as the daughter's "empty pack," while Owen inherits a legacy of violence. Owen is already considering his sister's proposal—that they murder their mother to punish her for supposedly killing their father—when he meets the revolutionary, Ulrich May, grandson of the architect who designed the Hallecks' home. Ulrich, who is also a member of the American Silver Doves Revolutionary Army, seduces Owen in a bedroom full of images of grotesque violence, furnishings that include a Uruguayan "flying carpet" made of human hair described as "crow's wing black" (201) and metal-framed photos of the bloody bodies of men killing and being killed all over the world. May insists that the photos are not those of terrorists but of revolutionaries, human beings capable of violent self-sacrifice: Ulrike Meinhof of the Bader-Meinhof Gang, a suicide in her cell at age thirty; Holger Meins, near dead of a hunger strike, Christ-like in skeletal repose; the bloodied corpses of school children; a smashed and flaming helicopter, the 1972 Olympics and the Black September Massacre. "Geniuses of the body—absolutely dedicated— fearless—the will made flesh" (245), according to May. May's seduction of Owen has obvious sexual overtones, though he employs a revolutionary rhetoric—"*A revolution moves at the pace of a dove*, the admirable Nietzsche said, which is absolutely true" (Oates's italics 243).

Despite May's belief in his own moral superiority, the American Silver Doves Revolutionary Army is the mirror image—the dark underside—of the homosocial Washington political order he condemns. The photographs surrounding May's bed illustrate the sadomasochism of this homosocial order in which a man's true desire is for other men; thus, according to May, a woman such as Isabel Halleck "isn't so much depraved and vicious and selfish as she is utterly worthless—litter—a piece of trash. I mean actual *litter* on the face of the earth" (242). In fact, Ulrich May's moral righteousness is a form of culturally inscribed misogyny, a fact evident in the body-hatred characteristic of the revolutionaries he idealizes. Within the context of May's revolutionary order, Owen's "private" violence toward his mother takes on public and historical meaning. Having been brought up to obey the patriarchal imperative, "*Away from the unconscious, away from the mother*," Owen's natural bond with his mother has become distorted, perverse: he dreams of having sexual intercourse with Isabel in the family swimming pool, as if immersing himself in amniotic fluid. Behind the son's sexual desire for his mother, his Oedipal wish, is the patriarchal imperative that bars mother-love. In such a society the image of the Goddess—the dove, the female soul[4]—is debased until it comes to mean, in May's words, something "utterly worthless—litter—a piece of trash" (242).

However, because the conclusion of *Angel of Light* alters the ending of *The Oresteia*, the novel suggests the possibility of social change. Whereas the House of Atreus, which is built upon the death of Clytemnestra, dramatizes the founding of patriarchy through the power vested in a legally "innocent" son, Orestes, the House of Halleck ends with the death of Owen. The death of Owen contrasts sharply with the fate of Orestes, who is, according to Zeitlin, freed by the gods "(as far as it is intellectually possible) from the irrefutable and often anguished fact of human existence that man is from woman born" (71). Furthermore, the House of Halleck can now continue only through the "fallen" (or transgressive) daughter, Kirsten. Furthermore, in contrast to Electra, Kirsten does not remain a father-identified daughter at the end of the novel; her decision to live with her maternal grandmother suggests a change of heart in the "angel of wrath," as Nick Martens describes her.[5] Kirsten's change of heart is also evident in her decision to abandon the revenge plot. Out of sympathy, sympathy stimulated by the sight of Nick's aging and bleeding body, she calls for help: "You'd better come get him, you'd better send an ambulance at once, she tells the policeman at the other end of the line. . . . He's bleeding to death" (420). However, only after the tragic action has run its course, only after her mother's death, does Kirsten finally begin to question the ethics of revenge.[6] In this novel, then, the daughter claims her voice at the cost of the mother's silence.

By contrast, in *You Must Remember This*, a novel set in the 1950s, both mother and daughter claim their voices. Like Marya Knauer in *Marya, a Life*, who is also a working-class daughter, Enid Stevick in *You Must Remember This* is an intelligent observer of family life who, having recognized the gender hierarchies in her family, is determined not to occupy the devalued and vulnerable place of the mother. Enid acts out her ambivalence toward becoming the mother through secret acts of rebellion. Adult expectations, especially in the 1950s—that Enid behave as a "good" girl, an obedient and submissive daughter—require that she act out her "bad" girl self only when she is away from home and school.[7] For this reason, she develops two selves: the dutiful and polite Enid who goes to Mass and gets good grades, and the rebellious Enid who steals from stores and attempts suicide to entice her attractive, wealthy uncle into a sexual relationship. Neither of

Enid's parents knows anything about this "other" Enid and, even when she almost succeeds in killing herself, they avoid any discussion of her death-wish. Death is, in fact, as taboo a topic as sex. Yet the "innocent" Enid has heard stories of sex and death; such as the story of a soldier and his lover who had been found dead in their car. The couple had poisoned themselves with carbon monoxide "for love" (13), according to Enid's older sister.

The motive for Enid's suicide attempt is actually quite similar: she wants her uncle's love, no matter what the cost. She thinks of her suicide as a dramatic form of revenge against Felix for his indifference to her after their first sexual encounter. This encounter had taken place after Enid had attracted her uncle's attention by playing the part of his (male) adversary: during a playful boxing lesson, she had actually landed a blow, splitting Felix's lip. The stratagem had worked. Felix had paid attention to his niece: "Want to go for a ride, sweetheart?" (100), he had asked. The affair had begun, however, only after Enid had almost succeeded in killing herself. Even though Enid desires a "romantic" relationship with her uncle, it is, nonetheless, a violation of the taboo against incest for which Felix, as the adult participant, must accept the great share of responsibility. Furthermore, as defined by Judith Lewis Herman, *incest* "mean[s] any sexual relationship between a child and an adult in a position of paternal authority" (70) in which the sexual contact must be kept a secret. Enid's secret and incestuous affair with her uncle begins and ends with her encounters with death: Enid's suicide attempt and, finally, her abortion. The necessity of having an abortion, however, finally leads Enid to integrate her fragmented selves. The "good" Enid meets her "bad" self, her shadow, and this meeting makes possible their integration into Enid, the aspiring pianist.

As in *Angel of Light*, the image of the dove in *You Must Remember This* signifies the relationship between private and public power relations, as well as the necessarily transitory nature of innocence. For example, when Enid, who is only seventeen, has an abortion—an abortion resulting from her Uncle Felix's carelessness—she remembers a dove that neighborhood boys had set on fire. During the abortion, following the injection of the anesthetic, she imagines: "Around her head a flaming nimbus appeared. There was a dove whose feathers were afire. Enid was the dove but she was also watching the dove flying upward in wild widening fiery circles out of her vision" (370). At this moment, Enid is the suffering dove, but she is also watching the suffering dove, as if she were one of the neighborhood boys, one of the persecutors of the dove, her unborn child. Both possibilities—of

Enid as victim and victimizer, of Enid as "good" and as "evil"—are suggested by the image of the dove. Through the image of the dove, this scene is linked to the Prologue of the novel where readers learn that, as fifteen-year-old Enid attempts suicide, "she remembered a mourning dove the boys caught in the vacant lot then doused with gasoline then lit with a match. The bird's wild wings flapping flying in looping crazy circles, ablaze, its beak opened emitting a terrible shriek. It flew up into the air higher and higher then suddenly fell to the ground" (5). In the act of suicide, Enid identifies with the boys' cruelty, but at the same time her suffering is like that of the vulnerable dove, "its beak opened emitting a terrible shriek."

This image of the burning dove mirrors the gender politics in both the private and public spheres: power relationships within the Stevick family that lead to Enid's suicide attempt, as well as the politics of the cold war era that almost force Lyle Stevick to attempt suicide. Fortunately, in contrast to other fathers in *Angel of Light* or *American Appetites*, Lyle Stevick comes to terms with mortality, with the death he carries within. Indeed, Lyle's honest confrontation with death—through his struggle to build a bomb shelter—teaches him to let go of his children, in particular to let go of his youngest daughter, Enid. When Lyle borrows money from Felix to build a bomb shelter, he also shares with his half-brother some of his feelings about being a father. In this way, Lyle establishes a healing bond with Felix, who is still engaged in an incestuous affair with Enid. Once the alienated brothers establish a direct, emotional relationship, they no longer need Enid to act as an object of exchange between them; hence, she is freed from their psychic projections. This fraternal relationship also enables Felix to overcome his incestuous obsession with Enid, through whose body he had attempted to reunite himself with the family of his dead father. Again, because Felix has known defeat as a boxer—defeat which teaches him, as it teaches Lyle, to recognize his mortality—he finally gives up the romantic desire to transcend human limitations. Such a mature recognition of human limitations, particularly of mortality, spells the end of innocence and, at the same time, the end of romance.

Fortunately, Hannah's increasing self-respect coincides with Lyle's willingness to acknowledge his need for her, a convergence that enables the aging couple to redefine their love for each other. This change, the maturation of parents, also makes it possible for Enid—more quickly than almost any daughter in Oates's oeuvre—to reclaim her matrilineal inheritance. As a result of Hannah's self-assertion, she changes the balance of power in

the Stevick family. As a working-class man, Lyle has already been forced
to acknowledge the limits of his power; just Hannah gains economic and
psychological power, however, Lyle has begun to confront the other limits
of his power: his aging and the inevitable loss of his children. In fact, just
as Enid had begun the process of separating from her mother, Hannah had
begun a sewing business. However, not until she begins to recover from
her abortion does Enid make the important discovery that her mother
is not only a mother but also an artist. "Lying in bed beneath an old
quilt Mrs. Stevick had made for her years ago," she begins to see and
admire her mother's artistry: "For comfort rubbing the quilt—Momma's
quilt, 'double wedding ring' the pattern was called, interlocking circles of
vari-textured white cloth on a plain white background with white applique
and white embroidery so finely done it fairly astonished—so many hours
of Hannah Stevick's life sewn into it, Enid was thinking, thinking too it
was beyond her even to calculate the jigsaw puzzle of hundreds of subtly
differing shades and textures of white. White upon white, the wedding
rings interlocking scarcely perceptible to the casual eye. She wondered if
anyone in the family had ever *seen* this quilt Momma had sewed? Really
seen it. Though looking wasn't enough, you had to touch too—like reading
Braille" (419). In this maternal heritage, which is not only biological but
cultural, Enid discovers firm ground for her own claims to subjectivity and
artistry.

And although Enid's life may not follow the same pattern as her mother's
—the pattern, for example, of the "double wedding ring"—she sees/touches
in her mother's sewing, just as Alice Walker sees in our "mothers' gardens,"
the value of commitment to something beyond the self, to one's family as
well as to one's art. By honoring her own gifts, rather than seeking them in
a man, Enid moves beyond the romance plot. Thus, it is primarily through
Enid's recognition of the value of her mother's art that she finds the courage
to claim her vocation as an artist.[8] Finally, then, Enid finds consolation not in
a relationship with a father-surrogate but in her art, her music. Fortunately,
because Hannah Stevick has claimed her own subjectivity and artistry, Enid
is free to pursue her study of the piano. Moreover, when she integrates the
repressed shadow—allowing the powerful (m)other to speak within—Enid
finally begins to acquire genuine artistic power as a pianist. Thus, as illustrated in this and other novels, innocence has little value for an adult, male
or female, and the demand that girls retain their innocence into womanhood
actually inhibits their development, both sexually and intellectually.

In this way, these novels introduce the myth of romantic innocence—especially the romantic myth of the father's possession of his virginal daughter—only to critique it. In *You Must Remember This*, as in *Angel of Light*, the loss of innocence that leads to self-knowledge is necessary if Americans are to revise their conception of the family romance and to mature as a nation. For example, in *Angel of Light* both the saintly Maurice Halleck, whose suicide forces his children to act out his revengeful desires, and Nick Martens, who takes Kirsten Halleck to bed, are examples of dangerously innocent fathers. Such innocence—specifically, the lack of self-knowledge that leads to incestuous desire—results in both public and private acts of violence. In such an Oedipal world, the daughter is forced to fulfill the father's incestuous desires rather than being given the freedom to see with her own eyes and act upon her own desires, sexual or artistic. By contrast, in *You Must Remember This*, Lyle Stevick wards off his fear of death, a fear widely shared in the U. S. during the 1950s, not by committing incest, but through the process of building a bomb shelter. Moreover, through images associated with the bomb shelter—a cavernous space that might be womb or tomb—the novel links Lyle's private fears to public paranoia over communism in the 1950s. Oates's title suggests that just as Lyle Stevick must remember his "personal" past, the loss of a father who divorced Lyle's mother to marry a younger woman, the nation must remember its repressed fear of mortality in order to recover from the "hysteria" of McCarthyism.[9]

As Abrams and Zweig explain, "The collective shadow takes the form of scapegoating, racism, or enemy-making. To anti-Communist Americans, the USSR is the evil empire. To Moslems, America is the great Satan. . . . In our minds, we turn these *others* into the containers of evil, the enemies of civilization" (xx). Oates emphasizes the dangers of such romantic innocence, innocence that necessitates the projection of personal and political evil onto the (m)other, when she describes the process of writing *You Must Remember This*, which had as its "working title" *The Green Island*: "During the approximately fifteen months of its composition, I thought of this chronicle of the Stevick family as suffused, in a sense, with greenness: green of romance, of nostalgia, of innocence; green of an epoch in our American history that, for all its hypocrisies, and its much-documented crimes against its own citizens, has come to represent an innocence of a peculiarly American kind." What is this peculiarly American kind of innocence? Oates defines it as "an island: insular, self-contained, self-referential, doomed. Passion plays itself out on both the collective and the personal scale, and is best contemplated at a distance, by way of memory" ([*Woman*] *Writer* 379). In both *Angel of Light* and *You Must Remember This*, the theme that "passion plays itself out on both the collective and the personal scale" is evident from Oates's transformation of the Oedipal plot, or family romance, and in her critique of America's romantic innocence. Through recurring poetic images, both novels also illustrate Kaschak's argument that "neither the antigonal nor the oedipal complex is a purely personal or familial drama, but each includes an interplay with those aspects of experience with the socio-cultural" (87). The interplay between the familial and the sociocultural dramas is most fully developed in *Because It Is Bitter, Because It Is My Heart*, which depicts four families, one of them African-American, representing different socioeconomic classes.

In a highly positive review of *Because It Is Bitter, Because It Is My Heart*,[10] Henry Louis Gates remarks that Oates "has taken on what Du Bois averred would be the defining problem of this century. Du Bois called it the 'color line,' but here it is figured as a wound, crusted with proud flesh and humbled spirits" (27). This wounded body, as I shall illustrate, is at once individual and social, a point the novel makes through its recurrent imagery as well as its fluid narrative technique. Through this technique, as Gates emphasizes, Oates creates "porous boundaries" between characters. Oates's "ear is unfailing across gradations of class and color," Gates says, and she "gives minor characters carefully limned personalities and histories where an impressionistic blur might have sufficed" (27), an effect he describes as "akin to the photographic technique of 'deep focus'" (27). This comparison of Oates's narrative with a photographic technique is especially suitable for *Because It Is Bitter*, since, as I shall illustrate, photomontage is the novel's trope for the art of a democratic society. Oates's emphasis upon the art of democracy—an art that celebrates people of all colors, genders, and social classes—is evident in the opening scene of *Because It Is Bitter*.

It is August 1955 when the female protagonist, Iris Courtney, visits her uncle at his photography studio. There, in the negatives clipped to a wire above her Uncle Leslie's work bench, Iris sees the "luridly black faces and arms" that tell her that this photograph is of "'white' people" (57). This observation, which is at once aesthetic and political, points to the author's critique of a racist society: just as the black of a negative becomes the white of a developed photograph, the two are not actually antagonistic opposites, but interdependent. Although Uncle Leslie is still hurt by customer criticism of his interracial collage, which had been captioned "Merry Christmas 1949,"

Iris understands why it had offended some of her uncle's customers. The collage not only mixes races, but the individuality of each child is lost in a sea of faces. When Iris suggests, "Maybe the faces are too small. For the parents' taste, I mean" (61), Leslie answers, "But that was the idea of the constellation as a form. And theme, too—individual faces are small, in the tree of life. Obviously!" (61). Like Uncle Leslie's collage, *Because It Is Bitter* portrays a collage of families not only to develop the theme of community but also to critique romantic individualism. Such a theme did not appeal to many of Oates's early readers[11] just as it did not appeal, during the 1950s, to Leslie's customers. Even at age thirteen, Iris Courtney understands that her uncle's mixing of races is not quite socially acceptable, and she says, "Uncle Leslie, you know, white and colored mixed . . . that offends some people. Some parents" (61).

Nevertheless, in the spirit of Walt Whitman, Leslie Courtney practices a democratic art, celebrating the American people "en masse," even though his customers don't appreciate it. What these customers want is exactly what Iris's parents want: not a democratic art but a romantic art that mirrors their desire to be "larger-than-life" figures at center stage, the brightest stars in the constellation. It is just such oversized desires, the novel illustrates, that prompt Iris's parents, the self-named Duke and the exotically named Persia, to disavow the past and reinvent themselves, and to gamble and drink and quarrel. When Duke betrays Persia, the marriage finally ends in divorce. Of course, Iris bears the burden of her parents' romanticism, first suffering abandonment by her father, who leaves the family deeply in debt as a result of his addictive gambling, and later, abandonment by her mother, who dies of alcoholism after years of neglecting Iris. At the same time, the multiplication of Iris's face on her uncle's Christmas tree collage, where her image is almost lost among the faces of many other children, black and white, makes the point that she is certainly not the only child who suffers from neglect.

The novel also makes the point that, however divided in appearance, these multiple lives are interconnected. For example, although only one family, the Savage family, is highlighted in the wedding ceremony that takes place in the novel's epilogue, the presence of Alan Savage's family underscores the absence of Iris Courtney's family. The kindly presence of Gwendolyn Savage, who presides as surrogate mother to Iris, also serves as a reminder of the painful absence of Iris's mother, Persia. Likewise, the presence of Leslie Courtney, the only "family" Iris invites to her wedding, reminds readers of the absence of her father, Duke. This play of presence/absence also highlights the fact that Iris is keenly aware of the absence of Jinx Fairchild, the young African American she loves, while in the presence of Alan. Finally, using the rhetoric of photography, the wedding itself acts as a "negative" of other ceremonies that take place in the novel. The novel reiterates this point by portraying not only Iris Courtney's family but three other families of different races and social classes. These three families produce three sons whose lives, in different ways, intersect with Iris's: Alan, son of Gwendolyn and Byron Savage, an upper-class white family; Verlyn or "Jinx," son of Minnie and Woodrow Fairchild, a working-class black family; and Patrick Wesley or "Little Red," son of Vesta and Vernon Garlock, a poor white family from the hills of West Virginia.

By the time Iris enters Syracuse University as a scholarship student, she has lost both her father and mother and, although she appears entirely self-sufficient, she yearns for a family. This desire for a family, a "good" family unlike her own, will determine Iris's choice of a husband.[12] Iris's desire is shaped not only by her experience of family life but also by oppressive societal forces—inequalities of class, sex, and race—as represented by the families whose sons' lives intersect hers in various ways. It is not surprising, for example, that in 1963, when Iris is a senior in college, she is willing to lie about her family heritage in order to become part of what she deems a "good" family. She has already come to know Professor Byron Savage, an art historian for whom she works as a research assistant, and his wife Gwendolyn, when their only son, Alan, returns from a stay in Paris. Swiftly, and with Gwendolyn's encouragement, Iris decides that she will marry Alan. With this objective in mind, Iris invites Alan into her tiny attic room, where he sees on her wall a collection of photographs, "the largest, a constellation of hundreds of children's faces in the shape of a Christmas tree" (343). However, when Alan exclaims, "Wherever did you find these," Iris answers in a manner that denies any kinship with her artist uncle: "Oh, I found them in a secondhand shop. In Hammond" (344).[13] Alan, an art historian who specializes in the photography of the modernist Man Ray, says he "likes" the constellation even though his father would not consider photographs to be "art" at all.

Yet Iris is unwilling to trust Alan with any revelation about her embarrassing family; she therefore denies her kinship not only with her Uncle Leslie but with her father and mother and with all the children on her uncle's tree of life collage. Shame isolates Iris from others, depriving her of a sense of family and community, as is often characteristic of adult children of alcoholics who become, according to Judith Seixas and Geraldine Youcha, "lonely islands" (8). But despite Iris's attempt to deny the past, even while Alan Savage is making love to her, she cannot avoid thinking of another young man who is part of that past, an African-American named Jinx Fairchild, the only man for whom Iris has felt love and genuine sexual desire. Even though Iris wants to marry Alan, a "good" white man from a well-educated and privileged family, she cannot give herself to him. Mysteriously, her body closes to Alan as "the thought of Jinx Fairchild passes through Iris's mind, for all men in their physical presence define Jinx Fairchild in his absence; she thinks, Oh Jinx, how I love you, but no, she is thinking of Alan Savage; she touches his hair, his fine lank hair, she strokes the nape of his neck, they're whispering and laughing together to forestall a terrible gathering urgency like the wind rising outside" (345). Soon, however, Alan senses that her body resists his, "as if all that this young man might offer her, all the passion and tenderness and beauty of his maleness, were being rejected beforehand for no reason either of them might name" (346). Because Iris has little hope of acting upon her desire for Jinx Fairchild, the man who saved her life, that desire takes a new object—not Alan, but instead his family, particularly his mother. Her secret longing is for a mother who will replace the lost Persia.

Invited for Thanksgiving dinner by the Savages, Iris feels, after a drink of sherry, "a curl of something in the pit of her belly, a tickle of sexual desire" (285). At this moment Iris's eyes are not on Alan Savage, whom she has yet to meet, but on Mrs. Savage.[14] This hunger for a (m)other, symptomatic of a hunger for community, defines the "bitter" heart of this novel, whose title comes from a poem by Stephen Crane.[15] Like many others, Iris is hungry, not only for heterosexual love but for communal love. We are told, for example, that Iris's body rejects Alan's "for no reason either of them might name," not only because she marries Alan for his mother, his family, but also because she cannot—given the racism of American society—marry the African-American man she loves. Since tragic divisions in American society have destroyed what Oates calls "the democratic essence of divinity," the tripartite structure of *Because It Is Bitter* ("Body," "Torsion," "Ceremony") depicts a society in which four American families—the Garlocks, the Fairchilds, the Courtneys, and the Savages—represent aspects of our fragmented social body. In contrast to traditional tragedy, however, our "democratic" society's "Body," "Torsion," and "Ceremony" are not embodied in a single (usually white aristocratic male) character. Instead, the novel's center shifts, its plots multiplying like the faces in Uncle Leslie's photomontage. As this multiplication implies, the democratic spirit reveals itself in the social body's torsion and its ceremonies, whether the individual body is male or female, white or black, rich or poor.

For example, the ceremony that unites Iris and Jinx is an act of violence: Jinx's accidental killing of "Little Red" Garlock to protect Iris. This moment of death functions as a shadow ceremony or mirror image of the wedding that takes place in the epilogue. Indeed, the fish-white body of Little Red that bobs to the surface of the river functions as an image of the guilt that finally puts an end to young Jinx's life. The novel also depicts Iris and Jinx as twins or doubles: as white and black, female and male. The death of Jinx in Vietnam functions as a shadow image of Iris's marriage to an upper-class white male who has degrees from Harvard and Yale rather than medals from Vietnam. However, even as social injustice becomes evident in the duplications, the novel itself is constructed as an act of resistance against privileges of class, gender and race. Like Uncle Leslie's collage, the novel has no single center but instead democratically multiplies its movement, its interplay of bodies, torsions, and ceremonies. For example, Alan Savage's presence makes palpable the absence of Jinx Fairchild; the duplication is "bitter," but the novel's imagery resists bitter inequities through its play of light and dark. As stated above, the interdependency of the races is also obvious in Iris's observation that a film negative with "luridly black faces and arms" indicates that the people in the photo are, in fact, white.

In short, the ceremony of marriage in the novel's epilogue is not a "happy ending" tacked onto the tragic story of Jinx Fairchild but rather a variation upon the theme of social injustice: what is possible for an Alan Savage, born into wealth and privilege, and what is possible even for Iris Courtney, a young woman born into a lower-middle-class white family, is impossible for a highly intelligent and talented young man born into a black family named Fairchild. It is true that Jinx Fairchild dies in the Vietnam War, but his fall from glory had actually come much earlier, at the moment his basketball career had ended, closing abruptly his only chance to fulfill the American dream, which is also his mother's dream for him, of winning a scholarship to college. In a ceremony of self-punishment performed on a basketball court in the presence of a large crowd, Jinx "comes down awkwardly, and hard, his ankle turns . . . and the *crack!* of the snapping bone sounds through the entire gym" (201). As if to fulfill his nickname, Jinx's body, in torsion, finally snaps, not only from the pressure to play well—to be a "performin' monkey" (191), as his brother puts it—but from the terrible burden of his guilt. For Jinx, the condition of being twisted or turned in opposite directions, the experience of torsion, is psychologically induced. Although Jinx's guilt should be shared by the entire community, as the novel makes clear, racism forces him to bear it alone.

Only one person, Iris Courtney, knows why Jinx acts out a ritual of self-punishment on the basketball court. Because she alone watched as he killed Little Red in her defense, some years later Iris tells Jinx, "Look, why did you do it? That 'accident'? I know you did it intentionally, I knew right away" (240). But Jinx, who has tried to avoid Iris since the death of Little Red Garlock, answers, "I don't know what you're talking about, girl. You better shut up your foolish mouth" (240). Iris persists, "Nobody knows, but I know. You never fooled me. And it was a mistake. We didn't do anything wrong. We don't deserve to be punished" (241), but she "isn't altogether real to Jinx: she's a kind of doll, doll-sister, little white doll-sister, not a woman" (243), and this conversation, which takes place during a date initiated by Iris, is their last. Jinx cannot recognize Iris as a soul mate; nevertheless, the secret they share unites them in spirit, and it changes both of them irrevocably. The different consequences of Little Red's death—which leads to death for Jinx and to "good" marriage for Iris—cannot be attributed to the fact that Jinx has a conscience, whereas Iris does not, as Marilynne Robinson suggests in a review of the novel. Even though Robinson claims that "Iris, in the manner of many of Ms. Oates's female protagonists, is notably unencumbered by guilt" (7),[16] in fact, it is *because* Iris has the audacity to feel "wed to Jinx by their secret" (7) that she can manage her guilt.

Tragically, because he is black, Jinx has been taught not to think of a white woman as an object of desire, and, because he is male, he has also been taught not to think of any woman as someone with whom to share his pain and guilt. The comfort Iris might offer, as a secret sharer, is thus doubly forbidden to Jinx; as a consequence, he feels more isolated than she, more alone with their so-called "crime." Jinx is a scapegoat, but his experience is also multiplied in the lives of his father, his brother, and other African-American men who experience brutality rather than the protection of their rights from officers of the law. Thus, the novel is a dramatization, in Oates's words, of "the abyss . . . established between blacks and whites [that] causes people to lose their completeness as human beings, to lose their souls" (Hersh 4). The novel's multiple depictions of injustice against

African-American men, such as John Elmo Ritchie, make it obvious that Jinx cannot go to the police, that he cannot confess to killing Little Red in an act of self-defense and be released, ceremoniously, from his guilt. He does try to talk to his parents, who are good and loving people, but he has the intelligence and sensitivity to recognize that their burdens are already too great, and he does not ask them to shoulder his.

Often the novel depicts young people—Iris and Jinx, as well as Little Red and Alan—through the dreams of their mothers; as a result, readers view the dismembering of the social body through the mothers' losses of their sons and daughters. The American dream cannot be fulfilled, this novel suggests, as long as mothers—of all classes and races—are unable to realize their own dreams or their children's dreams. This loss is most obvious in the tragic ceremonies of death, usually the deaths of sons, which are more often experienced by lower-class and/or black families. For example, because Vesta Garlock had seen a vision in which the Angel Gabriel held her last child in his hand as "a 'bright, shining' baby with flame-colored hair that skipped back a generation to Vesta's grandfather" (97), she had named him in honor of this man, who had died young in a world war. Yet the dirty, brutalized child, whom his mother tried to scrub in boiling water when he was six, had died before reaching adulthood.

Minnie Fairchild, a hard-working and determined mother, also had dreams for her sons, dreams reflected in the names she had chosen for her sons, Woodrow William and Verlyn Rayburn, which recall powerful political figures, President Woodrow Wilson and Speaker of the House Sam Rayburn. However, only her sons' nicknames, Sugar Baby and Jinx, had stuck, and their violent deaths seem to Minnie Fairchild a repudiation of her fair children, born of her body and dreams. As a "negative" image of these ceremonies of male death, Iris's wedding does not spell the end of a single "comic" plot, presumably, at the center of American society. An upper-middle-class white wedding does not have the power to mend such bloody tears in the body politic. Even if central to the plot of Iris's life, the wedding does not signify social unity, for Iris has learned, as readers are told, to ignore the promptings of her body. Nevertheless, in contrast to Vesta and Minnie, Persia has greater power, for, though she herself dies an alcoholic, her daughter lives out the dream implicit in the name "Iris," the name Persia had chosen.

As Iris learns, Persia did not name her for a flower, but rather for "something special: the iris of the eye" (39). Because Iris herself would have preferred being named more conventionally, she "doesn't know whether she likes her name" when she finds out its "special" meaning. Iris does flower into a beautiful woman, but by this time she has learned—from her father's betrayal and abandonment of the beautiful Persia—that beauty has little survival value. Instead, Iris learns to use her "feminine" beauty to attract only men of a certain kind, the "good" men—as Persia confesses to Iris on her deathbed—that her mother had mistakenly rejected. Out of necessity, the prematurely adult Iris becomes more than simply a delight for the male's gaze; she becomes a keen-eyed observer herself. Iris has, in fact, cultivated the habit of observation in her struggle to survive the blurry, chaotic world of her alcoholic parents. But Iris's vision is also transformed by the fact that she has seen Little Red Garlock die at the hands of Jinx Fairchild, who defends her when neither of her parents is available to help. After witnessing this event, Iris develops the capacity, rare in one so young, to see beyond simple (binary) terms of black and white, or good and evil. Just as the iris of the eye is itself composed of a rainbow of colors, Iris has the capacity to see her society in more complex terms. In fact, as a major in art history, Iris has more in common with the "iris diaphragm," that piece of the camera that regulates the amount of light admitted to a lens, than she does with the showy, variously colored flower, the iris.

Iris's camera-like capacity for observation enables her to regulate her emotions as she observes and then carefully modifies her behavior in order to appear "normal." Invited to a Thanksgiving dinner by Professor Savage, Iris carefully calculates her behavior until she is acceptable enough to marry into this white upper-class American family. The Savages, whose family name is quite carefully chosen, are a generous, even "magnanimous" family, but Iris understands that " 'her friends' very magnanimity is granted them by means of an infrastructure that surrounds and protects them yet remains unexamined as the air they breathe: their inherited wealth, their social position, the color of their skin" (312). They are "so good, so generous, yet so smug," Iris notes, taking their social position as "their God-given birth-right" (312). Early in her relationship with the Savage family, whom Iris thinks of as having adopted her, as if she were a "stray," she joins in the family's laughter "even as she's calmly calculating: Families like to laugh together: remember that" (320). Like other children of alcoholics, Iris has no idea what a "normal" family does; sadly, she must learn by watching.

Iris carefully watches the Savages for cues to the performance she is expected to play. When she suddenly "snatches up the empty wine bottles and bears them off in the black woman's wake . . . brazenly out into the kitchen where no guest is welcome," she thinks, "Why am I doing this?" (293). It is an act of loyalty to Jinx, no doubt, for his mother might have played the part of serving maid, but it is also an act of loyalty to her own mother, whose absence becomes poignant in the presence of the wine bottles. In fact, Iris can scarcely eat Gwendolyn's sumptuous Thanksgiving dinner, with its recipes handed down from "Mary Washington herself" (289), without thinking about her mother and, when the kindly Mrs. Savage asks her about her family, Iris quickly leaves the table after explaining that her mother is dead. In the bathroom "she vomits out her guts in the toilet" (296), something her alcoholic mother did frequently. During the Savages' dinner party, Iris thinks, *"Impossible for me to dissociate, since P., the spectacle of eating from the spectacle of vomiting"* (289), but still she tries to eat the lobster bisque, the turkey, "the two kinds of stuffings (mushroom, oyster), and two kinds of cranberry sauce (sweet, tart), and whipped potatoes, and candied yams, and diced carrots, and several kinds of hot breads including corn bread" (289).

As an adolescent, Iris had eaten her meals alone, and often, because of her mother's absences, away from home. However, as Persia had entered the late stages of alcoholism, Iris had tried to feed her, tried to mother her mother. Iris recalls "overseeing Persia's breakfast . . . a meal served at an odd hour, late afternoon of this windy April day. Scrambled eggs, lavishly buttered whole wheat toast, orange juice, weak Lipton's tea. Persia raises a forkful of egg to her mouth, lowers it to her plate; raises it as if it were something precious, or mysteriously heavy . . . then lowers it again to her plate. Iris is teasing, cajoling, begging, threatening, pleading. 'Try. Try. Just *try*. How do you know you can't keep it down if you don't *try*?'" (245). Even years later, when Iris eats, she cannot forget Persia's vomiting.[17] Nor can Iris marry without thinking of the loss of her mother. In the days prior to her wedding she continues to lose weight so that her gown—loaned by Gwendolyn—requires repeated alteration: "Evidently, since the last fitting, the bride-to-be has lost more weight. Another pleat or two will have to be taken in, another judicious tuck" (386). If the "negative" of the wedding ceremony is the ceremony of dying, calling up images of Jinx, then the "negative" of the dinner party is the tomb itself, calling up images of Iris's mother.

But images of eating are multiplied in the novel; for example, Virgil Starling makes "Galveston Gumbo" for Persia, describing it as "Just some messin' around my momma does, it ain't no recipe or anything" (146), and Minnie Fairchild prepares fish for dinner, reminding Jinx of the river, of the smell of death on his hands, "murderer's hands" (131), he thinks. Images of food and death mingle in Jinx's mind, as they do in Iris's. Noticing the change in Jinx, Minnie Fairchild does and yet does not want to know what the problem is. Is he sick? She questions her son while "chopping fish heads and tails, brisk, no-nonsense, squinching up her face as if she hates the smell but showing by her posture and pistonlike motions of her chopping arm, that, yes, there's a pleasure in this, chop! chop! chop! against the old weathered blood-stained breadboard, Minnie doesn't quite hear" (131). Minnie responds to her own question: "Make yourself useful, boy, get some newspaper and wrap up this offal and haul it out back; if there's one thing I can't stand more'n the stink of fish and scales all over everything it's the fish-eye starin' up at me like I'm the one to blame" (131). For Jinx, the smell of the river is associated with the smell of death and the image of Little Red rising to the surface of the water, rising to the surface of his conscience, refusing to stay down.

The web of poetic associations, as in the clustering of fish images and smells of the river and Little Red's death, suggests that not only do we deny the relationship between food and death but also the reality that we are all "kin." For example, Iris associates her uncle's photography shop with "doomed lobsters, black, spidery, giant-clawed, groping about in the bubbly water tank in the neighboring front window" 53), whose smell, "a sly stink of wet sand, brine, fish penetrating the walls" (56) of her uncle's studio, mingles with the odor of the chemicals in the developing fluid. The smell, together with the images of the lobsters, reminds Iris of her uncle's artistry; looking at the many photos in his shop window, some "flyspecked" and "discolored," Iris thinks, "What a jumble! It's like a common graveyard: photographs of unknown men, women, and children . . . black faces beside white . . . landscapes of the city of Hammond . . . the riverfront. . . . 'artistic' studies that yield their designs only after a long minute's scrutiny. It seems that Leslie never takes anything out of his display case, only adds" (Oates's ellipses 53–54). Like Whitman, Leslie's is an egalitarian art, an art of the graveyard in which all, great and small, white and black, human and animal, lie down together. In Leslie's art the stress falls on likeness rather than upon difference or social hierarchies. "His vision as an artist was to photograph every man, woman, and child living in Hammond, New York: 'every soul sharing a single instant of time' " (56). His romanticism seems to be reserved for Persia, his brother's wife, whom he photographs again and again, often in mother-daughter portraits: "the camera gaze is waist-high, a technical trick to make the subjects appear taller than the viewer, more exalted" (58).

However, after Persia's death, Leslie weans himself from both romanticism and alcoholism; he even moves his shop to "the sunny side of the street," one sign of ascent, socially and artistically. Still, photography reminds Iris, always, of mortality: just walking into her uncle's shop brings "that stab of visceral horror: *You are going to die, here's proof*" (58). For Iris, who is an art historian like her husband and his father, art bears a democratic message, which is also Oates's message: "You are going to die, here's proof." This is also the message of one of Iris's gifts to Jinx: an old photograph of the Civil War in which are posed "a band of Union soldiers, some on horseback, most on foot, and among the foot soldiers are several black men, uniformed like the rest" (188). Although Jinx "doesn't feel any kinship with the black soldiers," the photo is found among his "treasures" after his death in another war. During a discussion of art at the Savages' Thanksgiving dinner table, Iris, who has noticed that Byron Savage doesn't mention photography in his survey courses, had argued that Bosch's untitled triptych, "The Garden of Earthly Delights,"[18] is "a code of some kind," but that "the code of the work doesn't matter anyway, the 'Meaning' doesn't matter, it's the fact of the work, whether seeing it, you are stopped dead in your tracks . . . nothing else matters" (Oates's ellipsis 292). Afterward, Iris realizes "that she'd spoken disparagingly of the very enterprise of art history and of iconography, Dr. Savage's religion" (293), but he had seemed amused.

Of course, as Dr. Savage practices his religion, it would exclude photography completely, a point against which his son Alan rebels. Alan says, "Art is art for a specific time and a specific play; 'art for all the ages' is bogus," finally causing his father to explode when he argues, "As Man Ray says, what is art but 'the giving of restlessness a material form' " (327). Yet Alan also "described to Iris the way in which Man Ray 'designed' his mistress Kiki's face; the artist had shaved the young woman's eyebrows completely off, drew on artificial brows, painted on her a masklike face of stylized beauty, with eerily enlarged eyes and prominent darkly stained lips" (344). The views of father and son are not, after all, so far apart; it is unlikely that either would admit Leslie Courtney's photomontage into the "great tradition." Undoubtedly, that is why Iris had disowned her uncle's tree of life in Alan's presence. The novel explores the question of artistic value through poetic associations that democratically link the "high" with the "low." For example, Iris associates the images in Titian's classic painting "Marsyas Flayed by Apollo," which depicts "the skinning alive of a satyr who's in fact a human being" (378), with the news of President Kennedy's death when she imagines "objects, and we among them, objects in others' eyes, losing their shapes, definitions, names: the boundaries separating them gone, their very skins torn off or peeled deliberately away as in that deathly painting at which Iris stared for a very long time one day in Dr. Savage's library at his home" (378).

Through poetic association, the image of being skinned alive is associated with the ordinary act of cooking, of dropping lobsters into boiling water, and with acts of human cruelty almost beyond imagining: with mad Vesta's scouring of Little Red Garlock, age six, in boiling water; with Persia's scalding of her own body with boiling water that, in her alcoholic madness, she had intended for the cat; and with the blistering death of Sugar Baby, who, while in his own bath, is burned beyond recognition by boiling water that his tormentors pour over his skin, again and again.[19] Would Byron Savage consider Sugar Baby's savage death an appropriate subject for the artist? These haunting images demand that readers question the relationship between art and life, particularly between art and the lives of those who have been absent in "classic" literature. Like Leslie Courtney's photography, the art of Joyce Carol Oates is democratic and communal; again and again, her novels call attention to the fact that although we imagine ourselves isolated individuals, we are all, in fact, interconnected. We are all kin. It is the death of a president, the man who has traditionally represented the body politic, that reminds Iris of the truth of Titian's painting: that the boundaries that separate "us" from "them" are illusions that can be stripped away, if not by art, then by violence.[20]

How Does "I" Speak for "We"?: Violence and Representation in Foxfire, Confessions of a Girl Gang

Through its narrator, Madeleine "Maddy" Wirtz, *Foxfire, Confessions of a Girl Gang*[1] explores the complex relationship between language and violence. Fifty-year-old Maddy, a member of FOXFIRE (always spelled in caps) from age thirteen to age seventeen, uses her notes and memories—as well as some flights of imagination—to chronicle the gang's adventures from 1952 to 1956. "It was a time of violence against girls and women," Maddy explains, "but we didn't have the language to talk about it then" (100). In retrospect, Maddy—who has completed college and now works as an astronomer's assistant—understands that the girls in FOXFIRE had no language for the violence perpetrated against them; however, as narrator, Maddy has a different problem: how can she tell the gang's story—that is, how can an "I" speak for a "we"—without doing violence to, without denying the voices of, the women she once loved? This question is of critical importance because the gang was formed so that collectively its members would have the power to resist the violence perpetrated against them. Under the leadership of Margaret "Legs" Sadovsksy, the FOXFIRE gang devised a range of creative strategies, many of them verbal, to defend themselves against sexual harassment and violence. As Legs tells Maddy, "It's a state of undeclared war, them hating us, men hating us no matter our age or who the hell we are but nobody wants to admit it, not even *us*." (101).

To defend themselves against male violence, the girls in FOXFIRE must first admit what adults, especially males in positions of authority, refuse to acknowledge: institutionally sanctioned violence toward women, violence perpetuated by the silences in public discourses. As Teresa de Lauretis argues, the silence of male-dominated discourses—the way language "names certain behaviors and events as violent, but not others" (240)—is one way that "violence is en-gendered in representation" (240). To illustrate her point, de Lauretis cites the work of feminist social scientists Wini Breines and Linda Gordon, who explain that as long as no word existed for "family violence," medical professionals usually ignored the causes of a patient's injuries, returning wives and children to their abusers, thereby perpetuating domestic violence. Again citing Breines and Gordon, De Lauretis argues that the use of gender-neutral language in most studies of incest perpetuates sexual violence by obscuring the fact that "in cases of incest as well as cases of child sexual abuse, 92 per cent of the victims are female and 97 per cent of the assailants are male" (242). What is at stake, de Lauretis emphasizes, is whether the social order—in this case the family—is to be "maintained or to be dismantled" (242). The violence engendered by such presumably "neutral" institutional discourse has a direct bearing upon the lives of poor teenage girls, such as those depicted in *Foxfire*, many of whom, while running away from violent or neglectful families, become vulnerable to sexual violence on the street.

The traditional canon of literature also constitutes a form of violence, as Judith Fetterley asserts, because "through what is taught and how it is taught, our educational system ratifies boys' sense of agency and primacy, their sense of themselves as subjects, particularly as defined *against* their sense of girls as objects" (" 'Not in the Least American' " 880). By contrast, Maddy is striving to define her subjectivity, not by making the girls in FOXFIRE into mute objects, but by establishing their claims to language and agency, along with her own. Strictly speaking, Maddy's voice occupies an "intermediate" zone between personal and communal narration. Maddy is, in fact, not the protagonist—that role belongs to Legs—but she is telling her own story and, at the same time, the gang's. As Susan Lanser points out, narrative individualism has prevented analysis of this "intermediate" type of narrator: one who is "reconstructing the life of another woman but is in some sense the protagonist herself, not simply an eye witness or an autobiographer" (21). At the same time, Maddy's narrative authority comes from her membership in a community that, contradictorily, has authorized her to write the gang's history, but not to tell it. In my view, Maddy's style of communal narration, her attempt to create an "I" that can speak nonviolently for a "we," is born out of her recognition that violence, whether linguistic or physical, arises from a desire for stability, certainty, and control.

"For the violator," as Laura Tanner says in *Intimate Violence*, "violence may come to serve as a temporary affirmation of an unstable self, a material manifestation of a disembodied ideology, an expansion of one's own insubstantial form out into an alien world" (4). Even though Maddy's authority is already unstable because of her gender and class, she reveals her uncertainties as a narrator: she is striving to avoid representational violence by acknowledging that, even as she attempts to tell the "Truth," she doubts that it is possible to do so. She admits that, at times, she is not simply reporting an event, but inventing it, while at other times she admits to losing control over the narrative. As narrator, Maddy's voice is structurally superior to others in the gang, but she refuses to claim linguistic agency by denying other points of view. Sometimes, for example, Maddy makes it obvious that Legs has a different point of view. Furthermore, Maddy's authority is clearly contingent upon her position in the community; Legs is always first in command of the FOXFIRE gang.

As Maddy relates, the girls of FOXFIRE refuse to become the blank screens of male desire or violence. Working together, under the capable guidance of Legs, they devise a game called "hook and bait" to trap the men who would buy them for sex. Invented primarily to meet a desperate need—to raise capital to pay the gang's living expenses—the game also provides the pleasures of revenge. Their strategy is simple but effective: while one girl acts as the attractive "bait" with which to "hook" the male gaze—as if she were merely a blank screen for male desire—the rest of the gang watches, waiting for the right moment to attack. The object of the game is not to kill or injure, but to demand money from men willing to treat them as commodities. The tricky part of the game is, of course, timing the attack to catch the man with his pants down, just before the girl who is playing "bait" can be forced to turn a trick. It is Margaret "Legs" Sadovsky, the gang's remarkable leader, who invents the game following a job interview that turns into an attempted seduction. Because Legs was "fed up with the kinds of jobs available in Hammond for young women with her qualifications" (225), she had dressed as a man[2] to interview for a position as an encyclopedia salesman. When the interviewer, mistaking Legs for a young ("feminine") man, tries to seduce "him," she draws her knife. To save himself, the injured Mr. Rucke bribes Legs by giving her all he has.

"Just something that got snagged on my *hook*" (232), Legs explains upon returning to FOXFIRE with Rucke's money, watch, ring, camera, even some marijuana. Though she didn't get the job, the interview inspires the invention of the money-making game, "hook and bait." In a chapter called, "FOXFIRE HOOKING: A Miscellany, Winter 1955–56," Maddy describes the disguises worn by gang members who play "bait"—it may be "an alone-looking girl of about seventeen years of age, pretty freckled face and curly red hair" (233) or "the one with dead-white skin and luscious lips, big sloe eyes, sleek black hair" (234) or "a shapely girl with eye-catching platinum blond hair waved and curled like Marilyn Monroe's" (236). The gang stages the game in different settings—at a train depot, a hotel, and an inn—and they hook a variety of "fatherly" men: a man with "a fatherly, an avuncular look to him" (233), a man who takes "the hook in his smug little purse of a mouth" (234) with the comment, "I have a daughter myself" (235), and another man who is "a good Catholic husband and father" (236). When Maddy plays the bait, "sitting in the Trailways station glancing through a newspaper" (239), a man "with a fatherly-bullying smile" almost wins the game by leading Maddy, in a manner "snug and fatherly" (244) into an isolated alley. By the time FOXFIRE arrives to defend her, she is already swallowing blood.

Despite its dangers, the gang plays this tricky game quite successfully, hooking "fatherly" men who read them as blank screens, as bodies without voices, as "bad daughters" who function as currency to be circulated by the fathers. According to the homosocial rules of "hooking," the prostitute circulates as daughter/currency among men; however, FOXFIRE turns the tables, rewriting the rules of the game. As Elaine Scarry observes, voice and body historically have been understood as "paired opposites," a structural relationship "between the disembodied torturer (at times no more than a voice) and the (speechless) victim who is all body," a relationship that is "played out again in biblical history with a God who is all voice and in Marxist economic theory with its remote commands issued by a disembodied capitalist class" (quoted in Morris 251). Since these paired opposites—voice and body—are gendered, a (woman) writer finds herself in a different relationship to language; as de Lauretis points out, Nietzsche can speak from the position of woman, because that place is "vacant" (239). The novel makes this point most powerfully when Legs decides to kidnap a wealthy businessman and hold him for ransom. At this moment, when FOXFIRE attempts to turn a male body into a commodity—a body that the gang hopes to circulate like currency—the novel raises questions about the ethics of violence.

I will return to this ethical issue after first illustrating how the gang plays the language game—that is, how they fight sexual violence with words. I begin my analysis of the novel's word games with the gang's rewriting of the body in its ritual of membership. As Maddy reports, FOXFIRE is a linguistic creation, born during a formal swearing-in ceremony. The ceremony takes place on New Year's Day, 1953, when four girls arrive at the home of Legs (also "Sheena") Sadovsky: Goldie (also "Boom-Boom") Betty Siefried; Lana Loretta Maguire; Rita (also "Red or Fireball") Elizabeth O'Hagan; and Madeleine (also "Maddy," "Monkey" or "Killer") Faith Wirtz. All wear black, and all wear crosses around their necks, as instructed by Legs. Once all have entered her bedroom, which is darkened except for five burning candles, Legs distributes five shot glasses filled with whiskey, "with priestly decorum" (39). Next, in an "incantatory" voice, and in language she probably borrowed from conversations with a "retired" priest, she leads them in this secret oath: "Do you solemnly swear to consecrate yourself to your sisters in FOXFIRE *yes I swear* to consecrate yourself to the vision of FOXFIRE *I do, I swear* to think always of your sisters as you would they would think of you *I do* in the Revolution of the Proletariat that is imminent in the Apocalypse that is imminent in the Valley of the Shadow of Death and under torture physical or spiritual *I do*" (39–40). The girls must also swear, "never to betray your FOXFIRE sisters in thought word or deed never to reveal FOXFIRE secrets" (39–40), a promise Maddy clearly breaks by writing the FOXFIRE confessions.

Following this swearing-in ceremony—a playfully serious parody of religious, civic, and legal ceremonies that traditionally confer power on men—Legs produces an "elegant silver ice pick" (40) with which she writes the gang's emblem upon her own body. Maddy, who is last in the ceremony, asks Legs to tattoo her left shoulder: "At first it was a tattoo of blood, oozing blood-droplets, points of pain on the pale tender flesh of Maddy's left shoulder," but after the bleeding stopped, they rubbed alcohol into their wounds and used red dye to form the flame-tattoo; then, "while the bleeding was fresh, they pressed together eagerly to mingle their blood their separate bloods" (41). In this ceremony they become "blood sisters," as Legs says, in a serious parody of homosocial rituals in which men celebrate their collective power. And in the Dionysian frenzy that follows—when Goldie is pulling down Legs's bra and giving Lana "a jungle-cat bite of a kiss," when Rita is "pressing her grapefruit-sized bare breasts against Goldie's smaller taut breasts and someone dribbled whiskey on Rita's breasts and licked it off" (42). This parody of ceremonies—those rituals in which language is an action conferring power—is not a pale imitation, but an aggressive recontextualization, a carnivalization of language by which the FOXFIRE gang appropriates linguistic power for itself.

I deliberately choose Mikhail Bakhtin's term *carnivalization* because, as Patricia Yaeger points out in *Honey-Mad Women*, we must turn to Bakhtin, rather than Foucault, if we are to find a theory of transgressive practices that liberates not only words but speakers, speakers such as the young women in *Foxfire*. In Yaeger's view, as in mine, "There is little room in Foucault's system for the linguistic play affirmed, say, in Bakhtin's descriptions of insult and parody. According to Bakhtin, such transgressive practices allow not only words, but speakers themselves to be released 'from the shackles of sense,' to define moments within discourse when we are able 'to enjoy a period of play and complete freedom and to establish unusual relationships'" (Bakhtin, *Rabelais and His World* 423; qtd. in Yaeger 89). Although the gang enjoys only a short period of such playful freedom, they celebrate by writing on a variety of surfaces—on paper or placards, on cars, buildings, or cakes, as well as on their own flesh—and with a variety of materials— with crayons and ink, blood and frosting, paint and nail polish, ice picks and an old Underwood typewriter. They also use different genres—tattoos, graffiti, letters, and a ransom note. During these carnival moments, the gang radically reverses the position of women: FOXFIRE claims collective agency through acts of violent inscription, thereby rejecting the role of mute body, often violently inscribed by men. The novel depicts a number of these reversals.

One such reversal—also depicted as a scene of recognition between women—takes place in a chapter called "Black Eye" when Maddy's mother opens the bathroom door, which has a broken lock, to see her daughter standing before the mirror. Because it is early in the morning and both mother and daughter are half-naked, they can read what is written on the other's body: Maddy is inscribed with the "beautiful FOXFIRE tattoo . . . my tattoo so lurid and flamey red exposed for Momma to see," while her mother is inscribed with a "big purplish-orangish black eye as if a giant's fist has walloped her good on the right side of her face" (58).

Although both mother and daughter have been written upon, the flame on Maddy's shoulder is a reversal, a mirror image, of the black eye inscribed by the male "giant." Men possess the power of a giant, not only because of greater physical strength, but because of economic dominance. For example, Maddy's mother has been widowed by war, but she cannot earn enough to support herself and her daughter. Yet her husband's family offers her no financial help. In fact, when Maddy asks her uncle for a favor—she wants an old Underwood he has put out with the trash—he tries to force her into providing sexual favors in exchange for the typewriter.

A second scene occurs when Legs, newly released from a girls' detention center and employed by the Park Service, accidentally comes upon a "dwarf" woman named Yetta. Legs is helping to clear underbrush at the edge of Cassadaga Park when she grows thirsty. At that moment she spots a house attached to a tavern, that happens to be closed. When no one answers her knock on the door of the house, she goes to the back yard looking for an outside faucet. There she sees a strange woman "child-size but not child-proportioned with a long torso and a misshapen back, and her face, not ugly exactly, but strange, sort of twisted like her spine" (198). What is most shocking to Legs is that "this woman is wearing a dog collar around her neck and the collar is attached to a lightweight chain which is attached to a clothesline" (198). Although Legs is a "giant" in the eyes of her gang—a mythical figure with powers usually attributed only to heroic males—Yetta is actually a mirror image of the many "dwarfing" experiences of abuse that Legs has experienced at home, at school, at work, and in a girls' detention center. Drawn to those who cannot defend themselves, imagining herself as a protector of women, Legs returns with Goldie to observe what happens to Yetta at night. Hiding in the bushes, the girls are horrified by what they see: Yetta lying "naked, spread-eagle, a terrible sight to see her with her wrists and ankles tied to the bed's four posters so her deformed body is completely exposed and completely open . . . and one by one men come into the room" (200 Oates's ellipsis).

The attachment of the tavern to a house underscores the close relationship between commercial and family violence—the latter a form of violence that, as stated above, didn't even exist until feminists named it.[3] Legs and Goldie try to prevent family violence when they return to the house where they confront a "bear-size" man who identifies himself as Yetta's brother. Boldly, since the two girls are alone, Legs argues that "there are laws prohibiting such things, abuse, forced prostitution" (200), but Yetta's brother retorts angrily that "it's none of her fucking business what people do in the privacy of their own home" (200). Unfortunately, because Legs has been abused by many figures of authority—father, principal, judge, prison guards—she does not trust them enough to ask for their help. Nonetheless, she returns, alone, to the scene of the crime. Again she watches men enter Yetta's room where "one by one bare-assed their genitals swollen, penises stiffened into rods, mounting the dwarf-woman, the woman-that's-a-body, one by one pumping their life into her, evoking those cries" (202), and her rage flares. Recalling the words of Father Theriault, a defrocked and alcoholic priest who speaks "of capitalism of the curse of human beings apprehending one another as commodities the tragedy is that men and women not only use one another as things but use themselves, present themselves, sell themselves . . . as things" (202–3 Oates's ellipsis), Legs sets fire to the house and tavern. The fox's fire burns. In this instance, words of protest have proven to be useless. In the next chapter, called "FOXFIRE DREAM/FOXFIRE HOMESTEAD," Legs manages to finance a mortgage on an old farmhouse that, in sharp contrast to Yetta's, protects the FOXFIRE "family"—as they define themselves—from abusive men.

Almost all of the early FOXFIRE triumphs recorded by Maddy are to some degree verbal victories. For example, in their first adventure the girls cover with graffiti the car of a middle-aged math teacher who has been sexually harassing Rita "Red" O'Hagan. By age eleven, Rita had "the contours and proportions of a woman" (23), as well as a certain "conspicuous female helplessness" (25) and as a result had already begun attracting unwanted male attention. At age twelve, for example, her own brothers, along with older boys from the Viscounts gang, had made her "the object of certain acts performed upon her, or to her, or with her, for most of a long August afternoon" (25). However, when Mr. Buttinger, her ninth-grade teacher, not only made fun of Rita's mistakes but was observed "sometimes drawing his thick beefy hands against her breasts quickly and seemingly accidentally" (29), the gang decided to act. The next time Buttinger forced Rita to stay after school, they were ready: they painted "tall lurid red letters" on the back and passenger side of his 1949 Ford. During his drive home, Buttinger feels himself "running the gauntlet of witnesses, some of them students" (31), but, out of dread, waits until he arrives home to read the words that have made a "spectacle" of him: "I AM NIGGER LIPS BUTTINGER IM A DIRTY OLD MAN MMMMMM GIRLS!!! I TEACH MATH & TICKLE TITS IM BUTTINGER I EAT PUSSY" and mysteriously, on the bumper, "FOXFIRE REVENGE!" (31). Shortly afterward, Buttinger retires from teaching.

FOXFIRE's next triumph is also, in part, a matter of possessing the word—in this case, owning a typewriter. When Maddy Wirtz tries to buy her uncle's used Underwood, with which she plans to chronicle the gang's adventures, the gang saves her from his attempt at sexual blackmail. Uncle "Wimpy," as they call him, demands five dollars for the machine even though it had been put out on the curb with the garbage; "I'm a businessman, sweetie," he says, "I'm not the goddamed Salvation Army" (61). Maddy returns with borrowed money, but once again he raises the price—this time to eight dollars. Then, after teasing his niece for an hour, "He brought her hand against the front of his trousers: against his bulging crotch" (67). She manages to get away, and, after consulting with her gang, returns. Uncle Wirtz mistakenly interprets her return as signaling a willingness to submit to his sexual demands. This time, however, she has brought along the gang who wait, hidden, ready to attack when signaled. Just as Wimpy unzips his pants exposing "a red boiled sausage," Maddy "scrambles to her feet, tugs at the blind to release it so it flies up to the ceiling," calling for the attack: "they have a board they're using as a battering ram, within seconds the window is broken, shards of glass go flying, it's an explosion, it's festive, the girls of FOXFIRE piling through the window like young dogs eager for the kill, there's Legs, there's Goldie, there's Lana, there's fierce little hot-eyed Fireball, and Maddy's one of them, five girls springing on Wimpy Wirtz caught frozen in astonishment and disbelief, gaping, pants open and penis exposed, big as a club but already it's beginning to wilt, and retreat. And they're on him" (76).

Inflamed by their success, the gang finds great pleasure in writing FOX-FIRE's "secret flame-tattoo in red crayon or ink or nail polish just a few inches high on a locker or a desk or a window at school" (80), or drawing "a giant flame five feet in height in bright red-blood paint on these surfaces: the eastern side of the railroad viaduct above Mohawk Street; the southern side of the Sixth Street bridge; the wall facing Fairfax Avenue of the boarded-up Tuller Bros. warehouse; the brick wall facing Ninth Street of the high school; the tattered billboard high on stilts overlooking the Northern Pacific railroad yard!" (80). Their next adventure, a protest against a pet shop's mistreatment of animals, is also a triumph of words. They drive customers away by carrying picket signs bearing the words, "TYNE PETS IS CRUEL TO ANIMALS," "IF YOU LOVE ANIMALS DON'T SHOP HERE,"

"SHAME SHAME SHAME," "HAVE MERCY ON ME," and "HELP ME PLEASE" (92). It is a tactic they have learned from local unions, but they add an unusual twist, disguising their identities by wearing Halloween masks: "Legs has a crafty fox mask, Goldie has a snarling wolf mask, Lana has a snooty cat mask, Rita has a panda mask, and Maddy, naturally, has a puckish monkey mask" (92). This carnivalesque moment, in which the costumed young women assert the transformational power of the word, illustrates what Yaeger calls "the animality of the letter" even as the gang calls attention to the violence of representation: the fact that, historically, man's flight from the body has been predicated upon his identification of woman as body, animal, nature.

Of course, FOXFIRE does not define its protest in such academic rhetoric, yet Legs's sympathetic identification with Yetta, as well as the gang's with the animals at the Tyne Pet Shop, indicates a desire to transform that violent binary hierarchy: voice/body, writing/text, culture/nature, man/woman. Of course, the gang's desire for transformation includes economic hierarchies as well. As Legs understands, the power of words is not enough. FOXFIRE must have a home of its own and an adequate income. Indeed, the demise of FOXFIRE is brought about primarily (though not exclusively) by the gang's lack of a strong economic base. However, in its heady early days the gang usually managed to find ways, as well as words, to triumph over their oppressors. Halloween is such a triumphant occasion. "ITEM. Hallowe'en: the sisters of FOXFIRE in disguise as gypsies in long black skirts, exotic scarves and jewelry, wearing black domino masks travel miles away to uptown Hammond to go trick-or-treating in the affluent residential neighborhoods" (93). While trick-or-treating they acquire quite a bit of loot, "but their real mission as Legs envisions it is to familiarize themselves with alien territory—the world of the 'propertied bourgeoisie' " (95). They write their Halloween graffiti on the plate glass windows of business establishments: Lana writes, "SATAN LIVES," Maddy prints, "BEWARE THE CAT," and Legs scrawls, "NO ESCAPE NO MERCY $$$$ IS SHIT ABOMINATION DEATH" (94). In this and other episodes, the novel emphasizes the point that the gang performs its subversive acts not simply as women, but as poor women.[4]

Indeed, it is largely because she is poor and untrained in good-girl submissiveness that Legs is "detained" in Red Bank State Correctional Facility for Girls. Yes, she had pulled a knife to defend a new gang member from harassment by members of the Viscount gang, and, yes, she had stolen a car to make her getaway, but most of FOXFIRE had gone along for the ride. However, Legs is clearly their leader, and the judge must punish someone: "Legs drew what is called an indeterminate sentence, five months *minimum*, no stated *maximum*" (130) which she had the audacity to declare "*unconstitutional*" (131). In the eyes of her gang, the fact that Legs is incarcerated only raises her stature. As Oates comments, "She begins as a young girl and ascends to a kind of mythic state, at least in the minds of her Foxfire sisters" (Karpen 6). Despite her mythic attributes, Legs finally collides with the patriarchal power that cages young women—institutional power personified by principal Morton Wall, Judge Oldacker, and her father Ab Sadovsky. Though known for his public drinking and fighting, Ab Sadovsky appears in court not to support his daughter but to testify against her. Like Yetta, Legs is caged and—because she imagines herself always in flight, running like a horse,[5] climbing like a cat, even flying like a hawk—such confinement drives her almost mad.

As John Crowley says, "Legs Sadovsky is a brilliant creation—wholly heroic, wholly convincing, racing for her tragic consummation impelled by a finer sensibility and a more thoughtful daring than is usually granted to the tragic male outlaws we love and need" (6). In one legendary exploit, Legs climbs a sixty-foot water tower, defeating all male contenders for the prize money: seventy-five dollars. In another climbing exploit, Legs tries to escape from Red Bank: "skinny and snakey-agile she pushes herself through a crack between buildings" until she reaches "the wall—she doesn't hesitate, leaps up grasping at raw blunt featureless cinderblock, leaps up like a doe shot in the heart, leaps up, up, grabbing and grasping and falling back" (151). Once apprehended, her resistance only increases her prison time. However, Legs finally becomes "tractable; reasonable; obedient; good" (174) following a visit from her father, during which the sadistic man told Legs that her mother had tried to abort her. Meanwhile, the other Legs—though isolated, injured, and caged—watches "the sparrow hawks riding the air in the blue of morning," and "suddenly she was among them her arms that ached from being twisted up behind her back were wings dark-feathered powerfully muscled wings and she ascended the air, the cinderblock wall fell away" (170–71).

Legs vows, "*No one and nothing will touch me, ever again. If anybody is to kill it will be me*" (174). Although she loves Legs, Maddy cannot make such a vow. The division between Legs and Maddy over the attempt to kidnap a wealthy businessman is the result, to a large degree, of their different experiences:

because Maddy's father is dead, she has not experienced paternal violence as Legs has, nor has Maddy been subjected to the violence of prison as Legs has. But their conflict can also be attributed to differences in their personalities. Both yearn for escape, but Maddy's flights tend to be primarily verbal while Legs's are primarily physical. Oates says, "The book is supposed to be a kind of dialectic between romance and realism. . . . I had originally imagined Legs Sadovsky with a great deal of motion, flying across rooftops, able to jump long distances. Probably, in a larger sense, I was writing a romance, and Legs is one of those figures out of myth" (Karpen 6). Legs is the romantic figure, but the dialectic between romance and realism, between heavenly transcendence and earthly bonds, between the freedom of flight and the pull of gravity, is intensified by Maddy's narrative strategies. As an adolescent, Maddy, the voice of "realism," was no match for Legs. Maddy tells us, "Legs talked, I listened, always I was mesmerised listening to her, always and forever" (15); "I wasn't hoping to analyze Legs' account of what had befallen her, I never tried, those early years," she says. "I wouldn't have granted Maddy Wirtz such authority!" (16).

Maddy gradually acquires a sense of her own authority, not the authority of mastery but of the imagination. As a girl, she had "loved to study maps, maps of the solar system, and the Earth, but maps too of local regions" (8); she loved writing lunar names; and she had been excited by "numbers invisible and inviolate never to be contaminated nor even touched by their human practitioners" (28). Like Legs, Maddy loves freedom, but while Legs chooses the power of moving physically through space, Maddy prefers the power of moving mentally through time and space. Maddy does, in fact, become a scientist whose work is "the contemplation and quantification of rock-debris" (322), but she returns to earth—and to the body—through the act of writing her memoir. "Writing a memoir is like pulling your own guts out inch by slow inch" (99), she says. Sadly, since the gang had pledged itself to secrecy: "Never never tell" (3, 7, 319) the act of writing is itself a betrayal of Legs and of FOXFIRE. In fact, from the start, Legs had regarded Maddy's flights of imagination as a betrayal of their friendship. Once, observing a family buying a Christmas tree, Maddy had said innocently to Legs, "There's something about other people isn't there—you'd like to know who they are?—you'd like to know who they are—you'd like to *be* them, maybe?" (21). Legs had answered, "You'd betray your friends, huh, not giving a shit about anybody who knows you and your true friend not some fucking stranger, huh?" (21).

Conflict emerges once again when Legs is released from Red Banks. Maddy senses, not without jealousy, that Legs "knows things I don't know, now" (187). For example, Legs has been brutally beaten by a female guard, and she knows now, as she tells Maddy, "that we do have enemies, yeah men are the enemy but not just men, the shock of it is that girls and women are our enemies too sometimes" (180). However, the final break between Legs and Maddy occurs when Maddy refuses to participate in the plot to kidnap a wealthy capitalist. Since Maddy's rescue during the game of "hook and bait," she recognizes that the gang's use of violence has escalated—*"Since that terrible night. I was afraid of you I guess. You saved my life but I was afraid of you having seen you hit him the way you did"* (253)—and she rejects, finally, the very American—and very male—role of romantic outlaw. Here, I believe, Maddy speaks for her author. Although Maddy is not an autobiographical character, Oates acknowledges, "I'm very much like Maddy" (Karpen 6). It is through the narrator's voice, as well as Maddy's refusal to commit a violent (or potentially violent) criminal act, that the novel makes its ethical point: when women take power, they must not simply identify with it but redefine it. Maddy's refusal to write the ransom note constitutes a betrayal of FOXFIRE, but it also marks her rejection of violence as a tactic. Her decision is primarily ethical; however, it also turns out to be practical for, in this way, Maddy avoids becoming an accessory to kidnapping.

From the start, the crime seems doomed to fail. A major problem is that the gang's carefully chosen male victim—Whitney Kellogg, Jr.—refuses to cooperate: he refuses, for example, to speak to his wife on the phone, using words dictated by his captors. A strong-willed man, he simply refuses to speak to anyone and, in this instance, silence is, ironically, more powerful than words. Another problem is that, though Legs has promised not to use violence, a new member of the gang, V. V. the Enforcer, disobeys orders and shoots their stubborn captive, seriously injuring him. At this point Legs draws the line: she calls an ambulance, ending the game. Idealistic and protective to the end, she orders all those not directly involved to run away before she drives off with V. V., Lana, and Goldie in the gang's car, LIGHTNING BOLT. It is a conclusion reminiscent of and even more ambiguous than the movie *Thelma and Louise*. For, since LIGHTNING BOLT might actually have made it across the Cassadaga bridge—in fact, "is never sighted again, so far as law enforcement authorities can determine" (316)—Legs may still live. This mystery is heightened in the novel's "Epilogue," in which Maddy returns to Hammond some years later. At this time, a now-married Rita shows Maddy a newspaper photograph taken on April 22, 1961, in which a woman—"a figure distinctly American, tall, slender, blond, male? female?"—appears to be listening intently to "a stiff bearded military figure, Fidel Castro" (324). But they can't be certain. And since much of the action in *Foxfire* occurs in Maddy's narration, the ambiguities persist.

As Maddy records the adventures of FOXFIRE, it becomes evident that the gang has nurtured her gift for words. "Rightly or wrongly," as Maddy says, she was perceived as "having the power of words" because she got good grades in writing and because she could "talk fast" (5). The close relationship between a woman's ability to fight back and her ability to talk back is established not only in many of the gang's adventures but also through Maddy's narrative technique. For example, words play an important part in the gang's final adventure (or misadventure): Maddy's refusal to write the ransom note illustrates a refusal to turn a male body into a commodity. Because Maddy begins many chapters by commenting directly upon the act of writing, her narration not only heightens the dialectic between realism and romance, it also problematizes notions of authority and truth. For example, Maddy acknowledges that she may not achieve unity or consistency in her authorial role. She says, for example, "Whoever's reading this, if anyone is reading it: does it matter that our old selves are lost to us as surely as the past is lost, or is it enough to know yes we lived then, and we're living now, and the connection must be there?" (179). She also acknowledges that she does not have complete control of the writing process. For example, in the novel's final part, five chapters are given the same title: "The Plot (I)," "The Plot (II)," "The Plot (III)," "The Plot (IV)," and "The Plot (V)"—as if a single plot cannot tell the truth, the whole truth. And she begins one chapter: "I was certain this morning I'd be writing about our FOXFIRE DREAM/FOXFIRE HOMESTEAD" (195). In this chapter, called "The Paradox of Chronology/Dwarf-Woman," Maddy supposedly "records" the encounter between Yetta and Legs; however, Maddy admits that she did not witness the actual event. How reliable, then, is her "chronicle," as she sometimes calls it?

And what, exactly, is a "fact"? She speculates openly, "If it were not for language, could we lie?" (196). As a scientist—though she admits that she is not an astronomer, but only an astronomer's assistant—Maddy raises complex questions about the relationship between language, memory, imagination, and truth. For example, she says: "There's the paradox of chronology which arises when you try to record events of historical veracity; the problem of transcribing a document like this notebook is that it's a memoir or a confession where you have not the power to invent episodes, people, places, 'plot,' etc. but must set everything down as it occurred. Not imagination but memory is the agent but language is the instrument in all cases and can language be trusted?" (195–96). Admitting that the episode of the dwarf-woman was "never actually glimpsed by Maddy Wirtz," she hints at the desire prompting her to invent the dwarf-woman episode and to position it just before the chapter, "FOXFIRE DREAM/FOXFIRE HOMESTEAD." She says, "The paradox of chronology is hateful because you are always obliged to seek out earlier causes than what's at hand" (196). As Maddy knows, establishing causality is primarily a matter of careful sequencing: what happens first, it is assumed, causes what happens next. In this instance, Maddy's sequencing of events establishes the victimization of Yetta as a cause of the gang's desire for revenge against violent men. Here, by implying that revenge is the motive, Maddy contradicts an earlier statement that she is writing the gang's history to refute certain *"distortions and misunderstand-ings,"* such as, "Like we did evil for evil's sake, and for revenge" (3).

Of course, it is Maddy the fifty-year-old scientist-writer, not the thirteen-year-old gang member, who understands that language structures our no-tions of authority, truth, and social relationships. Looking at her record of the gang's adventures—defined by adolescent Maddy as a "historical docu-ment in which Truth would reside forever" (3)—the adult woman observes: "Never does Maddy record in her notebook her own doubts of herself, or of FOXFIRE" (239). Her youthful idealism—her still developing ethical sense and intense loyalty to FOXFIRE—would have made any confession of doubt difficult. While the adolescent Maddy grows intensely anxious during Legs's absence—and admits that without "certain interests of mine like reading about the stars, and Time, yes I guess and typing on the old Underwood typewriter I loved, I would not have known who I was at all. Even maybe, whether I *was*" (167)—the adult writer acknowledges, "For every fact transcribed in these CONFESSIONS there are a dozen facts, a hundred facts, my God maybe a thousand left out. . . . Can you tell the truth if it isn't the *entire* truth" (99). Even chronology, Maddy realizes, is a fiction, a language effect. She says, "Because one thing rises out of something that came before it, or many things that came before it, so it's like a big spiderweb in Time going back forever and ever, no true beginning or any promise of an end in the way in those years it was believed the Universe was" (99). While the adolescent Maddy desired certainty from math and science—"the world of Numbers that doesn't change, immutable facts, celestial bodies" (100)—the adult acknowledges: "For all material things, we have learned in the twentieth century, are but the processes of invisible force-fields" (221).

As an author, as a writer who is presumably confessing the Truth, Maddy's reflections upon the composing process point to the instability of self, truth, and authority. Even the heavens, which once promised Maddy a stable place to drift—the very names, "OCEAN OF STORMS SEA OF TRANQUIL-ITY LAKE OF DREAMS LAKE OF DEATH" (163) providing a sanctuary from her "scary loose slipping-down life" (166)—turn out to be constantly in flux. For the adult Maddy, the lunar names function instead as a code for the loneliness that Maddy felt in the absence of Legs but that she could not openly express. Another chapter, "A Short History of the Heavens," serves a similar metaphorical purpose. As an adolescent, Maddy had memorized certain facts—so desperate to *learn* to *memorize* things she believed to be permanent" (137)—which she now lists: reports of "fiery stones" falling from the sky in Rouen, France, in 1594; of "raining-burning rocks" falling in Salem Falls, Connecticut, in 1923; or of an object shaped like a "pineapple with wings" observed in Puce, Ontario, in 1951 (135–36). Now, such "facts" have become a code for Maddy to confess the powerful passions of her youth: her feeling, for example, that when Legs fell to the earth, it was as if the sky itself had fallen. "What is a meteorite?—it's the metallic substance of a meteoroid that has survived its swift, violent passage to earth through the earth's atmosphere. A meteoroid?—small planets or chunks of planets that, passing into the earth's atmosphere, become incandescent; sometimes trail flame" (136). To Maddy, Legs is a burning star, a meteorite or a meteoroid, an asteroid who fell to the earth.

Although science no longer provides certainty for Maddy, her use of scientific discourse allows Oates to create an evolutionary context in which to situate her analysis of human violence. As Oates says, the novel is a dialectic between romance and realism, a dialectic between the language of romance, in which giant-sized humans possess godlike powers, and the evolutionary language of science. While an individual life may appear gigantic in romantic contexts, the novel re-imagines an individual human life in an evolutionary context, as part of "a big spiderweb in Time." In a chapter called "Homo Sapiens," Oates situates the problem of human violence in just such an evolutionary context. Viewing "THE TREE OF LIFE: EVOLUTION" (102), Legs expresses indignation at such a vision of humanity—"Christ you'd think our hot-shit species would count for more than *that*" (102–3)! Maddy responds somewhat differently. At first "fascinated by how complex the tree is, how multiple its branches" (102), Maddy's faith in God is shaken by evidence that not just a single human being but an entire species can die out. The thought occurs to Maddy: "*Homo sapiens* is no big deal! and it doesn't look as if there's any logic to it, the TREE OF LIFE, man's position on the tree, *Homo sapiens: thinking man:* created by what humanoid God in His own image?" (102). What, exactly, does it mean for women to take on power within such an evolutionary context?

Through the novel's representation of violence—particularly as played out in the figures of Legs and Maddy—*Foxfire* considers a range of narrative possibilities. During their visit to the museum, for example, Legs and Maddy talk about the terrible things happening to females, things most girls didn't dare to think or talk about: the rape and strangling of a nineteen-year-old nursing student; a pregnant woman stabbed to death in her house; a serial killer charged with the death of eight girls; a little girl "slashed by some madman with a razor" (100). And Legs dares to say, "They hate us, y'know?—the sons of bitches! This is proof they hate us, they don't even know it probably, most of them, but they hate us" (101). Within an evolutionary context, the only sane option is for homo sapiens to give up romantic illusions—illusions of omnipotence, autonomy, and control. Maddy's communal narrative strategies, in concert with a plot that ends with the probable demise of FOXFIRE, emphasize the limits of human power, mental or physical. The plot also dramatizes how Legs's desire for revenge—the kidnapping plot is motivated by revenge, not just economic need—leads to destruction, to violence and death, while Maddy's communal narration encourages readers to reflect upon the possibility that fear, not strength, motivates Legs's desire for conquest of a "man." According to Jessica Benjamin, the desire for omnipotence—a desire evident in the self presented in psychology and philosophy—is rooted in the fear of dependency upon others.

The fear of dependency can also be discerned in the linguistic habit of splitting the self into a privileged disembodied (male) voice and a re-pressed (m)other. It is through this type of psychic splitting, as de Lau-retis points, that "violence is en-gendered in representation" (240). One consequence of such representational violence, as Carolyn Heilbrun says, is that "women have been deprived of the narratives, or the texts, plots, or examples by which they might assume power over—take control of—

their own lives" (17). As Heilbrun says, "Women's exercise of power and control, and admission and expression of anger necessary to that exercise, has until recently been declared unacceptable" (17). *Foxfire, Confessions of a Girl Gang* portrays women as capable of exercising power and control, capable of expressing the unacceptable. Just as Virginia Woolf recognized that, if she wished to write, she must "kill" the Victorian Angel in the House, Oates understands that to open a creative space for women's voices, she must transform those representations of "woman" as a speechless, tortured victim into representations of women who, together, claim their voices and their agency. Ironically, given *Foxfire*'s critique of the romantic outlaw, the novel's dialectical motion also advances the argument that in order to take power over her own life, a woman must become an outlaw; she must, in community with other women, transgress sociolinguistic codes that position her outside language. The dialectic between romance and realism in *Foxfire*, as represented in the figures of Legs and Maddy, illustrates the paradox, quoted in Heilbrun's *Writing a Woman's Life*, that "all women must destroy in order to create."[6]

Conclusion

Where Has Joyce Carol Oates Been, Where Is She Going?

Is Oates a naturalist or a postmodernist, a crime writer or a gothic novelist? My answer is that Oates eludes such categories, just as the novel, as a genre, eludes them.[1] How, then, are we to define her? The argument of *Lavish Self-Divisions* is that Joyce Carol Oates becomes visible through the manner in which she divides herself into the voices and texts in her novels. Sometimes, as I have illustrated, Oates openly pairs her voice with that of a character as, for example, when she signs a poem, published elsewhere above the name "Joyce Carol Oates" with the name "Trick Monk," a character in *Wonderland*. A similar pairing, or double-voicedness, is evident in a short essay called " 'JCO' and I" which, though signed by "Joyce Carol Oates," employs diction that might be that of Maddy Wirtz, the fifty-year-old narrator of *Foxfire, Confessions of a Girl Gang*. Maddy is a scientist, an astronomer's assistant, but as narrator of the FOXFIRE gang's confessions, she becomes a writer who in some ways resembles Joyce Carol Oates. For example, Maddy asks, "What is a meteorite?—it's the metallic substance of a meteoroid that has survived its swift, violent passage to earth through the earth's atmosphere. A meteoroid?—small planets or chunks of planets that, passing into the earth's atmosphere, become incandescent; sometimes trail flame" (136). In " 'JCO' and I," Oates uses similar diction as a metaphor for the writing process: the speaker asks, "Can a process be said to have an age?—an impulse a strategy, an obsessive tracery, like planetary orbits to which planets, 'real' planets, must conform?" (n.p.).

A study of the graphic traces of such self-division, I have argued, can make visible the imaginative process by which Joyce Carol Oates—not the visible woman, but the invisible writer—divides herself into different voices and texts. As Oates herself emphasizes, " 'JCO' is not a person, nor even a personality, but a process that has resulted in a sequence of texts" (n.p.). Why this emphasis on a (woman) writer's invisibility? The answer is, of course, that a woman is often defined in terms of her visible self, her body; therefore, writing becomes an imaginative activity by which she escapes that confining self. Writing allows her to assume other voices, whether the voice of scientist Maddy Wirtz, Kelly Kelleher in *Black Water*, or serial killer Quentin P., narrator of Oates's recent novel, *Zombie* (1995). "No one wants to believe this obvious truth: the 'artist' can inhabit any individual, for the individual is irrelevant to 'art' (" 'JCO' and I," n.p.), Oates says. At the same time, she does acknowledge that JCO "mines, and distorts" her own "personal history" (" 'JCO' and I," n.p.). Oates's novels are not autobiographical even though she sometimes "mines and distorts" material from her own life or from the lives of her friends. However, Oates's oeuvre does provide a graphic record of her imaginative life, her invisible life, over the past three decades—decades of dramatic change in the U.S. and in the world.

Since Oates's novels are the focus of *Lavish Self-Divisions*, I have not attempted to investigate Oates the short story writer, playwright, poet, critic, editor, or the pseudonymous mystery writer Rosamond Smith—each of whom may be considered a different author-self. As Lorna Sage says, "Joyce Carol Oates, who hardly seems to be one writer, and who writes enough to be several, may stand as a type of contemporary women's writing nonetheless. Who else, after all, could so exactly convey the subversive thought that there's *no end to it*?" (194). But is Joyce Carol Oates a subversive (woman) writer, as Sage asserts? The answer to this question can be found only by analyzing how Oates has "answered" the social struggles of American women during a particular historical era. My argument is that through Oates's revisionary conceptions of authorship—from anxious to dialogic to communal—she articulates an increasingly explicit feminist response to social conditions in the United States from 1964 to 1994. During the past three decades, this study demonstrates, Oates has become increasingly assertive in her linguistic practices, just as her fictional daughters have become increasingly assertive in their social behavior.

However, in the trilogy of the 1990s, Oates is once again depicting victimized women—a suggestion that she may be returning to the tragic vision of the 1960s. In Oates's tragic novels, the incestuous alliance between father and daughter prevails, as I have illustrated, as the power of the mother weakens, in both the family and in society. The mother-daughter bond is strong in the first novel of the trilogy, *I Lock My Door Upon Myself* (1990), but strikingly absent in *The Rise of Life on Earth* (1991) and *Black Water* (1992). All three female protagonists are strong women, but each, to different degrees, is victimized. The question is, why, after two decades, has Oates returned to writing stories about victimized women? Oates has responded to this question in political rather than aesthetic terms. For example, asked why she decided to write *Black Water*, she has explained repeatedly that she was disturbed by events indicating "a climate particularly inhospitable to women" (Hunnewell 29).[2] More specifically, she explained that she was "drawn back to the [Chappaquiddick] incident by Justice Thurgood Marshall's resignation from the Supreme Court and by accusations of rape against Senator Kennedy's nephew William K. Smith" (Hunnewell 29). Indeed, despite the civil rights movements and the women's movements, violence and injustice have not been eradicated in the United States. Violence against women has actually increased during the past two decades.

Hence, this change in Oates's novels of the early 1990s mirrors current sociopolitical realities—in particular, the widening gap between rich and poor, as well as the backlash against feminists, African Americans, and immigrants—along with a resulting increase in hostility and violence. Oates has answered this crisis, not by retreating from her ongoing analysis of the relationship between political and personal realities, but by intensifying it. For example, in her short story collection *Last Days* she continues to bear witness—on a global scale—to social injustices that lead to violence. As she told David Germain in 1988, "I'm more or less of the school of the writer as witness. Witness to history and society" (177). Even though the title of this collection may sound apocalyptic, as Greg Johnson says, "*Last Days* should be read, not as fatalistic but as hopeful, in the sense that a breaking down . . . is the necessary prelude to the 'communal consciousness' Oates has envisioned as replacing the divisive, ego-centered philosophies of the past" (*Understanding Joyce Carol Oates* 199). Furthermore, as if to balance her portrayal of victimized daughters in the trilogy, Oates portrays feisty females, some of whom tote weapons, in *Foxfire: Confessions of a Girl Gang* (1993) and in *What I Lived For* (1994). Yet the victimized women in the trilogy represent an equally powerful response to the growing hostility toward women in our present era. Indeed, just as Oates had no need to invent the violence in "Where are you going?," a fictionalized account of the actual murder of three young women reported in *Life* magazine in 1966, she had no need to invent the drowning of Kelly Kelleher in *Black Water*.[3]

However, Oates's emphasis on victimization in the trilogy suggests that she sees this as a dangerous era, a time when Americans must once again face the hard problems that will determine our collective identity and destiny. Hence, as in the famous "Where are you going?," each novel in the trilogy asks readers to examine the roots of violence in our society, a problem that can be understood only in terms of our past. In an analysis of "Where are you going?" Elaine Showalter points out that while "some have attributed such plots to the overheated and morbid imaginings of the author" (*Sister's Choice* 139–40), Oates has no need to invent the violence she depicts. Oates herself makes this point in her essay, "Why Is Your Writing So Violent?" She also said, following the publication of *Black Water*, "I write about the victims of violence . . . and yet my critics say I'm writing about violence. From my point of view, I've always been writing about its aftermath" (Hunnewell 29). Because of Oates's persistence in exploring violence, some critics describe her fiction as "gothic," but as Showalter explains, "Oates does not see the Gothic as a revelation of female hysteria, but rather as the indictment of an American social disorder, the romanticization of the violent psychopath and serial killer" (*Sister's Choice* 140). In *The Rise of Life on Earth* the serial killer happens to be female, but she is, like Arnold Friend before her, a challenge to the American habit of romanticizing the violent (usually male) psychopath.

As is evident from this example, Oates does not always depict women as feminist role models. This may be one reason why she continues to be excluded from feminist canons. Oates's name does not appear, for example, in any studies by the feminist critics who, according to Ellen Cronan Rose, are creating the canon of contemporary women writers: Linda Anderson, Rachel Blau Du Plessis, Rita Felski, Joanne S. Frye, Gayle Greene, Molly Hite,[4] Sally Robinson, Roberta Rubenstein, Melissa Walker, Nancy A. Walker, Jean Wyatt, and Bonnie Zimmerman. Yet there is substantial evidence, especially during the 1980s, that Oates supports feminist goals. This evidence can be found not only in her novels but also in her criticism,[5] as well as in letters to the editor.[6] In addition, a growing number of feminist critics have acknowledged that Oates is a feminist writer. This change began with the publication of Ellen Friedman's *Joyce Carol Oates* in 1980, followed by Elaine Showalter in 1983; Cara Chell in 1985; Eileen Teper Bender in 1987; and Marilyn Wesley, Joanne Creighton, and Lorna Sage in 1992. Teper Bender argues, for example, that Oates has been "subject to accusatory fire from some feminists," but she has, nevertheless, "anticipated and continues to share central feminist concerns" (*Joyce Carol Oates* x), and Creighton points out that "in both her fiction and her essays, [Oates] participates in feminist discourse by attempting to assess how women are made and unmade by male definitions of womanhood" (*Joyce Carol Oates: Novels of the Middle Years* 57).

Yet in 1986 Bonnie Zimmerman, in "Feminist Fiction and the Postmodern Challenge," describes Oates as "hostile to feminism," despite the fact that her fiction exhibits features that Zimmerman identifies as characteristic of feminist postmodern fiction: attentiveness to "an audience, to meaning, and to everyday life" and the use of the gothic "to create chilling views of social and private life" (177–80). Gayle Greene also omitted Oates from her 1991 study of women novelists, *Changing the Story: Women Writers and the Tradition*, simply by declaring that Oates is "not feminist" (25). Remarking on Oates's "troubled relationship" with "normative feminism," Henry Louis Gates suggests that feminists reject Oates's fiction because she "insists on exploring the nature of female masochism" (28). An equally plausible explanation for Oates's exclusion is, I think, competition among women. Oates depicts such competition in *Solstice* (1985) despite the fact that, as Rebecca Sinkler comments in a review of the novel, "The soft underbelly of feminist thought has promoted the idea that if women rule the world, cooperation, supportiveness, even love would replace patriarchal imperatives like competition, dominance and brute force" (4).

Feminist controversy over this novel mirrored the very competition—a power struggle between two women—depicted in the novel. When novelist Joanna Russ attacked *Solstice*, describing it as a "Sadistic Lesbian novel," because of its supposed appeal to "prurient appetites" (qtd. in Teper Bender, *Joyce Carol Oates* 158), Oates replied in a letter to the *Women's Review of Books*: "I have never written a sadistic lesbian novel," though she defended her right to do so. Ironically, *Solstice* confronts the very problems that Joanna Russ (or "Joanna," the first-person authorial voice of *The Female Man* describes as major problems in establishing a feminist identity: "the vanity training, the obedience training, the self-effacement training, the rivalry training, the stupidity training, the placation training" (151). Joanna asks, "How am I to put this together with my human life, my intellectual life, my solitude, my transcendence, my brains, and my fearful, fearful ambition?" (151). It is a question Russ answers, according to Annis Pratt, not only through imagery and plot in *The Female Man* but in her authorial comment: "To resolve contrarities . . . unite them in your own person" (111). Despite their conflict in *The Women's Review of Books*, Oates shares Russ's view; in fact, she prefaced a collection of critical essays called *Contraries* (1981) with Blake's dictum "Without contraries is no progression."

While this study concedes that not all the stories in Oates's novels depict positive female role models—such a strategy would make good propaganda but poor art—I believe that her novels illustrate brilliantly that by claiming the right of self-narration, the right of self-definition, women have the potential to liberate themselves, along with our entire society, from the violence engendered by unjust social hierarchies. However, as Oates recognizes, "Power does not reside with women—no more in the literary world than in the world of politics and finance—and power is never under the obligation to act justly" (*[Woman] Writer* 31–32). Furthermore, even in the late twentieth century, as Oates says, "only the (woman) writer is afflicted by her own essential identity" (*[Woman] Writer* 32). "How can the paradox be accommodated?" she asks, and answers, "with resilience, with a sense of humor, with stubbornness, with anger, with hope" (*[Woman] Writer* 32). I can think of no better way to conclude this study—which has examined Oates's struggle to accommodate this paradox—than with her emphasis on the resilience, the sense of humor, the stubbornness, the anger at injustice, and the hope for social change that sustain her.

Notes

INTRODUCTION

1. For a full discussion of Bakhtin's value to feminism, see Laurie Finke's *Feminist Theory, Women's Writing*, Dale Bauer's *Feminist Dialogics*, Patricia Yaeger's *Honey-Mad Women*, and Bauer and Susan McKinstry's *Feminism, Bakhtin, and the Dialogic.*

2. Critics attack Oates's productivity, charging that she writes too hastily, that she does not edit carefully. But Oates does revise carefully, as illustrated in *A Piece of Work: Five Writers Discuss Their Revisions*, edited by Jay Woodruf.

3. Following Oates's example, I place "woman" inside parentheses when it is used in the phrase "(woman) writer." With this practice, I underscore the fact that, linguistically, a writer is assumed to be masculine. In addition, I mean to emphasize the idea that gender is socially constructed rather than "natural." For more on this topic, see Oates's exchange with Elaine Showalter, following the publication of Showalter's "Women Who Write Are Women."

4. Oates's resistance to the notion of a unified (essentialist) self is illustrated not only in her fiction but in autobiographical pieces such as "Stories That Define Me" (5–16) as well as in essays such as "Does the Writer Exist?" or "Pseudonymous Selves" ([*Woman*] *Writer* 45–52; 383–97), where she explains that the pseudonymous "Rosamond Smith," author of crime novels, is another alternate self.

5. Both Eileen Teper Bender and Joanne Creighton discuss the theme of community in Oates's novels, but neither focuses, as I do, on multivocal narrative techniques in novels of the 1980s.

6. The short story, "The Girl," which appeared in *The Goddess and Other Women* (stories published individually between 1966 and 1974), was also printed in a special limited edition by Pomegranate Press—a fact suggesting its importance to Oates.

7. A number of critics have examined Oates's depictions of women—among them Mary Allen, Eileen Teper Bender, Cara Chell, Joanne Creighton, and Ellen Friedman, but few have focused specifically on daughters. However, see Marilyn C. Wesley's "Father-Daughter Incest as Social Transgression: A Feminist Reading of Joyce Carol Oates." Also see Pamela Smiley's "Incest,

Roman Catholicism, and Joyce Carol Oates" (*College Literature* 18 [Feb. 1991]: 39–49). Brief references to the daughters in Oates's fiction also appear in Thelma J. Shina's *Radiant Daughters: Fictional American Women* (158–87).

8. The title poem of Oates's collection, *Invisible Woman*, ends with these lines: "Because you know me, we have never met. / Because you see me, you cannot hear" (3). Alicia Ostriker locates this poem by Oates in an invisible woman tradition originating in Emily Dickinson's duplicitous "I'm Nobody!"

9. My work on father-daughter incest precedes Wesley's. See chapter 3, "The Central Nervous System of America: The Writer in/as the Crowd in *Wonderland*," which first appeared in *Feminism, Bakhtin, and the Dialogic* in 1991.

10. During the development of both genres, the daughter functioned as an object of homosocial exchange; however, according to Paula Cohen, the threat of father-daughter incest increased during the era of the novel's development because, as the power of the kinship system weakened, its ability to constrain the incestuous father diminished.

11. Both Cohen and Kristeva make this argument, although Kristeva suggests that the practice arose much earlier (*Desire in Language* 37–91). Cohen is, of course, describing the traditional canon, a canon that feminists began to challenge—by recovering the novels of women writers—just at the time Oates began to resist the practice of aesthetic unity.

12. Katha Pollitt suggests that promoters of "difference feminism" make essentialist arguments about " 'relational' women, [and] 'autonomous' men" (800–801). My point is that, while recognizing women's need for autonomy, Oates calls for a recognition of the relational nature of identity for *both* men and women.

13. See my *Narrating Mothers*, co-edited with Maureen Reddy.

PART ONE
Anxious Authorship in the 1960s: Daughters Leaving Home

1. In a study based almost entirely on Oates's early short fiction, Frank Cunningham identifies what he calls "The Enclosures of Identity in the Earlier Stories" (9–28). He locates these enclosures in Oates's mind, or in the minds of her characters. I locate these enclosures in sociolinguistic conventions that shape the consciousness of her characters. Oates critiques these enclosures in her early fiction while transgressing and transforming them in her later fiction.

2. This story—for which the full title is "How I Contemplated the World from the Detroit House of Correction and Began My Life Over Again: Notes for an English Class at Baldwin Country Day School; Poking Around in

Debris; Disgust and Curiosity; a Revelation of the Meaning of Life; a Happy Ending . . ." appears in *The Wheel of Love, and Other Stories.* It first appeared in *Triquarterly* (Spring 1969), and later in *Prize Stories: The O. Henry Awards* (1970), and also in *Cutting Edges: Young American Fiction for the '70s* (1973).

3. Oates also explores male-female relationships in many of her best-known short stories of this decade, many of which appear in *The Wheel of Love* (1970). See my "Sexual Politics in Two Short Story Collections by Joyce Carol Oates."

CHAPTER ONE
Not Strictly Parallel: The Sacrificial Plots of
Daughters and Sons in *With Shuddering Fall*

1. In a short story called "Ceremonies" (*By the North Gate*), a daughter's sexual awakening again triggers violence. The daughter in "Ceremonies" does marry, but only after the father acknowledges some loss of control. The story is narrated by a woman with the maturity to understand the destructiveness of such a possessive father.

2. According to Rose Marie Burwell, Oates wrote *With Shuddering Fall* while still an undergraduate at Syracuse (between 1955 and 1959) although the novel was not published until 1964.

3. *Homosocial* refers to the spectrum of male interaction. Eve Sedgwick explains it as the range from "men-promoting-the-interests-of-men" to "men-loving-men" (3).

4. Oates uses this phrase in a footnote to her essay on D. H. Lawrence, where she remarks, "If one sees that Lawrence *is* 'The Princess,' whose father's ethic of the cold, locked-in ego dooms her to frigidity, the story comes alive as drama and does not seem so flat and polarized in its elements of 'consciousness' and 'instinct' " (*New Heaven, New Earth* 278 n. 4).

5. In "(M)other Eve: Some Revisions of the Fall in Fiction by Contemporary Women Writers," Madelon Sprengnether finds what she describes as "a psychic disengagement from the biblical master plot that provides an aura of familiarity and from the oedipal master plot that sustains it" (298). This moment in *With Shuddering Fall*, when daughter Karen begins to think of herself as a mother, comes closest to the kind of psychic disengagement that Sprengnether describes. The mother-daughter relationship is not central in *With Shuddering Fall*, but it does portray what Sprengnether describes as the daughter's "incorporation of (m)other into her own self-image" (300).

6. Rosalind Miles interprets *With Shuddering Fall* as an analysis of "a woman's collapse into madness and despair, complicated in the case of her heroine, Karen, by the lethal cocktail of religious and sexual guilt" (296–97).

CHAPTER TWO
Yeats's Daughter: Images of "Leda and
the Swan" in the Trilogy of the 1960s

1. See, for example, Fossum's "Only Control: The Novels of Joyce Carol Oates," and Cunningham's "The Enclosure of Identity in the Earlier Stories."

2. See Oates's autobiographical essay, "My Father, My Fiction," in which she describes how her father inspired her, by his creative example, to write fiction.

3. In my view of the father's "unmitigated agency," I am probably closest to Ellen Friedman, who finds in Oates an "inveterate anti-romanticism" (7). By contrast, Joanne Creighton finds "more credence in [Gary] Waller's assessment of Oates as 'neo-romantic' than in Friedman's characterization of her as an 'inveterate antiromantic' " (*Joyce Carol Oates: Novels of The Middle Years* 110). Creighton adds, "We need a new term to encapsulate Oates's unique doubleness, her attraction to Blakean contraries, and her allegiance to, and skepticism about, the romantic tradition" (110). Creighton proposes the term *postmodern romantic*, but I prefer Bakhtin's term *dialogic*.

4. "Children of Freedom" is one of Richard's alternative titles for *Expensive People*, an ironic reference to a notion of freedom so extreme that, in Nada's case, it means a denial of family relationships. "Children of Silence" is the first of three subtitles in *them*.

5. During a personal conversation, Oates told me that her early novels were all variations on the Cronus myth (Detroit, Michigan, 14 April 1973).

6. Teper Bender compares Richard to Icarus rather than to Yeats's swan, but either allusion makes the same point: that the child cannot meet the overblown (romantic) expectations of his mother (*Joyce Carol Oates* 34).

7. This notion of the daughter as property is made explicit in *A Garden of Earthly Delights* when a man named Bert impregnates his daughter Rosalie. As men from a nearby town beat Bert to death, Bert's wife screams, "His property!" (79) and another migrant worker agrees, "The girl was his property" (81).

8. Oates explores this same theme—the theme of daughters attempting to leave home—in such short stories as "Pastoral Blood" (*By the North Gate* 75–92) and "How I Contemplated the World" (*The Wheel of Love* 149–65). Both stories end in failure.

9. Oates's own "class anger," which she acknowledges in "My Father, My Fiction" (108), may have prevented her from sympathizing with such women, at least early in her writing career. For example, Nadine Green, a type of blonde-haired "princess," is portrayed negatively, not only in *With Shuddering Fall*, but also in the short story, "The Expense of Spirit" (*By the North Gate* 179–93). On the other hand, the good middle-class daughter may also represent an aspect of Oates's psyche: the daughter for whom writing is a form of transgression.

CHAPTER THREE
"The Central Nervous System of America":
The Writer in/as the Crowd in *Wonderland*

1. *Wonderland* (1973). I quote only from this paperback edition, except where indicated.

2. Like Oates, Bakhtin insists that "The material bodily principle is contained not in the biologic individual, not in the bourgeois ego, but in the people, a people who are continually growing and renewed" (*Rabelais* 19).

3. Keller develops this argument more fully in *Reflections on Gender and Science* (1985).

PART TWO
Dialogic Authorship in the 1970s: Marriages and Infidelities

1. In Oates's novel *Cybele* (1979), however, the goddess has the final word when she says of the novel's hero, "There was a lover of mine who worshipped me, and became reckless of his life, which was soon taken from him—more abruptly than I would have wished, and more cruelly; for I came to pity him in the end" (11). During this decade, allusions to powerful goddess figures appear more frequently in Oates's fiction, as, for example, in *The Goddess and Other Women* (1974). Oates had begun revising patriarchal myths, alerting readers, even shocking them, into recognizing that we are "of woman born."

CHAPTER FOUR
Marriage as Novel: Beyond the Conventions of
Romance and Law in *Do with Me What You Will*

1. Elena's mother, whose male business associate trusts her because she thinks "like a man," actually assumes the paternal role in her dealings with Marvin Howe. In exchange for a certain amount of money, she gives up even the right to see her daughter. She illustrates, as do Nada in *Expensive People* and Nora in "The Goddess" (*The Goddess and Other Women* 402–20) the kind of "masculine" woman who destroys children. Although Ardis assumes a series of identities, these personas constitute a denial of time, especially the organic time of her aging body.

2. As Walter Clemons noted in his *Newsweek* review, this awakening is not a reenactment of "Sleeping Beauty." Elena's sexual response is awakened by her own activity, both imaginative and physical. Furthermore, Elena chooses to leave her husband, as does Nora in Ibsen's play, not so that she can become someone else's plaything, but rather to take charge of her own life.

3. Lynda Boose argues that "both the Judaic and the Christian myths of family genesis insistently refuse the nuclear family logic of four and just as repeatedly insist, through various transformations, that the three authorized roles within the family are father, son, and mother. The omission, however, creates a flaw in the structure that calls attention to itself. Every mythological system depends upon a persistent sequence of binary oppositions that discriminates categories in the form of 'x is what non-x is not' " (*Daughters and Fathers* 51). This denial of paternity of the daughter, says Boose, "leaves the woman who occupies that role in a strangely illegitimate relationship to the narrative." Oates takes up this problem again in *The Assassins* and *Childwold*.

CHAPTER FIVE

Wedding a (Woman) Writer's Voices: Dis-membering the
"I" in *The Assassins*, Re-membering "Us" in *Childwold*

1. In *Childwold*, as in Oates's "The Daughter" (*The Goddess and Other Women* 51–71), a strong mother intervenes when the father attempts to seduce the daughter.

2. This assumption informs Freud's case history of Dora, but as feminists reinterpret the narrative, Dora did not continue therapy because she rejected Freud's narrative, insisting upon her own interpretation of events. See, for example, Bernheimer and Kahane's *In Dora's Case: Freud, Hysteria, Feminism*.

3. Oates uses this term to define her hero's perversion in *Childwold*. Eileen Teper Bender remarks that Kasch uses the term *paedomorphosis* as a joke: "*Childwold* is itself paedomorphic, embracing primary data and sense impressions, an imaginative embodiment of the process of 'dreaming back,' the portrait of a young artist" (*Joyce Carol Oates* 91). I prefer Margaret Gullette's explanation that "behind every story of paedophilia is a drama of the normal human regret at growing older, distorted by the protagonist's illusory attempt to circumvent his aging in this particular way, by trying to possess youth vicariously through the bodies of the young" (215).

4. Later, Oates repudiated her public criticism of the "godly" Nabokov. In "Postscript to a Personal View of Nabokov," she wrote, "Nearly a decade later, while I still agree, more or less, with the 'personal view' here expressed, I'm not sure that I agree at all with the impulse to commit it to print; or with the generally reprehensible error of confusing opinions with literary criticism. Why I should have wished, or imagined I wished, the idiosyncratic and incontestably brilliant Vladimir Nabokov to be a species of *Dostoyevsky*, or *Mann*, or more egregiously yet, *myself*, I can't comprehend" (108).

5. Thurman failed to recognize Oates's feminist parody in *The Assassins*. After opening "Caviar and a Big Mac" with a disparaging comment upon the

twenty-four books Oates had written by then, she describes Oates as an elitist, a "hostess" at "a very long and elaborate dinner," over which she presides "in her evening dress, with her literary medals pinned to her breast . . . looking around at her guests with a fragile, an inscrutable, smile" (43). Even Joanne Creighton, a generally sympathetic critic of Oates, describes the novel as "not as illuminating as one would wish, even after repeated readings, because at a critical juncture, one is not given enough guidance" (*Joyce Carol Oates* 95). How much guidance is enough? How much guidance, for example, do critics expect from James Joyce? Is it possible that male authors are allowed to challenge readers, whereas female authors are expected to guide and nurture them?

6. As I interpret the dismemberment scene, Yvonne hallucinates her own dismemberment, recognizing herself as an archetype whose individuality and creativity are invisible to the Petrie men. This archetype also makes nature itself invisible; hence the scene invokes native American lore, suggesting the need for a redefinition of God, a God *in* nature.

7. The young scholars in "The Sacred Marriage" seek the dead father-artist through the body of his widow in a similar homosocial circuit (*Marriages and Infidelities* 3–36)

8. In a short story called "Psychiatric Services," Oates satirizes the egocentric psychiatrist who would willingly sacrifice a patient (son) to prove his superiority over a woman interning *under* him. "Oh, you romantic girl," he says, "you *baby!*" (396) when he learns she has taken a gun away from the male patient (*The Goddess and Other Women* 384–401.)

9. In romantic terms, "voice" is presumed to come from within the individual, while Oates locates the voices of *Childwold* both within and without, a dialogic (both/and) strategy. Such an internal voice, as Kristeva says in "Word, Dialogue, and Novel," is a "fiction" (*Desire in Language* 90).

CHAPTER SIX
Self-Narrating Woman: Marriage as
Emancipatory Metaphor in *Unholy Loves*

1. In "Art: Therapy and Magic," Oates describes writing as a form of therapy.

2. See Oates's "The Myth of the Isolated Artist," published in 1973.

3. Nina Auerbach's *Communities of Women: An Idea in Fiction*, published one year earlier, may have influenced Oates's conception of the novel. A more likely influence is Doris Lessing's *The Golden Notebook* (1973). Oates met Lessing during her stay in London in 1971–72, during the time she was writing "The Dead," along with other stories included in *Marriages and Infidelities*. (See Oates's "A Visit with Doris Lessing.")

4. If, as Oates suggests, the classroom is like "a little family," it is important to recognize, as the authors of *Gendered Subjects* emphasize, that "the classroom recapitulates the family in approximate ways only" (Culley and Portuges 14). The classroom may become a site of transference—as, for example, when the "alarmingly infantile" Kim transfers to her teacher, Brigit, an apparent unmet need for mothering. Such a moment might be described as "a highly charged, fantasy-laden recapitulation of the mother/daughter nexus" (Culley and Portuges 16).

5. Those who might consider Oates's imagination "prurient," after reading this scene in which menstrual blood flows onto the chapel floor, may be interested to know that a male professor at Dartmouth described feminist teachers as those women who "throw down their bloody tampons" ("Sixty Minutes" 30 Nov. 1988). This hysterical statement reveals a fear and hatred of the female body consistent with the belief that higher education is an intellectual territory where women, who must bear male projections of the body, do not belong. The Dartmouth professor believes a traditional division of labor—women give birth to children, men to ideas—should be maintained. Women may be tolerated in academia, but only if they act as if their bodies do not exist, as if minds transcend gender.

6. Oates told interviewer Jo Ann Levine that Maureen Wendall in *them* is a composite character "based on several students" (14). According to Teper Bender, Allen Weinstein in "In the Region of Ice" is based upon Oates's firsthand experience with a brilliant, troubled student named Richard Wishnetsky.

7. Freud argues in *Jokes and Their Relation to the Unconscious* that jokes reveal, by inversion, the values of a community. Laughter bonds members of the community by bringing low what is held in high esteem.

PART THREE
Communal Authorship in the 1980s: The (M)other in Us

1. Benjamin finds evidence of this same fear in the "self" presented in psychology and philosophy: "The hypothetical self presented by Hegel and Freud does not *want* to recognize the other, does not perceive him as a person just like himself. He gives up omnipotence only when he has no other choice" (53).

2. According to Oates, "*Marya* was an extremely difficult novel to write, perhaps because it is both 'personal' and 'fictional.' Many of Marya's thoughts and impressions parallel my own at her approximate age but the circumstances that provoke them have been altered. . . . What is most autobiographical about the novel is its inner kernel of emotion" ([*Woman*] *Writer* 376). She explains, "I am not Marya Knauer (who stopped writing fiction because it disturbed her

too deeply) and Marya is surely not I (who have been spared Marya's grimmer experiences with men)."

3. In this context the shadow may also be defined as "all the feelings and capacities that are rejected by the ego," in addition to "our infantile parts, emotional attachments, neurotic symptoms, as well as our undeveloped talents and gifts" (Abrams and Zweig xvi).

CHAPTER SEVEN
Daughters of the American Revolution: "Idiosyncratic"
Narrators in Three Postmodern Novels

1. For example, when Christine Di Stefano asks, "Why is it, just at the moment in Western history when previously silenced populations have begun to speak for themselves and on behalf of their subjectivities, that the concept of the subject and the possibility of discovering/creating a liberating 'truth' become suspect?" (75), she is reiterating a question asked previously by Nancy Hartsock. It is understandable, then, as Di Stefano notes (quoting Jane Flax 75) why some feminist critics are " 'deeply suspicious of the motives of those who counsel such a move at the moment when women have just begun to remember their selves and claim an *agentic* subjectivity' " (75).

2. Feminist emphasis upon the communal subject, the self-in-relationship, surfaces in a wide range of critical essays, and over a range of genres, including fiction, autobiography, and poetry. See, for example, Rubenstein's *Boundaries of the Self*; Hirsch's *The Mother/Daughter Plot;* and Du Plessis's *Writing Beyond the Ending.* See also Ostriker's *Stealing the Language.*

3. In an analysis of the nineteenth-century novel *Diana*, Oates quotes this passage from *Chamber's Journal*, 1857, as cited by Jennie Calder in *Women and Marriage in Victorian Fiction* (see "Pleasure, Duty, Redemption, Then and Now" in *[Woman] Writer* 422).

4. For an analysis of the politics of the gothic romance, see Michelle Masse's "Gothic Repetition: Husbands, Horrors, and Things That Go Bump in the Night" (673–709).

5. In "Jocoserious Joyce," Oates says that *Ulysses*, "the greatest novel in the English language," is "an immense sanctification of a city and its people" (*Contraries* 171). "The spirit of Dublin is the voice of *Ulysses,*" she says, and "all the narrators are aspects of this single voice" (176).

6. I am using the term *ecofeminist* rather than *ecological* to emphasize the distinction that Carol Christ articulates in "Rethinking Theology and Nature" (*Reweaving the World* 58–69).

7. Oates might be describing her own technique in *Bellefleur* when she says that *Wuthering Heights* "transcribes the gradual metamorphosis of the gothic

romance into its approximate opposite" as its characters grow from children into adults ("The Magnanimity of *Wuthering Heights*" 442).

8. See especially "Forms of Time and Chronotopes in the Novel" (*The Dialogic Imagination* 84–258).

9. In "Word, Dialogue, and Novel," Kristeva explains these terms: "With Bakhtin, who assimilates narrative discourse into epic discourse, narrative is a prohibition, a *monologism*, a subordination of the code to 1, to God. Hence, the epic is religious and theological; all 'realist' narrative obeying 0–1 logic is dogmatic. The realist novel, which Bakhtin calls monological (Tolstoy), tends to evolve within this space. Realist description, definition of 'personality,' 'character' creation, and 'subject' development—all are descriptive narrative elements belonging to the 0–1 interval and are thus *monological*. The only discourse integrally to achieve the 0–2 poetic logic is that of carnival. By adopting a dream logic, it transgresses rules of linguistic code and social morality as well" (*Desire in Language* 70).

10. Greek myths limit a woman to the role of housewife or celibate, as Mary Lefkowitz points out in *Heroines and Hysterics*, but Aphrodite escaped this destiny by abandoning her consorts. Leah also intends to escape this destiny as, seated in "The Walled Garden," she plots to restore the Bellefleur estate to its original grandeur.

11. Cats are mysterious creatures, long associated with witches and, in their lunar aspect, according to Ad de Vries in *Dictionary of Symbols*, associated with the Great Fertility Goddess, a deity who is sometimes a hater, sometimes a protector, of marriage. The name *Mahalaleel* also suggests *Mahat*, a term for the higher intellect, according to G. A. Gaskell's *Dictionary of All Scriptures and Myths*. *Aleel* is also the name of a famous character in Yeats's *The Countess Cathleen*, representative of the poet, and more famous than he would otherwise be because Stephen Dedalus, at the end of James Joyce's *A Portrait of the Artist as a Young Man* quotes "Bend down your faces, Oona and Aleel." The arrival of the cat in *Bellefleur* may be an allusion to Yeats's "The Second Coming," but, based on Oates's comments in "Jocoserious Joyce," *Bellefleur* is indebted primarily to *Ulysses*. Oates comments on the fact that Joyce "explicitly valued the 'comic' vision over the tragic" (*Contraries* 171). From Joyce's global perspective, the people of Dublin, Oates remarks, are "not really distinct from the complex pattern of relationships that is the human world at any given moment nor are they distinct from the landscape itself" (177). The same might be said of the people in Oates's "comic" novel, *Bellefleur.*

12. In *Wuthering Heights*, Oates points out, the childish Catherine is oblivious to the life she carries within her when she dies, just as Leah is oblivious to the needs of Germaine. According to Oates, reader identification with Heathcliff translates, in political terms, into admiration for "energy, evil, will, *action*. The

murderer who is really tender-hearted, the rapist whose victims provoke him, the fuhrer who is a vegetarian and in any case loves dogs. . . ." (See "The Magnanimity of *Wuthering Heights*" 444).

13. Other transformations include Raphael (in the present era) becoming a fish in order to escape an attack by the Doan boy; the Doan boy becoming a dog, following his rape of Yolande; Yolande becoming an actress following the rape; and Jedediah becoming an owl. There is also the transformation of Ewan, brother of Gideon and sheriff of Nautauga County into a born-again Christian following the revelation of his adultery and near "assassination." Gradual changes include the transformation of Nightshade from a dwarf— a figure from folklore—into a full-sized man, and the change of Emmanuel, family mapmaker, into a bird. Also, through the generations, Jean-Pierre I, founder of the family dynasty, becomes Jean-Pierre II, a mass-murderer, and over five generations, Raphael is transformed into a dreamy, perhaps autistic child, who disappears into his beloved Mink Pond. Through time, human beings become species or objects, and objects sometimes come alive. For example, Raphael Bellefleur is changed into "The Skin Drum," and his wife, Violet, into "The Clavichord." The transformation of "The Turquoise Room" into the "Room of Contamination" follows its use to house runaway slaves.

14. Bellefleur Manor resembles William Randolph Hearst's San Simeon. For example, at San Simeon there is a Bear House called The Gables that has walls decorated with the tale of a woman falling in love with a bear—similar to the fable of one of the Bellefleur daughters. See Loe's *William Randolph Hearst* (88–89).

15. Showalter first described the novel as a "feminist romance" during a presentation at the 1983 Modern Language Association session, "Drawing Our Skirts Across History, 1883–1983." *A Bloodsmoor Romance* is dedicated to Showalter.

16. As Lanser explains, "Where a distinction between the (implied) author and a public, heterodiegetic [or third-person] narrator is not textually marked, readers are invited to equate the narrator with the author and the narratee with themselves (or their historical equivalents)" (16).

17. Donoghue complains, "It is not clear from Oates's account of it what she means by voice" ("Wonder Woman" 16). If one assumes a unitary subject, as does Donoghue, a writer will have only one voice, but Oates persistently challenges this unitary conception of the self. For an analysis of Donoghue's review, see my "Misogynist Reviewers." Oates describes a writer-self that is multiple, consisting of many stories and voices in "Stories That Define Me." In "Does the Writer Exist?" she argues that the social-self differs from the writer-self, whose identity is fluid.

18. If the narrator's tone were not ironic, her language would fit the stereotype of "women's language": it is "polite, emotional, enthusiastic, gossipy, talkative, uncertain, dull, and chatty," as well as "weak, trivial, ineffectual, tentative, hesitant, hyperpolite, euphemistic, and . . . marked by gossip and gibberish" (Kramarae 50).

19. According to Lanser, Sarah Scott's *Millennium Hall* (1762) and Mary Wollstonecraft's *The Wrongs of Woman or, Maria* (1798) are early attempts to create both female communities and communal narrators.

20. As Marion Meade says in *Madame Blavatsky*, "In spite of the fact that the first full-scale investigation conducted by the Society for Psychical Research was an inquiry into theosophical phenomena, Madame Blavatsky's psi faculties were never tested. It is unclear whether the S. P. R. ever requested her to undergo testing, but it appears that they did not. If they had suggested the idea, she would not have cooperated because she refused to submit to even the simplest test when repeatedly urged to do so by some of her followers" (463).

21. Her rejection of Dr. Stoughton's proposal contrasts sharply with another of her nineteenth-century counterparts, Hawthorne's Priscilla in *The Blithedale Romance*. Readers may recall that Hawthorne's Priscilla and, later, James's Verena in *The Bostonians*, marry egocentric suitors; thus, both use their gifts to support men who are likely to become emotionally dependent, tyrannical husbands.

22. Jane Tompkins echoes Miner when, in her "Afterword" to *The Wide, Wide World*, she says, "Warner's heroine cannot be dismissed because she is us." Most women have felt "that our difficulties are undeserved, our efforts to overcome them heroic, our merits exceptional, and our misfortunes unique," according to Tompkins, and thus we still "inhabit the consciousness of this blameless, persecuted orphan." Because daughters today are still vulnerable to victimization, Tompkins argues, "The heroine's psycho-political situation is just as relevant today as it was in 1850" (584–608).

23. In a letter to her mother, a young Louisa Alcott writes about her sister Annie, "O she is so very very cross I cannot love her it seems as though she did every thing to trouble me but I will try to love her better, I hope you have spent a pleasant morning" (Myerson and Shealy 3).

24. Not until mothers become subjects in their own right—as Prudence Kiddemaster does—will the family romance, which remains an Oedipal narrative, be transformed. See Benjamin's *The Bonds of Love*, Hirsch's *The Mother/Daughter Plot*, as well as Daly and Reddy's *Narrating Mothers*.

25. The octagon house became quite popular in the nineteenth century, from the east coast to the west. As Madeleine B. Stern says in her introduction to *The Octagon House*, Orson Fowler was "a true innovator," and after the publication of his book, "octagonal houses rose up dotting the landscape of the eastern

United States," later moving west to Kansas where, in the 1850s, an "Octagon Settlement was projected" (vi).

26. See Adrienne Rich's "Jane Eyre: The Temptations of a Motherless Woman (1973)" in which she identifies the temptations of the motherless woman as the habit of depressive self-punishment (93), the tendency toward "romantic love and surrender" or "passive suicide" (96), and the habit of adopting a man's cause (103).

27. Edwina, Deirdre's writer-mother, pretends that her writing career is motivated by personal tragedy. According to Mary Kelley, nineteenth-century women writers believed that "No happy woman ever writes," at least not for a living. In this respect, Edwina Kiddemaster is fairly typical; nevertheless, her pleasure in the success of her own public life contradicts what she advocates in her conduct books: the confinement of women to the domestic sphere where "ladies" must practice submission to their husbands. Edwina's will revises this definition of a "lady."

28. Elizabeth Keyser argues that Edwina Kiddemaster may be the voice of Louisa May Alcott (220).

29. Oates has also published a collection of poems with the title *The Time Traveler* (1989). The outlaw balloon also suggests the time machine in Twain's "Connecticut Yankee."

30. Oates is certainly not the only feminist revising the crime novel, as is evident from studies of the genre, such as Reddy's *Sisters in Crime* and Klein's *The Woman Detective*. However, since the detective in *Mysteries of Winterthurn* is male, neither would define it as a feminist crime novel, while I would— particularly since the editor/writer is a feminist. Yet, according to Reddy and Klein, feminist writers often undermine the isolation and alienation of the detective-hero, as Oates does in this novel. In *Mysteries of Winterthurn*, the women are connected, not only by blood—they are half-sisters or cousins—but also through their writing: Sara Whimbrel's diary, Georgina Kilgarvan's poetry, the academic writing of Therese Kilgarvan, and her sister Perdita's editing of Xavier Kilgarvan's cases.

31. It is ironic, then, that Anna Katharine Green is credited with writing the detective novel that established the convention of excluding the "family" from analysis. Green created a detective who functions exclusively in the public realm, as if isolated from family and friends. At the same time, because Green included elements of romance, her novels were judged inferior. Oates revises the tradition of the isolated detective hero in *Mysteries of Winterthurn*, but she allows romance, as Green did in *Lost Man's Lane* and *The Circular Study*.

32. Under the pseudonym "Rosamond Smith," Oates continues to expose crimes against women, children, and the poor, in the guise of entertainment. Reviewers have been perplexed by Oates's use of a pseudonym. Linda Wolfe

is especially puzzled as to why Oates would use the pseudonym "Rosamond Smith" for *Soul/Mate*, since it was published after Oates's "cover was blown." For Oates, who imagines herself as plural, Smith is another self.

33. For example, Eloise Salholz claims that the first and third novellas are "choked by excesses of plot and excrescences of prose" (79), but she has not solved the mystery in either case; therefore she does not recognize the relevance of details of plot or prose that are, in fact, clues to the mystery of identity. Early reviews indicate that readers have difficulty solving the mysteries in the first and third tales in *Mysteries of Winterthurn*.

34. Oates confirmed my solution of the case in a letter to Joanne Creighton in which she identifies Perdita as "the murderess of the last mystery." Oates adds, "Like Lizzie Borden, who, as a lady, could not be imagined as having killed both her parents, Perdita is spared by the sexist attitudes of her era. For a while, Xavier successfully blocks this knowledge; then he succumbs to it, has a breakdown, but, in the end, recovers—and marries Perdita" (*Joyce Carol Oates: Novels of The Middle Years* 55).

35. Oates told Joanne Creighton that "the third mystery is based upon a notorious New Brunswick, N.J., case of the 1920s, sensationally known as the 'case of the minister and the choir singer.' That's to say, an amalgam of this case, and Lizzie Borden, and very likely one or two others" (qtd. in *Joyce Carol Oates: The Middle Years* 48). The case also bears some similarity to the famous nineteenth-century affair, made public by Victoria Woodhull in 1872, between Henry Ward Beecher and his parishioner, Elizabeth Tilton. The gothic sermons of Henry Ward Beecher may also have suggested Xavier's descent into the region of Paradise Hotel. See Karen Halttunen's "Gothic Imagination and Social Reform."

36. Oates has undoubtedly read *The New Feminist Criticism*, edited by her colleague and friend Elaine Showalter, which includes Annette Kolodny's "A Map for Rereading" (46–62). Kolodny's essay, which provides a map for reading "The Yellow Wallpaper" and "A Jury of Her Peers," also provides a map for reading the allusions in *Mysteries of Winterthurn*.

37. Oates alludes to and refashions works by Hawthorne, recreating Judge Pyncheon in *The House of Seven Gables* as Judge Kilgarvan and transforming Hollingshead from *The Blithedale Romance* into a cynical lawyer who defends a "lady killer." She also draws upon historical records not only to recreate crimes but also nineteenth-century attitudes toward female criminals. The novel alludes, for example, to Professor Caesar Lombrose's *The Female Offender* (1895), which eschews sociological explanation, locating the source of the crime in the physiognomy of violent women.

38. Georgina, like Emily Dickinson, is victimized by "invisible" patriarchal crimes. Also like Dickinson, Georgina uses her poetry to transform the prison

of "her father's house" into a creative space where she can have it out on her own premises. A number of autobiographical details suggest that Georgina is modeled upon Emily Dickinson. Like Dickinson, Georgina is called home from school and, though she has suitors, never marries. Also, like Dickinson, Georgina publishes few of her subversive poems during her lifetime. Her freedom from the responsibilities of marriage, from the burden of caring for husband and children, provides her an opportunity for a sacred marriage to poetry, and her poetry becomes a rich inheritance for her half-sisters, Perdita and Therese, both of whom, as revealed in the novel's final case, exhibit some of their stepsister's writing ability. See Helen McNeil's *Emily Dickinson* and Vivian R. Pollack's *Dickinson: The Anxiety of Gender.*

39. Perdita was the daughter of a jealous (and potentially incestuous) father in Shakespeare's *The Winter's Tale.* In many of Shakespeare's romances, Charles Frey finds "repeated images of fathers trying to dominate their daughters as well as learn from them" (301).

CHAPTER EIGHT
Porous Boundaries: Daughters, Families, and the
Body Politic in Realistic Novels of the 1980s

1. In this chapter I omit *Marya, a Life*, which I have already discussed in the introduction to Part 3. I also omit *Solstice*, which I discuss briefly in my Conclusion. I have not included *American Appetites* because its center of gravity is more often the father than the daughter.

2. In *American Appetites* Bianca McCullough becomes her father's ally in trivializing the domestic arts, especially her mother's cooking.

3. In her analysis of *Angel of Light*, Marianthe Colakis notes that the role of Clytemnestra has also been altered since, politically, Isabel Halleck is not as overtly active and aware as Clytemnestra. In my view, this difference is historical: *The Oresteia* dramatizes the founding act of patriarchy in a plot that brings a powerful, undomesticated woman under control, whereas *Angel of Light* dramatizes the misogyny of Washington, D.C., in the Watergate era, long after women have been domesticated by patriarchal politics.

4. In these novels the image of the dove, associated with sexual innocence and transcendence in Christian symbolism, is a feminist image that, as in ancient goddess cultures, signifies the transformational power of bodily experience. (See Elinor Gadon's *The Once and Future Goddess.*) Recurring images of the dove, in association with birth, sexual union, and death, remind readers that we are, as Rich's allusive title reminds us, "of woman born."

5. While Marianthe Colakis thinks "feminists may be disappointed" that Oates "has not assigned a dominant role to the Electra figure," having chosen

instead to "focus on Orestes" (127), I view the daughter's part in *Angel of Light* as equal to, if not more important than, the son's.

6. In *Angel of Light*, when the daughter moves beyond *lex talionis*, Oates is again re-visioning Aeschylus's play in which, according to Zeitlin, "the principle of vengeance itself is posed as wholly female and female in its blackest and most negative manifestation" (61).

7. The same parental expectations govern Connie's behavior in "Where are you going, where have you been?" In this story, set in the 1960s, Connie "looked one way when she was at home and another way when she was away from home. Everything about her had two sides to it" (*The Wheel of Love* 30).

8. In contrast to Nathaniel Hawthorne's dove-like and virginal Hilda in *The Marble Faun*, Enid does not find contentment as a copyist of work by other artists; at the novel's conclusion, she is a serious piano student who has won a scholarship to a prestigious school of music.

9. When John Updike says, in a review of *You Must Remember This*, that "some of the historical themes (such as that of bomb shelters) feel rubbed into the plot with a bit too much determination" (11), he fails to recognize that it is the bomb shelter that enables Oates to establish the complex interplay between the familial and public political unconscious.

10. The positive reception of *Because It Is Bitter, Because It Is My Heart* by many African American readers is evident, not only from Gates's review, but also from the fact that African-American critic Shirley Jordan includes Oates in her collection of interviews *Broken Silences* (150–58).

11. As Richard Ohmann demonstrates in "The Shaping of a Canon: U.S. Fiction, 1960–1975," the "premise of individualism" is not challenged by the mostly white, male canon shaped by publishers, critics, and professors during this period (219). Significantly, although Oates won the National Book Award in 1970, and although she received some attention from critics during this period, her fiction did not become part of this contemporary canon.

12. Judith Seixas and Geraldine Youcha point out that "the longing for consistent care and nurturing seems to go on and on, so they continue to search for the mother and father they never had. And they remain children to their peers, which in turn blocks or hampers any mature relationship they may attempt" (13).

13. This lie, in which Iris hides her bitter past, is characteristic of adult children of alcoholics. Seixas and Youcha attribute this behavior in adulthood to the habit, acquired in childhood, of "covering up" for the drinking parent. "Hiding becomes a way of life that goes unchallenged," they say (4). Iris's unwillingness to trust Alan in this scene, as well as her fear of loss of control while making love, are characteristic of adults who grew up with alcoholic parents.

14. The theme of mother-hunger may be especially pronounced in adults who grew up in homes with alcoholic parents, but it is also a characteristic subplot in romances by women, not only formula romances, as Madonne Miner argues in "Guaranteed to Please," but also in such "classics" as Chopin's *The Awakening*. Adrienne Rich argues that all women are unmothered in our patriarchal society; see her "Jane Eyre: The Temptations of a Motherless Women" and *Of Woman Born*.

15. The novel's only explicit allusion to the poem, "In the Desert," occurs when Iris's father, Duke, says, "Been missing my little girl, all this time . . . those months. Like apiece of my heart was bittenout, y'know?" (71). Duke is, of course, more responsible than anyone for Iris's bitter heart.

16. In fact, at one point Iris thinks, "More than Jinx Fairchild, I'm guilty" (156). She understands that "the whiteness of her skin has something to do with it, but what?" (156). It is by telling the lie that diverts police suspicion from Jinx that Iris begins to learn the "extraordinary power of duplicity" (156).

17. Alcohol irritates the stomach; high doses can cause delay of food absorption and vomiting, according to the Camberwell Council on Alcoholism. Iris observes these symptoms in her mother.

18. In *A Garden of Earthly Delights*, as in *Because It Is Bitter*, images of food are associated not only with socioeconomic inequities but also with spiritual/sexual desires.

19. In Oates's "Miracle Play" (*Three Short Plays* 53–99) sugar is added to the boiling water to make it stick and continue to burn the African-American male victim.

20. In the unconscious, according to Kristeva, the social body is associated with the maternal body. See, for example, her "Place Names" (*Desire in Language*), in which a child unconsciously associates space, laughter, and the maternal body.

C H A P T E R   N I N E
How Does "I" Speak for "We"? Violence and Representation in *Foxfire: Confessions of a Girl Gang*

1. According to Oates, a movie based on *Foxfire* will be out in 1996. The name "Foxfire" may be an allusion to the original *Foxfire Books*, edited by Eliot Wigginton. Written by Eliot's students, the stories and articles in the *Foxfire Books* are about their own working-class mountain community. Tragically, although Wigginton mentored his young writers and found a publisher for them, he was later imprisoned for sexually molesting some of them. On the topic of Wigginton's sexual abuse of children, see Guy Osborne's "Eliot Wigginton: A Meditation."

2. This cross-dressing is reminiscent of Constance Philippa Zinn's transformation into a man called Philippe Fox in Oates's *A Bloodsmoor Romance*.

3. See Breines and Gordon's "The New Scholarship on Family Violence." They open by saying, "Only a few decades ago, the term 'family violence' would have had no meaning: child abuse, wife beating, and incest would have been understood but not recognized as serious social problems" (490).

4. The fact that they are white women does not become a divisive issue until later, following Legs's release from a girls detention center, when the members of FOXFIRE do not welcome her new African-American friends, Marigold and Tama. In the detention center itself, as Legs observes, some women are white, some black, but all are poor.

5. Legs is described as "running now, leaping and flying across the rooftops of the brownstone row houses descending the street toward the invisible river, she's a horse, a powerful stallion all hooves, flying mane, tail, snorting and steamy-breathed" (12). For an earlier version of Legs, see the story "The Witness," which opens Oates's collection *Last Days*. Significantly, an even earlier occurrence of this image of the horse can be found in *A Garden of Earthly Delights*, but in association with a male, Carleton Walpole.

6. Heilbrun is quoting Myra Jehlen's "Archimedes and the Paradox of Feminist Criticism" (583).

Conclusion
Where Has Joyce Carol Oates Been, Where Is She Going?

1. Even as I write this conclusion, Joyce Carol Oates eludes me: she has just published another novel, *Zombie* (1995).

2. Oates repeated this statement in an interview with Katherine Couric on the CBS "Today Show," 29 April 1992, and during a television interview with Dick Cavett on 23 May 1992. When confronted with harsh accusations that she had evaded the ethical responsibilities of both journalism and fiction, as she was by Katie Couric, Oates responded, unapologetically, that writers have always taken events from the real world and "transmogrified" them in various ways.

3. For example, Connie in "Where are you going, where have you been?" is a composite of three women whose murders were reported in a *Life* magazine article (1966), and Kelly in *Black Water* is a fictional counterpart to Mary Jo Kopechne, who died in a car driven by Sen. Edward Kennedy in 1969. For a discussion of Oates's sources for Connie, see my " 'An Unfilmable Conclusion.' "

4. Molly Hite cites Oates, but only as a critic (41–42).

5. Oates has, for example, participated in the feminist project of recovering the work of "lost" literary foremothers. In 1971, she published an essay on

Harriet Arnow, which was later included in *New Heaven, New Earth* (97–108), and in 1987 she published an essay on Susan Warner, included in *(Woman) Writer* (190–97). She has also participated in the feminist critique of male images of women. See, for example, " 'At Least I have Made a Woman of Her': Images of Women in Yeats, Lawrence, Faulkner," first published in 1983, later published in *The Profane Art*.

6. In a letter to *Critical Inquiry*, for example, Oates criticizes Richard Stern's sexist depiction of the 1988 PEN Writers Congress. Her critique begins, "No more grotesquely homosocial piece of writing—one can hardly call such a hodgepodge of impressions an essay—has appeared in *Critical Inquiry* than Richard Stern's 'Some members of the Congress.' " "Is the punning title intentional?" she asks. "Most of the piece exudes gushing over men" (193). "Naturally," she asserts, "I am most offended by the vicious portrait of me as a neurasthenic female. The most sexist charge has to do with my presumed helplessness" (194–95). She criticizes Stern's use of the term "fucking bitches" to describe those women writers who had protested the exclusion of women from the PEN Congress. "A pig-souled sexism," she concludes, "is hardly dissolved in a perfunctory word or two as one signs off" (195).

Works Cited

O N E
Works by Joyce Carol Oates

A. Novels

A Bloodsmoor Romance. New York: E. P. Dutton, 1982.
American Appetites. New York: E. P. Dutton, 1989.
Angel of Light. New York: E. P. Dutton, 1981.
The Assassins: A Book of Hours. New York: Vanguard, 1975.
Because It Is Bitter, and Because It Is My Heart. New York: E. P. Dutton, 1990.
Bellefleur. New York: E. P. Dutton, 1980.
Childwold. New York: Vanguard, 1976.
Cybele. Santa Barbara, CA: Black Sparrow, 1979.
Do with Me What You Will. New York: Vanguard, 1973.
Expensive People. New York: Fawcett, 1968.
Foxfire: Confessions of a Girl Gang. New York: E. P. Dutton, 1993.
A Garden of Earthly Delights. New York: Fawcett, 1967.
Marya, a Life. New York: E. P. Dutton, 1986.
Mysteries of Winterthurn. New York: E. P. Dutton, 1984.
them. New York: Fawcett, 1969.
Son of the Morning: A Novel. New York: Vanguard, 1978.
Solstice. New York: E. P. Dutton, 1985.
The Triumph of the Spider Monkey. New York: Fawcett, 1976.
Unholy Loves: A Novel. New York: Vanguard, 1979.
What I Lived For. New York: E. P. Dutton, 1994.
With Shuddering Fall. New York: Fawcett, 1964.
Wonderland. New York: Vanguard Press, 1971; Rpt. New York: Fawcett, 1973.
You Must Remember This. New York: E. P. Dutton, 1987.
Zombie. New York: E. P. Dutton, 1995.

Novels written under the pseudonym Rosamond Smith

Lives of the Twins. New York: Avon Books, 1987.

Soul/Mate. New York: E. P. Dutton, 1989.
Nemesis. New York: E. P. Dutton, 1990.
Snake Eyes. New York: E. P. Dutton, 1992.
You Can't Catch Me. New York: E. P. Dutton, 1995.

B. Novellas
Black Water. New York: E. P. Dutton, 1992.
I Lock My Door Upon Myself. New York: Ecco Press, 1990.
The Rise of Life on Earth. New York: New Directions, 1991.

C. Collected Short Stories
By the North Gate. New York: Fawcett, 1963.
Crossing the Border: Fifteen Tales. New York: Vanguard, 1976.
The Goddess and Other Women. New York: Vanguard, 1974.
Haunted: Tales of the Grotesque. New York: E. P. Dutton, 1994.
The Hungry Ghosts: Seven Allusive Comedies. Santa Barbara, CA: Black Sparrow Press, 1975.
Last Days: Stories. New York: E. P. Dutton, 1984.
Marriages and Infidelities. New York: Vanguard, 1972.
A Sentimental Education: Stories. New York: E. P. Dutton, 1980.
Upon the Sweeping Flood. New York: Fawcett, 1966.
The Wheel of Love. New York: Fawcett, 1970.
Where are you going, Where have you been? Stories for Young America. New York: Fawcett, 1974.

D. Collected Poems and Plays
Invisible Woman: New & Selected Poems, 1970–1982. Princeton, NJ: Ontario Review Press, 1982.
The Time Traveler. New York: E. P. Dutton, 1989.
Three Short Plays. Princeton, NJ: Ontario Review Press, 1980.

E. Critical Essays
"Afterword: *Wonderland* Revisited." *Wonderland.* Princeton, NJ: Ontario Review Press, 1992. 507–11.
"Appendix." *Cutting Edges: Young American Fiction for the '70s.* Ed. Jack Hicks. New York: Holt, Rinehart and Winston, 1973. 542–43.
"Art: Therapy and Magic." *American Journal* (3 July 1973): 17–21.
Contraries: Essays. New York: Oxford University Press, 1981.
"Delirium and Detachment: The Secret of Being a Writer." *The New Yorker.* 27 June–3 July 1995: 134, 136.

"Does the Writer Exist?" *New York Times Book Review*, 22 April 1984: 1, 17. Rpt. in *(Woman) Writer*. New York: E. P. Dutton, 1988. 45–52.

The Edge of Impossibility: Tragic Forms in Literature. New York: Vanguard Press, 1971.

"Frankenstein's Fallen Angels." *Critical Inquiry* 10.3 (March 1984): 543–54. Rpt. in *(Woman) Writer*. New York: E P. Dutton, 1988. 106–22.

" 'JCO' and I" (a keepsake specially printed to accompany a loan exhibition of the Hannelore and William Heyen Collection of works by Joyce Carol Oates). Rochester, NY: University of Rochester Library, 1994.

"The Magnanimity of *Wuthering Heights*." *Critical Inquiry* 9.2 (Dec. 1982): 435–49. Rpt. in *The Profane Art: Essays and Reviews*. New York: E. P. Dutton, 1983. 63–81.

"My Father, My Fiction." *The New York Times Magazine*, 19 March 1985: 44–45, 80, 84–85, 89, 108.

"The Myth of the Isolated Artist." *Psychology Today*, 6 May 1973: 74–75.

"New Heaven, New Earth." *Saturday Review*, 4 Nov. 1972: 51–54.

New Heaven, New Earth: The Visionary Experience in Literature. New York: Vanguard Press, 1974; New York: Fawcett, 1974.

"Oates on Marriage." Letter to the editor. *Time*, 12 Nov. 1973: 12.

"Postscript to a Personal View of Nabokov." *Critical Essays on Vladimir Nabokov*. Ed. Phyllis Roth. Boston: G. K. Hall, 1984. 108–9.

The Profane Art. New York: E. P. Dutton, 1983.

Reply to Joanna Russ. *Women's Review of Books* 2.10 (July 1985), 18.

"Response to Richard Stern." *Critical Inquiry* 15 (Autumn 1988): 193–95.

"Stories That Define Me: The Making of a Writer." *New York Times Book Review*, 11 July 1982: 3, 15–16.

"A Visit with Doris Lessing." *Southern Review* 9 (Oct. 1973): 873–82.

"Why Is Your Writing So Violent?" *New York Times Book Review*, 29 March 1981: 15, 35.

(Woman) Writer: Occasions and Opportunities. New York: E. P. Dutton, 1988.

Two
Works by Others

Abrams, Jeremiah, and Connie Zweig. *Meeting the Shadow: The Hidden Power of the Dark Side of Human Nature*. New York: Putnam, 1991.

Alcott, Louisa. *Behind the Mask: Her Unknown Thrillers*. Ed. Madeline Stern. London: Hogarth Press, 1985.

Allen, Mary I. "The Terrified Women of Joyce Carol Oates." *The Necessary Blankness: Women in Major American Fiction of the Sixties*. Urbana: University of Illinois Press, 1976. 133–59.

Allen, Paula Gunn. "The Woman I Love Is a Planet. The Planet I Love Is a Tree." *Reweaving the World: The Emergence of Ecofeminism.* Ed. Irene Diamond and Gloria Feman Orenstein. San Francisco: Sierra Club Books, 1990. 52–57.

Anderson, Linda. *Plotting Change: Contemporary Women's Fiction.* London: Edward Arnold, 1990.

Auerbach, Nina. *Communities of Women: An Idea in Fiction.* Cambridge: Harvard University Press, 1978.

Bakan, David. *The Duality of Human Existence: An Essay on Psychology and Religion.* Chicago: Rand McNally, 1966.

Bakhtin, Mikhail M. *The Dialogic Imagination: Four Essays.* Trans. Caryl Emerson and Michael Holquist; ed. Michael Holquist. Austin: University of Texas Press, 1981.

———. *Rabelais and His World.* Trans. Helene Iswolsky. Bloomington: Indiana University Press, 1984.

Batterberry, Michael, and Ariane Batterberry. "Focus on Joyce Carol Oates." *Conversations with Joyce Carol Oates.* Ed. Lee Milazzo. Jackson: University Press of Mississippi, 1989. 42–46.

Bauer, Dale M. *Feminist Dialogics: A Theory of Failed Community.* Albany: State University of New York Press, 1988.

Bauer, Dale M., and S. Jaret McKinstry, eds. *Feminism, Bakhtin, and the Dialogic.* Albany: State University of New York Press, 1991.

Baym, Nina. *Woman's Fiction: A Guide to Novels by and about Women in America, 1820–1870.* Ithaca, NY: Cornell University Press, 1978.

Bedell, Madelon. *The Alcotts: Biography of a Family.* New York: Clarkson N. Potter, 1980.

Belensky, Mary Field, Blythe McVicker Clinchy, Nancy Rule Goldberger, and Jill Mattuck Tarute. *Women's Ways of Knowing: The Development of Self, Voice, and Mind.* New York: Basic Books, 1986.

Bender, Eileen Teper. *Joyce Carol Oates, Artist in Residence.* Bloomington: Indiana University Press, 1987.

———. "Autonomy and Influence: Joyce Carol Oates's *Marriages and Infidelities.*" *Joyce Carol Oates.* Ed. Harold Bloom. New York: Chelsea House, 1987. 45–59.

Benjamin, Jessica. *The Bonds of Love: Psychoanalysis, Feminism, and the Problem of Domination.* New York: Pantheon Books, 1988.

Bernheimer, Charles, and Claire Kahane, eds. *In Dora's Case: Freud-Hysteria-Feminism.* New York: Columbia University Press, 1985.

Bloom, Harold, ed. *Joyce Carol Oates.* New York: Chelsea House, 1987.

Boose, Lynda E. "The Father's House and the Daughter in it: The Structures of Western Culture's Daughter-Father Relationship." *Daughters and Fathers.*

Ed. Lynda E. Boose and Betty S. Flowers. Baltimore: Johns Hopkins University Press, 1989. 19–74.

Breines, Wini, and Linda Gordon. "The New Scholarship on Family Violence." *Signs* 8.3 (1983): 490–531.

Burwell, Rose Marie. "*With Shuddering Fall* and the Process of Individuation." *Joyce Carol Oates.* Ed. Harold Bloom. New York: Chelsea House, 1987. 38–97.

Camberwell Council on Alcoholism. *Women and Alcohol.* New York: Tavistock, 1980.

Campbell, Joseph. *The Masks of the God.* New York: Viking, 1968.

Chell, Cara. "Untricking the Eye: Joyce Carol Oates and the Feminist Ghost Story." *Arizona Quarterly* 41.1 (Spring 1985): 5–23.

Chernin, Kim. *The Hungry Self: Women, Eating & Identity.* New York: Harper & Row, 1985.

Chodorow, Nancy. *The Reproduction of Mothering: Psychoanalysis and the Sociology of Gender.* Berkeley: University of California Press, 1978.

Christ, Carol. "Rethinking Theology and Nature." *Reweaving the World: The Emergence of Ecofeminism.* Ed. Irene Diamond and Gloria Feman Orenstein. San Francisco: Sierra Club Books, 1990. 58–69.

Clemons, Walter. "Joyce Carol Oates: Love and Violence." *Newsweek*, 11 Dec. 1972, 72–77. Rpt. *Conversations with Joyce Carol Oates.* Ed. Lee Milazzo. Jackson: University Press of Mississippi, 1989. 32–41.

———. "Sleeping Princess." Review of *Do with Me What You Will. Newsweek*, 15 Oct. 1973: 107.

Coales, Samuel. "Joyce Carol Oates: Contending Spirits." *Joyce Carol Oates.* Ed. Harold Bloom. New York: Chelsea House, 1987. 119–36.

Cohen, Paula. *The Daughter's Dilemma: Family Process and the Nineteenth-Century Domestic Novel.* Ann Arbor: University of Michigan Press, 1991.

Colakis, Marianthe. "The House of Atreus Myth in the Seventies and Eighties: David Rabe's *The Orphan* and Joyce Carol Oates's *Angel of Light.*" *Classical and Modern Literature* 9.2 (Winter 1985): 125–30.

Craig, Patricia. "Philosophical Tale of Gore." Review of *Mysteries of Winterthurn. New York Book Review*, 12 Feb. 1984: 7.

Creighton, Joanne V. *Joyce Carol Oates.* Boston: Twayne, 1979.

———. *Joyce Carol Oates: Novels of the Middle Years.* Boston: Twayne, 1992.

Cronan, Rose Ellen. "American Feminist Criticism of Contemporary Women's Fiction." *Signs* 18.2 (Winter 1993): 346–75.

Crowley, John. "Outlaw Girls on the Rampage." *New York Times Book Review*, 15 Aug. 1993: 6.

Culley, Margo, and Catherine Portuges, eds. *Gendered Subjects: The Dynamics of Feminist Teaching.* Boston: Routledge & Kegan Paul, 1985.

Cunningham, Frank. "The Enclosure of Identity in the Earlier Stories." *Amer-*

ican Women Writing Fiction: Memory, Identity, Family, Space. Lexington: University of Kentucky Press, 1989. 9–44.

Daly, Brenda O. "The Central Nervous System of America: The Writer in/as the Crowd in Joyce Carol Oates's *Wonderland.*" *Feminism, Bakhtin, and the Dialogic.* Ed. Dale M. Bauer and S. Jaret McKinstry. Albany: State University of New York Press, 1991. 155–80.

——. "Misogynist Reviewers: Tiny Gunmen Take Shots at That Siren, Joyce Carol Oates." *Misogyny in Literature.* Ed. Katherine Ackley. New York: Garland, 1992. 265–87.

——. "Sexual Politics in Two Short Story Collections by Joyce Carol Oates." *Studies in Short Fiction* 32 (1995): 83–93.

——. " 'An Unfilmable Conclusion': Joyce Carol Oates at the Movies." *The Journal of Popular Culture* 23.3 (Winter 1989): 101–14. Rpt. *Where Are You Going, Where Have You Been?* Ed. Elaine Showalter. New Brunswick, NJ: Rutgers University Press, 1994. 145–62.

Daly, Brenda O., and Maureen T. Reddy, eds. *Narrating Mothers: Theorizing Maternal Subjectivities.* Knoxville: University of Tennessee Press, 1991.

De Lauretis, Teresa. "The Violence of Rhetoric: Considerations on Representation and Gender." *The Violence of Representation.* Ed. Nancy Armstrong and Leonard Tennenhouse. New York: Routledge, 1989. 239–56.

DeMott, Benjamin. "The Necessity in Art of a Reflective Intelligence." *Critical Essays on Joyce Carol Oates.* Ed. Linda W. Wagner. Boston: G. K. Hall, 1979. 19–23.

de Vries, Ad. *Dictionary of Symbols.* London: North-Holland Publishing Company, 1974.

Diamond, Irene, and Gloria Feman Orenstein, eds. *Reweaving the World: The Emergence of Ecofeminism.* San Francisco: Sierra Club Books, 1990.

Di Stefano, Christine. "Dilemmas of Difference: Feminism, Modernity, and Postmodernism." *Feminism/Postmodernism.* Ed. Linda J. Nicholson. New York: Routledge, 1990. 63–82.

Donoghue, Denis. "A Criticism of One's Own." *Men in Feminism.* Ed. Alice Jardine and Paul Smith. New York: Methuen, 1987. 146–52.

——. "Wonder Woman." Review of *A Bloodsmoor Romance. New York Review of Books,* 21 Oct. 1982: 12, 14, 16, 18.

Du Plessis, Rachel Blau. *Writing Beyond the Ending: Narrative Strategies of Twentieth-Century Women Writers.* Bloomington: Indiana University Press, 1985.

Ebert, Teresa L. "The 'Difference' of Postmodern Feminism." *College English* 53.8 (Dec. 1991): 886–904.

Edwards, Thomas. "The House of Atreus Now." Review of *Angel of Light. New York Times Book Review,* 16 Aug. 1981: 1, 18.

Ellis, Peter Berresford. *The Dictionary of Irish Mythology*. London: Constable, 1987.

Fagles, Robert. Introduction. *Aeschylus/The Oresteia*. New York: Viking, 1975.

Felski, Rita. *Beyond Feminist Aesthetics: Feminist Literature and Social Change*. Cambridge: Harvard University Press, 1989.

Fetterley, Judith. " 'Not in the Least American': Nineteenth-Century Literary Regionalism." *College English* 56.8 (Dec. 1994): 877–95.

———. *The Resisting Reader: A Feminist Approach to American Literature*. Bloomington: Indiana University Press, 1978.

Finke, Laurie A. *Feminist Theory, Women's Writing*. Ithaca, NY: Cornell University Press, 1992.

Flanders, Robert. "On Love, Law, and Innocence." Review of *Do with Me What You Will. Harvard Law Record*. 57.5 (2 Nov. 1973): 14.

Flax, Jane. "Postmodernism and Gender Relations in Feminist Theory." *Feminism/Postmodernism*. Ed. Linda J. Nicholson. New York: Routledge, 1990. 39–62.

Fossum, Robert H. "Only Control: The Novels of Joyce Carol Oates." *Studies in the Novel* 7 (Summer 1975): 295–97.

Foucault, Michel. "What Is an Author?" (1969). *The Critical Tradition: Classic Texts and Contemporary Trends*. Ed. David H. Richter. New York: St. Martin's Press, 1989. 978–89.

Fowler, Orson S. *The Octagon House: A Home for All*. New York: Dover, 1973.

Freud, Sigmund. *Jokes and Their Relation to the Unconscious*. Trans. James Strachey. New York: W. W. Norton, 1960.

Frey, Charles. " 'O sacred, shadowy, cold and constant green': Shakespeare's Imperiled and Chastening Daughters of Romance." *The Woman's Part: Feminist Criticism of Shakespeare*. Ed. Carolyn Ruth Swift Lenz, Gayle Green, and Carol Thomas Neely. Urbana: University of Illinois Press, 1980. 295–313.

Friedman, Ellen G. *Joyce Carol Oates*. New York: Frederick Ungar, 1980.

———. "Joyce Carol Oates." *Modern American Women Writers*. Ed. Elaine Showalter, Lea Baechler, and A. Walton Litz. New York: Collier, 1991, 1993.

———. "Where Are the Missing Contents? (Post) Modernism, Gender, and the Canon." *PMLA* 108.2 (March 1993): 240–52.

Froula, Christine. "When Eve Reads Milton: Undoing the Canonical Economy." *Critical Inquiry* 10 (1983): 321–48.

Frye, Joanne S. *Living Stories, Telling Lives: Women and the Novel in Contemporary Experience*. Ann Arbor: University of Michigan Press, 1986.

Frye, Northrop. *The Secular Scripture: A Study of the Structure of Romance*. 1976. Cambridge: Harvard University Press, 1978.

Furman, Nelly. "The Politics of Language: Beyond the Gender Principle?"

Making a Difference: Feminist Literary Criticism. Ed. Gayle Greene and Coppelia Kahn. New York: Methuen, 1985. 59–79.

Gadon, Elinor W. *The Once and Future Goddess: A Symbol for Our Time.* San Francisco: Harper & Row, 1989.

Gallop, Jane. *Around 1981: Academic Feminist Literary Theory.* New York: Routledge, 1992.

———. *The Daughter's Seduction: Feminism and Psychoanalysis.* Ithaca, NY: Cornell University Press, 1982.

Gardiner, Judith Kegan. "On Female Identity and Writing by Women." *Writing and Sexual Difference.* Ed. Elizabeth Abel. Chicago: University of Chicago Press, 1982. 177–92.

Gaskell, G. A. *Dictionary of All Scriptures and Myths..* New York: Julian Press, 1960.

Gates, Henry Louis, Jr. "Murder She Wrote." Review of *Because It Is Bitter, and Because It Is My Heart." The Nation,* 2 July 1990: 27–29.

Germain, David. "Author Oates Tells Where She's Been, Where She's Going." *Conversations with Joyce Carol Oates.* Ed. Lee Milazzo. Jackson: University Press of Mississippi, 1989. 173–80.

Gilbert, Sandra M. "Life's Empty Pack: Notes Toward a Literary Daughteronomy." *Daughters and Fathers.* Ed. Lynda E. Boose and Betty S. Flowers. Baltimore: Johns Hopkins University Press, 1989. 256–77.

Gilbert, Sandra M., and Susan Gubar. *The Madwoman in the Attic: The Woman Writer and the Nineteenth-Century Literary Imagination.* New Haven, CT: Yale University Press, 1979.

Goodman, Charlotte. "The Lost Brother, the Twin: Women Novelists and the Male-Female Double Bildungsroman." *Novel: A Forum on Fiction* 17 (1983): 28–43.

Grant, Mary Kathryn. *The Tragic Vision of Joyce Carol Oates.* Durham, NC: Duke University Press, 1978.

Gray, Paul. "Nice People in Glass Houses." Review of *American Appetites. Time* (9 Jan. 1989): 64.

Green, Anna Katharine. *The Circular Study.* New York: Doubleday, Page, 1914.

———. *Lost Man's Lane.* New York: Doubleday, Page, 1928.

Greene, Gayle. *Changing the Story: Feminist Fiction and the Tradition.* Bloomington: Indiana University Press, 1991.

———. "Feminist Fiction and the Uses of Memory." *Signs* 16.2 (Winter 1991): 290–321.

Griffin, Susan. "Curves along the Road." *Reweaving the World: The Emergence of Ecofeminism.* Ed. Irene Diamond and Gloria Feman Orenstein. San Francisco: Sierra Club Books, 1990. 87–99.

———. *Pornography and Silence: Culture's Revenge against Nature.* New York: Harper & Row, 1981.

Grumet, Madeleine R. *Bitter Milk: Women and Teaching.* Amherst: University of Massachusetts Press, 1988.

Gullette, Margaret. "The Exile of Adulthood: Paedophilia in the Midlife Novel" *Novel* 17.3 (Spring 1984): 215–32.

Halttunen, Karen. "Gothic Imagination and Social Reform: The Haunted Houses of Lyman Beecher, Henry Ward Beecher, and Harriet Beecher Stowe." *New Essays on Uncle Tom's Cabin.* Ed. Eric J. Sundquist. Cambridge: Cambridge University Press, 1986. 107–34.

Hawthorne, Nathaniel. *The Blithedale Romance.* Ed. Seymour Gross and Rosalie Murphy. New York: W. W. Norton, 1978.

Heilbrun, Carolyn. *Writing a Woman's Life.* New York: Ballantine Books, 1988.

Herman, Judith Lewis, with Lisa Hirschman. *Father-Daughter Incest.* Cambridge: Harvard University Press, 1981.

Hersh, Pam. "Ordinary People." *Time Off/Princeton Packet,* 16 May 1990: 3–4.

Hirsch, Marianne. *The Mother/Daughter Plot: Narrative, Psychoanalysis, Feminism.* Bloomington: Indiana University Press, 1989.

Hite, Molly. *The Other Side of the Story: Structures and Strategies of Contemporary Feminist Narrative.* Ithaca, NY: Cornell University Press, 1989.

Holquist, Michael. "Answering as Authoring: Mikhail Bakhtin's Trans-Linguistics." *Bakhtin: Essays and Dialogics on His Work.* Ed. Gary Saul Morson. Chicago: University of Chicago Press, 1986. 59–71.

Hunnewell, Susannah. "A Trusting Young Woman." *New York Times Book Review,* 10 May 1992: 29.

Hutcheonson, Linda. *The Politics of Postmodernism.* New York: Routledge, 1989. 140–68.

James, Henry. *The Bostonians.* New York: Random House, 1956.

Jameson, Frederic. *The Political Unconscious: Narrative as a Socially Symbolic Act.* Ithaca, NY: Cornell University Press, 1981.

Jehlen, Myra. "Archimedes and the Paradox of Feminist Criticism." *Feminist Theory: A Critique of Ideology.* Ed. Nannerl O. Keohane, Michelle A. Rosaldo, and Barbara C. Gelpi. Chicago: University of Chicago Press, 1982. 189–215.

Johnson, Diane. "Balloons and Abductions." Review of *A Bloodsmoor Romance. The New York Times Book Review,* 5 Sept. 1982: 1.

Johnson, Greg. *Joyce Carol Oates: A Study of the Short Fiction.* Boston: Twayne, 1994.

———. *Understanding Joyce Carol Oates.* Columbia: University of South Carolina Press, 1987.

Jordan, Shirley M., ed. "Joyce Carol Oates." *Broken Silences: Interviews with*

Black and White Women Writers. New Brunswick, NJ: Rutgers University Press, 1993. 150–58.

Karpen, Lynn. "Legs Sadovsky Goes Mythic." *New York Times Book Review,* 15 Aug. 1993: 6.

Kaschak, Ellyn. *Engendered Lives: A New Psychology of Women's Experience.* New York: Basic Books, 1992.

Keller, Evelyn Fox. "Feminism and Science." *Feminist Theory: A Critique of Ideology.* Ed. Nannerl O. Keohane, Michelle A. Rosaldo, and Barbara C. Gelpi. Chicago: University of Chicago Press, 1982. 113–26.

———. *Reflections on Gender and Science.* New Haven, CT: Yale University, 1985.

Kelley, Mary. *Private Woman, Public Stage: Literary Domesticity in Nineteenth-Century America.* New York: Oxford University Press, 1984.

Keyser, Elizabeth Lennox. "*A Bloodsmoor Romance:* Joyce Carol Oates's *Little Women.*" *Women's Studies: An Interdisciplinary Journal* 4.3 (Feb. 1988): 211–23.

King, Ynestra. "Healing the Wounds: Feminism, Ecology, and the Nature/Culture Dualism." *Reweaving the World: The Emergence of Ecofeminism.* Ed. Irene Diamond and Gloria Feman Orenstein. San Francisco: Sierra Club Books, 1990. 106–21.

Klein, Kathleen Gregory. *The Woman Detective: Gender and Genre.* Chicago: University of Chicago Press, 1988.

Kolodny, Annette. "A Map for Rereading: Gender and the Interpretation of Literary Texts." *The New Feminist Criticism.* Ed. Elaine Showalter. New York: Pantheon Books, 1985. 46–62.

Koppelman Cornillon, Susan, ed. *Images of Women in Fiction.* Bowling Green, OH: Bowling Green University Press, 1972.

Kramarae, Cheris. "Proprietors of Language." *Women and Language in Literature and Society.* Ed. Sally McConnell-Ginet, Ruth Borker, and Nelly Furman. New York: Praeger, 1980. 58–68.

Kristeva, Julia. *Desire in Language: A Semiotic Approach to Literature and Art.* Trans. Thomas Gora, Alice Jardine, and Leon S. Roudiez; ed. Leon S. Roudiez. New York: Columbia University Press, 1980.

———. "Women's Time." *Signs* 7.1 (Autumn 1981): 13–35.

Kuehl, Linda. "An Interview with Joyce Carol Oates." *Commonweal,* 5 Dec. 1969, 307–10. Rpt. *Conversations with Joyce Carol Oates.* Ed. Lee Milazzo. Jackson: University Press of Mississippi, 1989. 7–13.

Lanser, Susan Sniader. *Fictions of Authority: Women Writers and Narrative Voice.* Ithaca, NY: Cornell University Press, 1992.

Lefkowitz, Mary. *Heroines and Hysterics.* New York: St. Martin's Press, 1981.

Lessing, Doris. *The Golden Notebook.* New York: Bantam, 1973.

Levine, Jo Ann. "'Part-time' writer with full-time commitment to art." *The Christian Science Monitor,* 3 Aug. 1976: 14.

Loe, Nancy E. *William Randolph Hearst: An Illustrated Biography*. San Simeon, CA: ARA Leisure Services, 1988. 88–89.

Masse, Michelle A. "Gothic Repetition: Husbands, Horrors, and Things That Go Bump in the Night." *Signs* 15.4 (Summer 1990): 673–709.

McCaffrey, Larry, ed. *Postmodern Fiction: A Bio-Bibliographical Guide*. Westport, CT: Greenwood Press, 1986.

McNeil, Helen. *Emily Dickinson*. London: Virago Press, 1986.

Meade, Marion. *Madame Blavatsky: The Woman behind the Myth*. New York: G. P. Putnam's Sons, 1980.

Medvedev, P. N., and M. M. Bakhtin. *The Formal Method in Literary Criticism: A Critical Introduction to Sociological Poetics*. Trans. Albert J. Wehrle. Baltimore: Johns Hopkins University Press, 1978.

Meese, Elizabeth. *Crossing the Double-Cross: The Practice of Feminist Criticism*. Chapel Hill: University of North Carolina Press, 1986.

Michie, Helena. *Sororophobia: Differences among Women in Literature and Culture*. New York: Oxford University Press, 1992.

Mickelson, Anne Z. "Sexual Love in the Fiction of Joyce Carol Oates." *Reaching Out: Sensitivity and Order in Recent Fiction by Women*. Metuchen, NJ: Scarecrow Press, 1979. 15–34.

Milazzo, Lee, ed. *Conversations with Joyce Carol Oates*. Jackson: University Press of Mississippi, 1989.

Miles, Rosalind. *The Female Form: Women Writers and the Conquest of the Novel*. New York: Routledge & Kegan Paul, 1987.

Miner, Madonne M. "Guaranteed to Please: Twentieth Century Bestsellers." *Gender and Reading: Essays on Readers, Texts, and Contexts*. Ed. Elizabeth A. Flynn and Patrocinio P. Schweickart. Baltimore: Johns Hopkins University Press, 1986. 187–211.

Morris, David B. *The Culture of Pain*. Berkeley: University of California Press, 1993.

Myerson, Joel, and Daniel Shealy, eds; Madeleine Stern, associate ed. *The Selected Letters of Louisa May Alcott*. Boston: Little, Brown, 1987.

Nicholson, Linda J., ed. *Feminism/Postmodernism*. New York: Routledge, 1990.

Nodelman, Perry. "The Sense of Unending: Joyce Carol Oates's *Bellefleur* as an Experiment in Feminine Storytelling." *Breaking the Sequence*. Ed. Ellen G. Friedman and Miriam Fuchs. Princeton, NJ: Princeton University Press, 1989. 250–64.

Ohmann, Richard. "The Shaping of a Canon: U.S. Fiction, 1960–1975." *Critical Inquiry* 10.1 (Sept. 1988): 199–223.

Osborne, Guy L. "Eliot Wigginton: A Meditation." *Now and Then* 10.1 (Spring 1993): 39.

Ostriker, Alicia. *Stealing the Language: The Emergence of Women's Poetry in America.* Boston: Beacon Press, 1986.

Phillips, Robert. "Joyce Carol Oates." *Writers at Work.* Ed. George Plimpton. New York: Penguin, 1981. 361–84.

———. "Joyce Carol Oates: The Art of Fiction LXXII." *Conversations with Joyce Carol Oates.* Ed. Lee Milazzo. Jackson: University Press of Mississippi, 1989. 62–81.

Pitt-Rivers, Julian. *The Fate of Sechem, Or the Politics of Sex.* Cambridge Studies in Social Anthropology. Cambridge: Cambridge University Press, 1977.

Pollack, Vivian R. *Dickinson: The Anxiety of Gender.* Ithaca, NY: Cornell University Press, 1984.

Pollitt, Katha. "Are Women Morally Superior to Men?" *The Nation* 28 Dec. 1992: 799–807.

Pratt, Annis, with Andrea Loewenstein. "Love and Friendship between Women." *Archetypal Patterns in Women's Fiction.* Bloomington: Indiana University Press, 1981.

Prescott, Peter. "Varieties of Madness." Review of *The Assassins. Time,* 17 Oct. 1975: 100.

Quinn, Sally. "Joyce Carol Oates, an 'Observer of Life.'" *International Herald Tribune,* 8 May 1975: 6.

Radway, Janice A. *Reading the Romance: Women, Patriarchy and Popular Culture.* Chapel Hill: University of North Carolina Press, 1984.

Reddy, Maureen T. *Sisters in Crime: Feminism and the Crime Novel.* New York: Frederick Ungar, 1988.

Rich, Adrienne. "Jane Eyre: The Temptations of a Motherless Woman (1973)." *On Lies, Secrets, and Silence: Selected Prose 1966–1978.* New York: W. W. Norton, 1979. 89–106.

———. *Of Woman Born: Motherhood as Experience and Institution.* New York: W. W. Norton, 1976.

———. "Vesuvius at Home: The Power of Emily Dickinson." *On Lies, Secrets, and Silence: Selected Prose, 1966–1978.* New York: W. W. Norton, 1979. 157–83.

———. "When We Dead Awaken: Writing as Re-Vision," *On Lies, Secrets, and Silences, 1966–1978.* New York: W. W. Norton, 1979. 33–49.

Robinson, Marilynne. "The Guilt She Left Behind." Review of *Because It Is Bitter, Because It Is My Heart. The New York Times Book Review,* 22 April 1991: 7, 9.

Robinson, Sally. *Engendering the Subject: Gender and Self-Representation in Contemporary Women's Fiction.* Albany: State University of New York Press, 1991.

———. "Heat and Cold: Recent Fiction by Joyce Carol Oates." Review of *The*

Rise of Life on Earth; I Lock My Door Upon Myself ; and *Heat and Other Stories. Michigan Quarterly Review* 31.3 (Summer 1992): 400–414.

Rubenstein, Roberta. *Boundaries of the Self: Gender, Culture, Fiction.* Urbana: University of Illinois Press, 1987.

Ruddick, Sara. *Maternal Thinking: Toward a Politics of Peace.* Boston: Beacon Press, 1989.

Russ, Joanna. Letter to the Editor. *Women's Review of Books* 2.9 (June 1985), n.p.

Sage, Lorna. *Women in the House of Fiction: Post-War Women Novelists.* New York: Routledge, 1992.

Salholz, Eloise. "Gothic Horrors." Review of *Mysteries of Winterthurn. Newsweek,* 6 Feb. 1984: 79.

Scarry, Elaine. *The Body in Pain: The Making and Unmaking of the World.* New York: Oxford University Press, 1985.

Sedgwick, Eve Kosofsky. *Between Men: English Literature and Male Homosocial Desire.* New York: Columbia University Press, 1985.

Seixas, Judith S., and Geraldine Youcha. *Children of Alcoholism: A Survivor's Manual.* New York: Harper & Row, 1985.

Shina, Thelma J. *Radiant Daughters: Fictional American Women.* Westport, CT: Greenwood Press, 1986.

Showalter, Elaine. "Joyce Carol Oates: A Portrait." *Ms.,* March 1986: 44–50. Rpt. *Joyce Carol Oates.* Ed. Harold Bloom. New York: Chelsea House, 1987. 137–42.

———. "Joyce Carol Oates's *The Dead* and Feminist Criticism." *Faith of a (Woman) Writer.* Ed. Alice Kessler-Harris and William McBrien. Westport, CT: Greenwood Press, 1988. 13–19.

———. "My Friend, Joyce Carol Oates: An Intimate Portrait." *Ms.,* March 1986: 44–46, 50. Rpt. in *Conversations with Joyce Carol Oates.* Ed. Lee Milazzo. Jackson: University Press of Mississippi, 1989. 128–34.

———. "Women Who Write Are Women." *The New York Times Book Review,* 16 Dec. 1984: 1, 31. 33.

Showalter, Elaine, ed. *The New Feminist Criticism: Essays on Women, Literature, Theory.* New York: Pantheon Books, 1985.

———. *Sister's Choice: Tradition and Change in American Women's Writing.* New York: Oxford University Press, 1992.

Sinkler, Rebecca Pepper. "Time and Her Sisters." Review of *Solstice. New York Times Book Review,* 20 Jan. 1985: 4.

Skow, John. "Deafening Roar." Review of *Angel of Light. Time,* 17 Aug. 1981, 83.

Spanos, William V. *Repetitions: The Postmodern Occasion in Literature and Culture.* Baton Rouge: Louisiana State University Press, 1987.

Spelman, Elizabeth V. "Theories of Race and Gender: The Erasure of Black Women." *Quest: A Feminist Quarterly* 5.4 (1982): 36–62.

Spender, Dale. *Mothers of the Novel: One Hundred Good Women Writers Before Jane Austen.* New York: Pandora Press, 1986.

Sprengnether, Madelon. "(M)other Eve: Some Revisions of the Fall in Fiction by Contemporary Women Writers." *Feminism and Psychoanalysis.* Ed. Richard Feldstein and Judith Roof. Ithaca, NY: Cornell University Press, 1989. 298–322.

Stanton, Domna, ed. *The Female Autograph: Theory and Practice in Autobiography from the Tenth to the Twentieth Century.* Chicago: University of Chicago Press, 1984.

Stern, Madeline, ed. *Behind a Mask: Her Unknown Thrillers.* London: Hogarth Press, 1985.

Stern, Richard. "Some Members of the Congress." *Critical Inquiry* 14 (Summer 1988): 860–91.

Strandberg, Victor. "Sex, Violence, and Philosophy in *You Must Remember This.*" *Studies in American Fiction* 17.1 (Spring 1989): 2–17.

Sword, Helen. "Leda and the Modernists." *PMLA* 107.2 (March 1992): 305–18.

Tanner, Laura. *Intimate Violence: Reading Rape and Torture in Twentieth-Century Fiction.* Bloomington: Indiana University Press, 1994.

Thurman, Judith. "Joyce Carol Oates: Caviar and a Big Mac." Review of *The Assassins. Ms.,* Feb. 1976: 42–43.

Todorov, Tzvetan. *Mikhail Bakhtin: The Dialogic Principle.* Trans. Wlad Godzich. Minneapolis: University of Minnesota Press, 1984.

Tompkins, Jane. "Afterword." *The Wide, Wide World.* 1850. Rpt. New York: Feminist Press, 1987. 584–608.

"Transformations of Self: An Interview with Joyce Carol Oates." *Ohio Review* 15.1 (Fall 1963): 51–61. Rpt. in *Conversations with Joyce Carol Oates.* Ed. Lee Milazzo. Jackson: University Press of Mississippi. 47–58.

Upchurch, Michael. "Unpleasant Dreams." Review of *Haunted: Tales of the Grotesque. The New York Times Book Review,* 13 Feb. 1994: 34.

Updike, John. "What You Deserve Is What You Get." Review of *You Must Remember This. The New Yorker,* 28 Dec. 1981: 119–23.

Wagner, Linda, ed. *Critical Essays on Joyce Carol Oates.* Boston: G. K. Hall, 1979.

Walker, Melissa. *Down from the Mountaintop: Black Women's Novels in the Wake of the Civil Rights Movement, 1966–1989.* New Haven, CT: Yale University Press, 1991.

Walker, Nancy A. *Feminist Alternatives: Irony and Fantasy in the Contemporary Novel by Women.* Jackson: University Press of Mississippi, 1990.

Wall, Cheryl. "Feminist Literary Criticism and the Author." *Critical Inquiry* 16.3 (Spring 1990): 551–71.

Waller, Gary. *Dreaming America: Obsession and Transcendence in the Fiction of Joyce Carol Oates.* Baton Rouge: Louisiana State University Press, 1979.

Warner, Susan. *The Wide, Wide World.* 1850. Rpt. New York: Feminist Press, 1987.

Waugh, Patricia. *Feminine Fictions: Revisiting the Postmodern.* New York: Routledge, 1989.

Wesley, Marilyn C. "Father-Daughter Incest as Social Transgression: A Feminist Reading of Joyce Carol Oates." *Women's Studies* 21.3 (1992): 251–63.

———. *Refusal and Transgression in Joyce Carol Oates' Fiction.* Westport, CT: Greenwood Press, 1993.

Wigginton, Eliot, ed. *The Foxfire Book.* Garden City, NY: Doubleday, 1972.

Wolcott, James. "Stop Me Before I Write Again." Review of *A Bloodsmoor Romance. Harper's,* Sept. 1982: 67–69.

Woodruff, Jay, ed. "Joyce Carol Oates." *A Piece of Work: Five Writers Discuss Their Revisions.* Iowa City: University of Iowa Press, 1993. 149–227.

Wyatt, Jean. *Reconstructing Desire: The Role of the Unconscious in Women's Reading and Writing.* Chapel Hill: University of North Carolina Press, 1990.

Yaeger, Patricia. *Honey-Mad Women: Emancipatory Strategies in Women's Writing.* New York: Columbia University Press, 1988.

Zeitlin, Froma I. "The Dynamics of Misogyny: Myth and Mythmaking in the *Oresteia.*" *Aeschylus's "The Oresteia."* Ed. Harold Bloom. New York: Chelsea House, 1988. 47–71.

Zimmerman, Bonnie. "Feminist Fiction and the Postmodern Challenge." *Post-Modern Fiction: A Bio-Bibliographical Guide.* Ed. Larry McCaffery. Westport, CT: Greenwood Press, 1986. 175–188.

Index

93; divided according to gender conventions, 4; divided by gender in *With Shuddering Fall*, 15; different for female, 7; dialogic in the 1970s, 69; gender and power of, xiii; gendered in *them*, 44; "godly privilege" of masculine authorship, x; historical and intersubjective, ix; males assume the right of in *Expensive People* and *them*, 4; masculine, individualistic, xi; new in *Bellefleur*, 142; Oates as male impersonator, xi; Oates's desire for alternative model of, xi; Oates's redefinition of, xi; projected onto male characters, 4

Autobiography, xiv

Autographic: conflict between desire for knowledge and communion in *With Shuddering Fall*, 12; Oates's description of her play *Ontological Proof of My Existence*, 8; Oates's return to *The Assassins* in *Marya, a Life*, 130

Bakan, David, 26, 137
Bakhtin, Mikhail, ix, x, xviii, xx, xxii, 6, 48, 49, 70, 92, 136, 142, 149, 153, 155, 210, 233 n. 2
Balloon, as metaphor for writing, as time travel, 165
Bauer, Dale, 129, 229 n. 1
Baym, Nina, 160
Belenky, Mary Field, *et al*, 114. See also *Women's Ways of Knowing*
Bender, Eileen Teper, xiii, 22, 26, 31 80, 92, 95, 110, 154, 236 n. 6
Benjamin, Jessica, xxii, 128, 185–86, 236 n. 1, 240 n. 24
Blavatsky, Madame, 158, 240 n. 20
Blithedale Romance, The, 174, 242 n. 37
Body: aging, 233, Ch. 4 n. 1; of beautiful woman, site of male competition, 185; communal in *Wonderland*, 68; dismemberment in *Because It Is Bitter, Because It Is My Heart*, 197; history

written on bodies of, exploited in *Bellefleur*, 143; intellectual assassins of, 99; Maddy's return to, in *Marya, a Life*, 216; maternal vulnerabilities of, 126; maternal and social, 245 n. 20; not individual, 233, Ch. 3 n. 2; pathologic in *The Assassins*, 96; rewritten in *Foxfire, Confessions of a Girl Gang*, 209; socio-political in *Because It Is Bitter, Because It Is My Heart*, 197, 204; wounded in *Because It Is Bitter, Because It Is My Heart*, 193
Boose, Lynda, 3, 16, 78–79, 233, Ch. 4 n. 3
Boose, Lynda, and Betty Flowers, 6
Borden, Lizzie, 171, 242 nn. 34, 35
Boundaries: of discourses, location of Oates's voice, 49; porous in *Because It Is Bitter, Because It Is My Heart*, 193, 204
Bernheimer, Charles, and Clare Kahane, 234 n. 2
Breines Wini, and Linda Gordon, 246 n. 3
Bronte, Emily, 237–38 n. 7, 238 n. 12
Brown, John, 182
Broyard, Anatole, 155
Bounded text, 77
Burwell, Rose Marie, 231 n. 2

Campbell, Joseph, 103
Canons: exclusion of Oates's foremothers, 154; feminist, Oates's exclusion from, 226
Carnival: in the grotesque realism of *Wonderland*, 50, 53
Carroll, Lewis, x
Caufield, Holden, 5–6
Center: moves in *Because It Is Bitter, Because It Is My Heart*, 180; multiplies in *Because It Is Bitter, Because It Is My Heart*, 197
Characters: aggressive males, 8; author Oates as "Miss Oates" in *them*, 45;

boundary, a threat to father, what
the father desires, 10; exchangeable
figure in *With Shuddering Fall*,
10, 15–16; exchange foregrounds
socio-economic issues in *A Garden of
Earthly Delights*, 31; father's favorite
in *With Shuddering Fall*, 14; father's
incestuous desire for, in Shakespeare,
243 n. 39; father's search for, in
Wonderland, 64; "good" and "bad"
in *You Must Remember This*, 188;
function to save family, theory of
representation, xviii; idealize father,
xxiii; imprisoned by father in *With
Shuddering Fall*, 16; as heroes,
narrators in novels of the 1970s,
75; inheritance not parallel to son's,
6; Laney, as Oates's "alter ego" in
Childwold, 92; leaving, failing to leave,
3–4, 232 n. 8; lies, fantasizes paternal
abuse, 92; loss of name, 16; her part,
xii; mirror for father's desire, denial
of mortality, in *Do with Me What You
Will*, 86; mistaken by father as his
enemy, xvii; Nadine, captive of father
in *them*, 40; as narrator in *Childwold*,
92; needs a democratic society within
and beyond family, 181; not equal
to son, 6; Oates's revisioning of,
xviii; obedient to, ventriloquated by
father, 74; plot of daughter's return
to mother in *Childwold*, xviii; point
of contact between father and son
in *Do with Me What You Will*, 82;
as property, 232 n. 7; as property in
Do with Me What You Will, 83; in
postmodern novels, 139; rejection of
Christianity in *With Shuddering Fall*,
21; return to maternal past in novels
of the 1980s, 125; riddle for Oates,
78; as sacrifice, 11; saved by mother,
234 n. 1; "Seductive Daughter,"
rewritten in *Childwold*, 92; see with
own eyes, 128; self-authoring in

Do with Me What You Will, 89;
site of competition among men of
different generations and classes,
78; sociolinguistic parallels between
Oates and female characters, xiv;
surplus authorial consciousness in
With Shuddering Fall attaches to
daughter, 11; survival depends on
alliances with other women, 130;
as a thing, a spoil of masculine
warfare, 88; transformation of, in
Oates's oeuvre, xix; transgressive
in *A Bloodsmoor Romance*, 129;
transgressive in *Angel of Light*, 188;
voices resistance to father-lover, 73;
as wife in "The Sacred Marriage"
and *Do with Me What You Will*, 73;
wears father's too-large shoes in *With
Shuddering Fall*, 15–16
Daughter-centricity: privileging of
daughter's perspective over mother's,
xxiii; feminists collude in repressing
identification with mother, 127
Daughters and fathers: *Childwold* and
Do with Me What You Will investigate
relationship, 69; father-daughter
incest in the romance, 79. *See also*
Incest
"Dead, The," xiv, 72, 111, 129
De Lauretis, Teresa, 206
Democratic: authorship in *The Assassins*,
93; authorship in *Childwold*, 93
DeMott, xv, 24
Detective: acknowledges "Will to
Power" in *Mysteries of Winterthurn*,
170; feminists challenge conventions
of, 168; twinned with criminal
in *Mysteries of Winterthurn*, 168;
upper-class, according to convention,
177
Dialogic: announced in "The Sacred
Marriage," 73; authorship in *The
Assassins*, 93; in the decade of 1970s,
69; consciousness in *Marriages and*

criticism, 246 n. 5; studied father-son canon, xiii; transgressive, along with her female characters, in *A Bloodsmoor Romance*, 162; Shelley as author's "exaggerated self-portrait," xix; transgressive, 232 n. 9

Objectivity: "criminal" in *Mysteries of Winterthurn*, 167; illusion in *Wonderland*, 49

Octagon house, 163, 240 n. 25

Oedipal fathers, incestuous, seductive, sense of entitlement, 128

Oedipal identity, unique, whole, coherent, 7

Oedipal model, silences maternal voice, 127

Oedipal narrative, constraints of, xxiii

Oedipal plot, 5, 37, 76, 193, 231 n. 5

Ohmann, Richard, 244 n. 11

Ontological Proof of My Existence, xii, 8

Ontological puzzle, xi, xii, xiv, 88

Oresteia, The, 182, 243 n. 3

Orphan girl, scrutinized in *A Bloodsmoor Romance*, 160, 240 n. 22

Osborne, Guy, 245 n. 1

Ostriker, Alicia, 230 n. 8, 237 n. 2

Paradise Lost, parody of Miltonic structure in *With Shuddering Fall*, 17, 25

Patriarchal plot, sacrificial in *With Shuddering Fall*, 9, 10

Parody: of assassin novels in *The Assassins*, 99; of homosocial ceremonies in *Foxfire, Confessions of a Girl Gang*, 209; of Henry James's "The Aspern Papers," 74; of narrative voice, of *Jane Eyre* in *A Bloodsmoor Romance*, 156, 158; of monologic author in *Do with Me What You Will*, 85; Oates's use of, xiii; of restrictive gender codes in the postmodern novels, 138

Paranoia, of patriarch, Lear, xvii

Patriarchs, wealthy, suffer from disease of unmitigated agency, 26

Phillips, Robert, 94, 96

Place, voices of, 140, 178, 237 n. 5

Plath, Sylvia, 26, 72, 96, 130

Plots: Oedipal, 5, 37, 76, 193, 231 n. 5; patriarchal, 9, 10; postmodern, 125–26; romance, 22, 42–43, 79, 111, 125, 165, 191; tragic, 15

Poe, Edgar Allan, 160

Pollit, Katha, 230 n. 12

Politics: art, 179; interplay with personal, familial, 129; of representation, 180

Political unconscious: the body, the feminine, 104; the (m)other in us, 180; the social body in *Wonderland*, 66

Polyphonic, voices of place in the postmodern novels, 140

Postmodern plots, in novels of the 1980s, 125–26

Postmodern novels, 136–78

Pratt, Annis, 228

Productivity, x, 229 n. 2

Quilt, in *Bellefleur*, 142, 150

Quinn, Sally, xiv

Realism: obedient to law of one (monologic), 144; feminist, in novels of the 1980s, 180

Reddy, Maureen T., 166, 167, 173, 241 n. 30

Renaissance ego, 26

Resistance postmodernism, 136

Readers: Oates as resisting, 75; resisting, 172

Revenge, against time, in *Bellefleur*, 150, 152

Re-visionary: dialogic strategies in novels of the 1970s, 70; feminist techniques in novels of the 1980s, 180; novel, *Childwold*, 92; strategies to transform binary morality, 25

DATE DUE